Shojo Beat

ORESAMA TEACHER

top-heaviness

Vol. 10

Story & Art by
Izumi Tsubaki

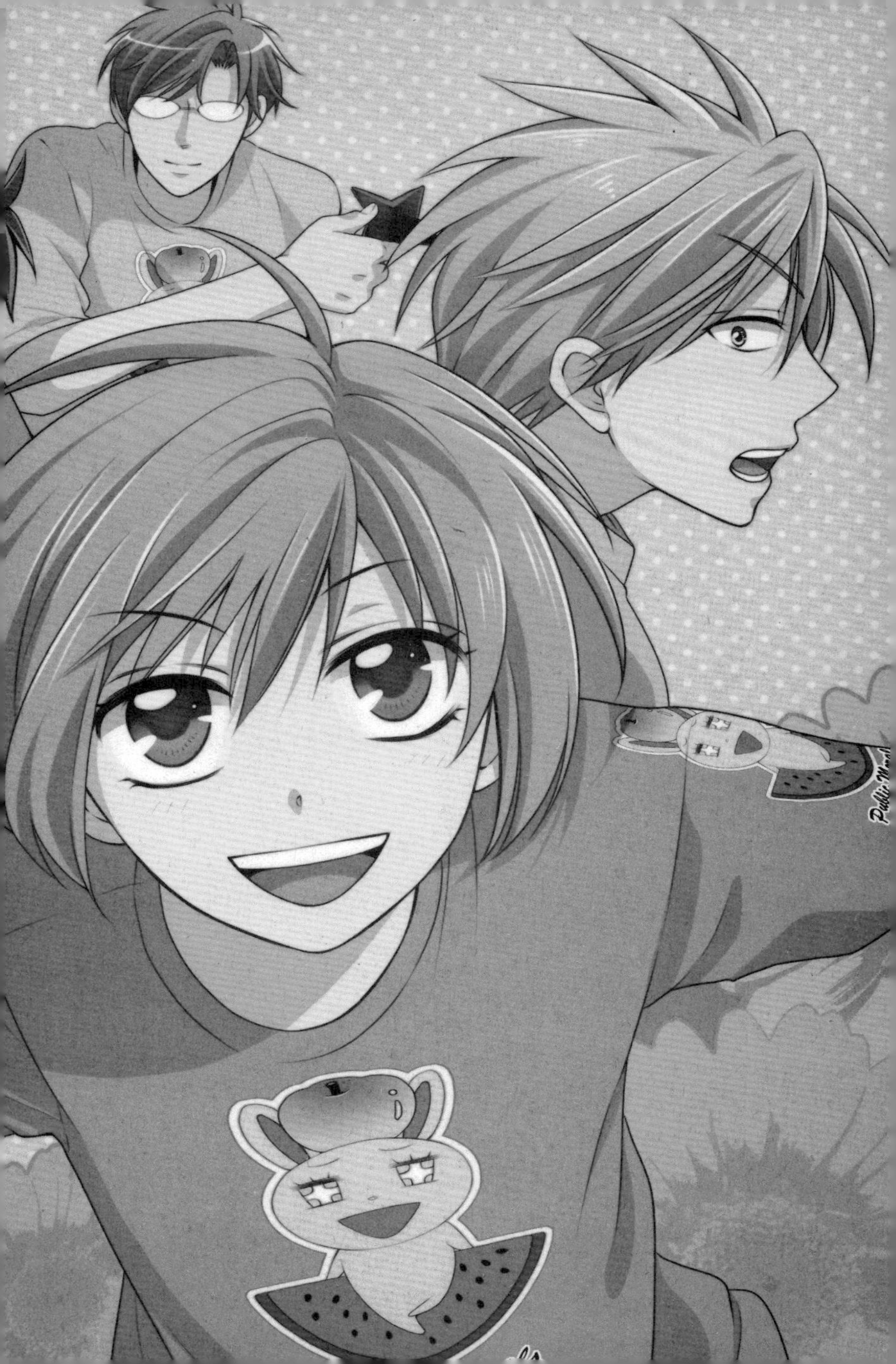

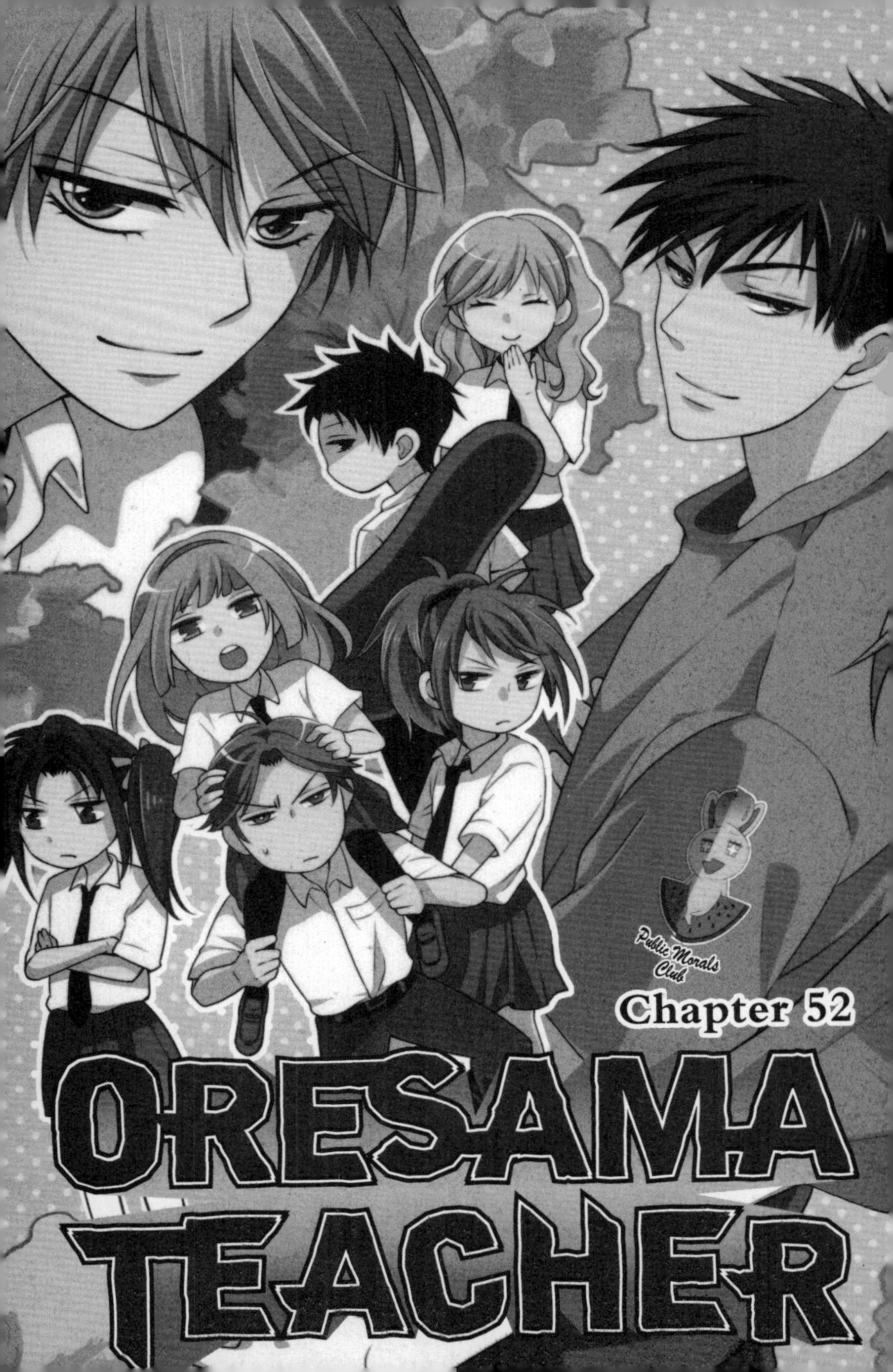
Public Morals Club
Chapter 52
ORESAMA TEACHER

ORESAMA TEACHER

Volume 10
CONTENTS

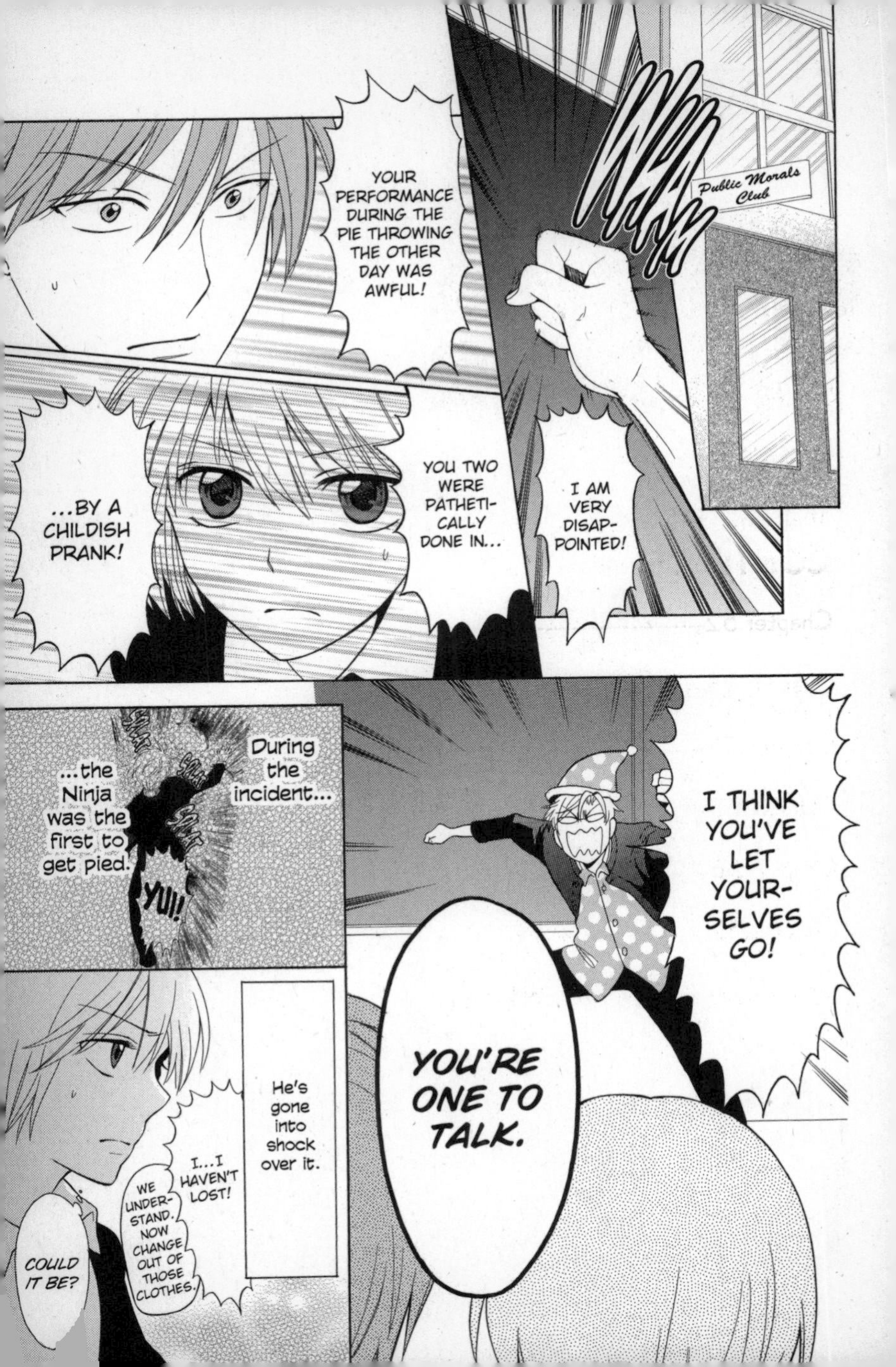
Public Morals Club
I AM VERY DISAPPOINTED!
YOUR PERFORMANCE DURING THE PIE THROWING THE OTHER DAY WAS AWFUL!
YOU TWO WERE PATHETICALLY DONE IN...
...BY A CHILDISH PRANK!
I THINK YOU'VE LET YOURSELVES GO!
YOU'RE ONE TO TALK.
During the incident...
...the Ninja was the first to get pied.
YUI!
He's gone into shock over it.
I...I HAVEN'T LOST!
WE UNDERSTAND. NOW CHANGE OUT OF THOSE CLOTHES.
COULD IT BE?

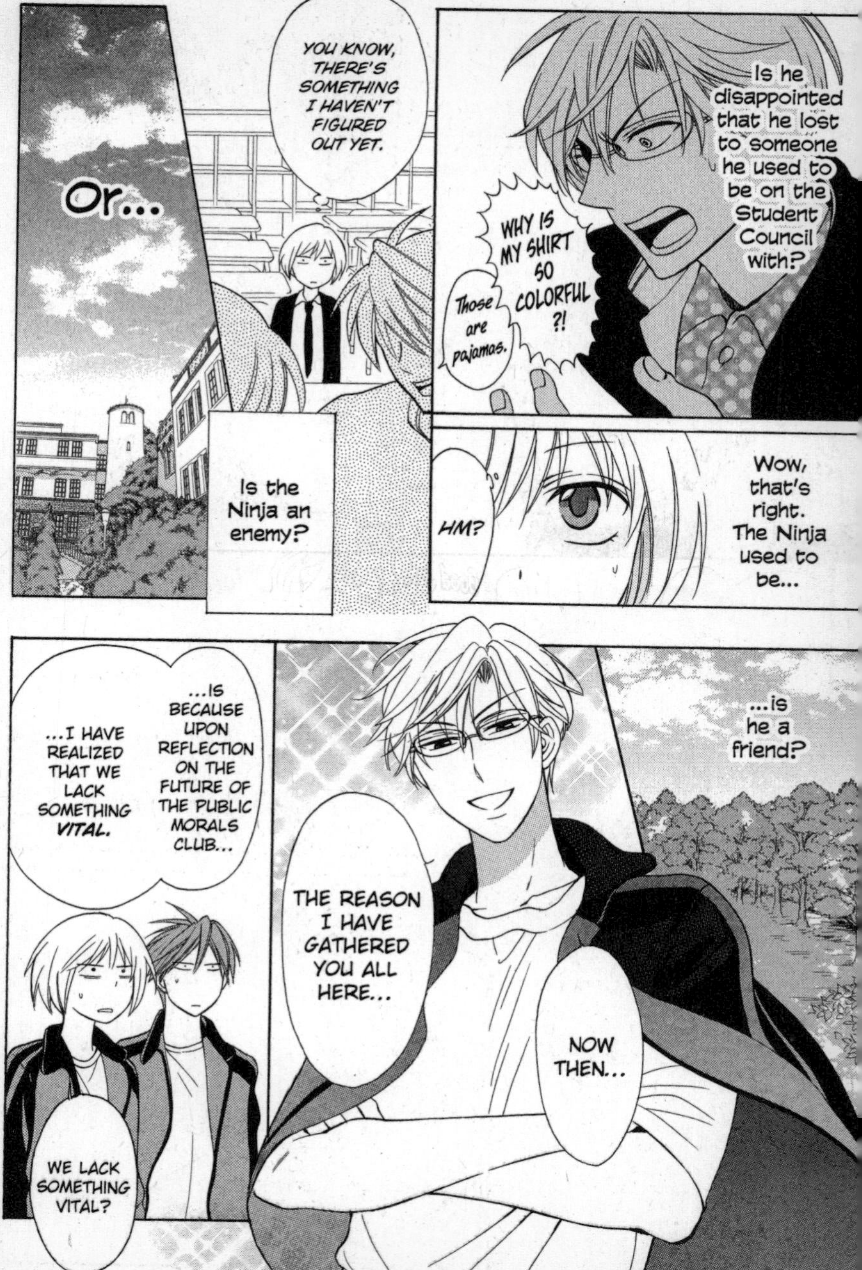
Is he disappointed that he lost to someone he used to be on the Student Council with?
WHY IS MY SHIRT SO COLORFUL?!
Those are pajamas.
Wow, that's right. The Ninja used to be...
HM?
YOU KNOW, THERE'S SOMETHING I HAVEN'T FIGURED OUT YET.
Is the Ninja an enemy?
Or...
...is he a friend?
NOW THEN...
THE REASON I HAVE GATHERED YOU ALL HERE...
...IS BECAUSE UPON REFLECTION ON THE FUTURE OF THE PUBLIC MORALS CLUB...
...I HAVE REALIZED THAT WE LACK SOMETHING VITAL.
WE LACK SOMETHING VITAL?

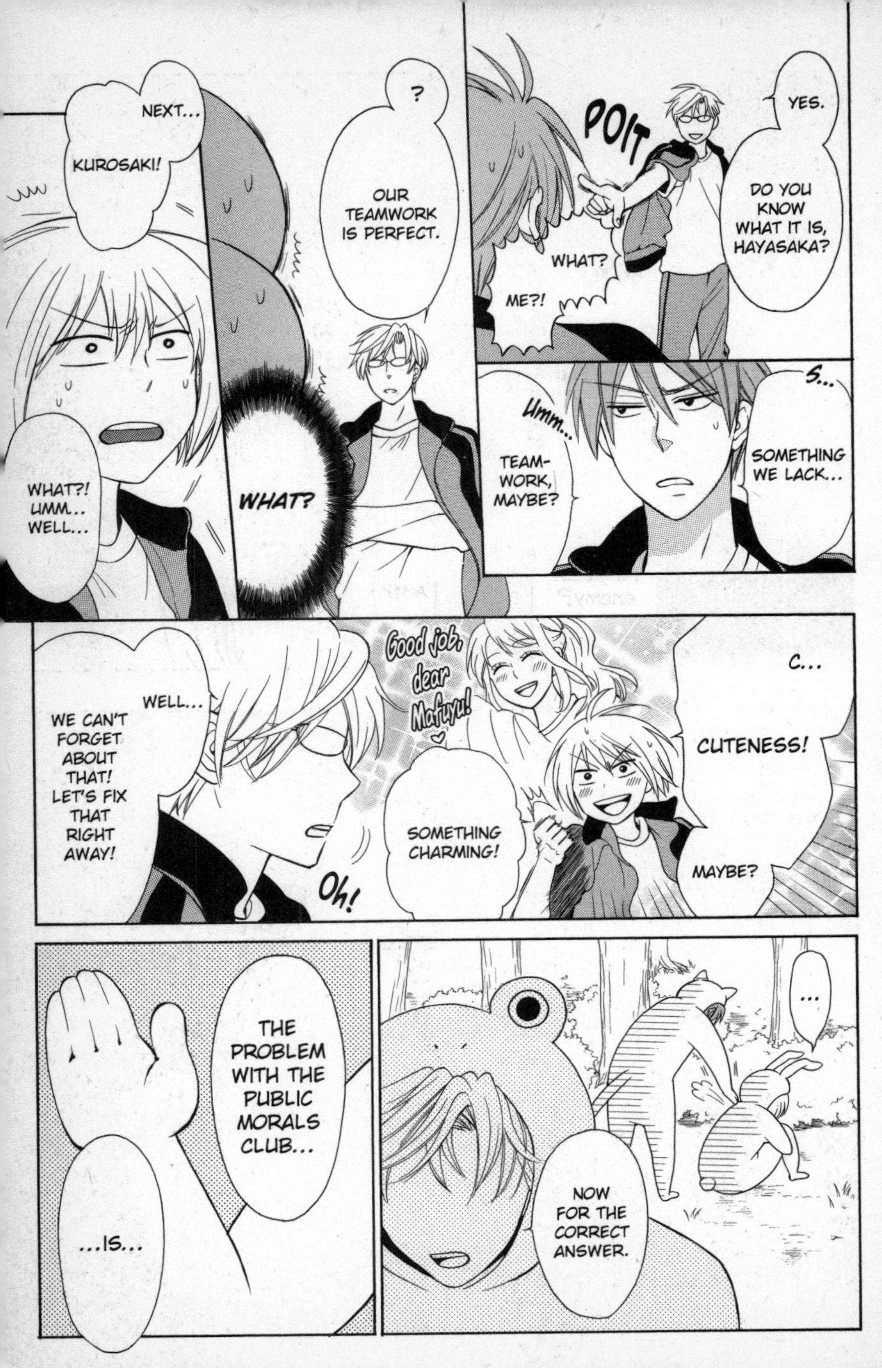
YES.
DO YOU KNOW WHAT IT IS, HAYASAKA?
POIT
WHAT?
ME?!
S...
SOMETHING WE LACK...
Umm...
TEAM-WORK, MAYBE?
?
OUR TEAMWORK IS PERFECT.
WHAT?
NEXT...
KUROSAKI!
WHAT?! UMM.. WELL...
C...
CUTENESS!
MAYBE?
Good job, dear Mafuyu!
SOMETHING CHARMING!
Oh!
WELL...
WE CAN'T FORGET ABOUT THAT! LET'S FIX THAT RIGHT AWAY!
...
NOW FOR THE CORRECT ANSWER.
THE PROBLEM WITH THE PUBLIC MORALS CLUB...
...IS...

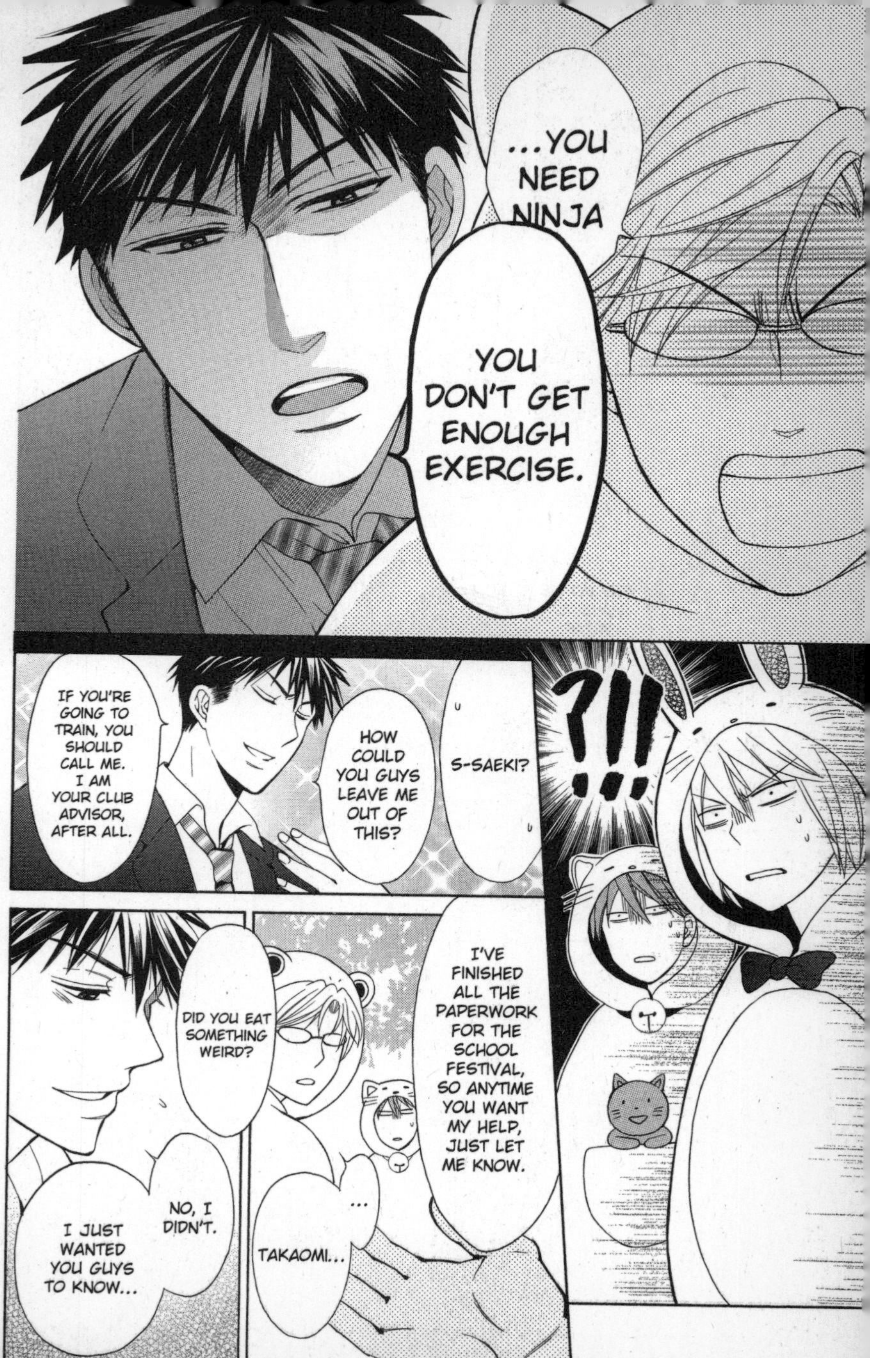
...YOU NEED NINJA
YOU DON'T GET ENOUGH EXERCISE.
?!!
S-SAEKI?
HOW COULD YOU GUYS LEAVE ME OUT OF THIS?
IF YOU'RE GOING TO TRAIN, YOU SHOULD CALL ME. I AM YOUR CLUB ADVISOR, AFTER ALL.
I'VE FINISHED ALL THE PAPERWORK FOR THE SCHOOL FESTIVAL, SO ANYTIME YOU WANT MY HELP, JUST LET ME KNOW.
DID YOU EAT SOMETHING WEIRD?
...
TAKAOMI...
NO, I DIDN'T.
I JUST WANTED YOU GUYS TO KNOW...

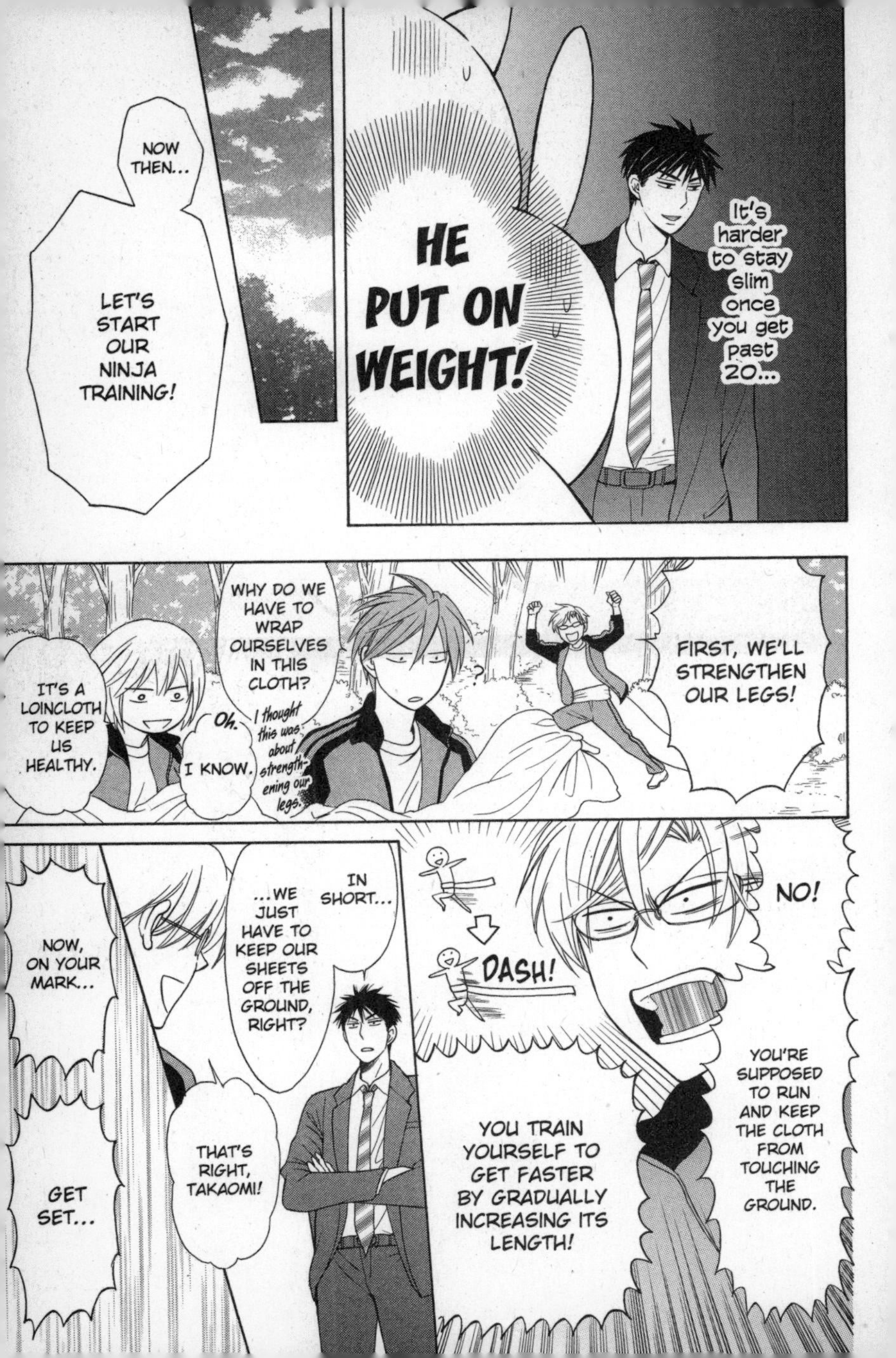
It's harder to stay slim once you get past 20...
HE PUT ON WEIGHT!
NOW THEN...
LET'S START OUR NINJA TRAINING!
FIRST, WE'LL STRENGTHEN OUR LEGS!
WHY DO WE HAVE TO WRAP OURSELVES IN THIS CLOTH?
I thought this was about strengthening our legs.
IT'S A LOINCLOTH TO KEEP US HEALTHY.
Oh.
I KNOW.
NO!
DASH!
YOU'RE SUPPOSED TO RUN AND KEEP THE CLOTH FROM TOUCHING THE GROUND.
YOU TRAIN YOURSELF TO GET FASTER BY GRADUALLY INCREASING ITS LENGTH!
IN SHORT...
...WE JUST HAVE TO KEEP OUR SHEETS OFF THE GROUND, RIGHT?
THAT'S RIGHT, TAKAOMI!
NOW, ON YOUR MARK...
GET SET...

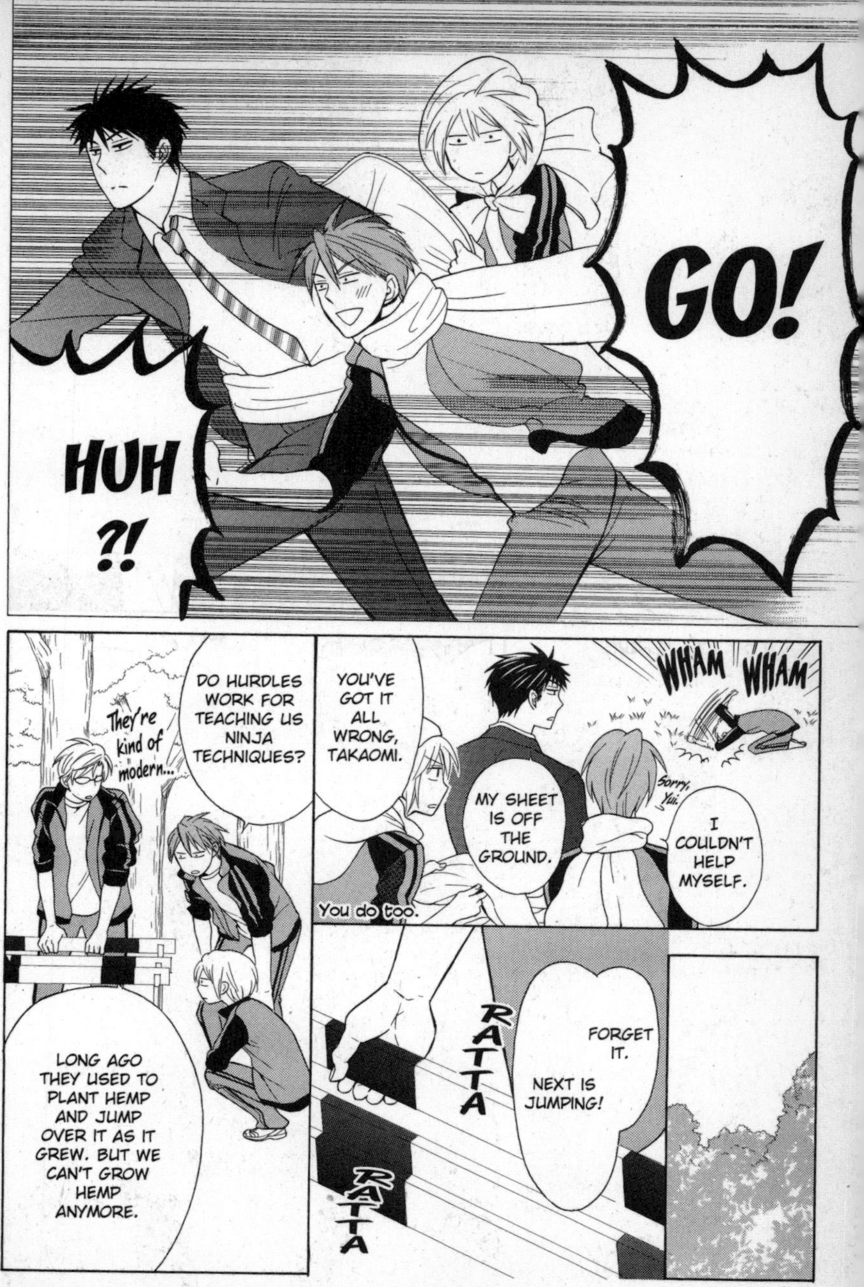
GO!
HUH ?!
WHAM WHAM
Sorry, Yui.
I COULDN'T HELP MYSELF.
MY SHEET IS OFF THE GROUND.
YOU'VE GOT IT ALL WRONG, TAKAOMI.
You do too.
RATTA
FORGET IT.
NEXT IS JUMPING!
RATTA
DO HURDLES WORK FOR TEACHING US NINJA TECHNIQUES?
They're kind of modern...
LONG AGO THEY USED TO PLANT HEMP AND JUMP OVER IT AS IT GREW. BUT WE CAN'T GROW HEMP ANYMORE.

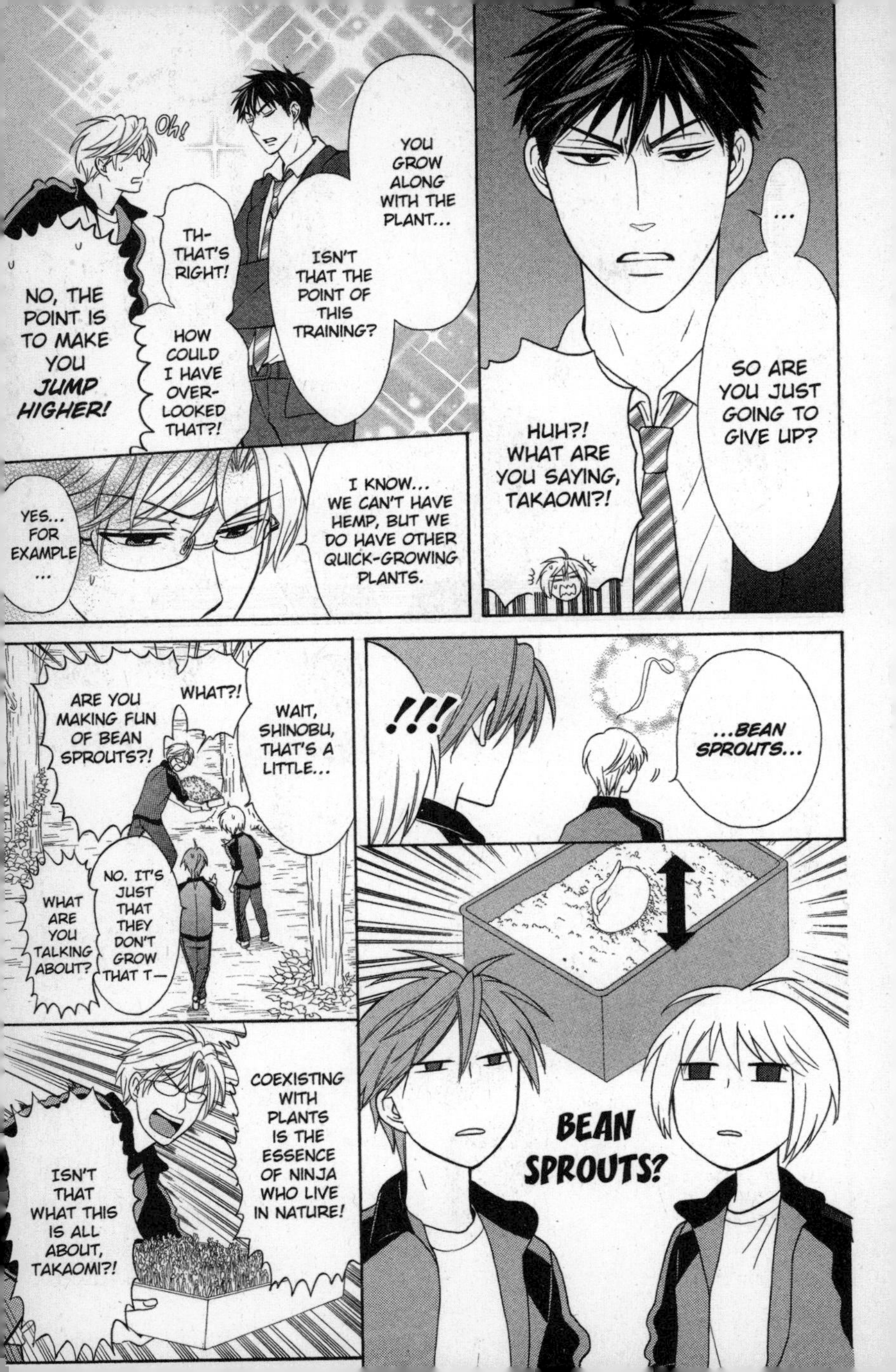
...
SO ARE YOU JUST GOING TO GIVE UP?
HUH?! WHAT ARE YOU SAYING, TAKAOMI?!
YOU GROW ALONG WITH THE PLANT...
ISN'T THAT THE POINT OF THIS TRAINING?
Oh!
TH-THAT'S RIGHT!
HOW COULD I HAVE OVER-LOOKED THAT?!
NO, THE POINT IS TO MAKE YOU JUMP HIGHER!
I KNOW... WE CAN'T HAVE HEMP, BUT WE DO HAVE OTHER QUICK-GROWING PLANTS.
YES... FOR EXAMPLE ...
...BEAN SPROUTS...
!!!
WAIT, SHINOBU, THAT'S A LITTLE...
WHAT?!
ARE YOU MAKING FUN OF BEAN SPROUTS?!
NO. IT'S JUST THAT THEY DON'T GROW THAT T—
WHAT ARE YOU TALKING ABOUT?
BEAN SPROUTS?
COEXISTING WITH PLANTS IS THE ESSENCE OF NINJA WHO LIVE IN NATURE!
ISN'T THAT WHAT THIS IS ALL ABOUT, TAKAOMI?!

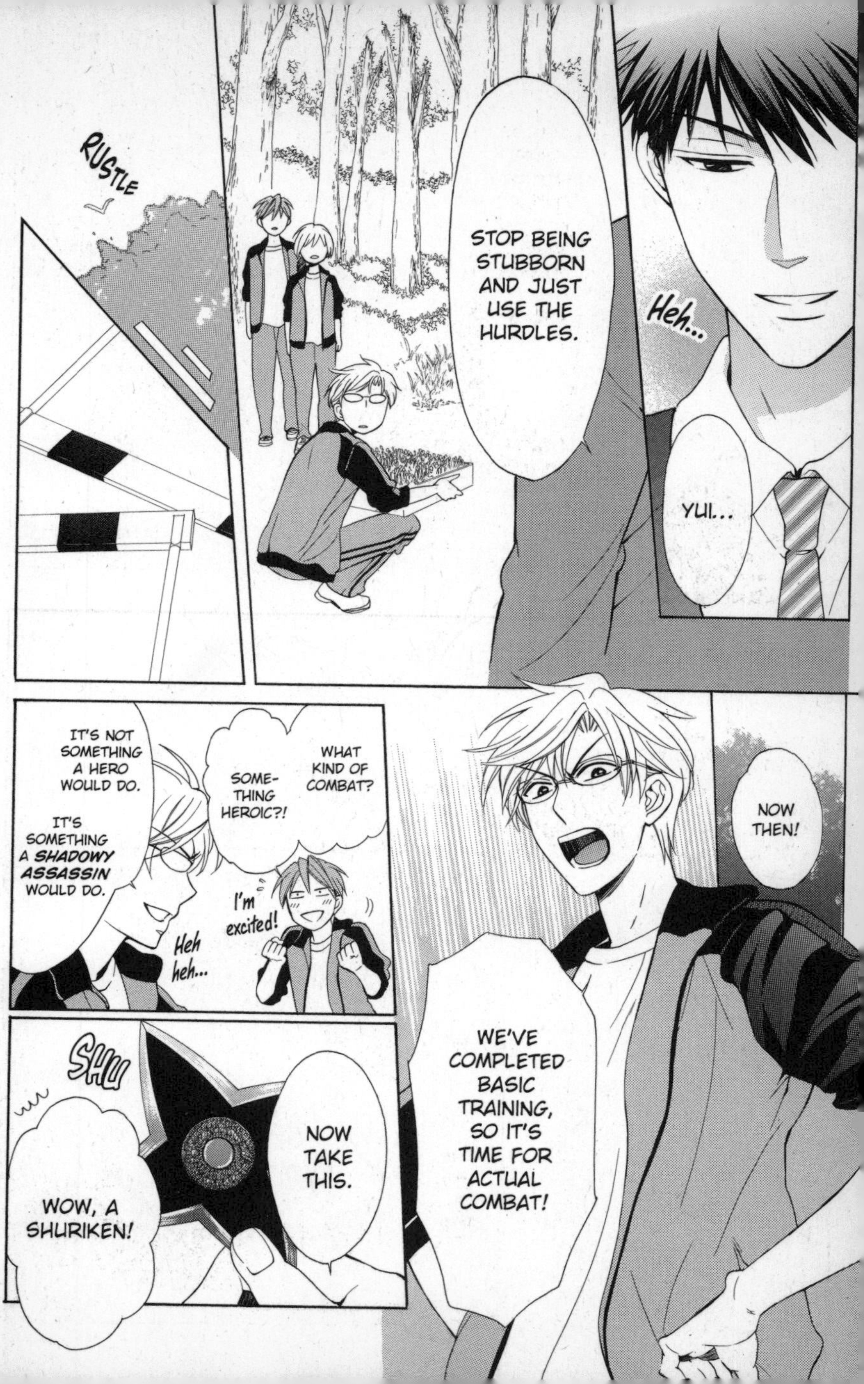
STOP BEING STUBBORN AND JUST USE THE HURDLES.
Heh...
YUI...
RUSTLE
NOW THEN!
WE'VE COMPLETED BASIC TRAINING, SO IT'S TIME FOR ACTUAL COMBAT!
WHAT KIND OF COMBAT?
SOME-THING HEROIC?!
I'm excited!
IT'S NOT SOMETHING A HERO WOULD DO.
IT'S SOMETHING A *SHADOWY ASSASSIN* WOULD DO.
Heh heh...
SHU
NOW TAKE THIS.
WOW, A SHURIKEN!

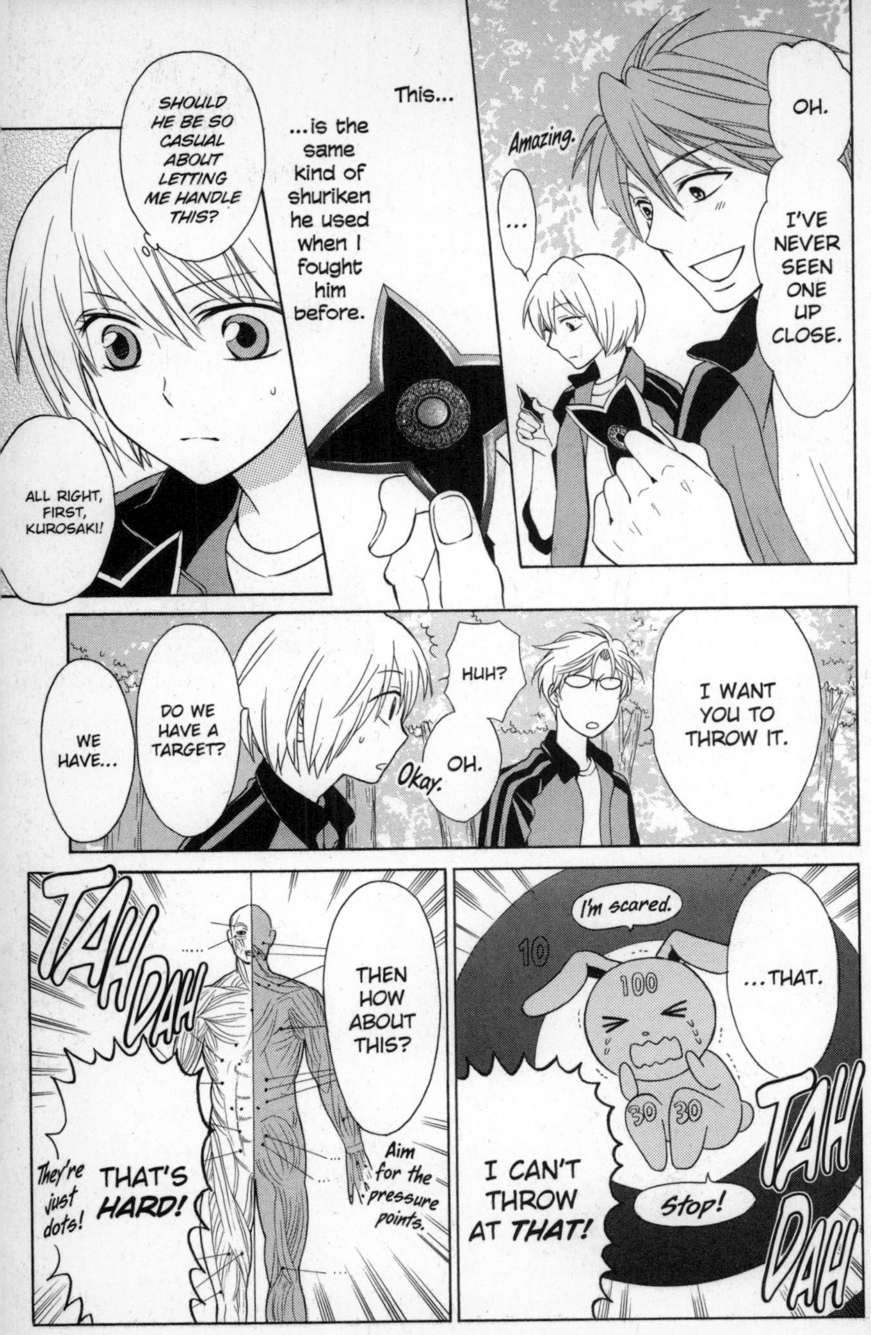
OH.
I'VE NEVER SEEN ONE UP CLOSE.
Amazing.
...
This...
...is the same kind of shuriken he used when I fought him before.
SHOULD HE BE SO CASUAL ABOUT LETTING ME HANDLE THIS?
ALL RIGHT, FIRST, KUROSAKI!
I WANT YOU TO THROW IT.
HUH?
OH.
Okay.
DO WE HAVE A TARGET?
WE HAVE...
...THAT.
I'm scared.
10
100
30 30
TAH DAH
Stop!
I CAN'T THROW AT THAT!
THEN HOW ABOUT THIS?
Aim for the pressure points.
TAH DAH
THAT'S HARD!
They're just dots!

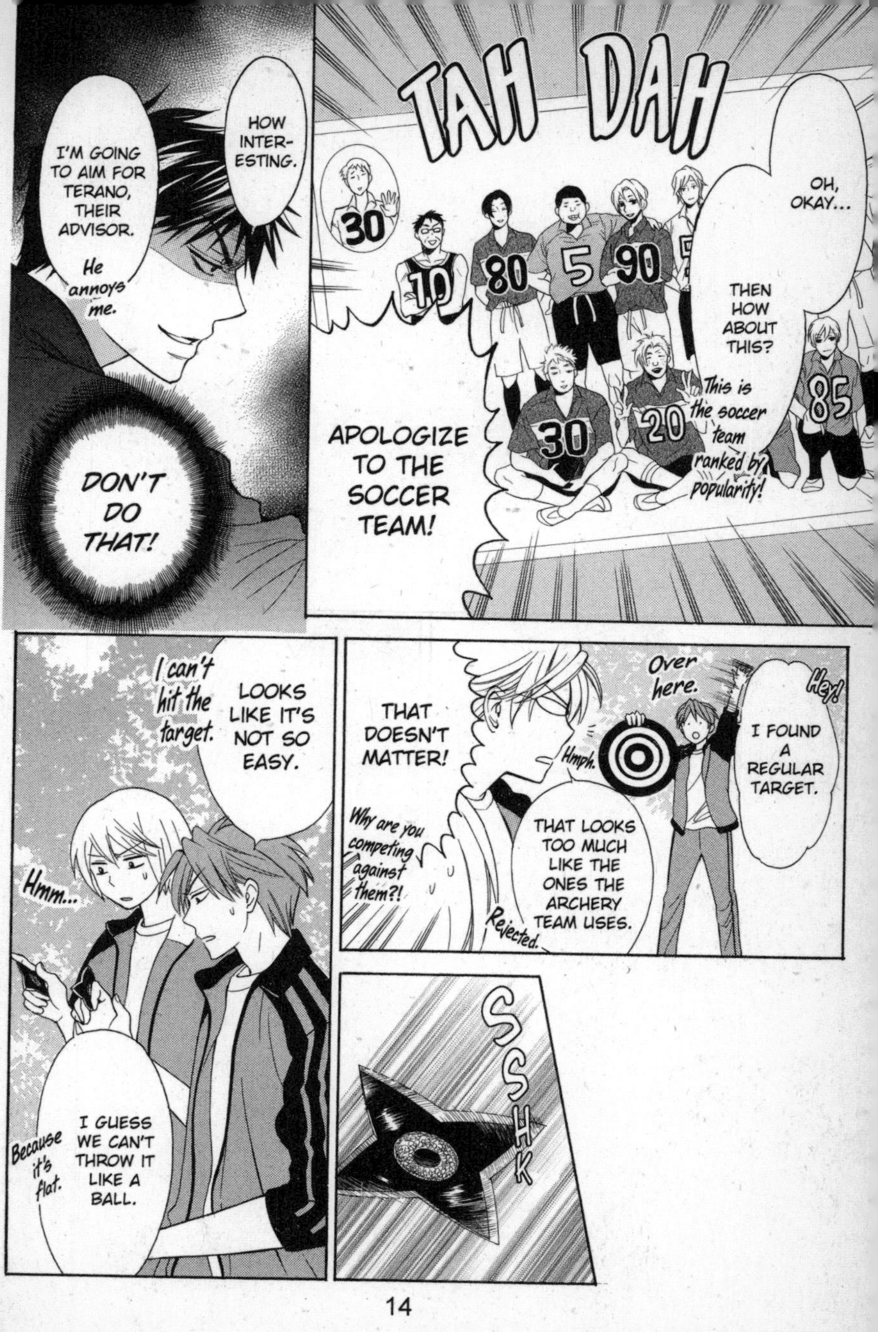
OH, OKAY...
THEN HOW ABOUT THIS?
This is the soccer team ranked by popularity!
TAH DAH
APOLOGIZE TO THE SOCCER TEAM!
HOW INTERESTING.
I'M GOING TO AIM FOR TERANO, THEIR ADVISOR.
He annoys me.
DON'T DO THAT!
Hey!
I FOUND A REGULAR TARGET.
Over here.
Hmph.
THAT LOOKS TOO MUCH LIKE THE ONES THE ARCHERY TEAM USES.
Rejected.
THAT DOESN'T MATTER!
Why are you competing against them?!
SSHK
LOOKS LIKE IT'S NOT SO EASY.
I can't hit the target.
Hmm...
I GUESS WE CAN'T THROW IT LIKE A BALL.
Because it's flat.

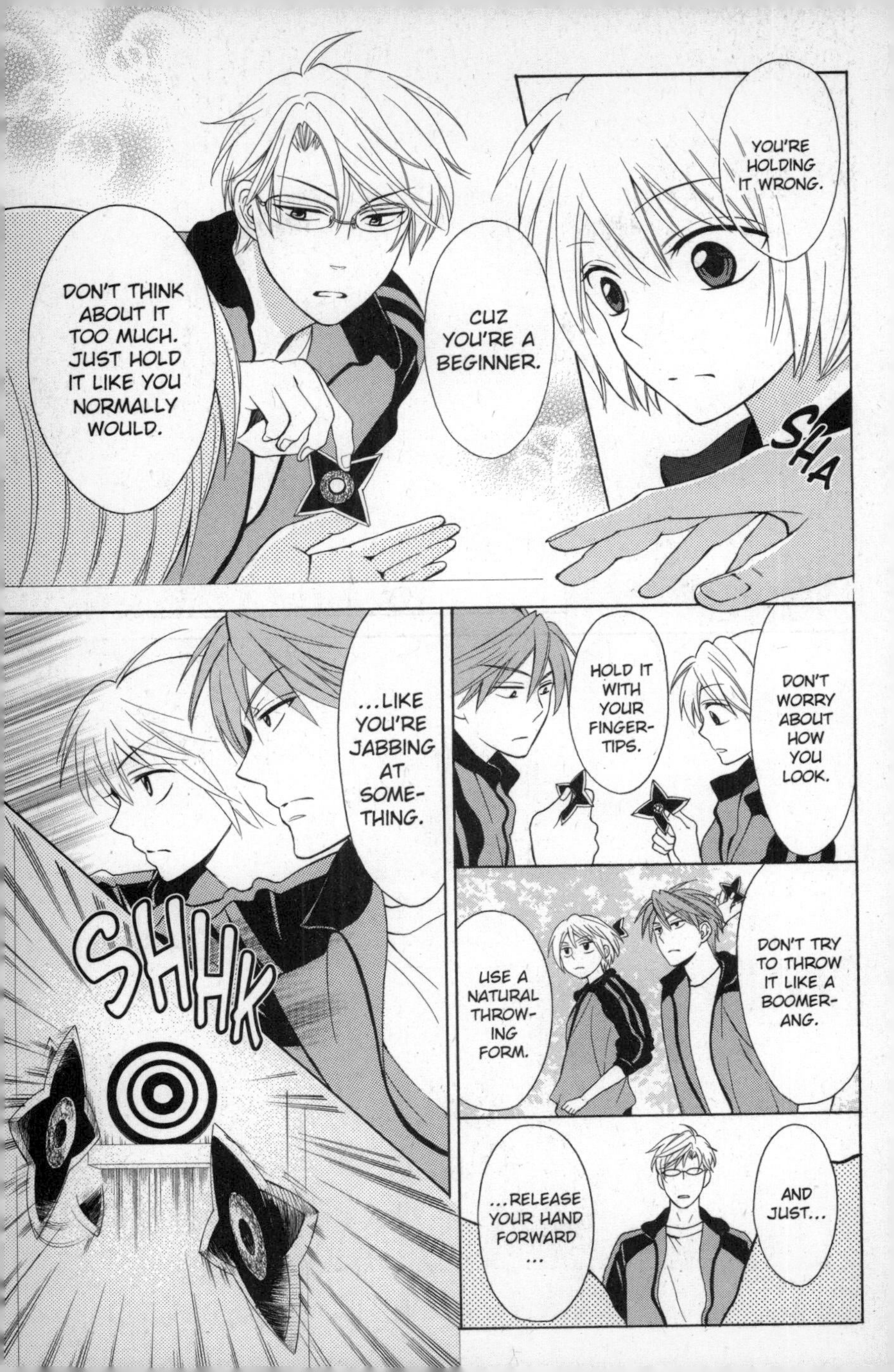

YOU'RE HOLDING IT WRONG.
SHA
CUZ YOU'RE A BEGINNER.
DON'T THINK ABOUT IT TOO MUCH. JUST HOLD IT LIKE YOU NORMALLY WOULD.
DON'T WORRY ABOUT HOW YOU LOOK.
HOLD IT WITH YOUR FINGER-TIPS.
DON'T TRY TO THROW IT LIKE A BOOMER-ANG.
USE A NATURAL THROW-ING FORM.
AND JUST...
...RELEASE YOUR HAND FORWARD ...
...LIKE YOU'RE JABBING AT SOME-THING.
SHHK

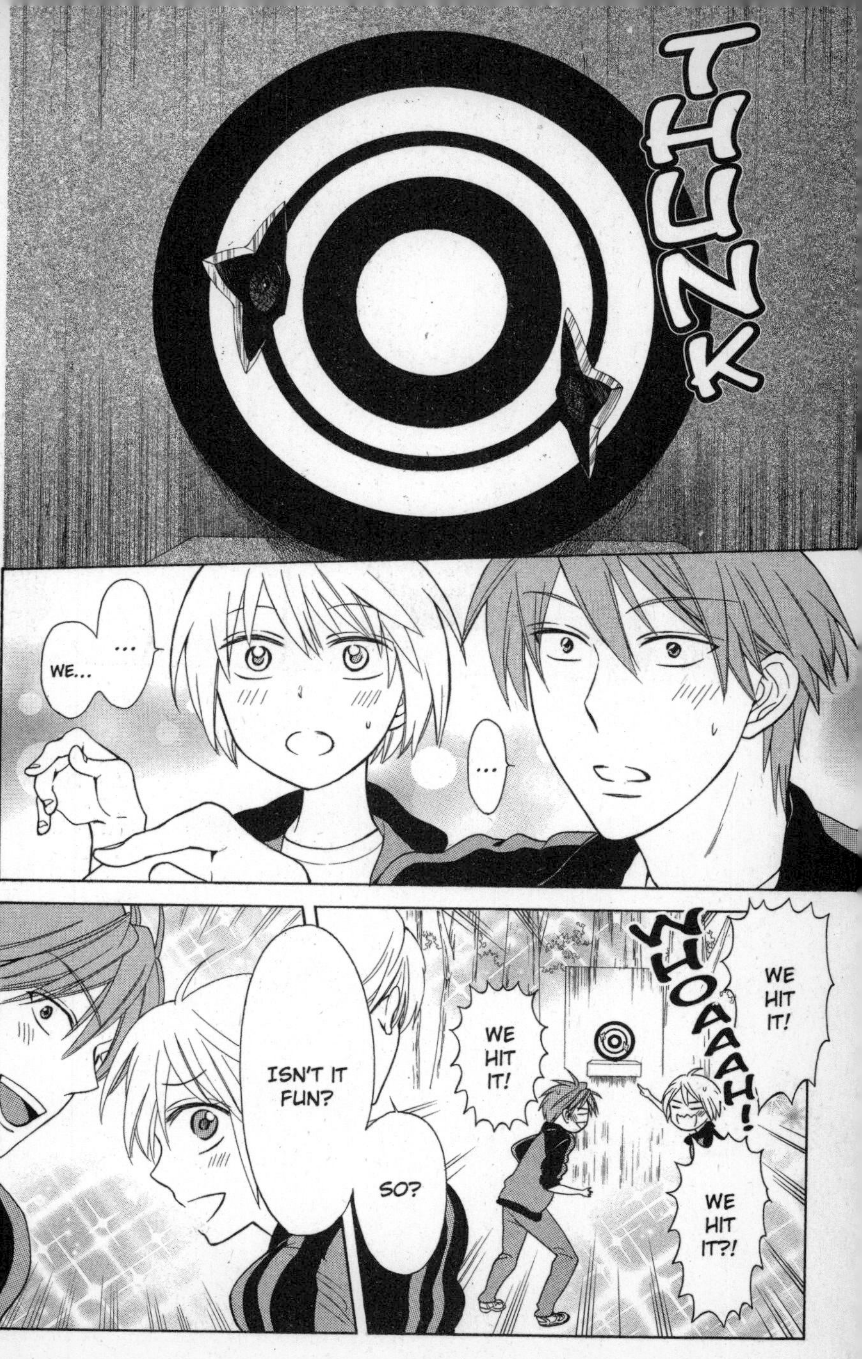
THUNK
...
...
WE...
WE HIT IT!
WHOAAAAH!
WE HIT IT?!
WE HIT IT!
ISN'T IT FUN?
SO?

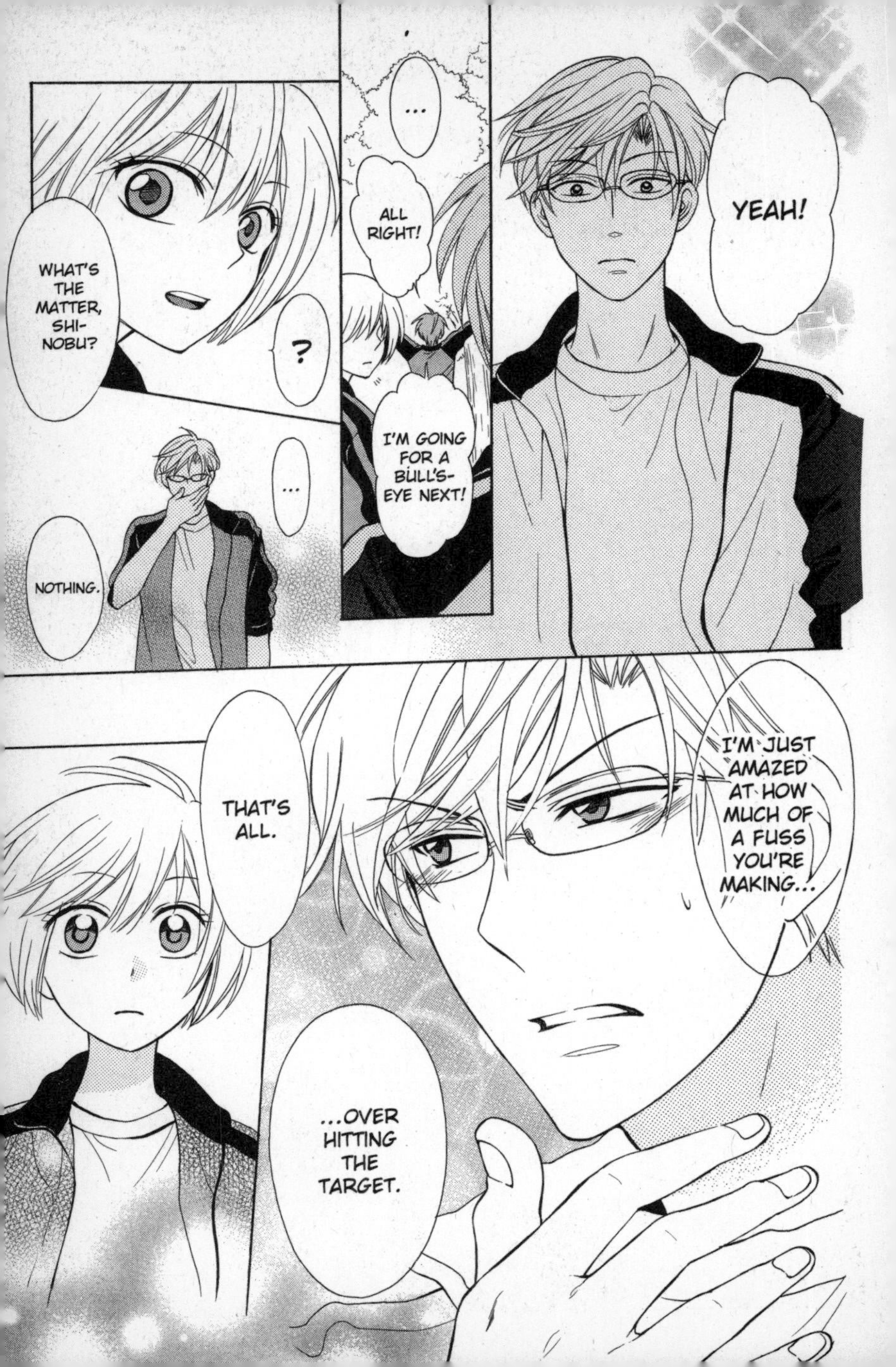
YEAH!
...
ALL RIGHT!
I'M GOING FOR A BULL'S-EYE NEXT!
?
WHAT'S THE MATTER, SHI-NOBU?
...
NOTHING.
I'M JUST AMAZED AT HOW MUCH OF A FUSS YOU'RE MAKING...
THAT'S ALL.
...OVER HITTING THE TARGET.

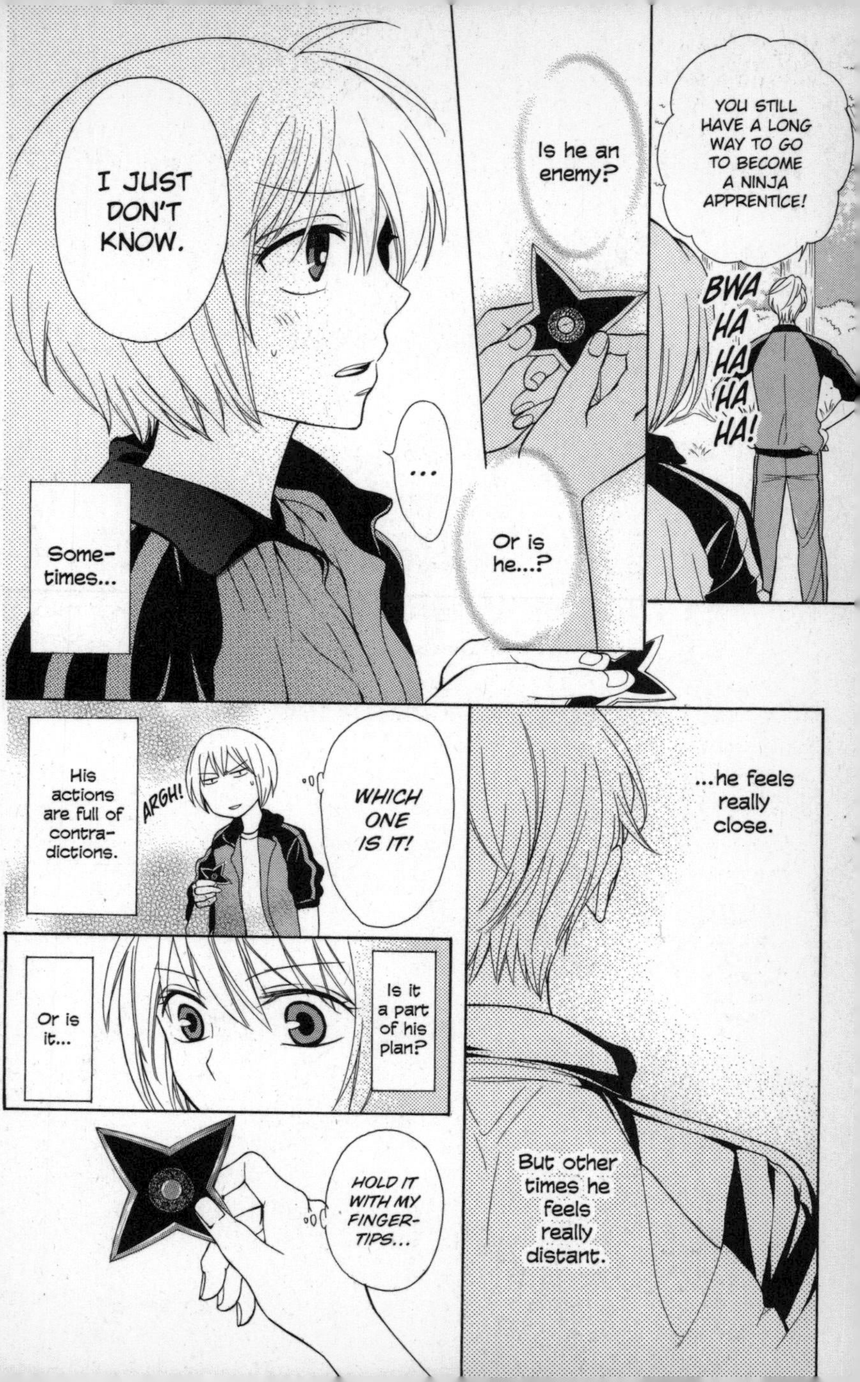

YOU STILL HAVE A LONG WAY TO GO TO BECOME A NINJA APPRENTICE!
BWA HA HA HA HA!
Is he an enemy?
Or is he...?
I JUST DON'T KNOW.
...
Some-times...
...he feels really close.
But other times he feels really distant.
WHICH ONE IS IT!
ARGH!
His actions are full of contra-dictions.
Is it a part of his plan?
Or is it...
HOLD IT WITH MY FINGER-TIPS...

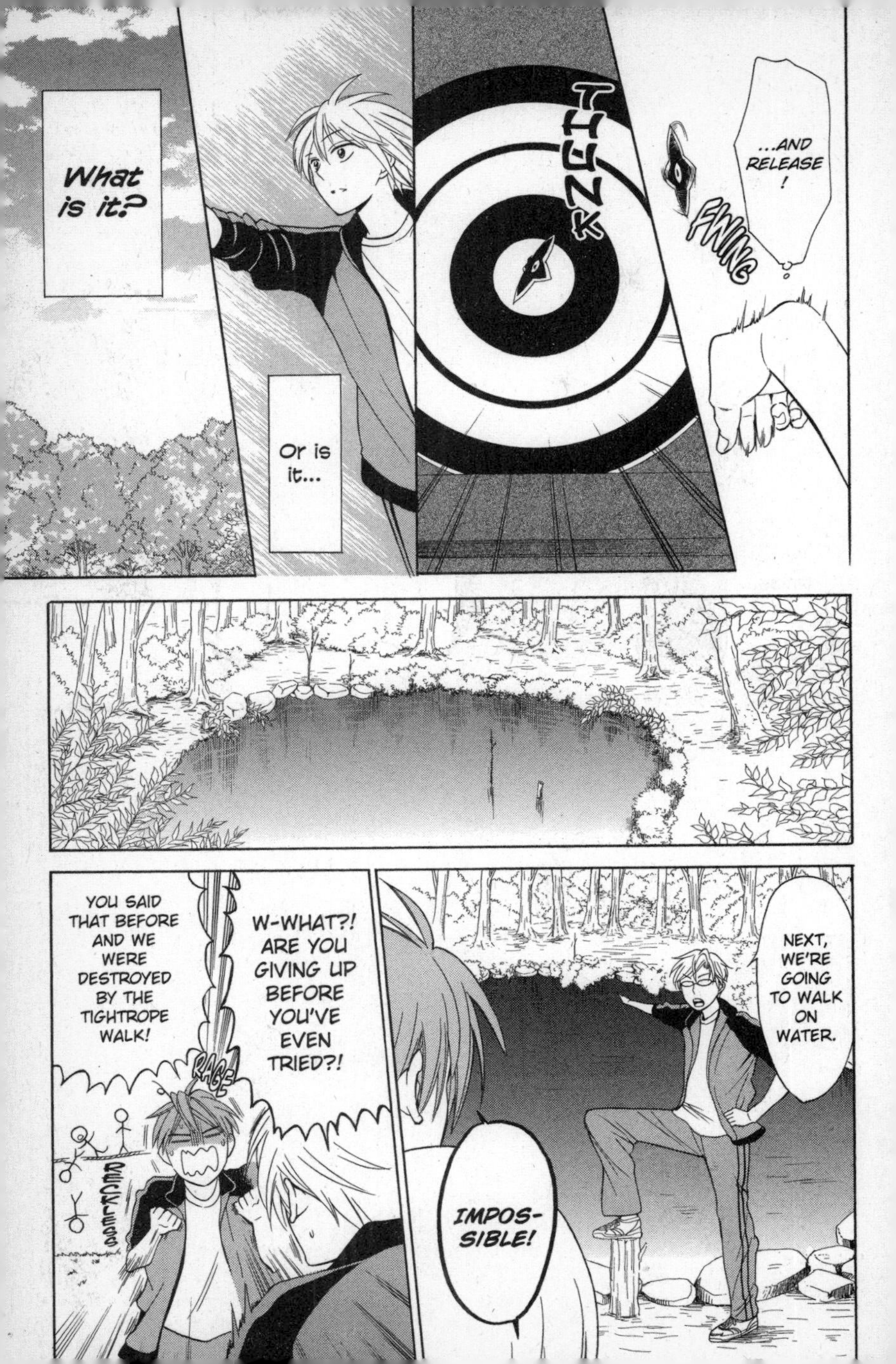
...AND RELEASE!
FWING
THUNK
Or is it...
What is it?
NEXT, WE'RE GOING TO WALK ON WATER.
IMPOSSIBLE!
W-WHAT?! ARE YOU GIVING UP BEFORE YOU'VE EVEN TRIED?!
RAGE
YOU SAID THAT BEFORE AND WE WERE DESTROYED BY THE TIGHTROPE WALK!
RECKLESS

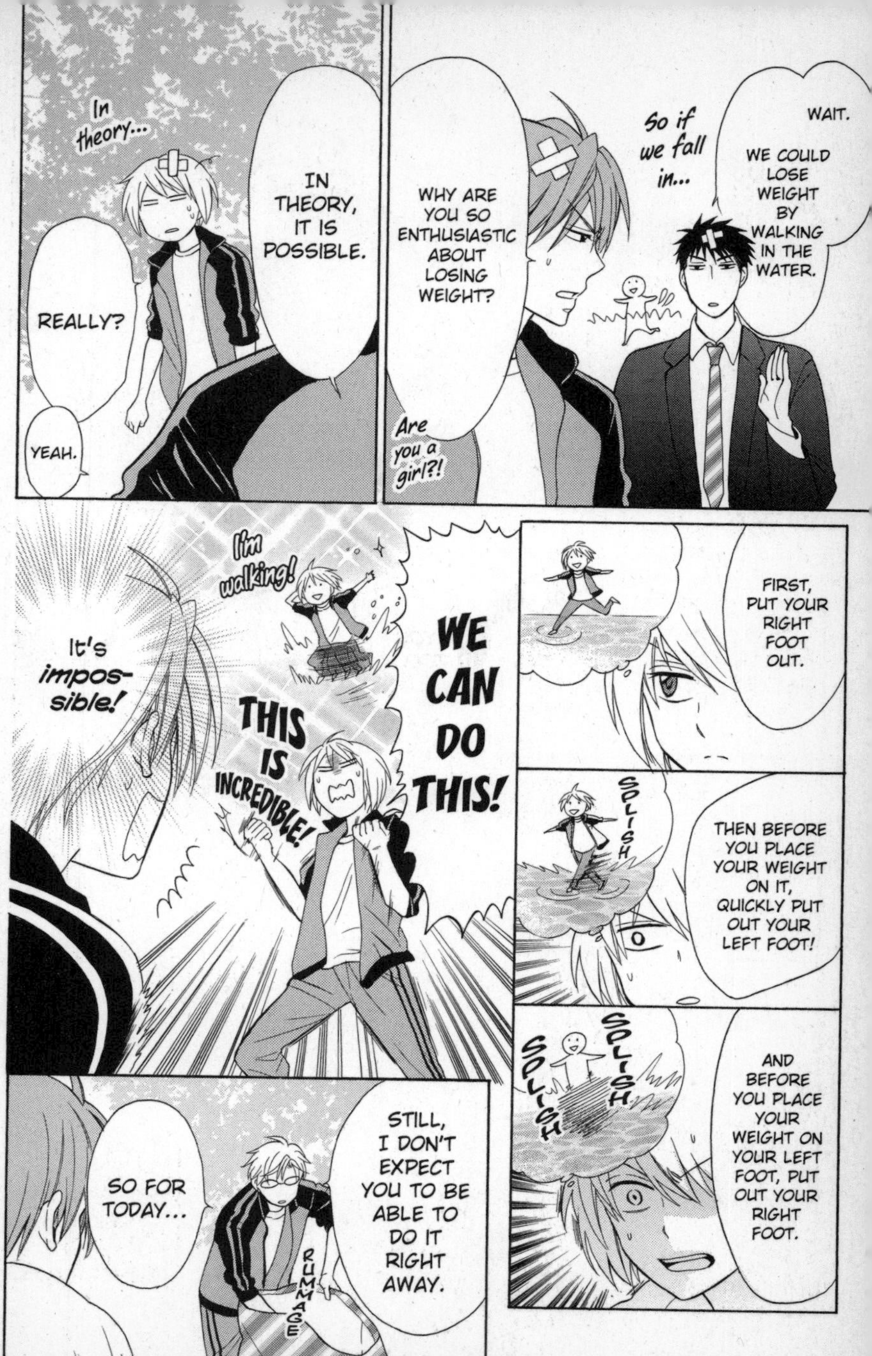
WAIT.
WE COULD LOSE WEIGHT BY WALKING IN THE WATER.
So if we fall in...
WHY ARE YOU SO ENTHUSIASTIC ABOUT LOSING WEIGHT?
Are you a girl?!
IN THEORY, IT IS POSSIBLE.
In theory...
REALLY?
YEAH.
FIRST, PUT YOUR RIGHT FOOT OUT.
SPLISH
THEN BEFORE YOU PLACE YOUR WEIGHT ON IT, QUICKLY PUT OUT YOUR LEFT FOOT!
SPLISH
SPLISH
AND BEFORE YOU PLACE YOUR WEIGHT ON YOUR LEFT FOOT, PUT OUT YOUR RIGHT FOOT.
I'm walking!
WE CAN DO THIS!
THIS IS INCREDIBLE!
It's impossible!
STILL, I DON'T EXPECT YOU TO BE ABLE TO DO IT RIGHT AWAY.
RUMMAGE
SO FOR TODAY...

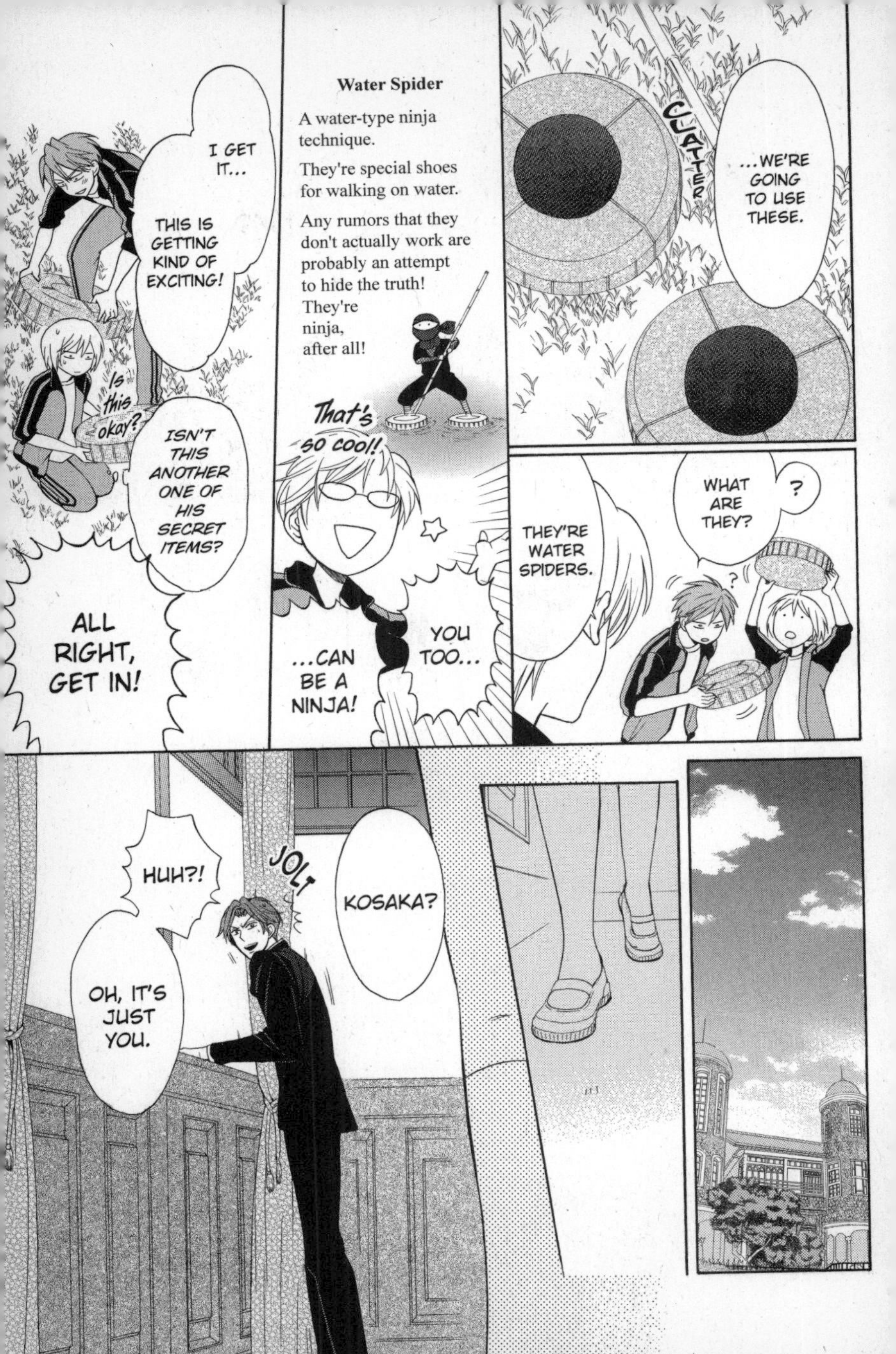
CLATTER
...WE'RE GOING TO USE THESE.
?
WHAT ARE THEY?
?
THEY'RE WATER SPIDERS.
Water Spider
A water-type ninja technique.
They're special shoes for walking on water.
Any rumors that they don't actually work are probably an attempt to hide the truth! They're ninja, after all!
That's so cool!!
YOU TOO...
...CAN BE A NINJA!
I GET IT...
THIS IS GETTING KIND OF EXCITING!
Is this okay?
ISN'T THIS ANOTHER ONE OF HIS SECRET ITEMS?
ALL RIGHT, GET IN!
KOSAKA?
JOLT
HUH?!
OH, IT'S JUST YOU.

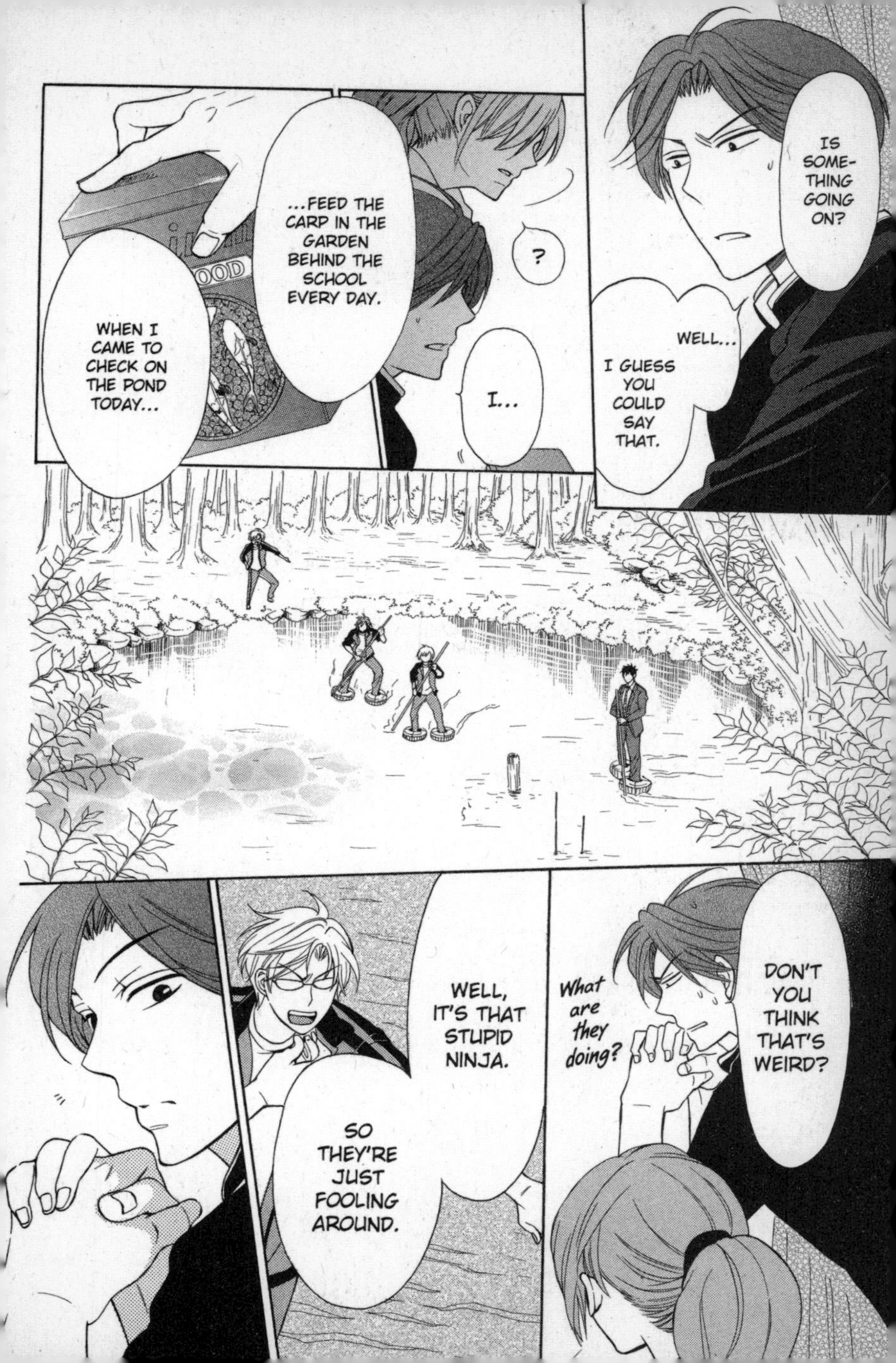
IS SOMETHING GOING ON?
WELL... I GUESS YOU COULD SAY THAT.
?
I...
...FEED THE CARP IN THE GARDEN BEHIND THE SCHOOL EVERY DAY.
WHEN I CAME TO CHECK ON THE POND TODAY...
DON'T YOU THINK THAT'S WEIRD?
What are they doing?
WELL, IT'S THAT STUPID NINJA.
SO THEY'RE JUST FOOLING AROUND.

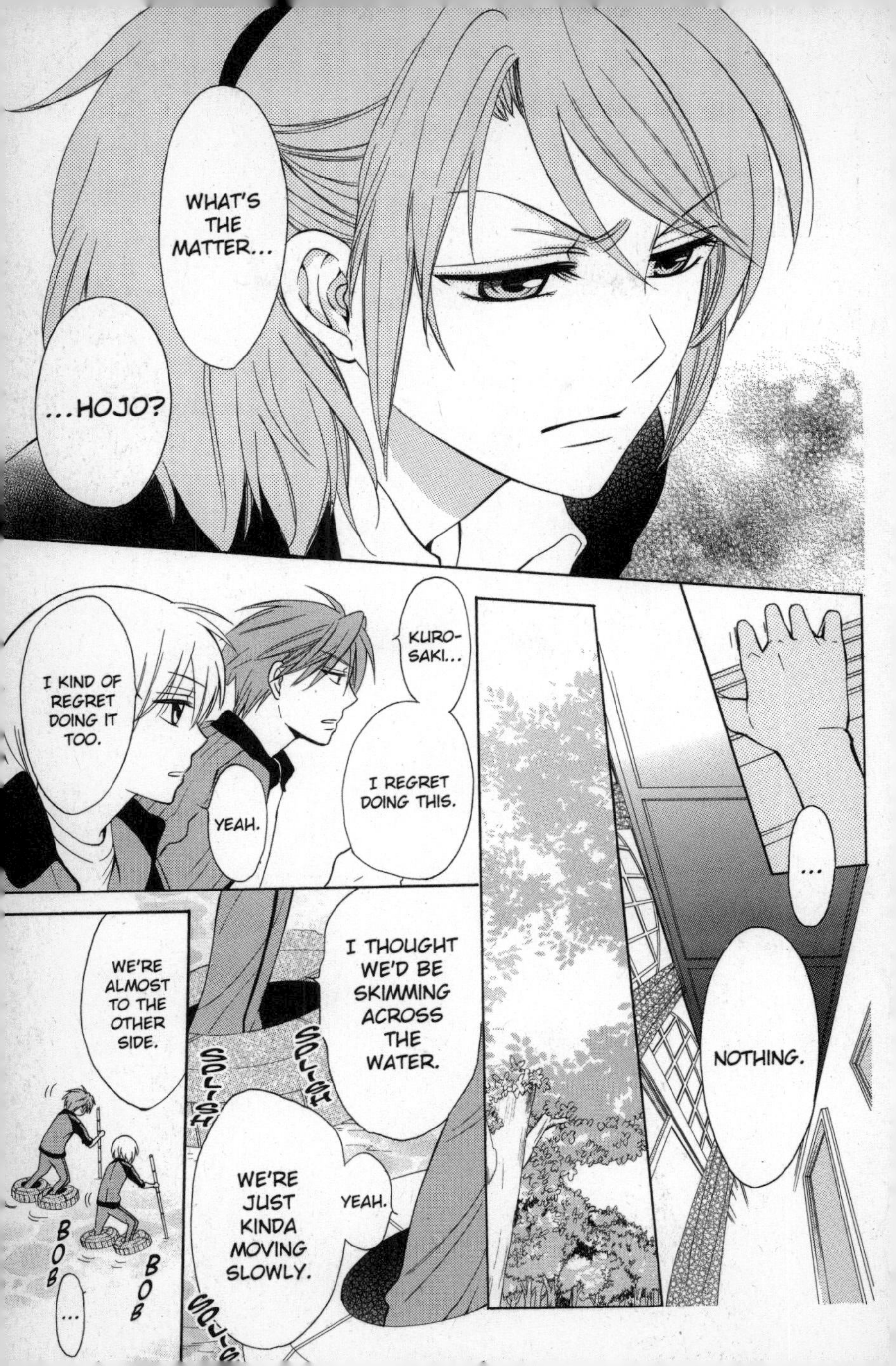
WHAT'S THE MATTER...
...HOJO?
...
NOTHING.
KURO-SAKI...
I REGRET DOING THIS.
YEAH.
I KIND OF REGRET DOING IT TOO.
I THOUGHT WE'D BE SKIMMING ACROSS THE WATER.
SPLISH
SPLISH
WE'RE ALMOST TO THE OTHER SIDE.
YEAH.
WE'RE JUST KINDA MOVING SLOWLY.
BOB
BOB
...

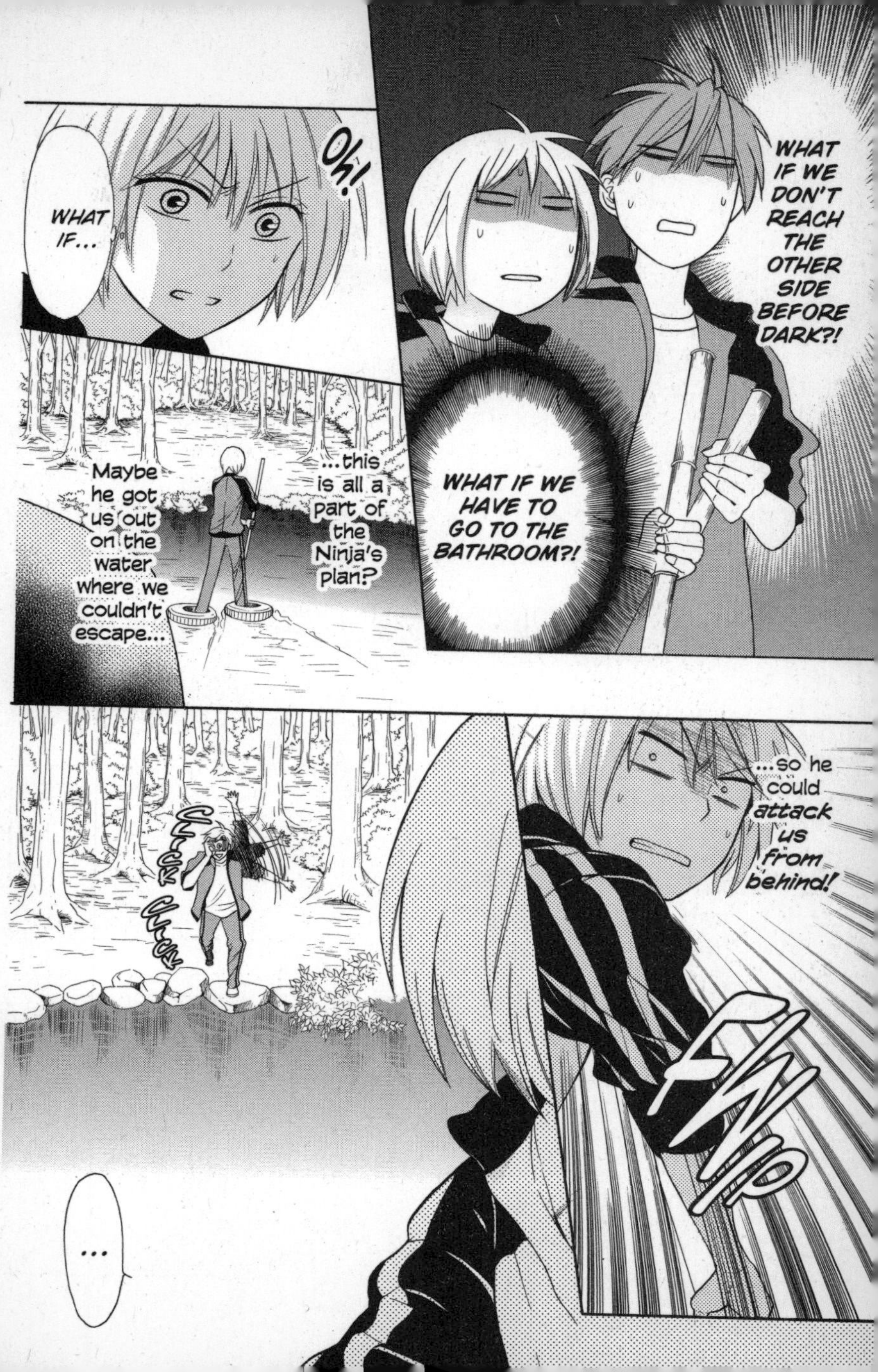
WHAT IF WE DON'T REACH THE OTHER SIDE BEFORE DARK?!
WHAT IF WE HAVE TO GO TO THE BATHROOM?!
Oh!
WHAT IF...
...this is all a part of the Ninja's plan?
Maybe he got us out on the water where we couldn't escape...
...so he could attack us from behind!
FWIP
...

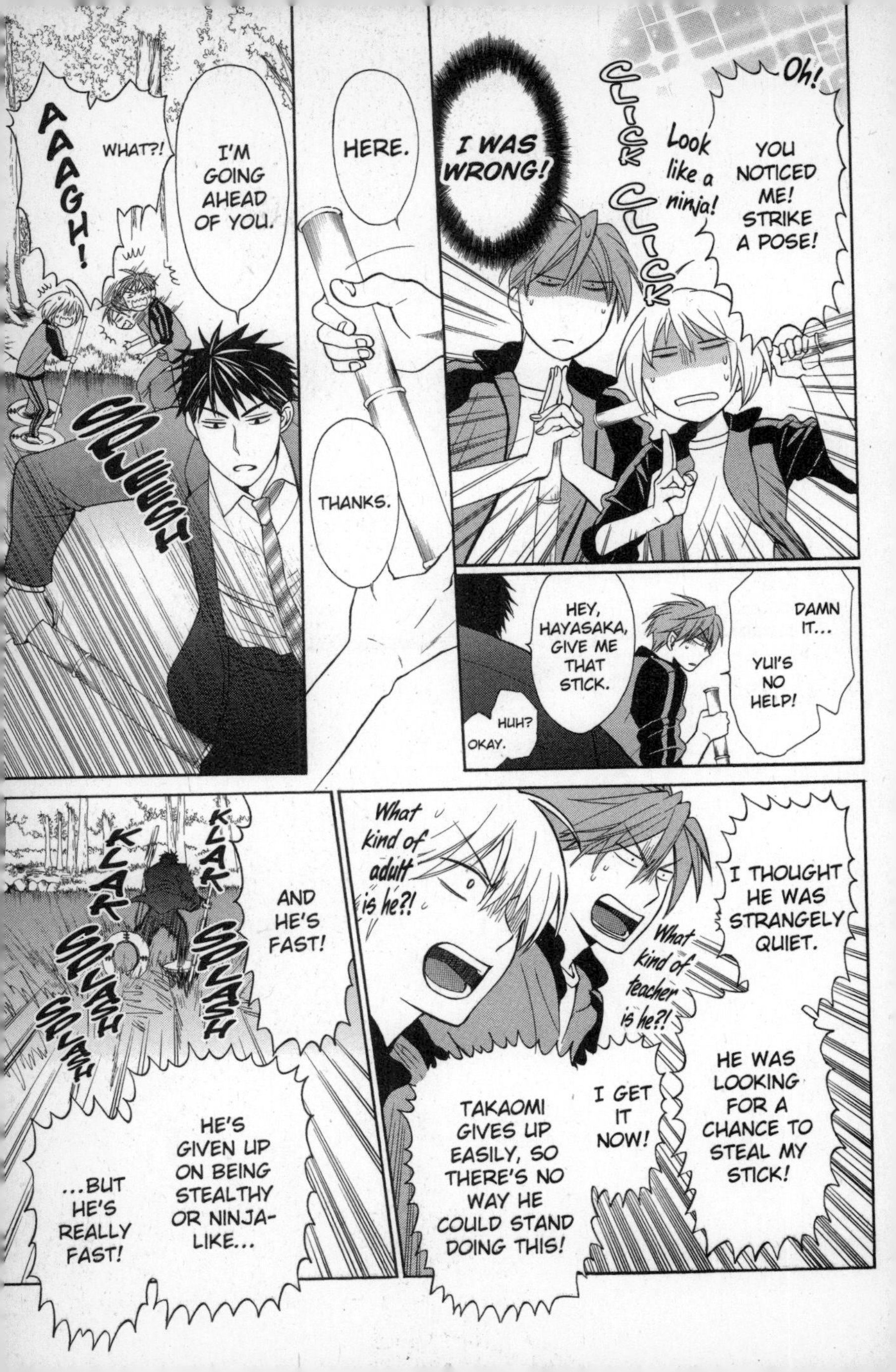
Oh!
YOU NOTICED ME! STRIKE A POSE!
Look like a ninja!
CLICK CLICK CLICK
I WAS WRONG!
DAMN IT...
YUI'S NO HELP!
HEY, HAYASAKA, GIVE ME THAT STICK.
HUH? OKAY.
HERE.
THANKS.
I'M GOING AHEAD OF YOU.
WHAT?!
AAAGH!
SQUEESH
I THOUGHT HE WAS STRANGELY QUIET.
What kind of teacher is he?!
What kind of adult is he?!
HE WAS LOOKING FOR A CHANCE TO STEAL MY STICK!
I GET IT NOW!
TAKAOMI GIVES UP EASILY, SO THERE'S NO WAY HE COULD STAND DOING THIS!
AND HE'S FAST!
KLAK KLAK
SPLASH SPLASH SPLASH SPLASH
HE'S GIVEN UP ON BEING STEALTHY OR NINJA-LIKE...
...BUT HE'S REALLY FAST!

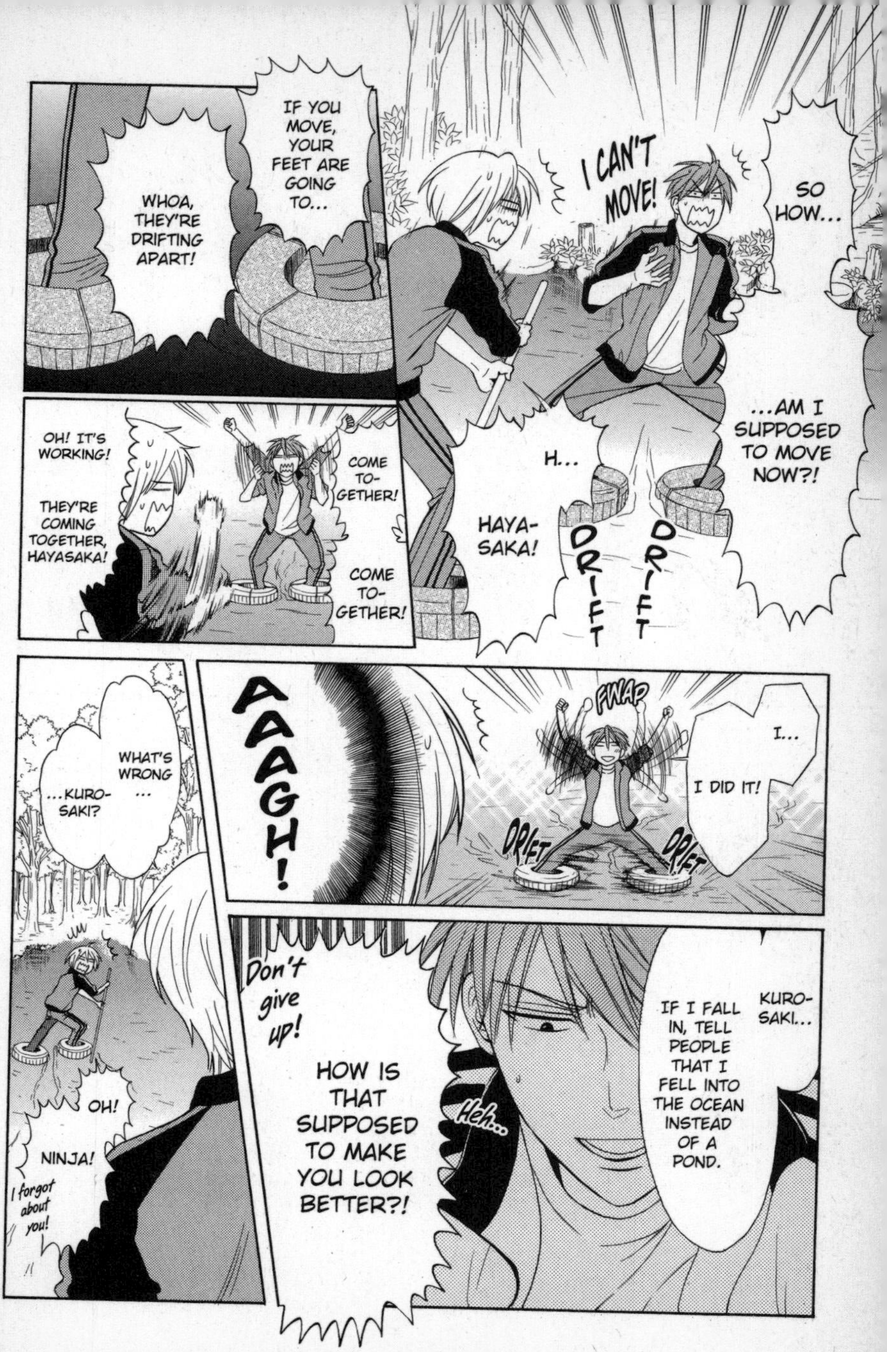
SO HOW...
I CAN'T MOVE!
...AM I SUPPOSED TO MOVE NOW?!
H...
HAYA-SAKA!
DRIFT
DRIFT
IF YOU MOVE, YOUR FEET ARE GOING TO...
WHOA, THEY'RE DRIFTING APART!
COME TO-GETHER!
COME TO-GETHER!
OH! IT'S WORKING!
THEY'RE COMING TOGETHER, HAYASAKA!
I...
I DID IT!
FWAP
DRIFT
DRIFT
AAAGH!
KURO-SAKI...
IF I FALL IN, TELL PEOPLE THAT I FELL INTO THE OCEAN INSTEAD OF A POND.
Heh...
HOW IS THAT SUPPOSED TO MAKE YOU LOOK BETTER?!
Don't give up!
WHAT'S WRONG...
...KURO-SAKI?
OH!
NINJA!
I forgot about you!

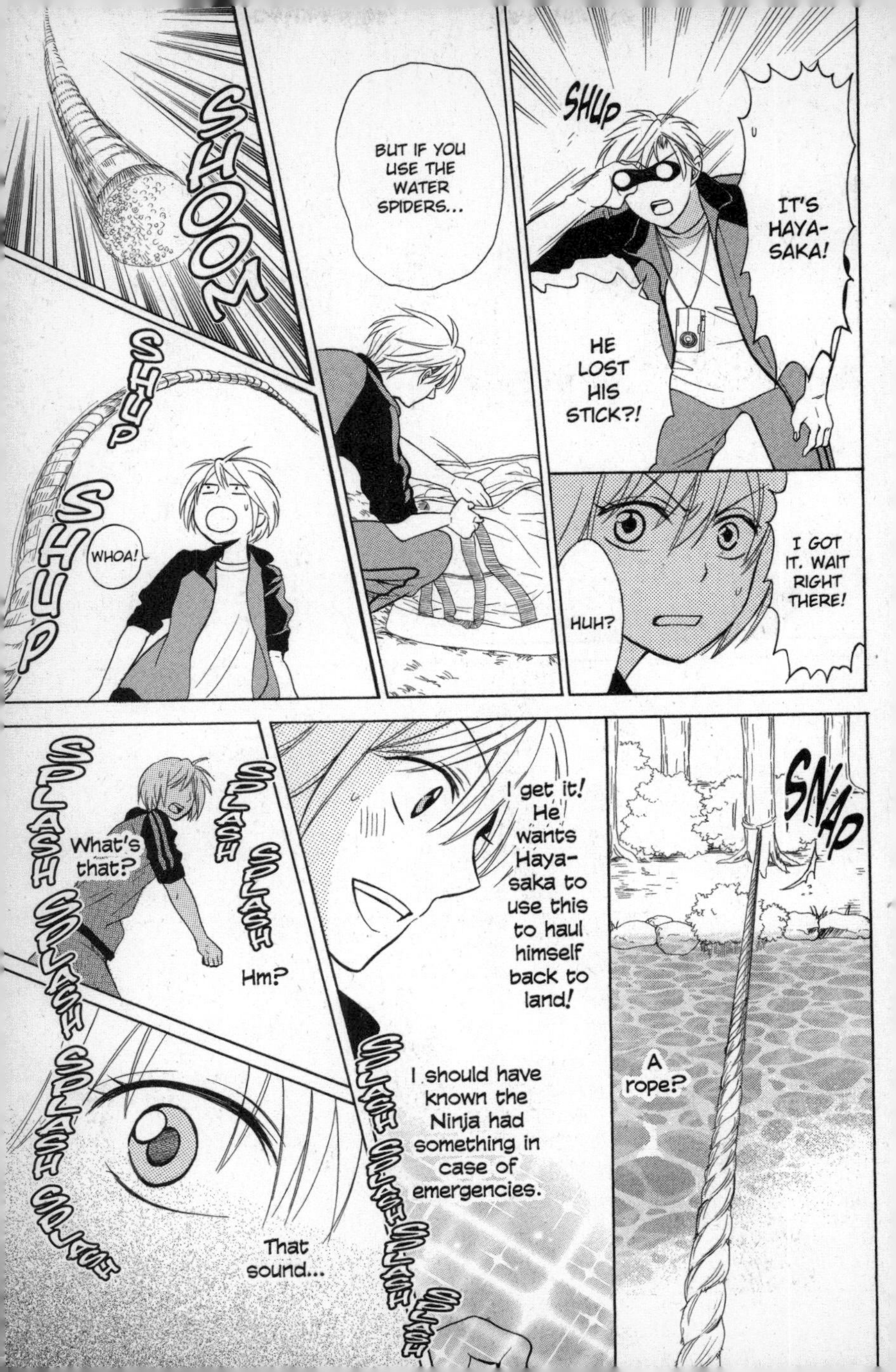

SHUP
IT'S HAYA-SAKA!
HE LOST HIS STICK?!
I GOT IT. WAIT RIGHT THERE!
HUH?
BUT IF YOU USE THE WATER SPIDERS...
SHOOM
SHUP
SHUP
WHOA!
SNAP
A rope?
I get it! He wants Haya-saka to use this to haul himself back to land!
I should have known the Ninja had something in case of emergencies.
SPLASH SPLASH SPLASH
SPLASH
SPLASH
What's that?
Hm?
That sound...
SPLASH SPLASH SPLASH

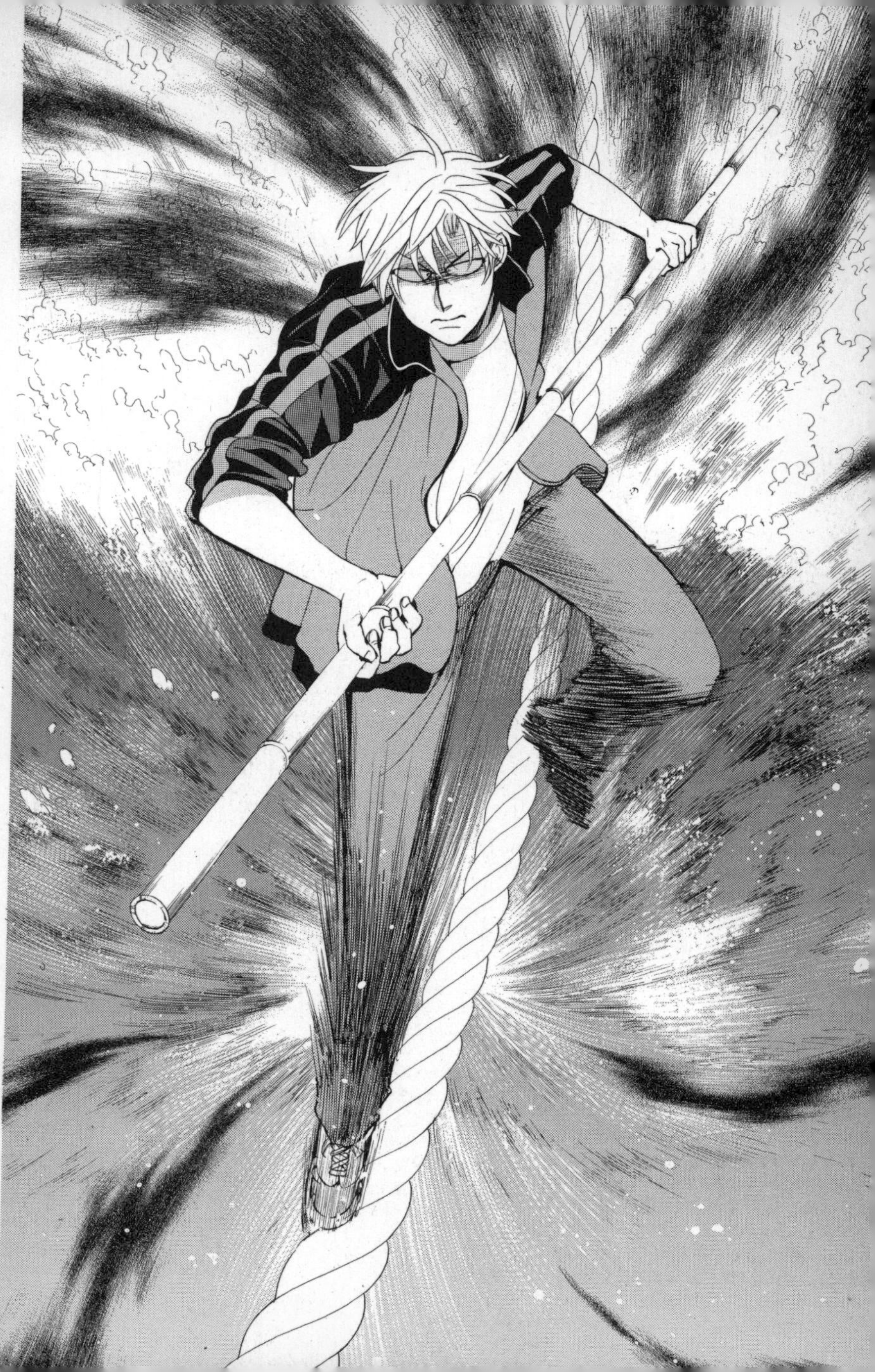

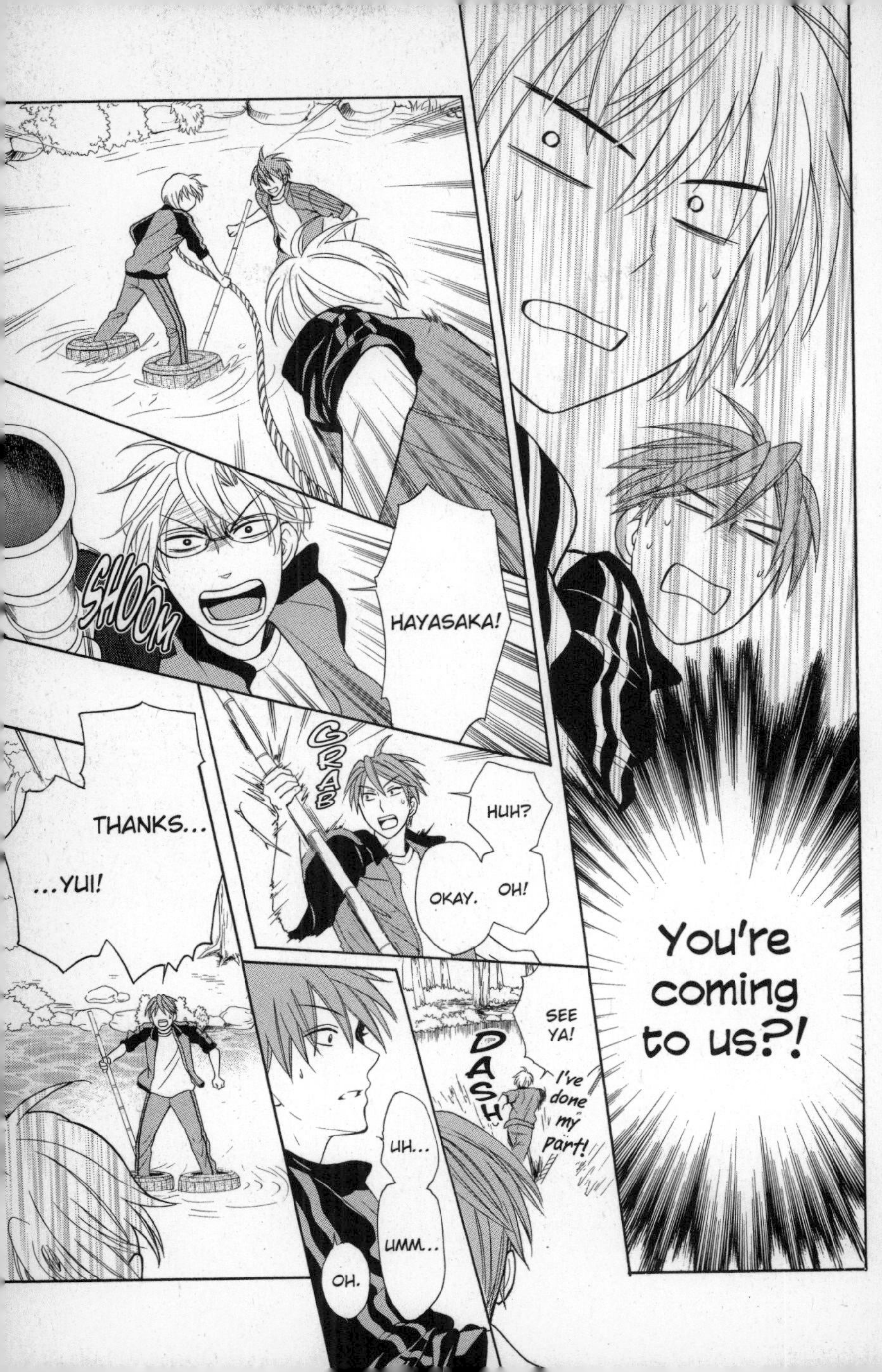
You're coming to us?!
SHOOM
HAYASAKA!
GRAB
HUH?
OH!
OKAY.
THANKS...
...YUI!
SEE YA!
DASH
I've done my part!
UH...
UMM...
OH.

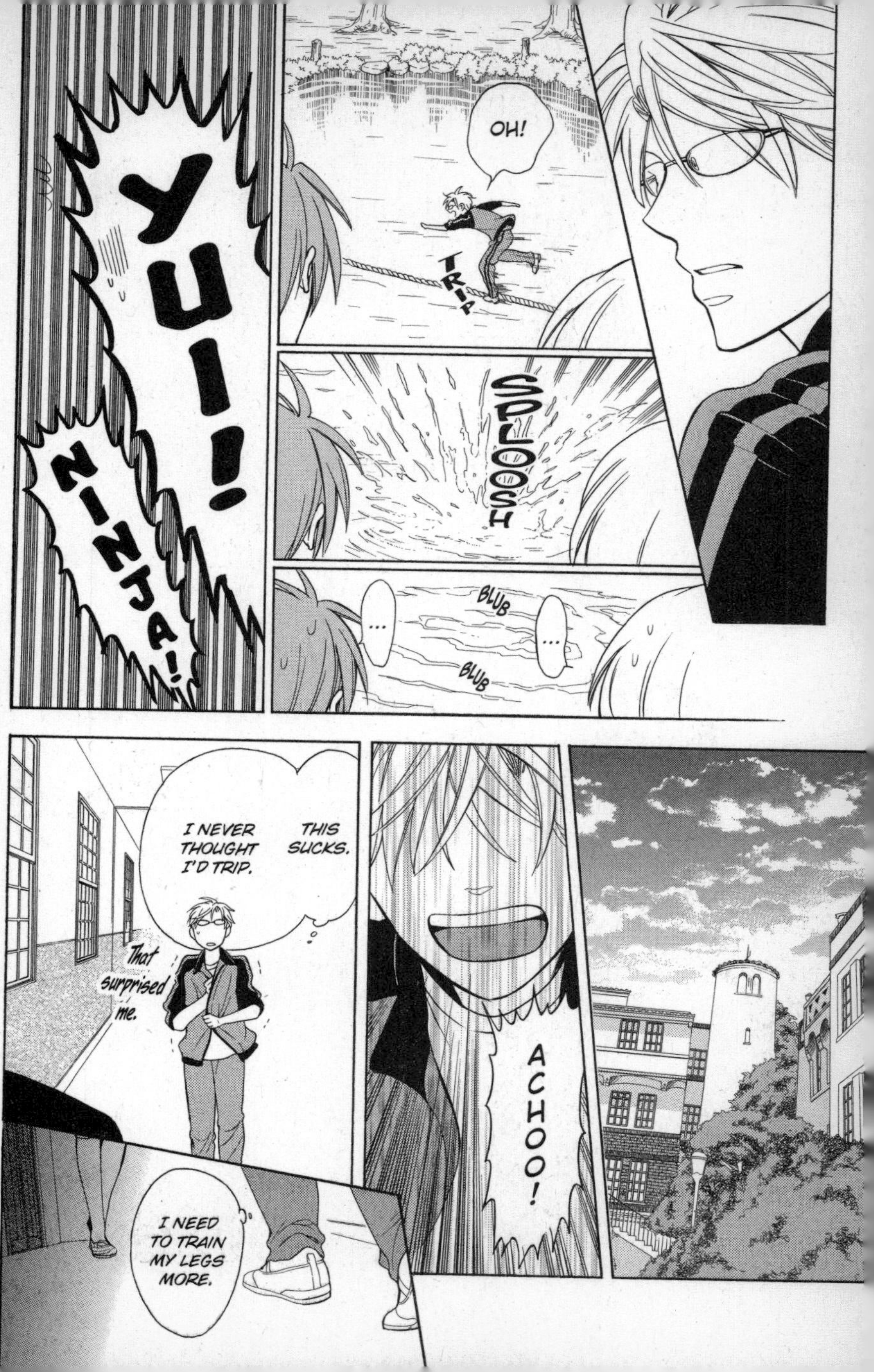
OH!
TRIP
SPLOOSH
...
...
BLUB
BLUB
YUI!!
NINJA!!
ACHOO!
THIS SUCKS.
I NEVER THOUGHT I'D TRIP.
That surprised me.
I NEED TO TRAIN MY LEGS MORE.

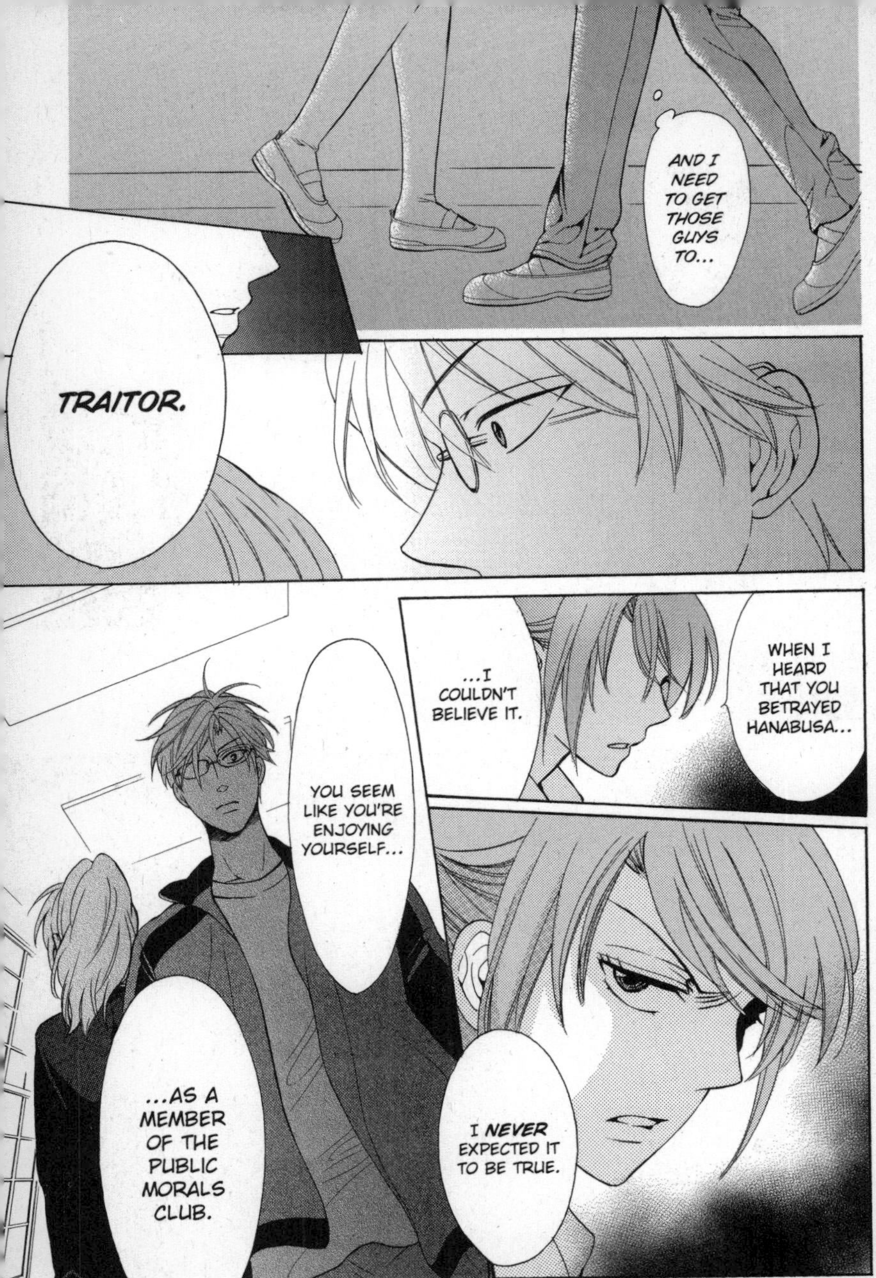
AND I NEED TO GET THOSE GUYS TO...
TRAITOR.
WHEN I HEARD THAT YOU BETRAYED HANABUSA...
...I COULDN'T BELIEVE IT.
I *NEVER* EXPECTED IT TO BE TRUE.
YOU SEEM LIKE YOU'RE ENJOYING YOURSELF...
...AS A MEMBER OF THE PUBLIC MORALS CLUB.

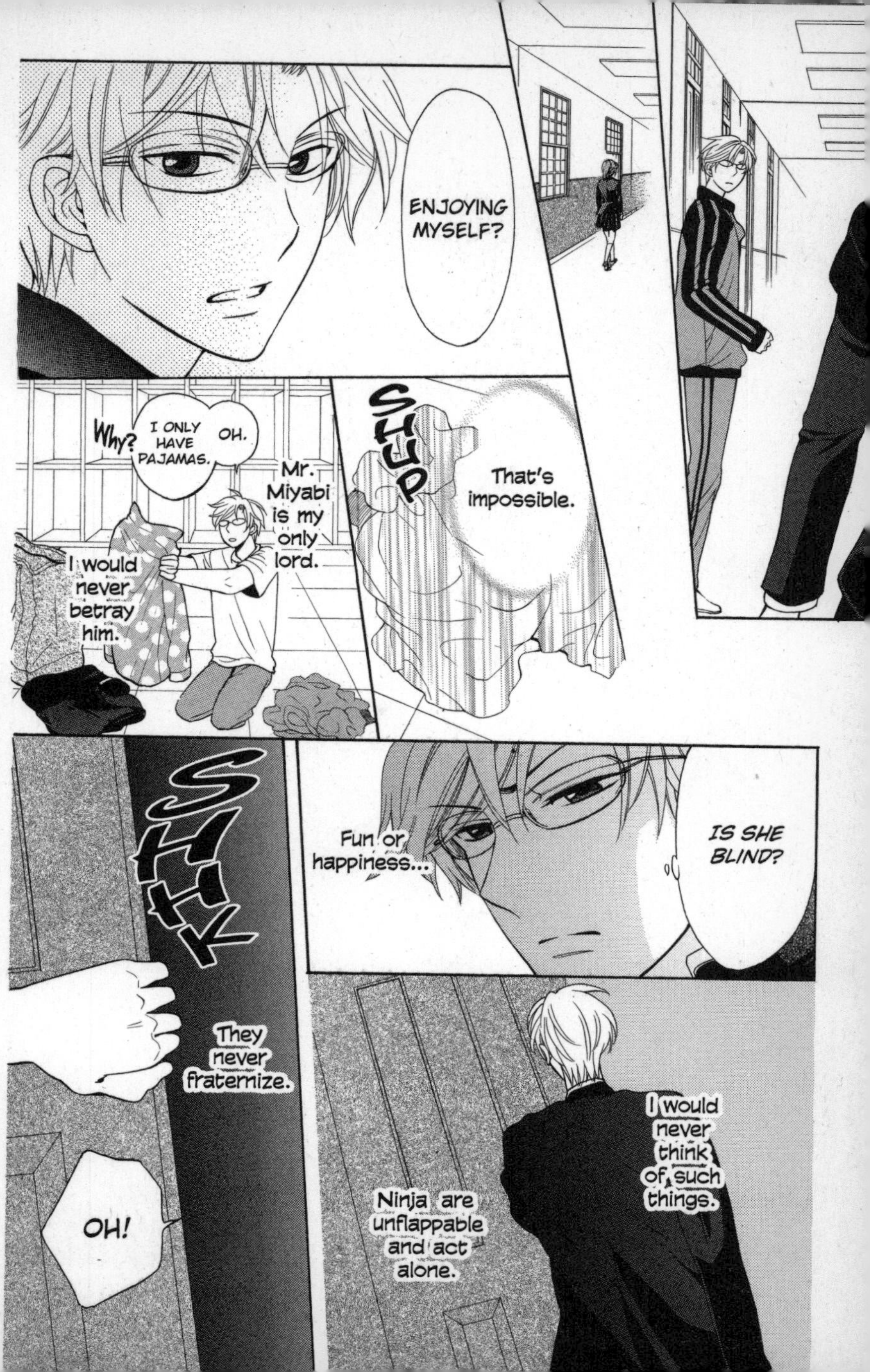
ENJOYING MYSELF?
SHUP
That's impossible.
OH.
I ONLY HAVE PAJAMAS.
Why?
Mr. Miyabi is my only lord.
I would never betray him.
IS SHE BLIND?
Fun or happiness...
I would never think of such things.
Ninja are unflappable and act alone.
SHKK
They never fraternize.
OH!

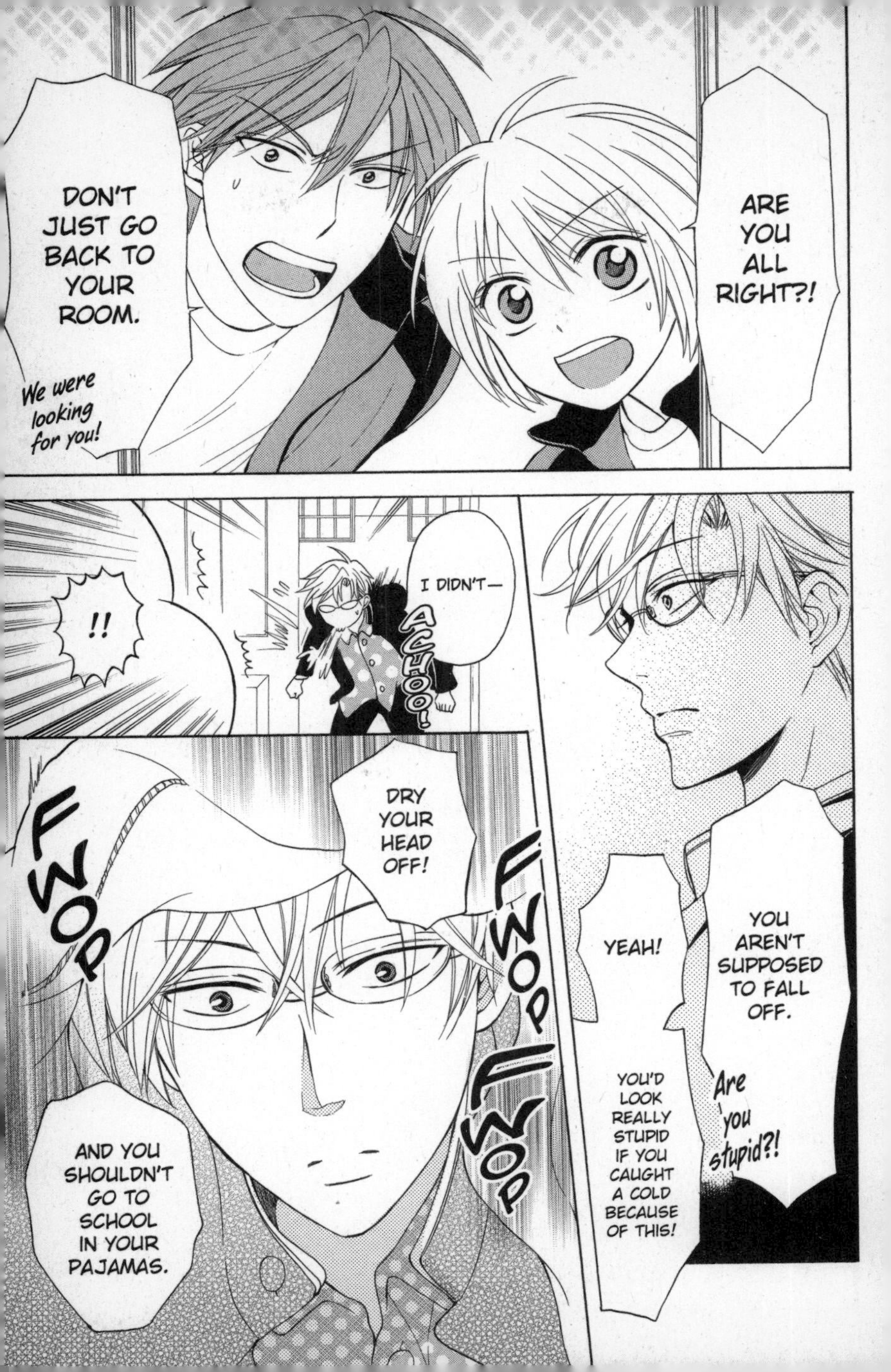
ARE YOU ALL RIGHT?!
DON'T JUST GO BACK TO YOUR ROOM.
We were looking for you!
YOU AREN'T SUPPOSED TO FALL OFF.
YEAH!
Are you stupid?!
YOU'D LOOK REALLY STUPID IF YOU CAUGHT A COLD BECAUSE OF THIS!
I DIDN'T—
ACHOO!
!!
DRY YOUR HEAD OFF!
FWOP
FWOP
FWOP
FWOP
AND YOU SHOULDN'T GO TO SCHOOL IN YOUR PAJAMAS.

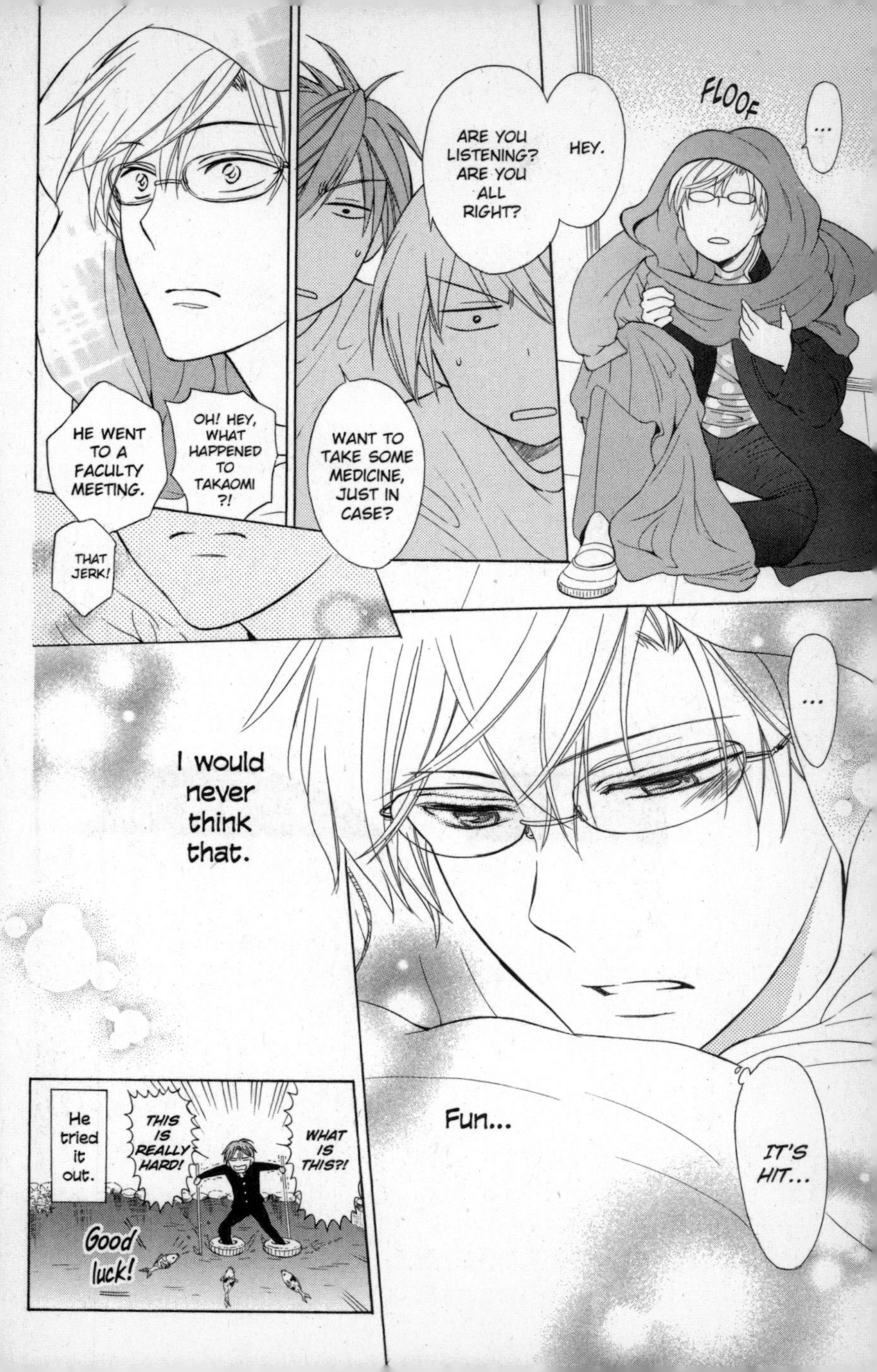
FLOOF
...
HEY.
ARE YOU LISTENING? ARE YOU ALL RIGHT?
WANT TO TAKE SOME MEDICINE, JUST IN CASE?
OH! HEY, WHAT HAPPENED TO TAKAOMI ?!
HE WENT TO A FACULTY MEETING.
THAT JERK!
...
I would never think that.
IT'S HIT...
Fun...
He tried it out.
WHAT IS THIS?!
THIS IS REALLY HARD!
Good luck!

Chapter 53

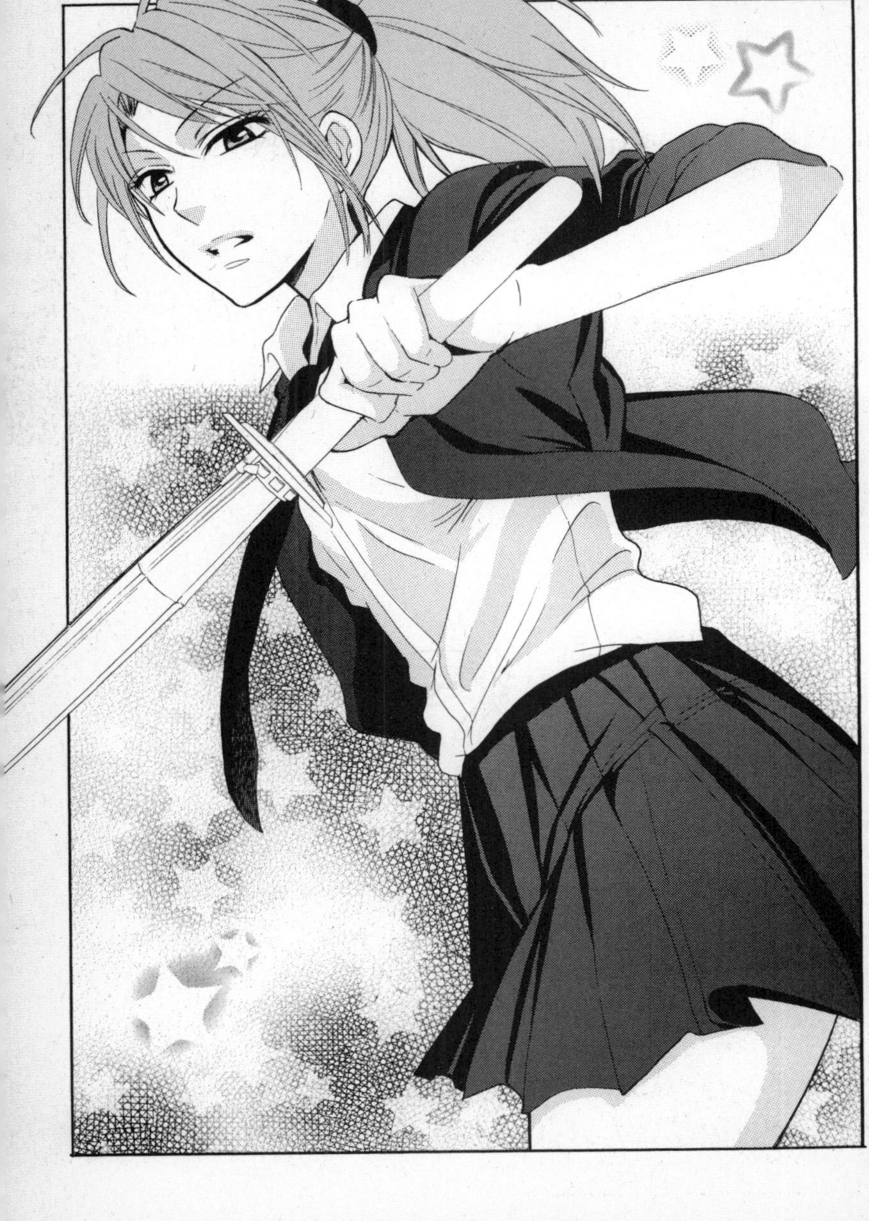

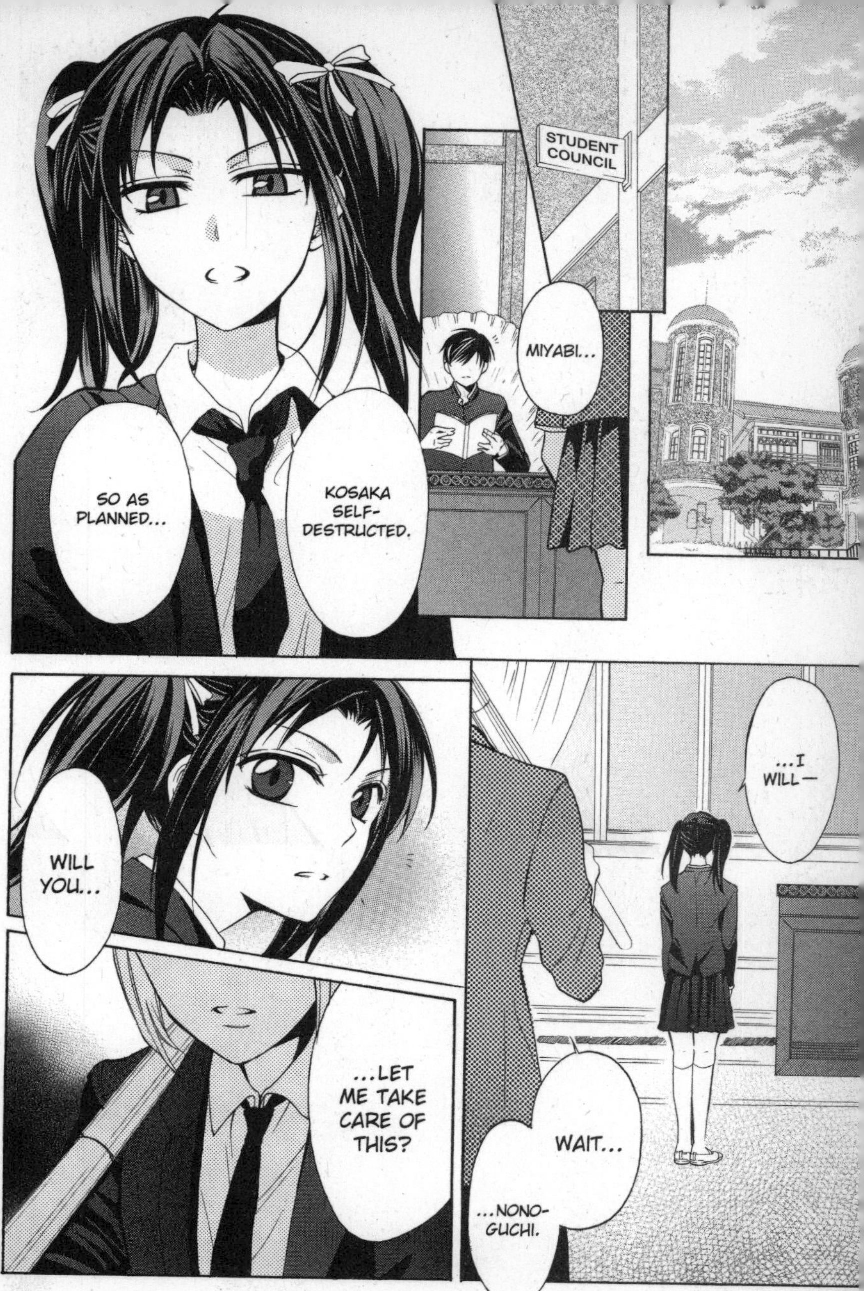
STUDENT COUNCIL
MIYABI...
KOSAKA SELF-DESTRUCTED.
SO AS PLANNED...
...I WILL—
WAIT...
...NONO-GUCHI.
WILL YOU...
...LET ME TAKE CARE OF THIS?

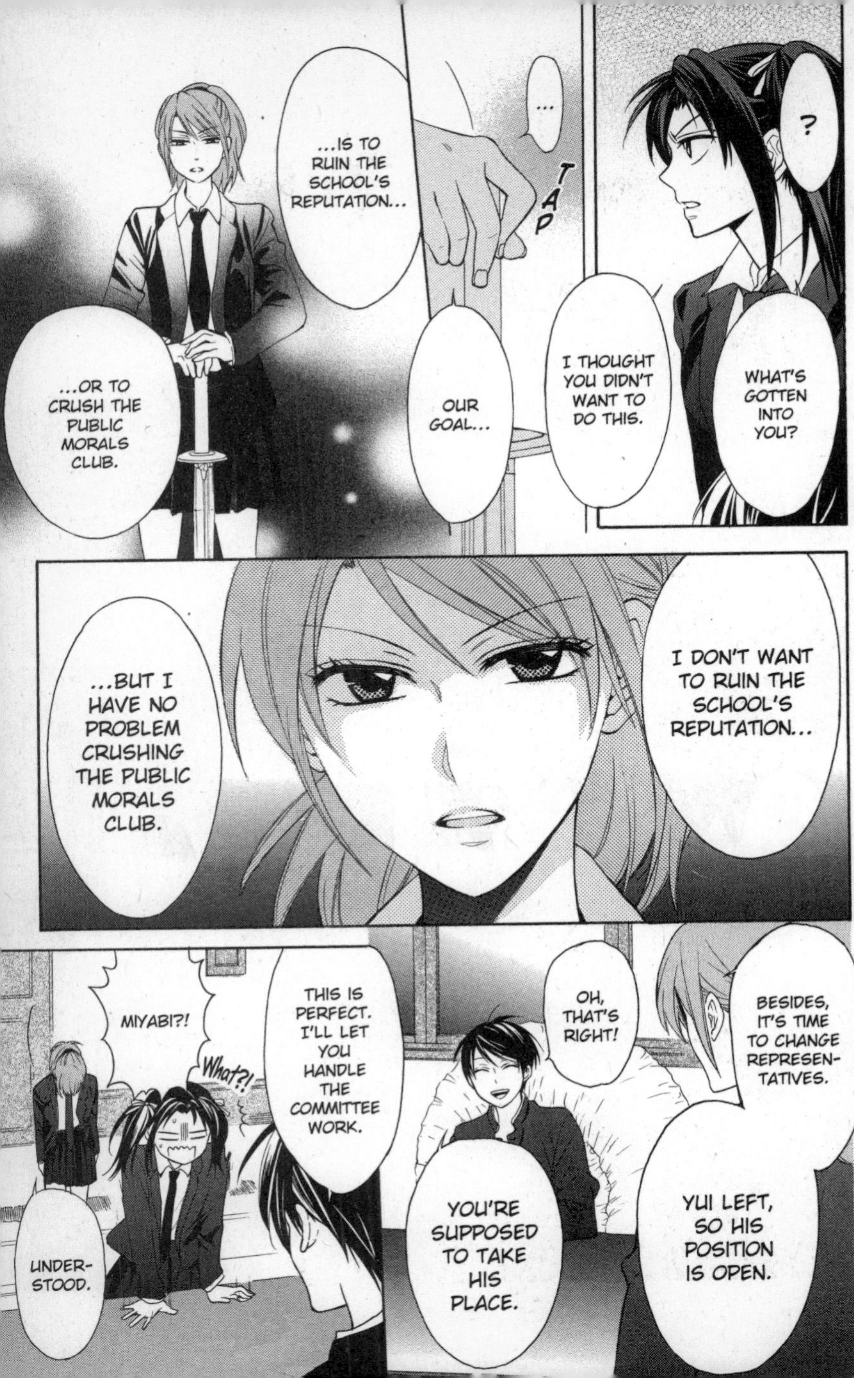
?
WHAT'S GOTTEN INTO YOU?
I THOUGHT YOU DIDN'T WANT TO DO THIS.
...
TAP
OUR GOAL...
...IS TO RUIN THE SCHOOL'S REPUTATION...
...OR TO CRUSH THE PUBLIC MORALS CLUB.
I DON'T WANT TO RUIN THE SCHOOL'S REPUTATION...
...BUT I HAVE NO PROBLEM CRUSHING THE PUBLIC MORALS CLUB.
BESIDES, IT'S TIME TO CHANGE REPRESEN-TATIVES.
YUI LEFT, SO HIS POSITION IS OPEN.
OH, THAT'S RIGHT!
YOU'RE SUPPOSED TO TAKE HIS PLACE.
THIS IS PERFECT. I'LL LET YOU HANDLE THE COMMITTEE WORK.
What?!
MIYABI?!
UNDER-STOOD.

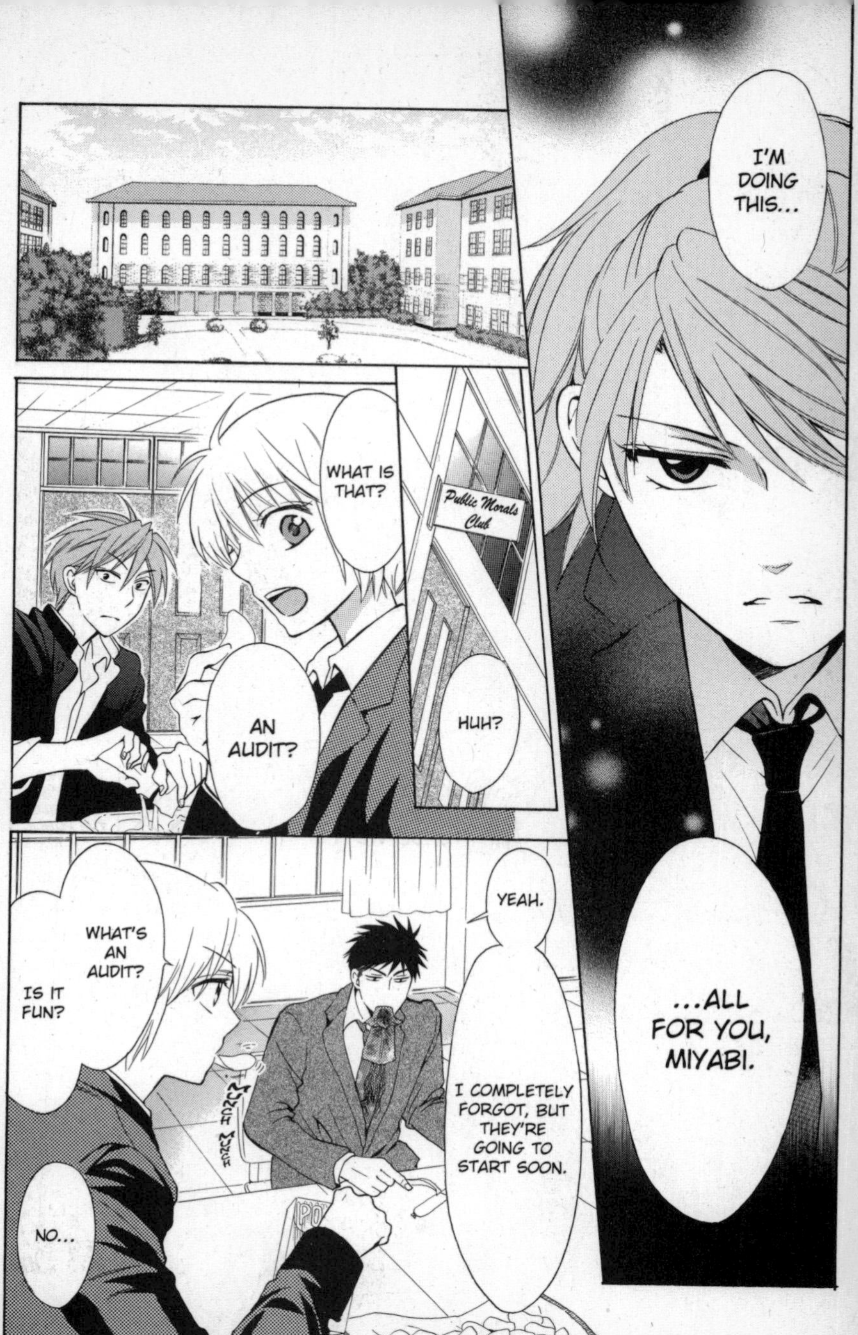
I'M DOING THIS...
...ALL FOR YOU, MIYABI.
Public Morals Club
HUH?
WHAT IS THAT?
AN AUDIT?
YEAH.
I COMPLETELY FORGOT, BUT THEY'RE GOING TO START SOON.
WHAT'S AN AUDIT?
IS IT FUN?
MUNCH MUNCH
NO...

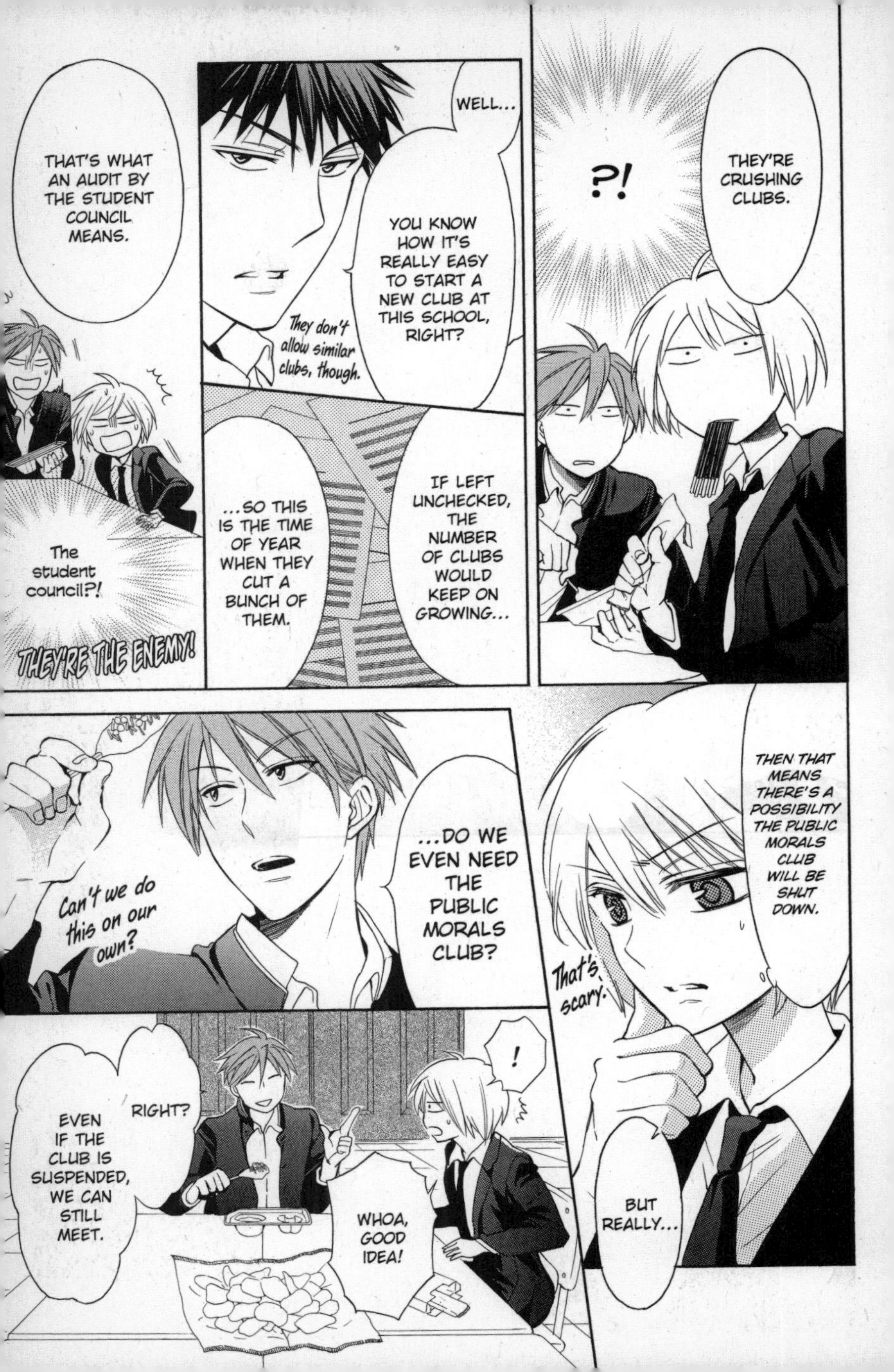

THEY'RE CRUSHING CLUBS.
?!
WELL...
YOU KNOW HOW IT'S REALLY EASY TO START A NEW CLUB AT THIS SCHOOL, RIGHT?
They don't allow similar clubs, though.
IF LEFT UNCHECKED, THE NUMBER OF CLUBS WOULD KEEP ON GROWING...
...SO THIS IS THE TIME OF YEAR WHEN THEY CUT A BUNCH OF THEM.
THAT'S WHAT AN AUDIT BY THE STUDENT COUNCIL MEANS.
The student council?!
THEY'RE THE ENEMY!
THEN THAT MEANS THERE'S A POSSIBILITY THE PUBLIC MORALS CLUB WILL BE SHUT DOWN.
That's scary.
BUT REALLY...
...DO WE EVEN NEED THE PUBLIC MORALS CLUB?
Can't we do this on our own?
!
RIGHT?
EVEN IF THE CLUB IS SUSPENDED, WE CAN STILL MEET.
WHOA, GOOD IDEA!

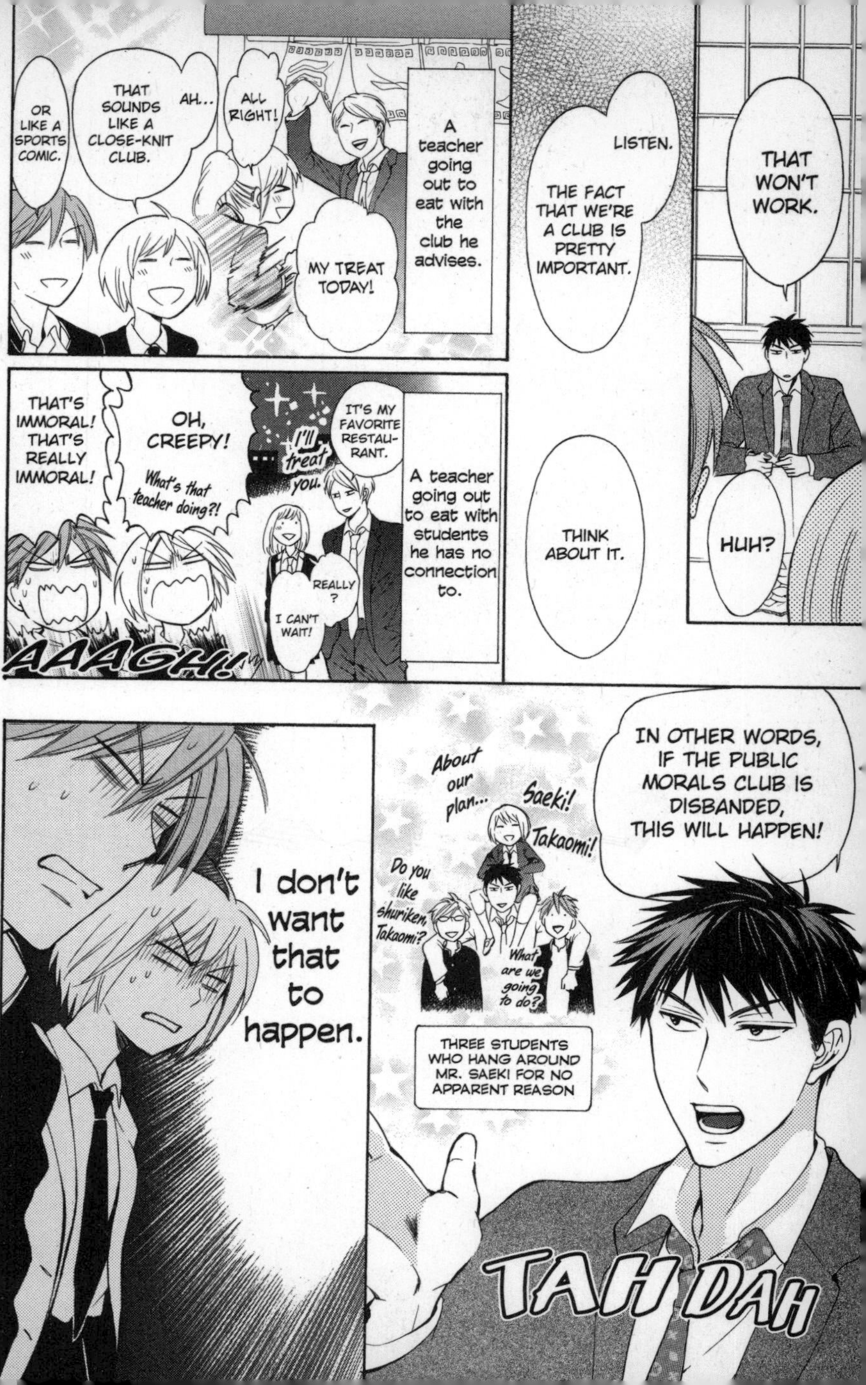
THAT WON'T WORK.
HUH?
LISTEN.
THE FACT THAT WE'RE A CLUB IS PRETTY IMPORTANT.
THINK ABOUT IT.
A teacher going out to eat with the club he advises.
ALL RIGHT!
MY TREAT TODAY!
AH...
THAT SOUNDS LIKE A CLOSE-KNIT CLUB.
OR LIKE A SPORTS COMIC.
A teacher going out to eat with students he has no connection to.
IT'S MY FAVORITE RESTAU-RANT.
I'll treat you.
REALLY?
I CAN'T WAIT!
OH, CREEPY!
What's that teacher doing?!
THAT'S IMMORAL! THAT'S REALLY IMMORAL!
AAAGH!
IN OTHER WORDS, IF THE PUBLIC MORALS CLUB IS DISBANDED, THIS WILL HAPPEN!
Saeki!
Takaomi!
About our plan...
Do you like shuriken, Takaomi?
What are we going to do?
THREE STUDENTS WHO HANG AROUND MR. SAEKI FOR NO APPARENT REASON
TAH DAH
I don't want that to happen.

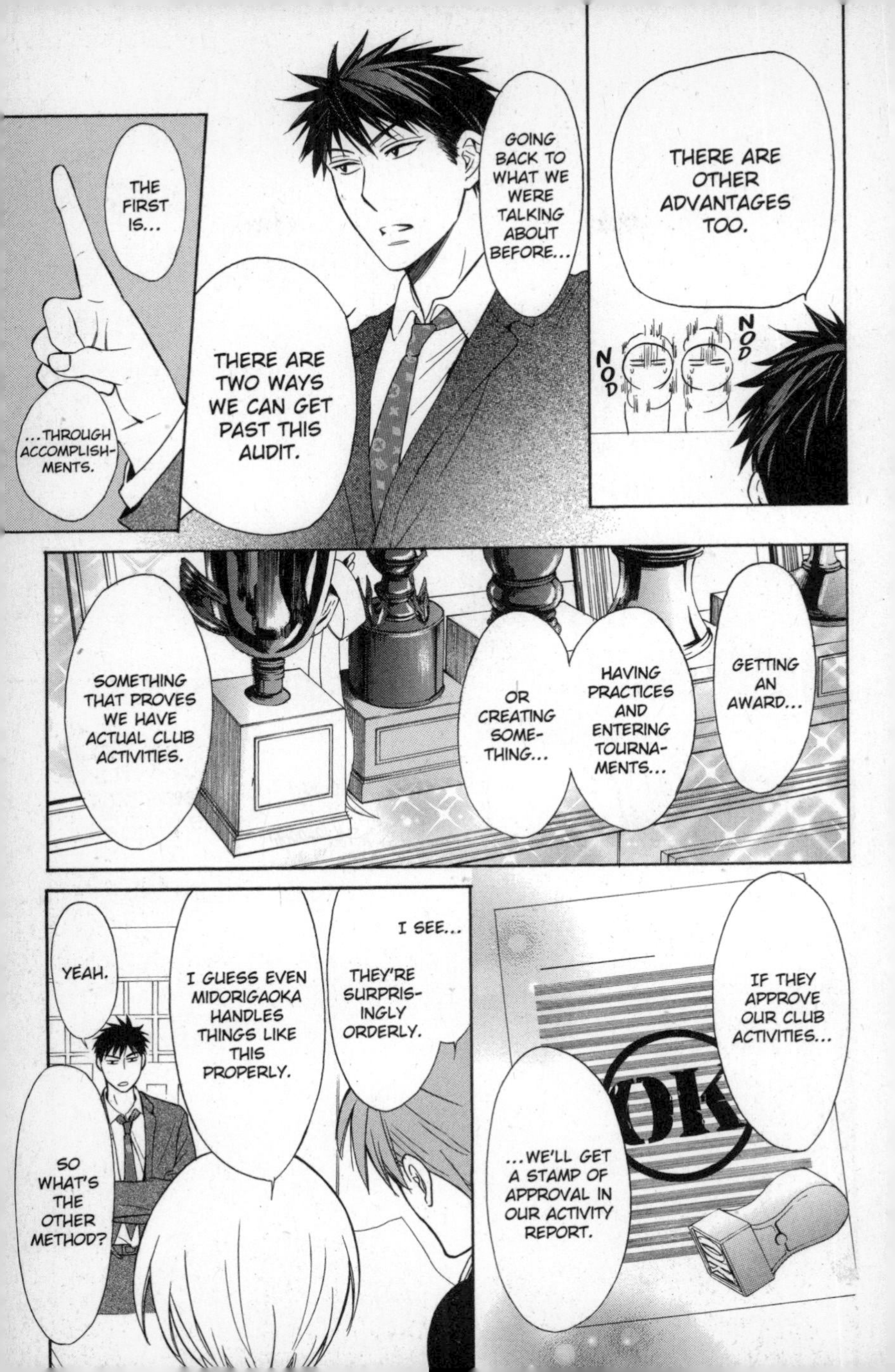
THERE ARE OTHER ADVANTAGES TOO.
NOD
NOD
GOING BACK TO WHAT WE WERE TALKING ABOUT BEFORE...
THERE ARE TWO WAYS WE CAN GET PAST THIS AUDIT.
THE FIRST IS...
...THROUGH ACCOMPLISH-MENTS.
GETTING AN AWARD...
HAVING PRACTICES AND ENTERING TOURNA-MENTS...
OR CREATING SOME-THING...
SOMETHING THAT PROVES WE HAVE ACTUAL CLUB ACTIVITIES.
IF THEY APPROVE OUR CLUB ACTIVITIES...
...WE'LL GET A STAMP OF APPROVAL IN OUR ACTIVITY REPORT.
OK
I SEE...
THEY'RE SURPRIS-INGLY ORDERLY.
I GUESS EVEN MIDORIGAOKA HANDLES THINGS LIKE THIS PROPERLY.
YEAH.
SO WHAT'S THE OTHER METHOD?

GETTING THAT STAMP OF APPROVAL BY FORCE!

IS THAT WHAT IT COMES DOWN TO?!

BUT THAT'S JUST A LAST RESORT.

Don't worry.

THE OTHER CLUBS ARE SCRAMBLING TO PUT TOGETHER THEIR REPORTS,

PUBLIC MORAL CLUB

Advisor

LET'S START ON OURS. FIRST OFF, OUR ACCOMPLISH- MENTS...

...esday
...ursday
Friday
...mes A Month
...eeting Place

CLUB ACCOMPLISHMENTS

o Took down Bancho

o Took down Yojimbo Club

o Dealt with other school...

o Reinstated Banch...

...

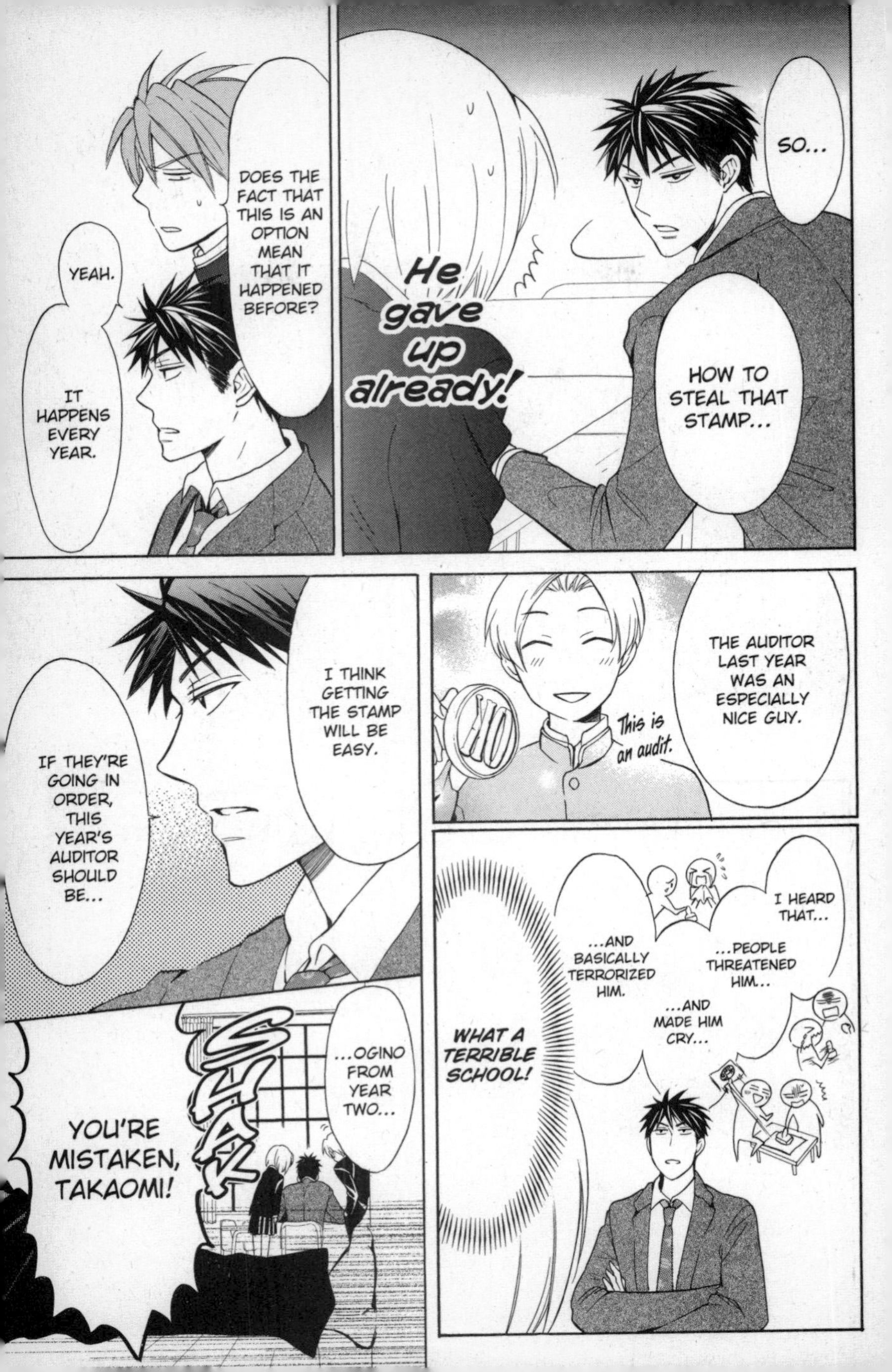

SO...
HOW TO STEAL THAT STAMP...
He gave up already!
DOES THE FACT THAT THIS IS AN OPTION MEAN THAT IT HAPPENED BEFORE?
YEAH.
IT HAPPENS EVERY YEAR.
THE AUDITOR LAST YEAR WAS AN ESPECIALLY NICE GUY.
This is an audit.
I HEARD THAT...
...PEOPLE THREATENED HIM...
...AND BASICALLY TERRORIZED HIM.
...AND MADE HIM CRY...
WHAT A TERRIBLE SCHOOL!
I THINK GETTING THE STAMP WILL BE EASY.
IF THEY'RE GOING IN ORDER, THIS YEAR'S AUDITOR SHOULD BE...
...OGINO FROM YEAR TWO...
SHAK
YOU'RE MISTAKEN, TAKAOMI!

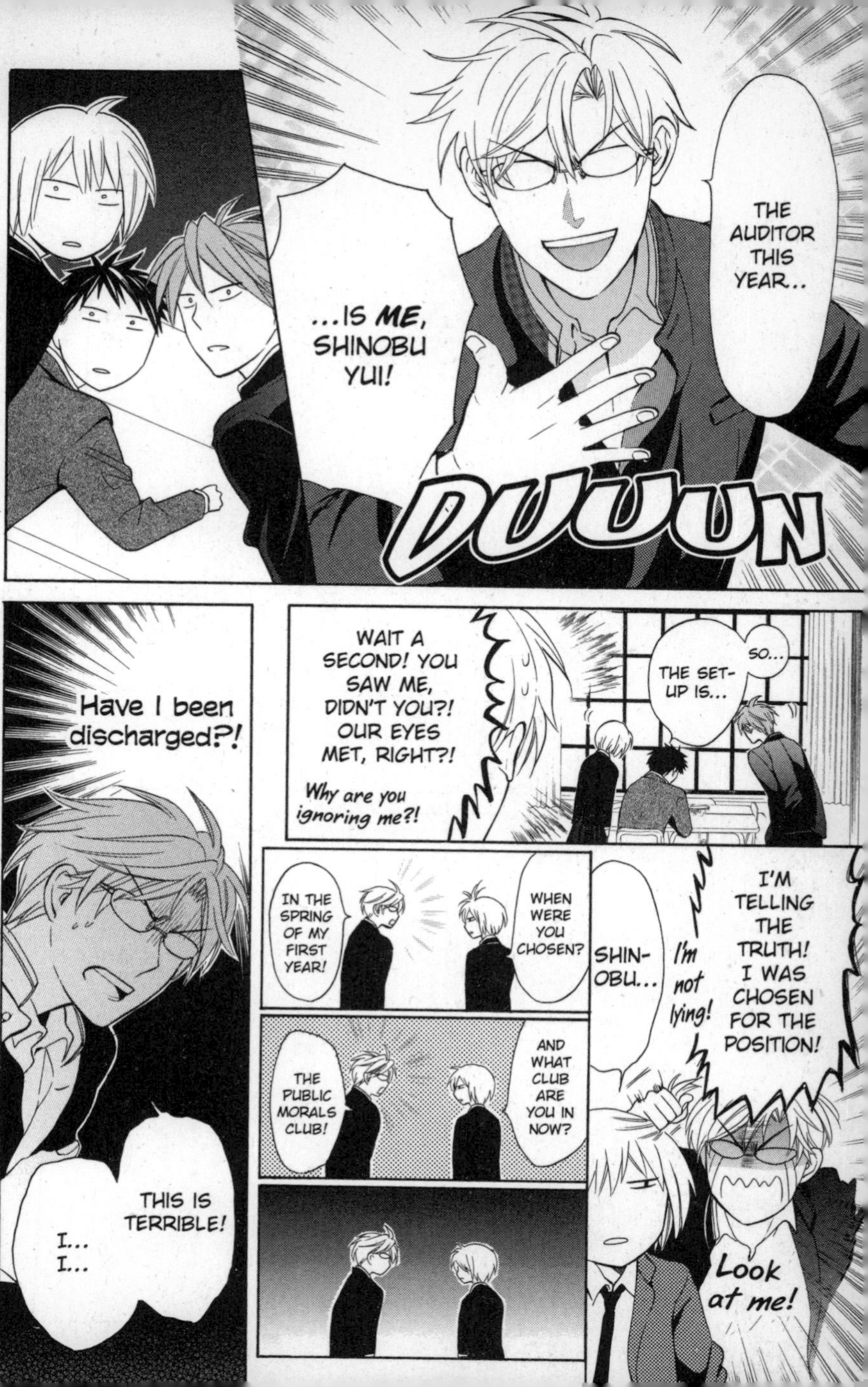
THE AUDITOR THIS YEAR...
...IS ME, SHINOBU YUI!
DUUUN
SO...
THE SET-UP IS...
WAIT A SECOND! YOU SAW ME, DIDN'T YOU?! OUR EYES MET, RIGHT?!
Why are you ignoring me?!
I'M TELLING THE TRUTH! I WAS CHOSEN FOR THE POSITION!
I'm not lying!
SHIN-OBU...
Look at me!
WHEN WERE YOU CHOSEN?
IN THE SPRING OF MY FIRST YEAR!
AND WHAT CLUB ARE YOU IN NOW?
THE PUBLIC MORALS CLUB!
Have I been discharged?!
THIS IS TERRIBLE!
I... I...

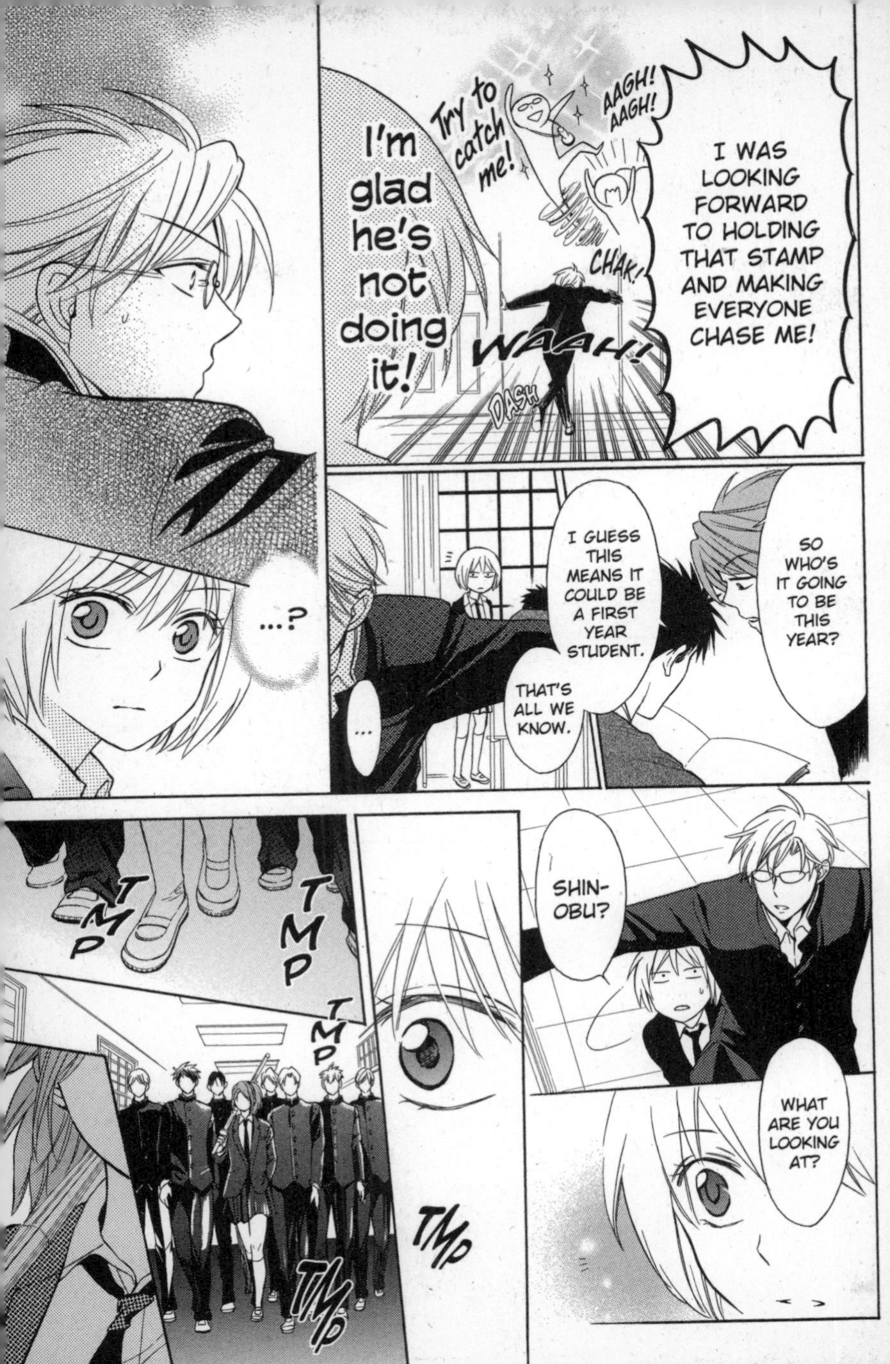
I WAS LOOKING FORWARD TO HOLDING THAT STAMP AND MAKING EVERYONE CHASE ME!
AAGH! AAGH!
Try to catch me!
CHAK!
WAAH!
DASH
I'm glad he's not doing it!
SO WHO'S IT GOING TO BE THIS YEAR?
I GUESS THIS MEANS IT COULD BE A FIRST YEAR STUDENT.
THAT'S ALL WE KNOW.
...
...?
SHIN-OBU?
WHAT ARE YOU LOOKING AT?
TMP
TMP
TMP
TMP
TMP
TMP

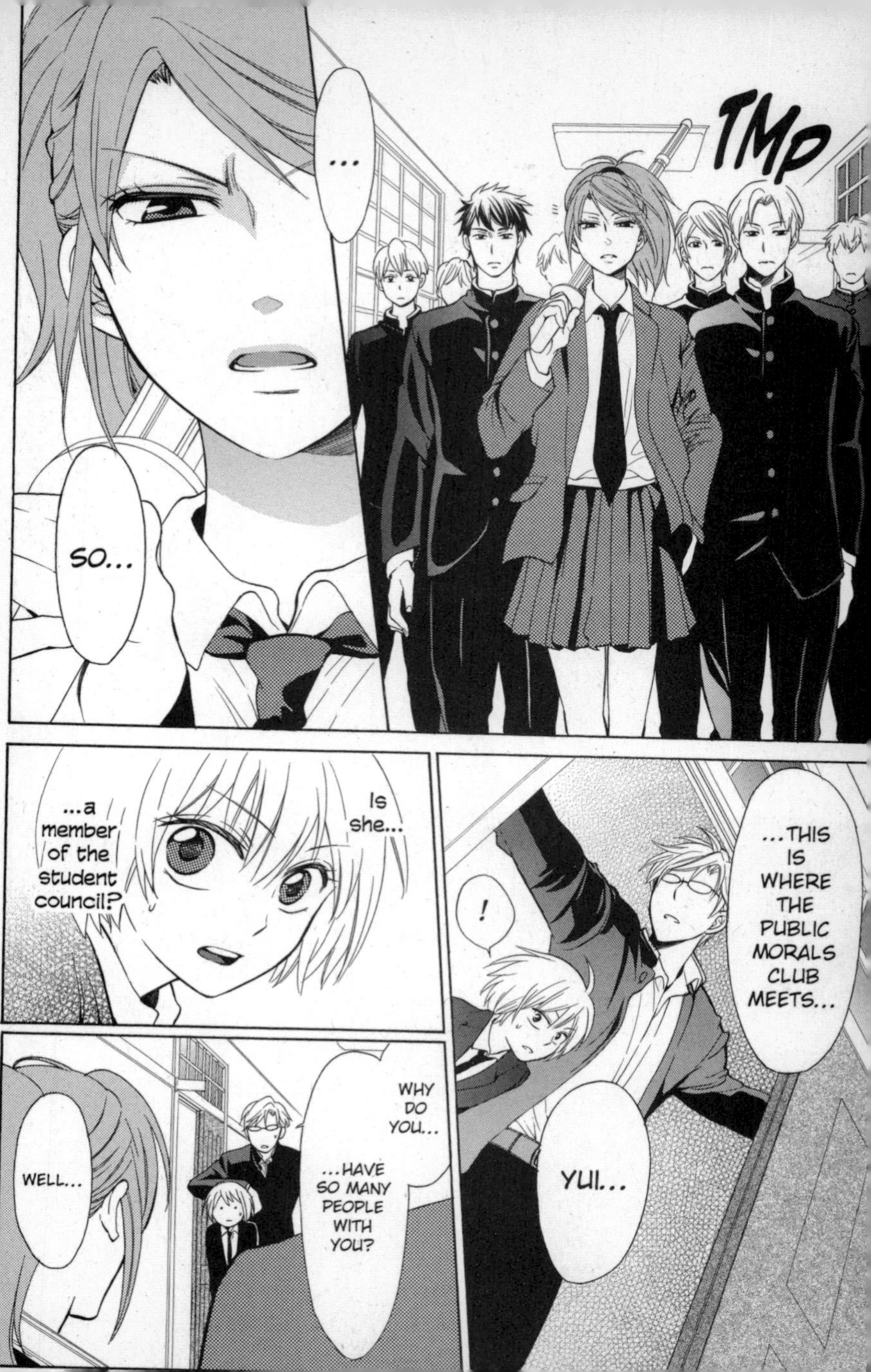
TMP
...
SO...
...THIS IS WHERE THE PUBLIC MORALS CLUB MEETS...
!
YUI...
Is she...
...a member of the student council?
WHY DO YOU...
...HAVE SO MANY PEOPLE WITH YOU?
WELL...

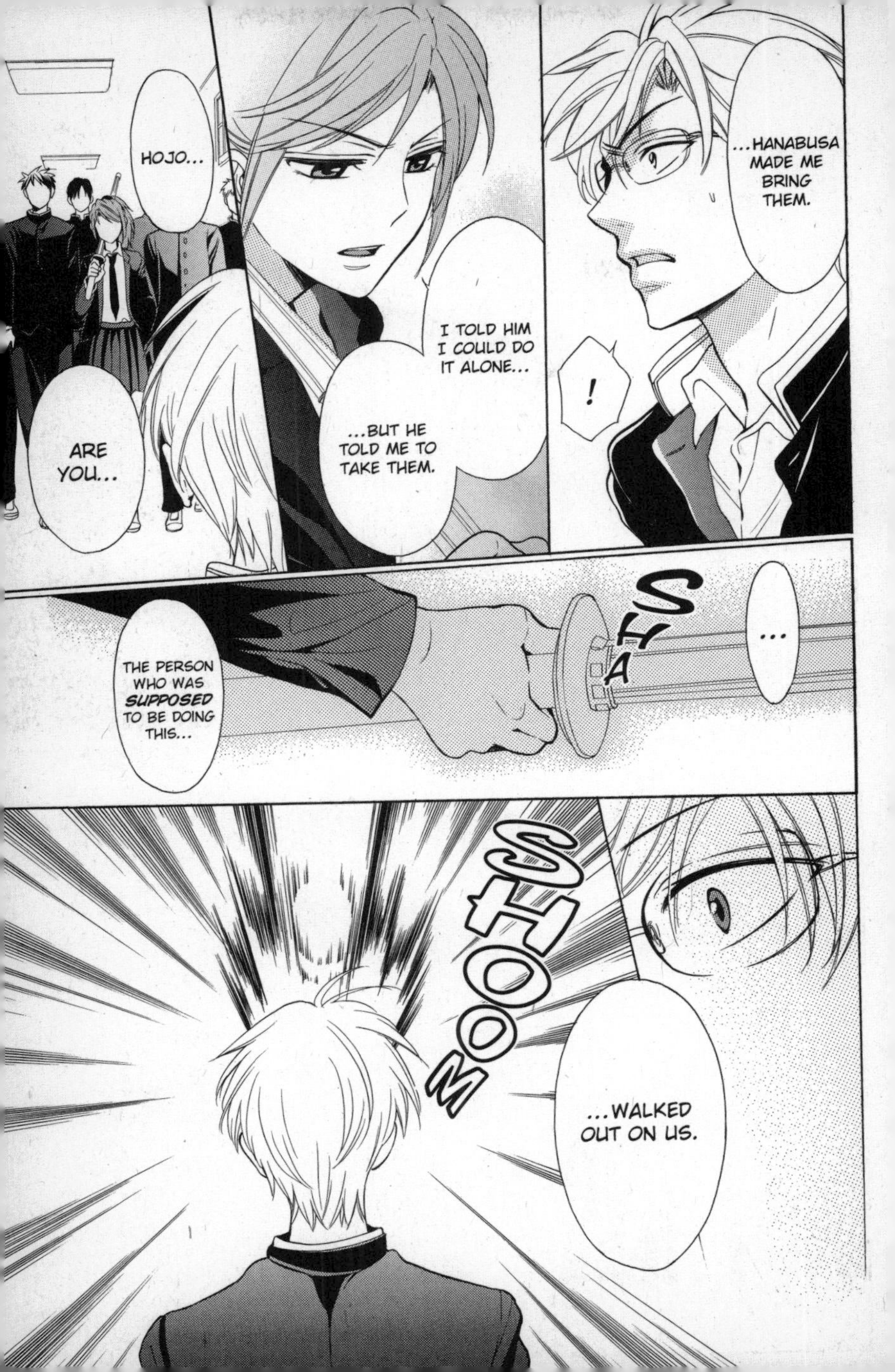
...HANABUSA MADE ME BRING THEM.
!
I TOLD HIM I COULD DO IT ALONE...
...BUT HE TOLD ME TO TAKE THEM.
HOJO...
ARE YOU...
...
SHA
THE PERSON WHO WAS SUPPOSED TO BE DOING THIS...
SHOOOM
...WALKED OUT ON US.

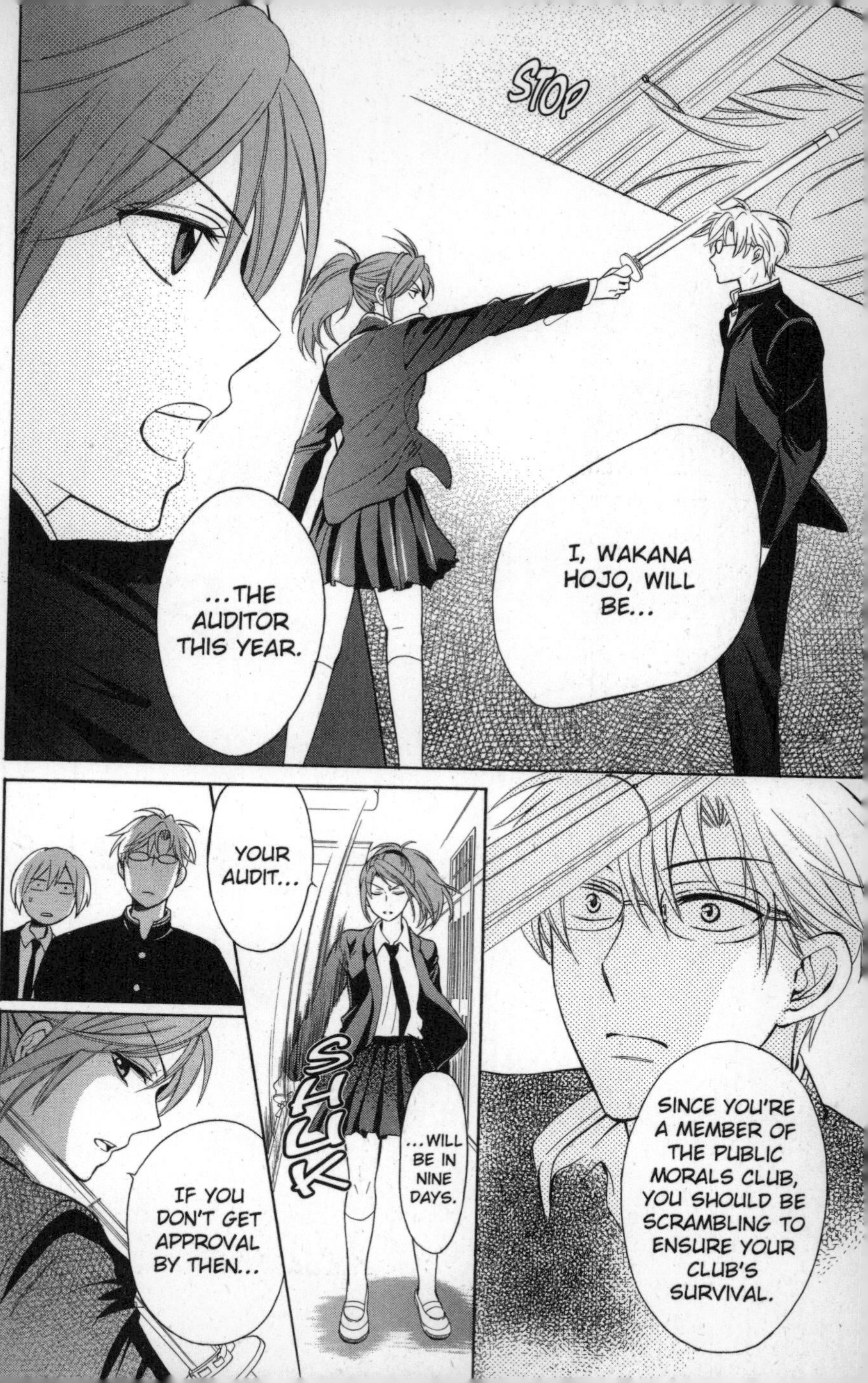
STOP
I, WAKANA HOJO, WILL BE...
...THE AUDITOR THIS YEAR.
SINCE YOU'RE A MEMBER OF THE PUBLIC MORALS CLUB, YOU SHOULD BE SCRAMBLING TO ENSURE YOUR CLUB'S SURVIVAL.
YOUR AUDIT...
SHUK
...WILL BE IN NINE DAYS.
IF YOU DON'T GET APPROVAL BY THEN...

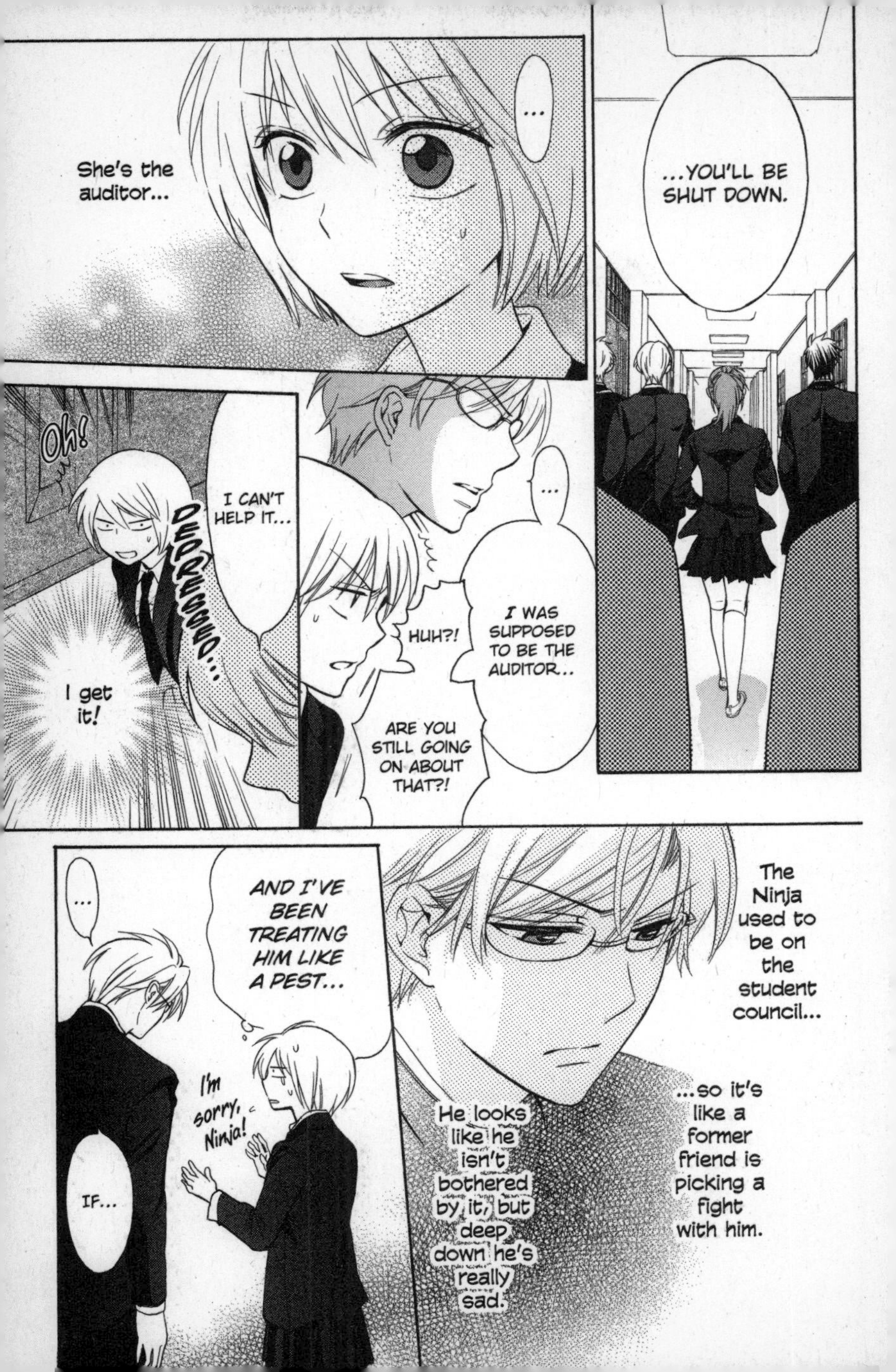
...YOU'LL BE SHUT DOWN.
...
She's the auditor...
...
I WAS SUPPOSED TO BE THE AUDITOR...
HUH?!
ARE YOU STILL GOING ON ABOUT THAT?!
I CAN'T HELP IT...
DEPRESSED...
Oh!
I get it!
The Ninja used to be on the student council...
...so it's like a former friend is picking a fight with him.
He looks like he isn't bothered by it, but deep down he's really sad.
AND I'VE BEEN TREATING HIM LIKE A PEST...
...
I'm sorry, Ninja!
IF...

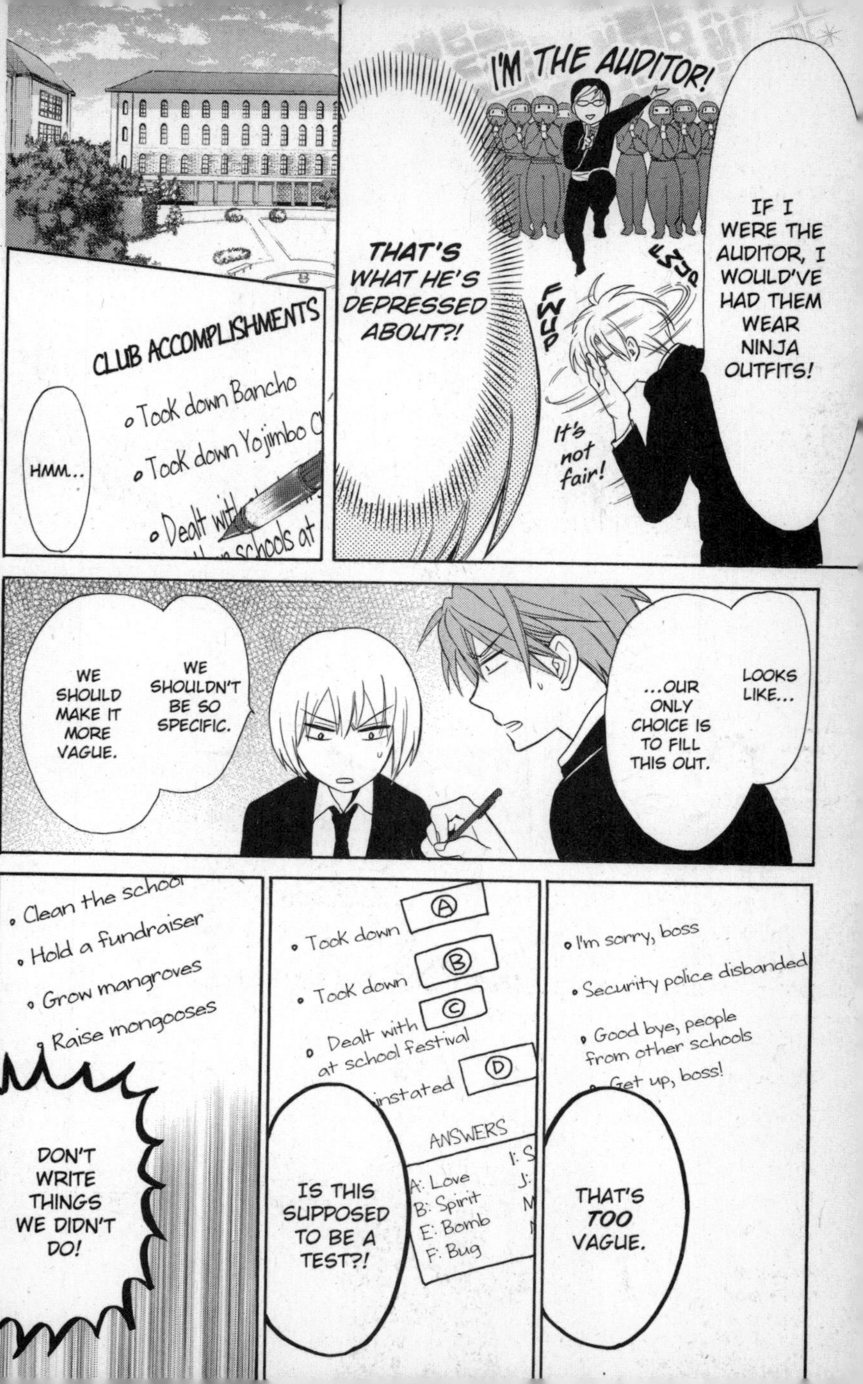

IF I WERE THE AUDITOR, I WOULD'VE HAD THEM WEAR NINJA OUTFITS!
I'M THE AUDITOR!
FWUP
It's not fair!
THAT'S WHAT HE'S DEPRESSED ABOUT?!
CLUB ACCOMPLISHMENTS
Took down Bancho
Took down Yojimbo C
Dealt with
schools at
HMM...
LOOKS LIKE...
...OUR ONLY CHOICE IS TO FILL THIS OUT.
WE SHOULDN'T BE SO SPECIFIC.
WE SHOULD MAKE IT MORE VAGUE.
I'm sorry, boss
Security police disbanded
Good bye, people from other schools
Get up, boss!
THAT'S TOO VAGUE.
Took down A
Took down B
Dealt with C at school festival
instated D
ANSWERS
A: Love
B: Spirit
E: Bomb
F: Bug
IS THIS SUPPOSED TO BE A TEST?!
Clean the school
Hold a fundraiser
Grow mangroves
Raise mongooses
DON'T WRITE THINGS WE DIDN'T DO!

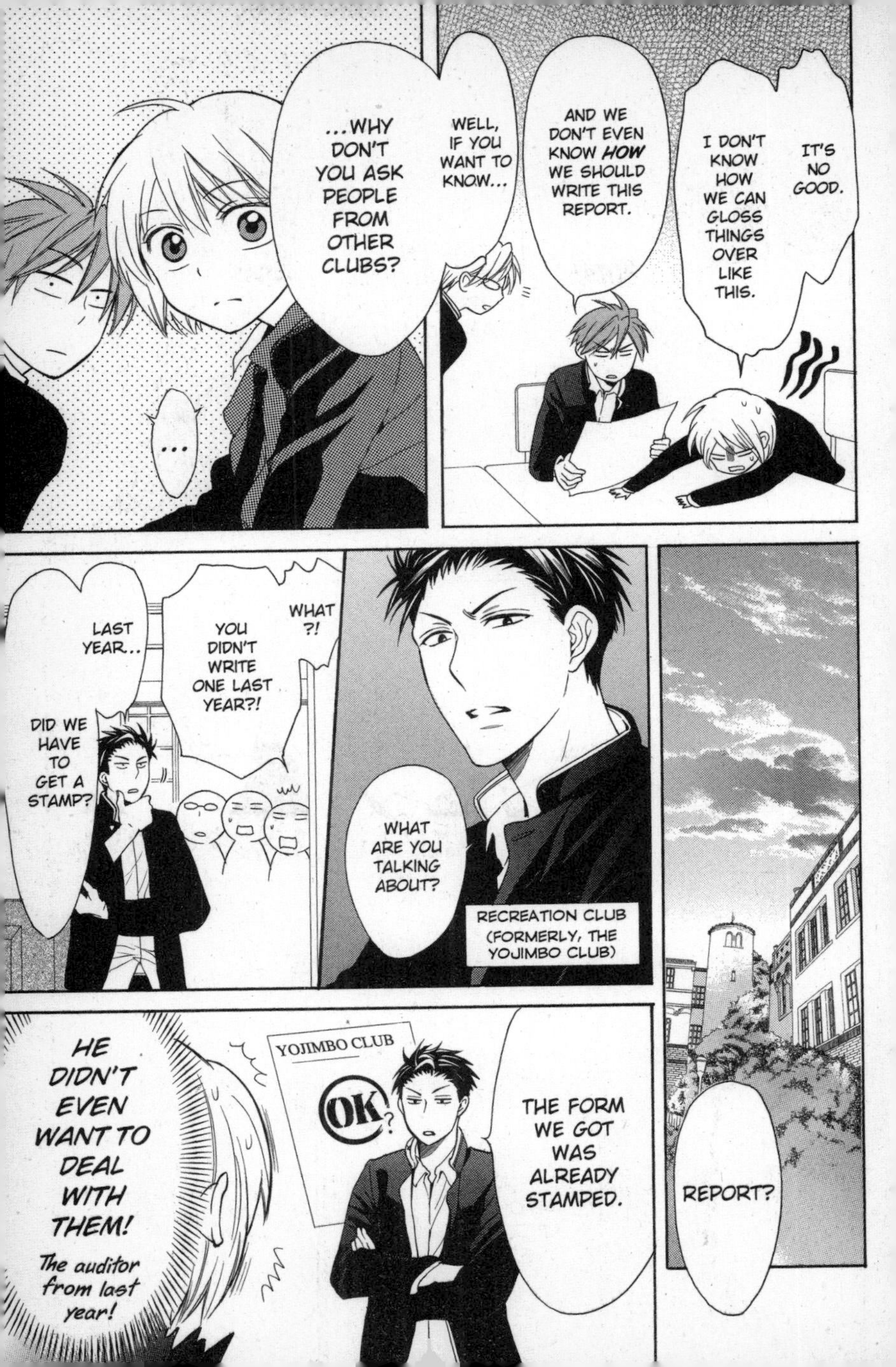
IT'S NO GOOD.
I DON'T KNOW HOW WE CAN GLOSS THINGS OVER LIKE THIS.
AND WE DON'T EVEN KNOW *HOW* WE SHOULD WRITE THIS REPORT.
WELL, IF YOU WANT TO KNOW...
...WHY DON'T YOU ASK PEOPLE FROM OTHER CLUBS?
...
REPORT?
WHAT ARE YOU TALKING ABOUT?
RECREATION CLUB (FORMERLY, THE YOJIMBO CLUB)
WHAT?!
YOU DIDN'T WRITE ONE LAST YEAR?!
LAST YEAR...
DID WE HAVE TO GET A STAMP?
THE FORM WE GOT WAS ALREADY STAMPED.
YOJIMBO CLUB
OK
?
HE DIDN'T EVEN WANT TO DEAL WITH THEM!
The auditor from last year!

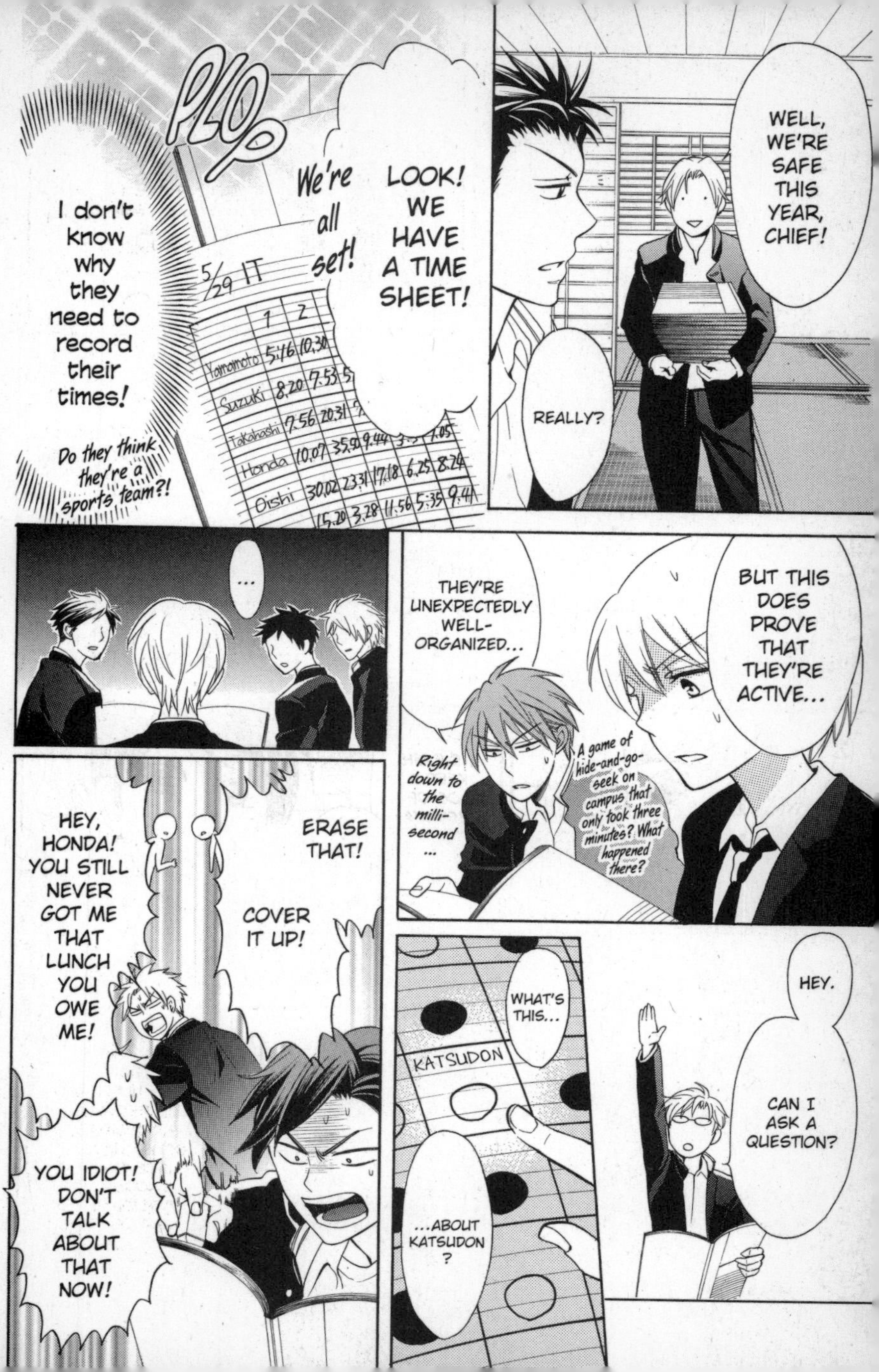
WELL, WE'RE SAFE THIS YEAR, CHIEF!
REALLY?
LOOK! WE HAVE A TIME SHEET!
We're all set!
PLOP
I don't know why they need to record their times!
Do they think they're a sports team?!
BUT THIS DOES PROVE THAT THEY'RE ACTIVE...
THEY'RE UNEXPECTEDLY WELL-ORGANIZED...
A game of hide-and-go-seek on campus that only took three minutes? What happened there?
Right down to the milli-second ...
...
HEY.
CAN I ASK A QUESTION?
WHAT'S THIS...
KATSUDON
...ABOUT KATSUDON?
ERASE THAT!
COVER IT UP!
HEY, HONDA! YOU STILL NEVER GOT ME THAT LUNCH YOU OWE ME!
YOU IDIOT! DON'T TALK ABOUT THAT NOW!

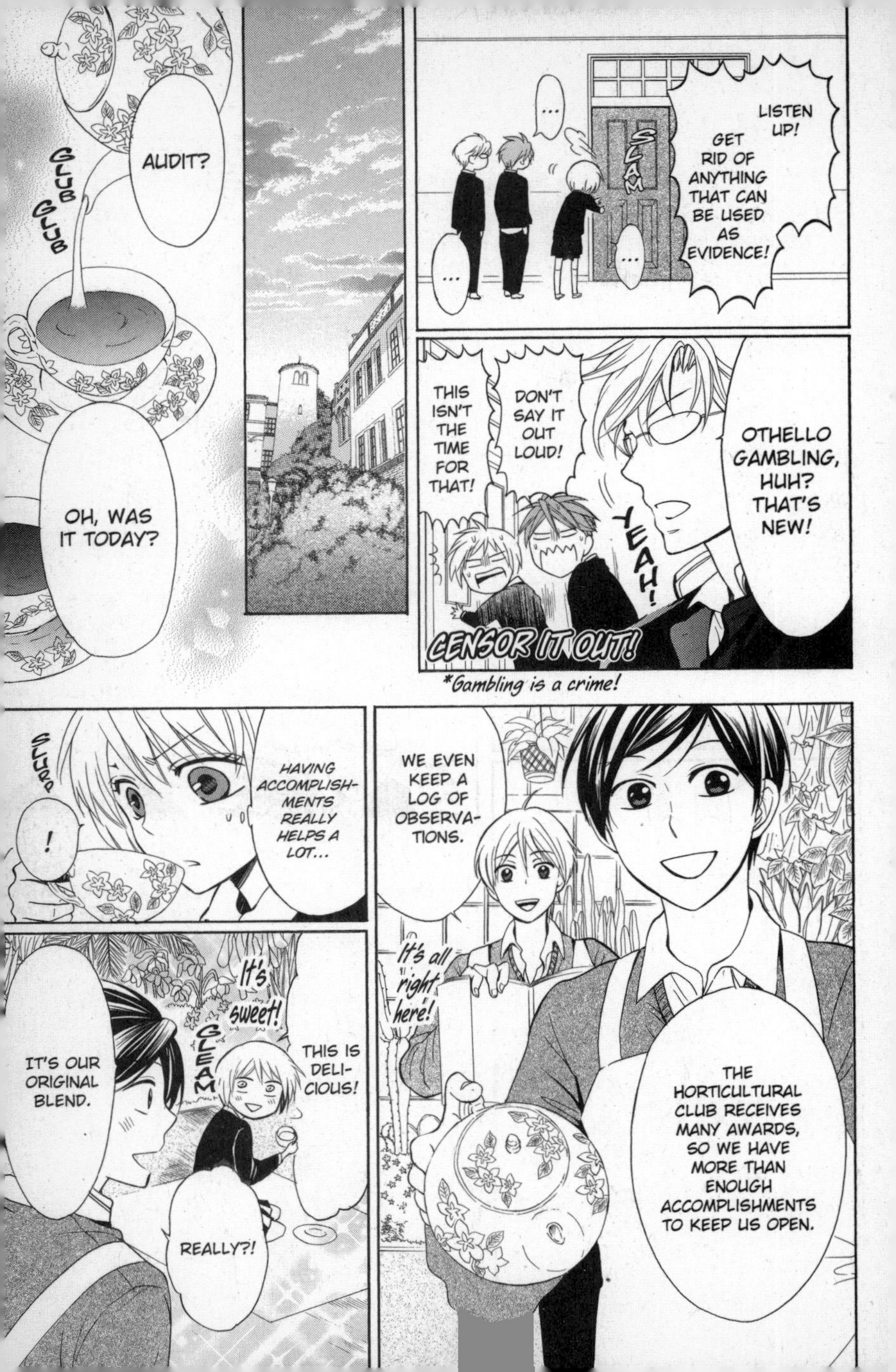
LISTEN UP! GET RID OF ANYTHING THAT CAN BE USED AS EVIDENCE!
SLAM
...
...
...
OTHELLO GAMBLING, HUH? THAT'S NEW!
YEAH!
DON'T SAY IT OUT LOUD!
THIS ISN'T THE TIME FOR THAT!
CENSOR IT OUT!
*Gambling is a crime!
AUDIT?
GLUB GLUB
OH, WAS IT TODAY?
THE HORTICULTURAL CLUB RECEIVES MANY AWARDS, SO WE HAVE MORE THAN ENOUGH ACCOMPLISHMENTS TO KEEP US OPEN.
WE EVEN KEEP A LOG OF OBSERVATIONS.
It's all right here!
HAVING ACCOMPLISHMENTS REALLY HELPS A LOT...
SLURP
!
It's sweet!
GLEAM
THIS IS DELICIOUS!
IT'S OUR ORIGINAL BLEND.
REALLY?!

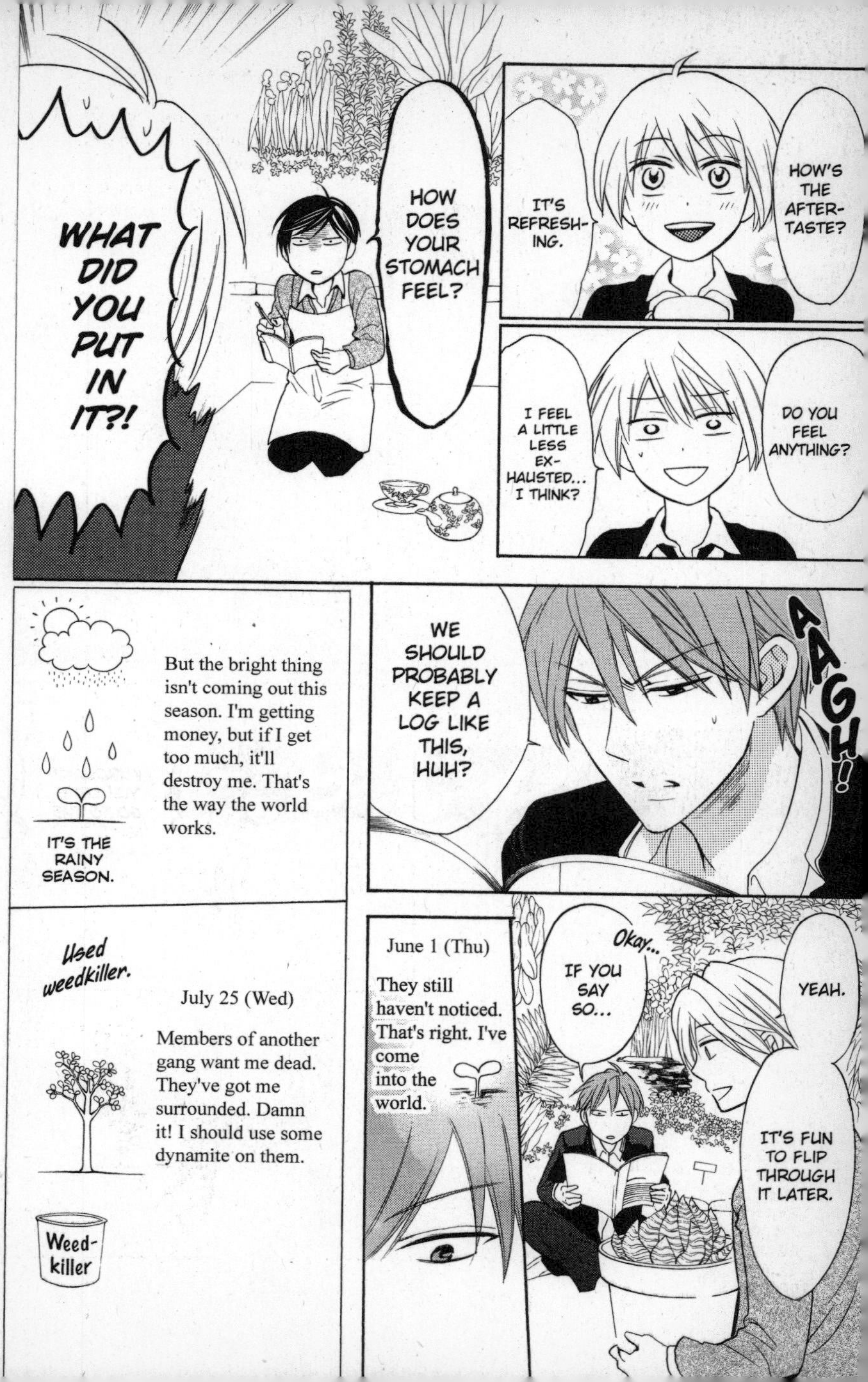
HOW'S THE AFTER-TASTE?
IT'S REFRESH-ING.
DO YOU FEEL ANYTHING?
I FEEL A LITTLE LESS EX-HAUSTED... I THINK?
HOW DOES YOUR STOMACH FEEL?
WHAT DID YOU PUT IN IT?!
AAGH!
WE SHOULD PROBABLY KEEP A LOG LIKE THIS, HUH?
But the bright thing isn't coming out this season. I'm getting money, but if I get too much, it'll destroy me. That's the way the world works.
IT'S THE RAINY SEASON.
YEAH.
IT'S FUN TO FLIP THROUGH IT LATER.
Okay...
IF YOU SAY SO...
June 1 (Thu)
They still haven't noticed. That's right. I've come into the world.
Used weedkiller.
July 25 (Wed)
Members of another gang want me dead. They've got me surrounded. Damn it! I should use some dynamite on them.
Weed-killer

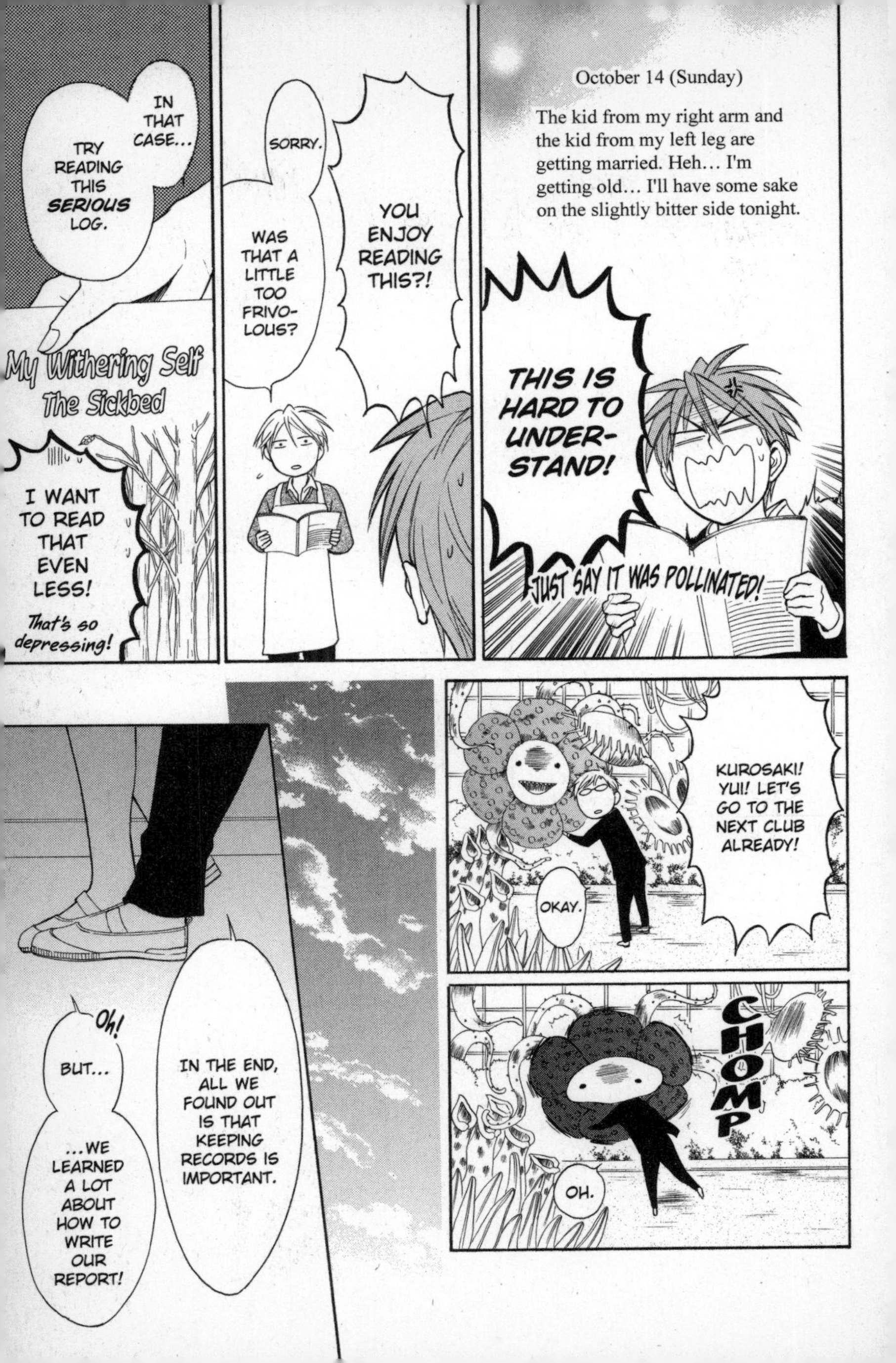
October 14 (Sunday)
The kid from my right arm and the kid from my left leg are getting married. Heh… I'm getting old… I'll have some sake on the slightly bitter side tonight.
THIS IS HARD TO UNDER-STAND!
JUST SAY IT WAS POLLINATED!
YOU ENJOY READING THIS?!
SORRY.
WAS THAT A LITTLE TOO FRIVO-LOUS?
IN THAT CASE...
TRY READING THIS SERIOUS LOG.
My Withering Self
The Sickbed
I WANT TO READ THAT EVEN LESS!
That's so depressing!
KUROSAKI! YUI! LET'S GO TO THE NEXT CLUB ALREADY!
OKAY.
CHOMP
OH.
IN THE END, ALL WE FOUND OUT IS THAT KEEPING RECORDS IS IMPORTANT.
Oh!
BUT...
...WE LEARNED A LOT ABOUT HOW TO WRITE OUR REPORT!

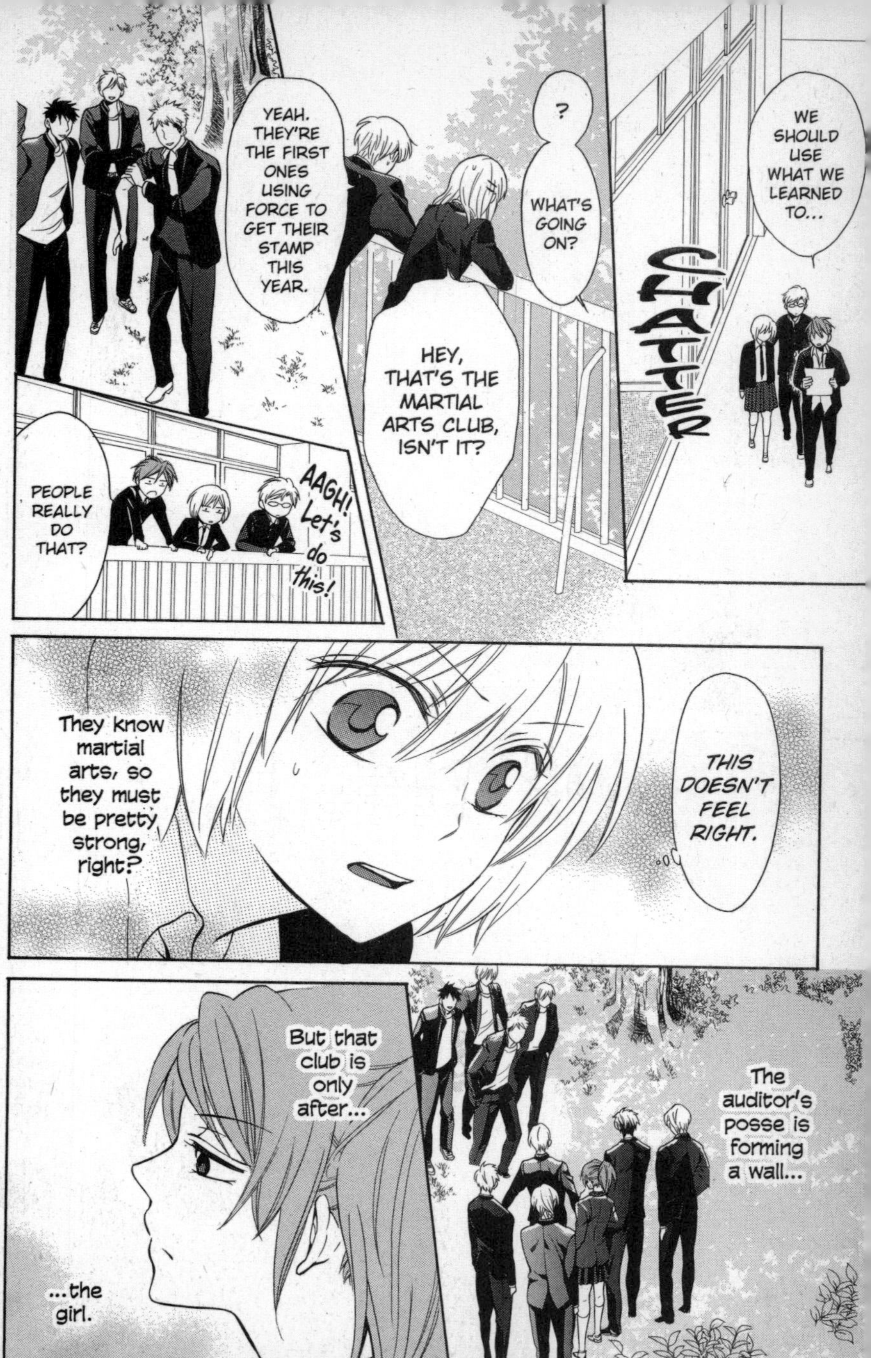
WE SHOULD USE WHAT WE LEARNED TO...
CHATTER
?
WHAT'S GOING ON?
HEY, THAT'S THE MARTIAL ARTS CLUB, ISN'T IT?
YEAH. THEY'RE THE FIRST ONES USING FORCE TO GET THEIR STAMP THIS YEAR.
AAGH! Let's do this!
PEOPLE REALLY DO THAT?
THIS DOESN'T FEEL RIGHT.
They know martial arts, so they must be pretty strong, right?
The auditor's posse is forming a wall...
But that club is only after...
...the girl.

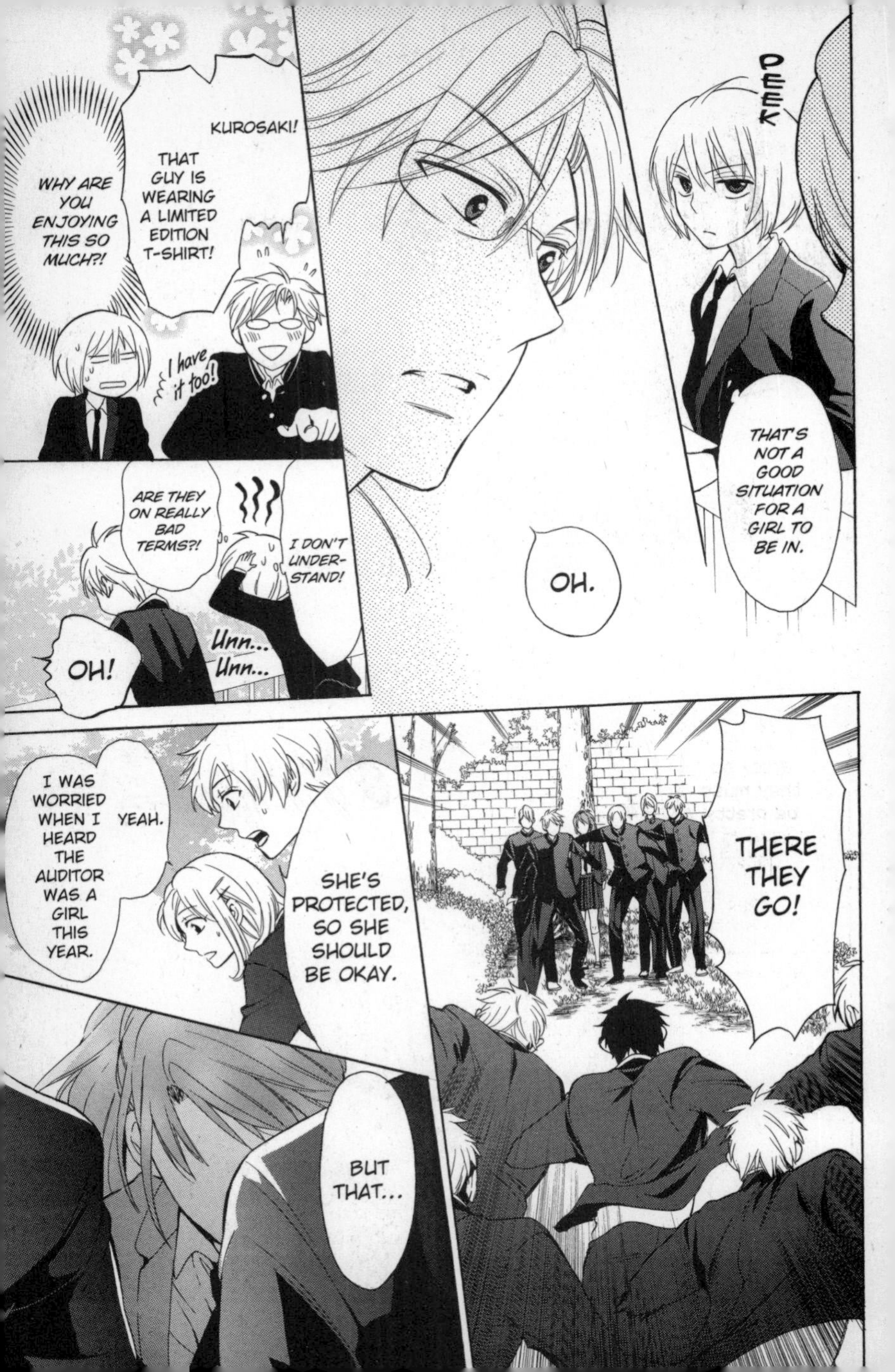
PEEK
THAT'S NOT A GOOD SITUATION FOR A GIRL TO BE IN.
OH.
KUROSAKI!
THAT GUY IS WEARING A LIMITED EDITION T-SHIRT!
I have it too!
WHY ARE YOU ENJOYING THIS SO MUCH?!
I DON'T UNDERSTAND!
ARE THEY ON REALLY BAD TERMS?!
Unn... Unn...
OH!
THERE THEY GO!
SHE'S PROTECTED, SO SHE SHOULD BE OKAY.
YEAH.
I WAS WORRIED WHEN I HEARD THE AUDITOR WAS A GIRL THIS YEAR.
BUT THAT...

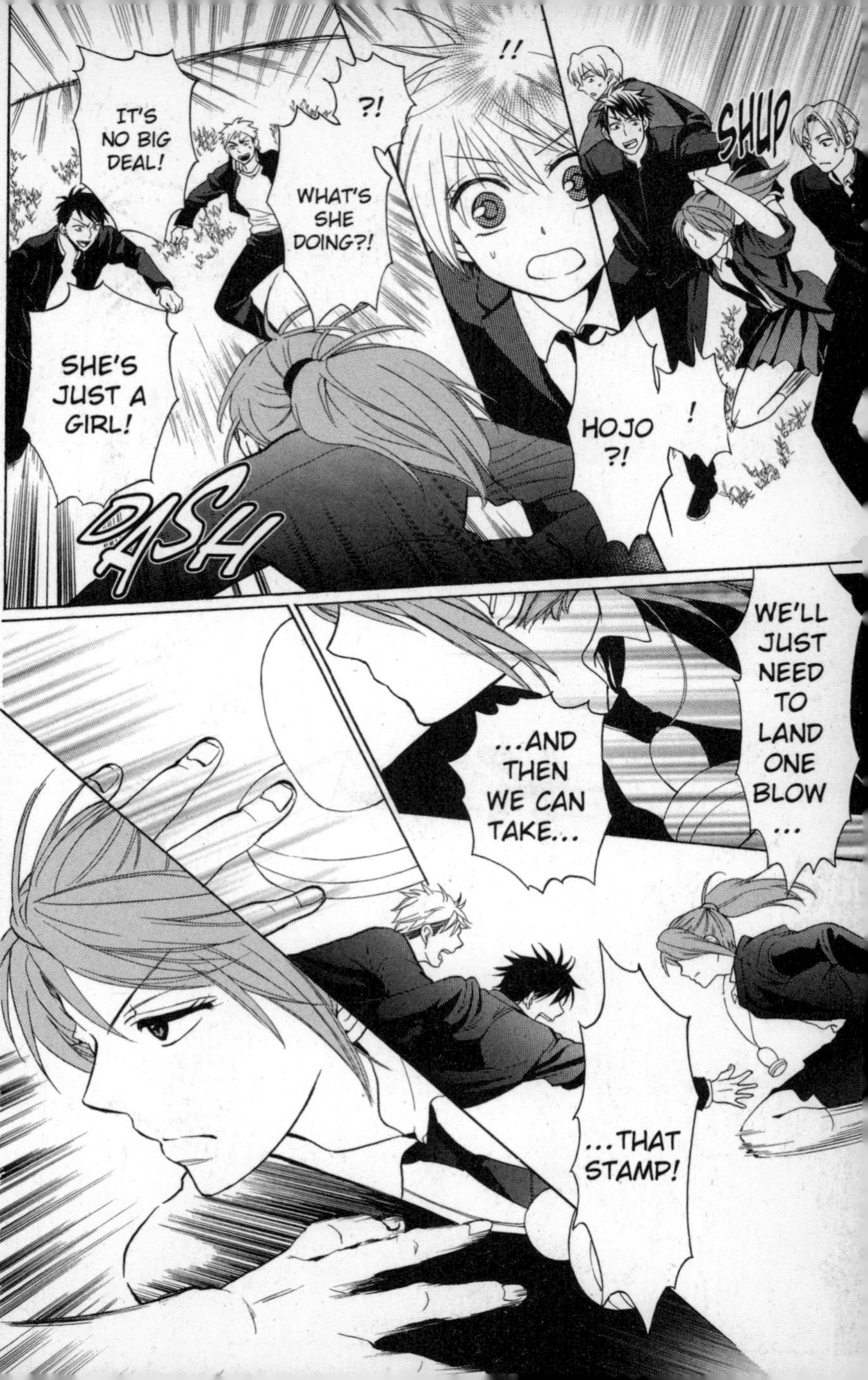
SHUP
!
!!
HOJO ?!
?!
WHAT'S SHE DOING?!
IT'S NO BIG DEAL!
SHE'S JUST A GIRL!
DASH
WE'LL JUST NEED TO LAND ONE BLOW...
...AND THEN WE CAN TAKE...
...THAT STAMP!

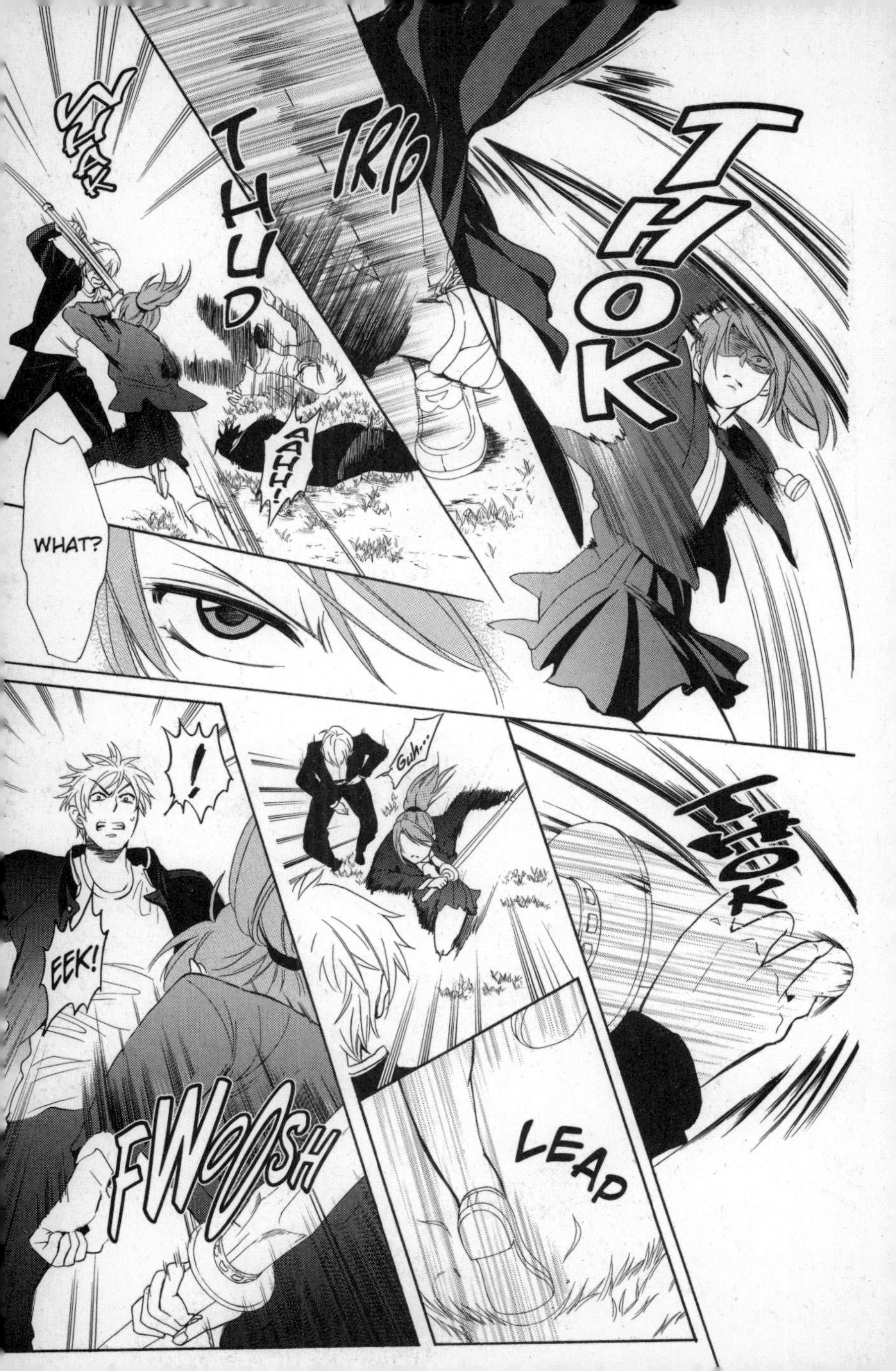
THOK
TRIP
THUD
AAHH!
WHAT?
THOK
LEAP
Guh...
!
EEK!
FWOOSH

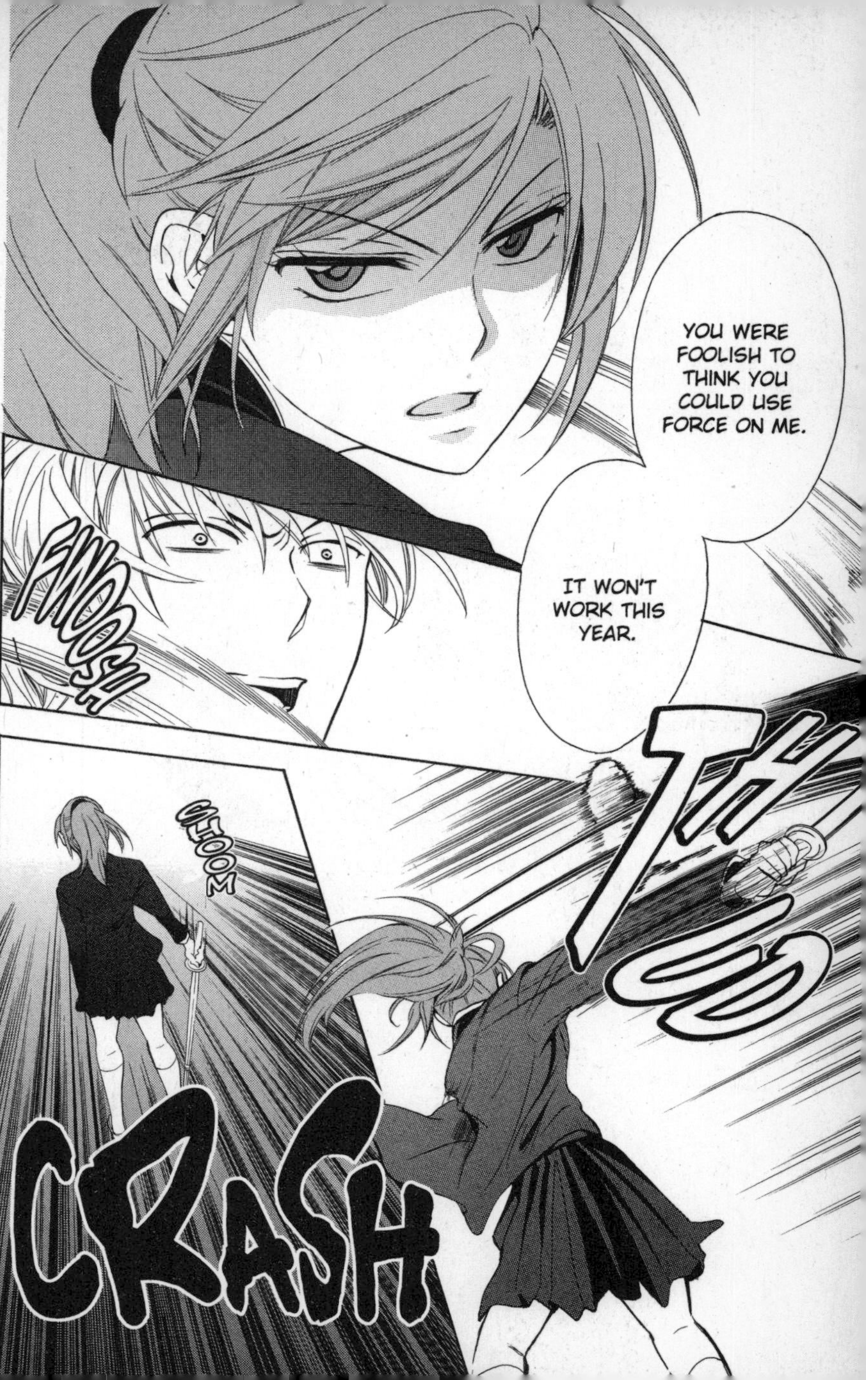
YOU WERE FOOLISH TO THINK YOU COULD USE FORCE ON ME.
IT WON'T WORK THIS YEAR.
FWOOSH
THUD
WHOOM
CRASH

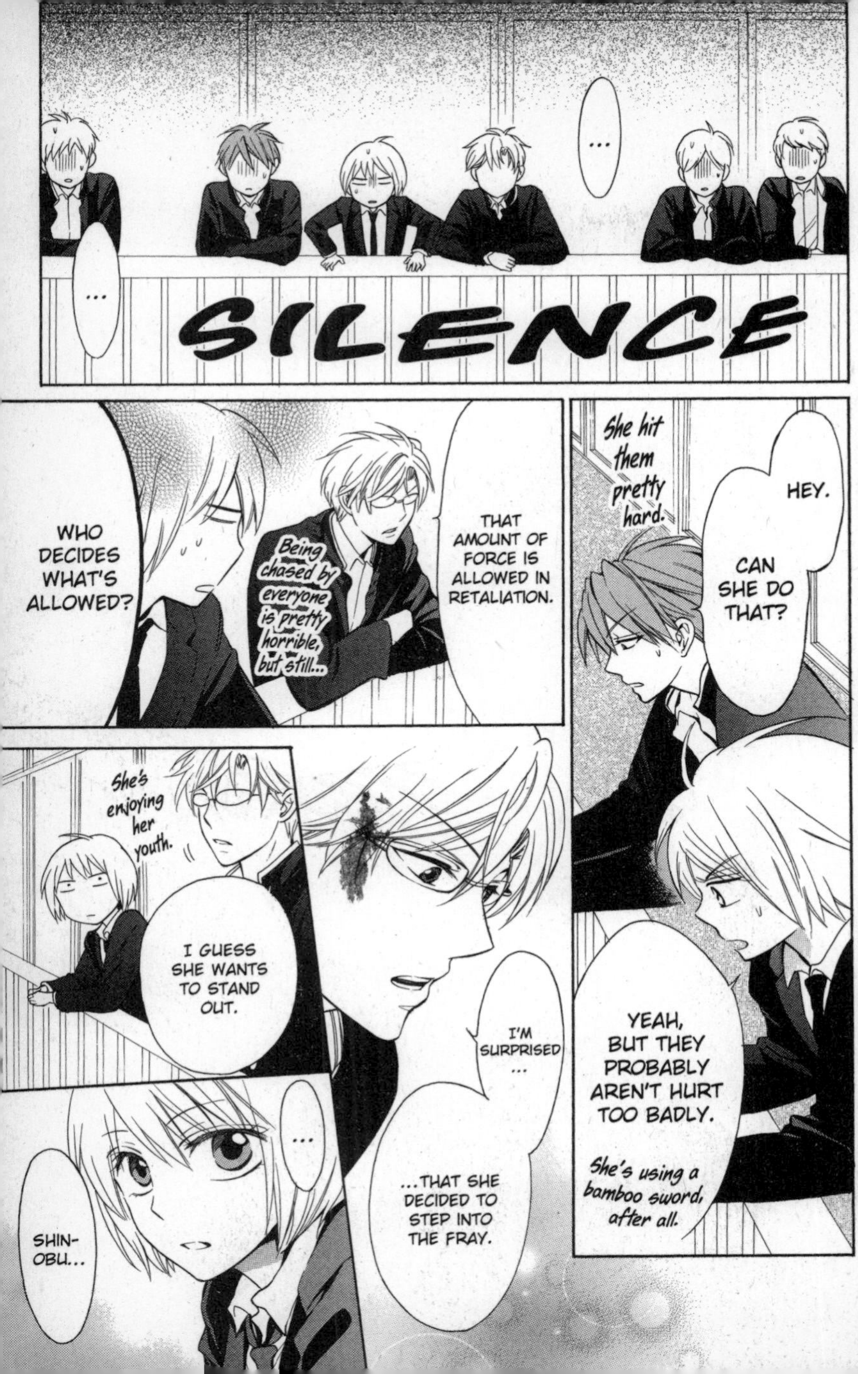
...
...
SILENCE
She hit them pretty hard.
HEY.
CAN SHE DO THAT?
YEAH, BUT THEY PROBABLY AREN'T HURT TOO BADLY.
She's using a bamboo sword, after all.
THAT AMOUNT OF FORCE IS ALLOWED IN RETALIATION.
Being chased by everyone is pretty horrible, but still...
WHO DECIDES WHAT'S ALLOWED?
I'M SURPRISED...
...THAT SHE DECIDED TO STEP INTO THE FRAY.
She's enjoying her youth.
I GUESS SHE WANTS TO STAND OUT.
...
SHIN-OBU...

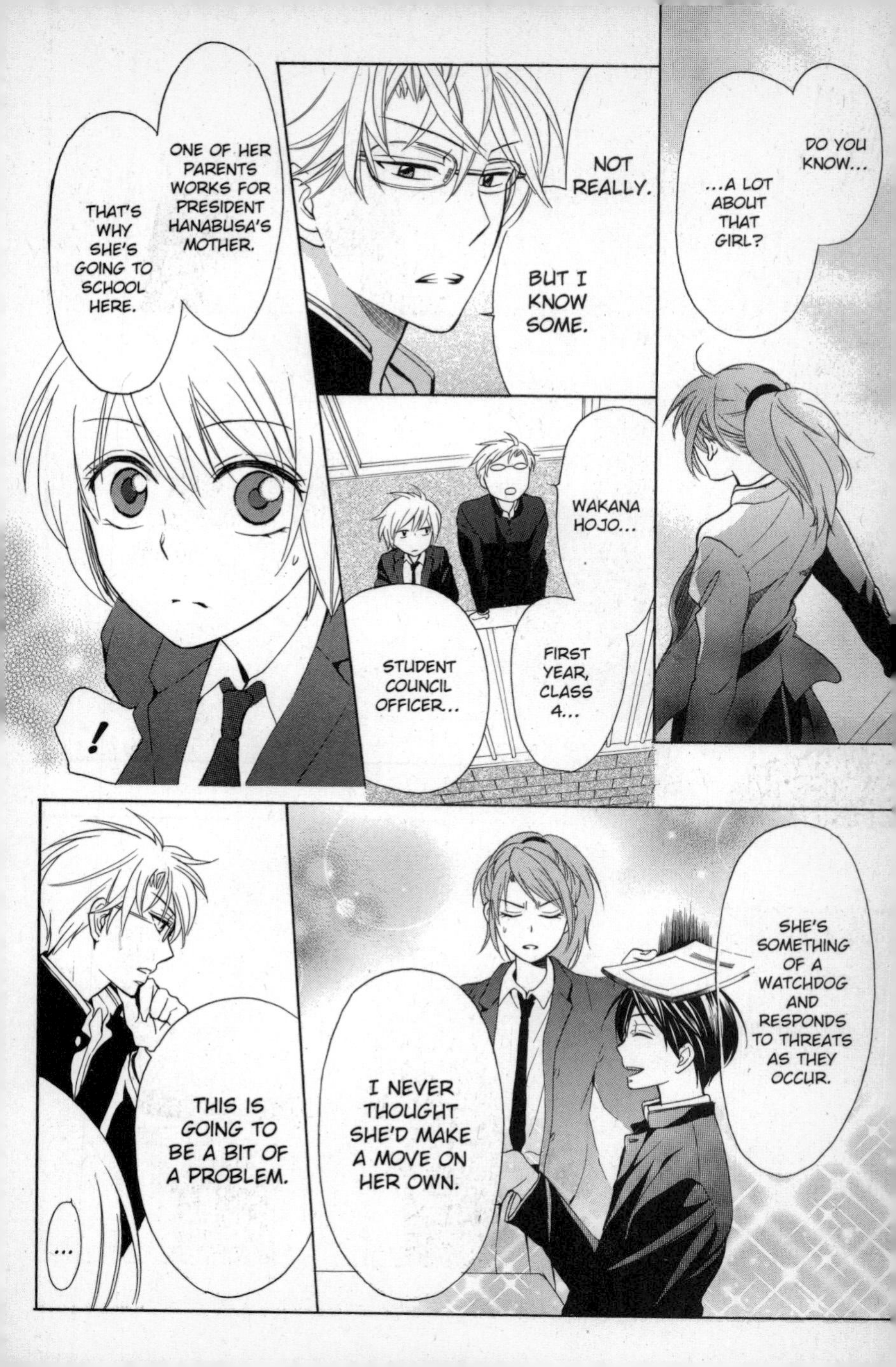

DO YOU KNOW...
...A LOT ABOUT THAT GIRL?
NOT REALLY.
BUT I KNOW SOME.
WAKANA HOJO...
FIRST YEAR, CLASS 4...
STUDENT COUNCIL OFFICER...
ONE OF HER PARENTS WORKS FOR PRESIDENT HANABUSA'S MOTHER.
THAT'S WHY SHE'S GOING TO SCHOOL HERE.
!
SHE'S SOMETHING OF A WATCHDOG AND RESPONDS TO THREATS AS THEY OCCUR.
I NEVER THOUGHT SHE'D MAKE A MOVE ON HER OWN.
THIS IS GOING TO BE A BIT OF A PROBLEM.
...

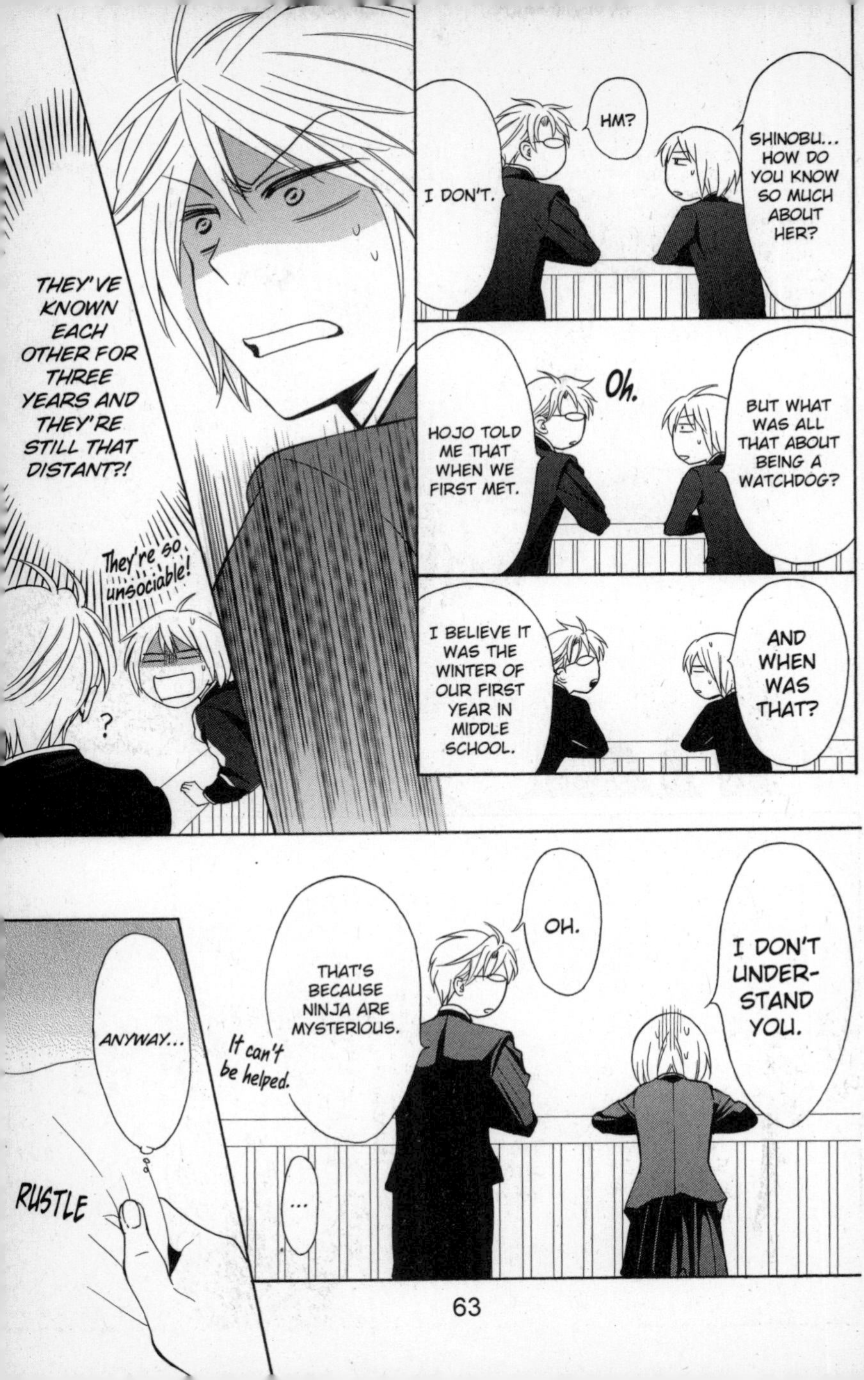
SHINOBU... HOW DO YOU KNOW SO MUCH ABOUT HER?
HM?
I DON'T.
BUT WHAT WAS ALL THAT ABOUT BEING A WATCHDOG?
Oh.
HOJO TOLD ME THAT WHEN WE FIRST MET.
AND WHEN WAS THAT?
I BELIEVE IT WAS THE WINTER OF OUR FIRST YEAR IN MIDDLE SCHOOL.
THEY'VE KNOWN EACH OTHER FOR THREE YEARS AND THEY'RE STILL THAT DISTANT?!
They're so unsociable!
?
I DON'T UNDER-STAND YOU.
OH.
THAT'S BECAUSE NINJA ARE MYSTERIOUS.
It can't be helped.
...
ANYWAY...
RUSTLE

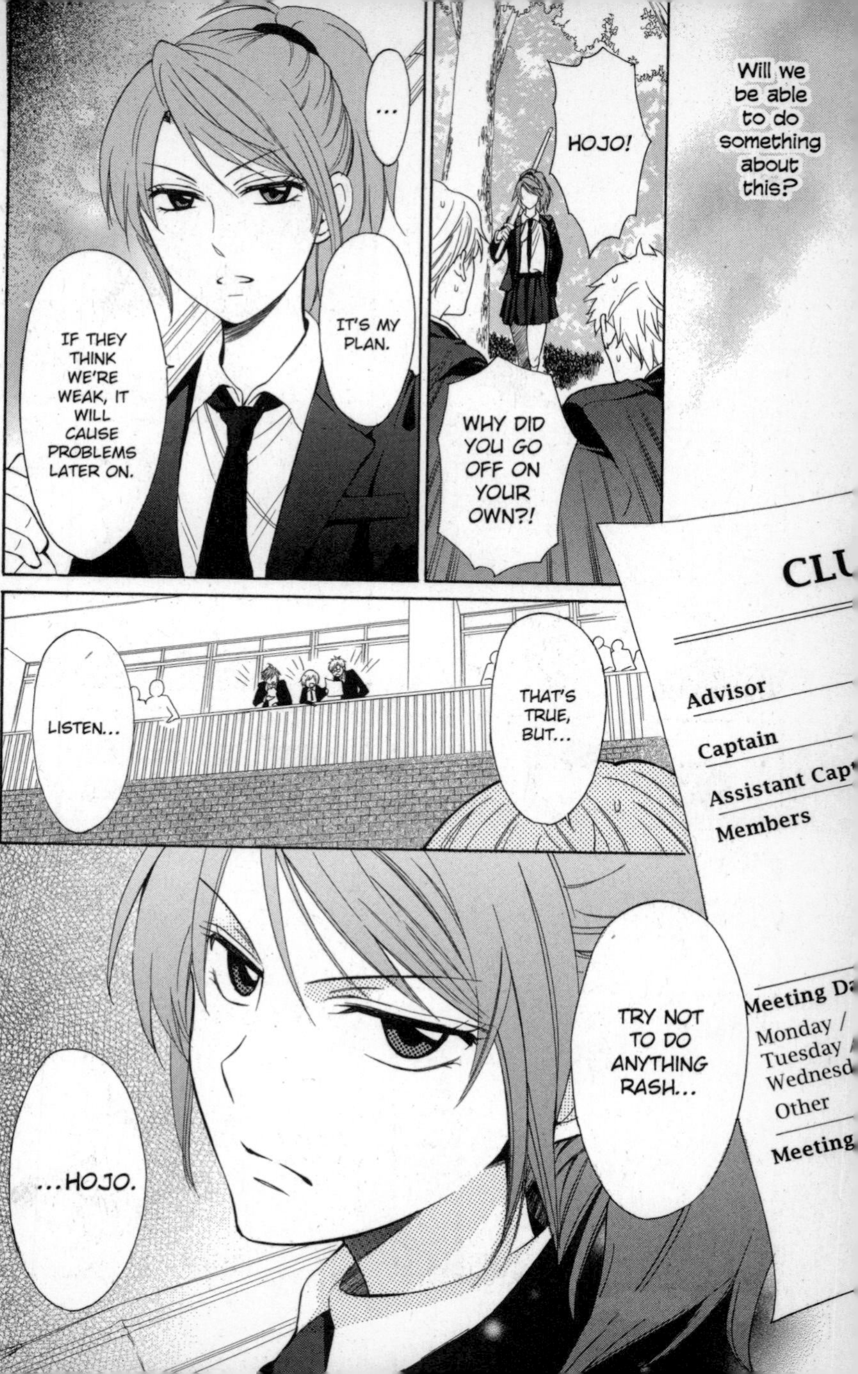
Will we be able to do something about this?
HOJO!
WHY DID YOU GO OFF ON YOUR OWN?!
...
IT'S MY PLAN.
IF THEY THINK WE'RE WEAK, IT WILL CAUSE PROBLEMS LATER ON.
Advisor
Captain
Members
THAT'S TRUE, BUT...
LISTEN...
Monday /
Tuesday
Other
TRY NOT TO DO ANYTHING RASH...
...HOJO.

A TRADITION UPHELD

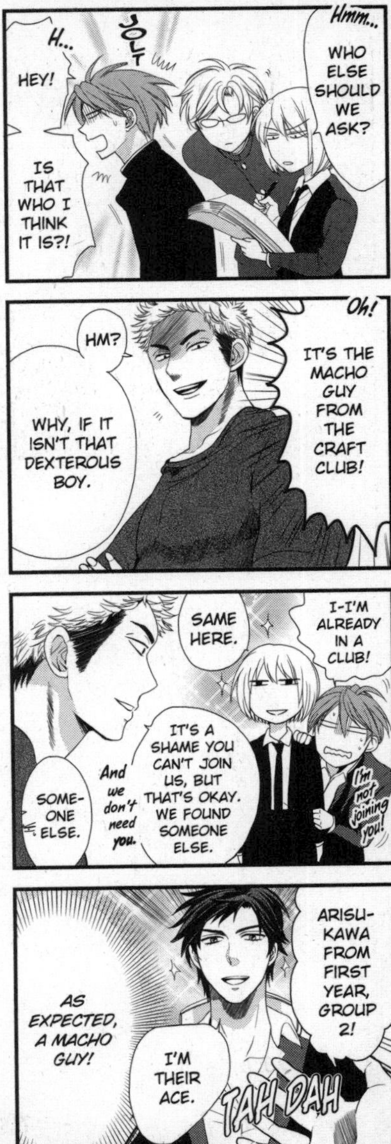
Hmm...
WHO ELSE SHOULD WE ASK?
JOLT
H... HEY!
IS THAT WHO I THINK IT IS?!
Oh!
IT'S THE MACHO GUY FROM THE CRAFT CLUB!
HM?
WHY, IF IT ISN'T THAT DEXTEROUS BOY.
I-I'M ALREADY IN A CLUB!
I'm not joining you!
SAME HERE.
IT'S A SHAME YOU CAN'T JOIN US, BUT THAT'S OKAY. WE FOUND SOMEONE ELSE.
And we don't need you.
SOME-ONE ELSE.
ARISU-KAWA FROM FIRST YEAR, GROUP 2!
TAH DAH
AS EXPECTED, A MACHO GUY!
I'M THEIR ACE.

CRAFT CLUB FUN

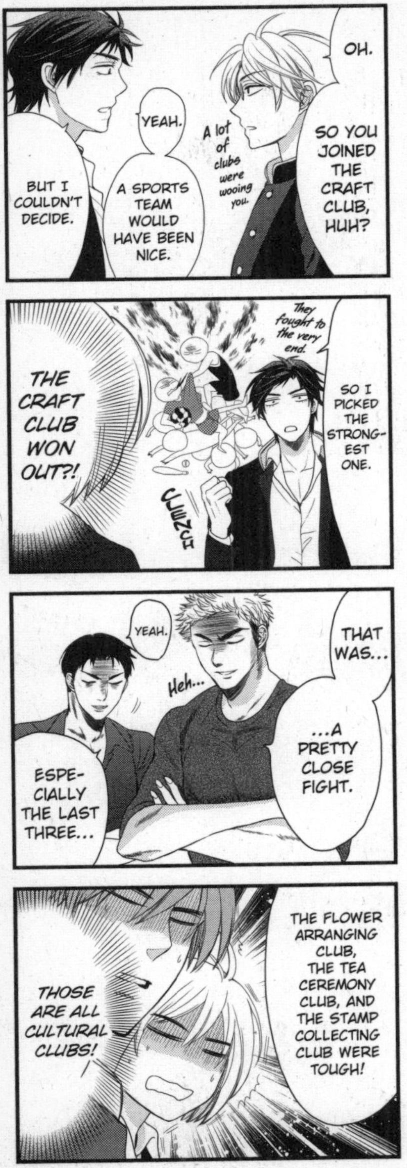
OH.
SO YOU JOINED THE CRAFT CLUB, HUH?
A lot of clubs were wooing you.
YEAH.
A SPORTS TEAM WOULD HAVE BEEN NICE.
BUT I COULDN'T DECIDE.
They fought to the very end.
SO I PICKED THE STRONG-EST ONE.
CLENCH
THE CRAFT CLUB WON OUT?!
THAT WAS...
...A PRETTY CLOSE FIGHT.
YEAH.
Heh...
ESPE-CIALLY THE LAST THREE...
THE FLOWER ARRANGING CLUB, THE TEA CEREMONY CLUB, AND THE STAMP COLLECTING CLUB WERE TOUGH!
THOSE ARE ALL CULTURAL CLUBS!

AS A DELINQUENT

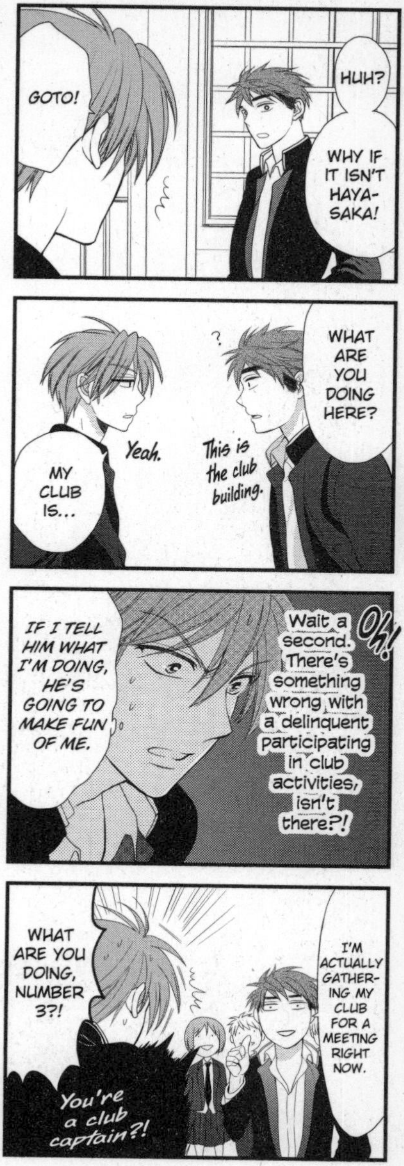
HUH?
WHY IF IT ISN'T HAYA-SAKA!
GOTO!
WHAT ARE YOU DOING HERE?
This is the club building.
Yeah.
MY CLUB IS...
Oh!
Wait a second. There's something wrong with a delinquent participating in club activities, isn't there?!
IF I TELL HIM WHAT I'M DOING, HE'S GOING TO MAKE FUN OF ME.
I'M ACTUALLY GATHER-ING MY CLUB FOR A MEETING RIGHT NOW.
WHAT ARE YOU DOING, NUMBER 3?!
You're a club captain?!

THINGS I WANT

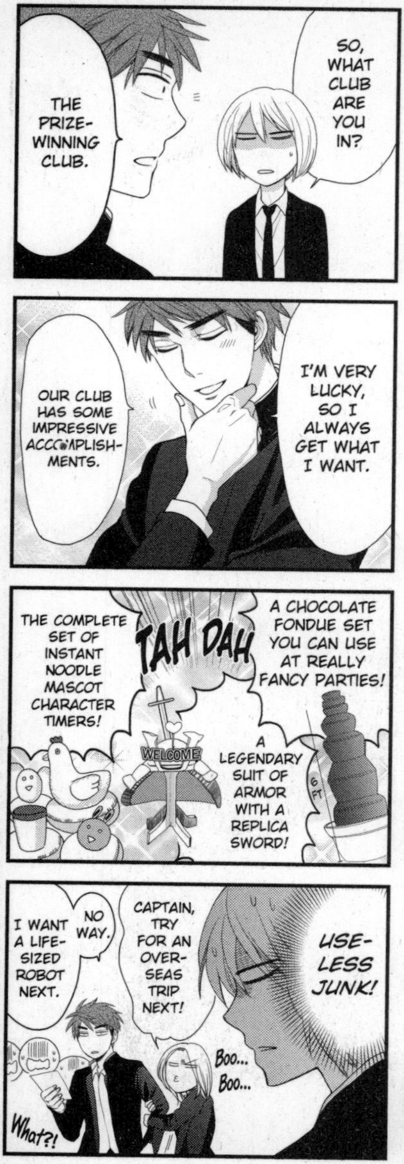
SO, WHAT CLUB ARE YOU IN?
THE PRIZE-WINNING CLUB.
I'M VERY LUCKY, SO I ALWAYS GET WHAT I WANT.
OUR CLUB HAS SOME IMPRESSIVE ACCOMPLISH-MENTS.
A CHOCOLATE FONDUE SET YOU CAN USE AT REALLY FANCY PARTIES!
TAH DAH
THE COMPLETE SET OF INSTANT NOODLE MASCOT CHARACTER TIMERS!
WELCOME
6 FT
A LEGENDARY SUIT OF ARMOR WITH A REPLICA SWORD!
USE-LESS JUNK!
CAPTAIN, TRY FOR AN OVER-SEAS TRIP NEXT!
Boo... Boo...
NO WAY.
I WANT A LIFE-SIZED ROBOT NEXT.
What?!

Chapter 54

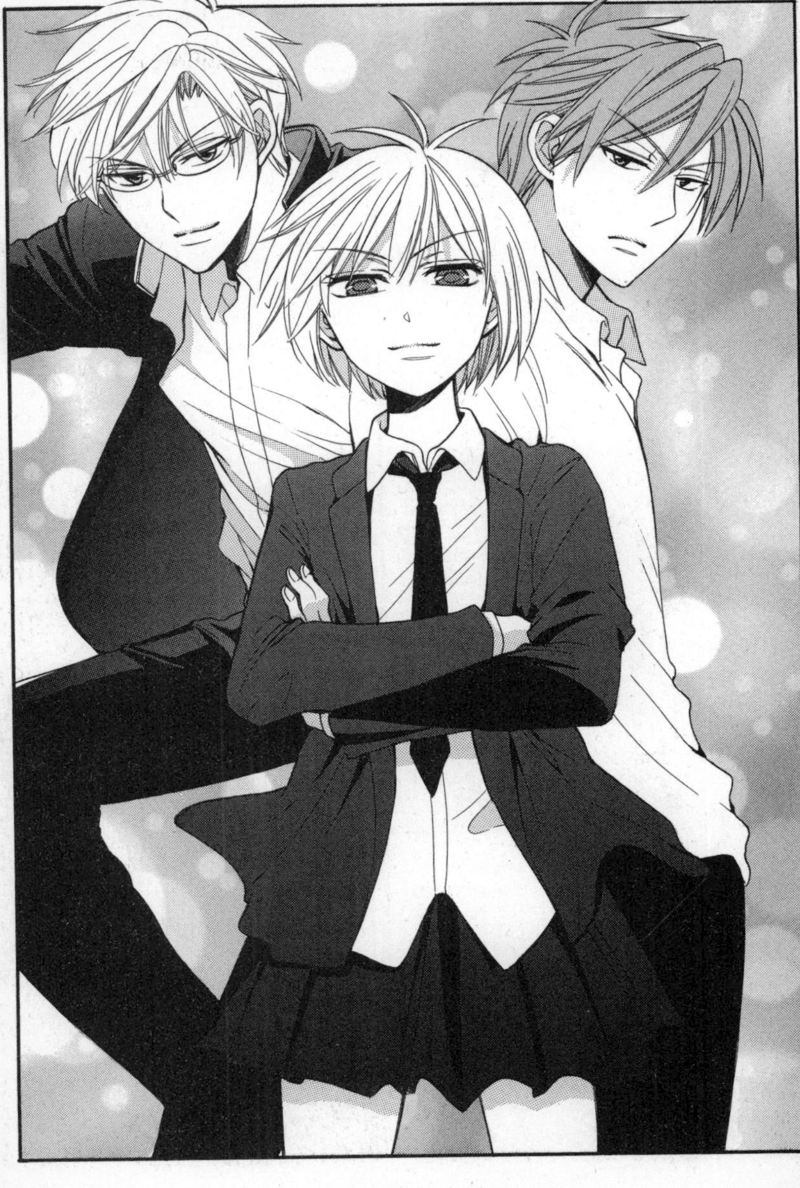

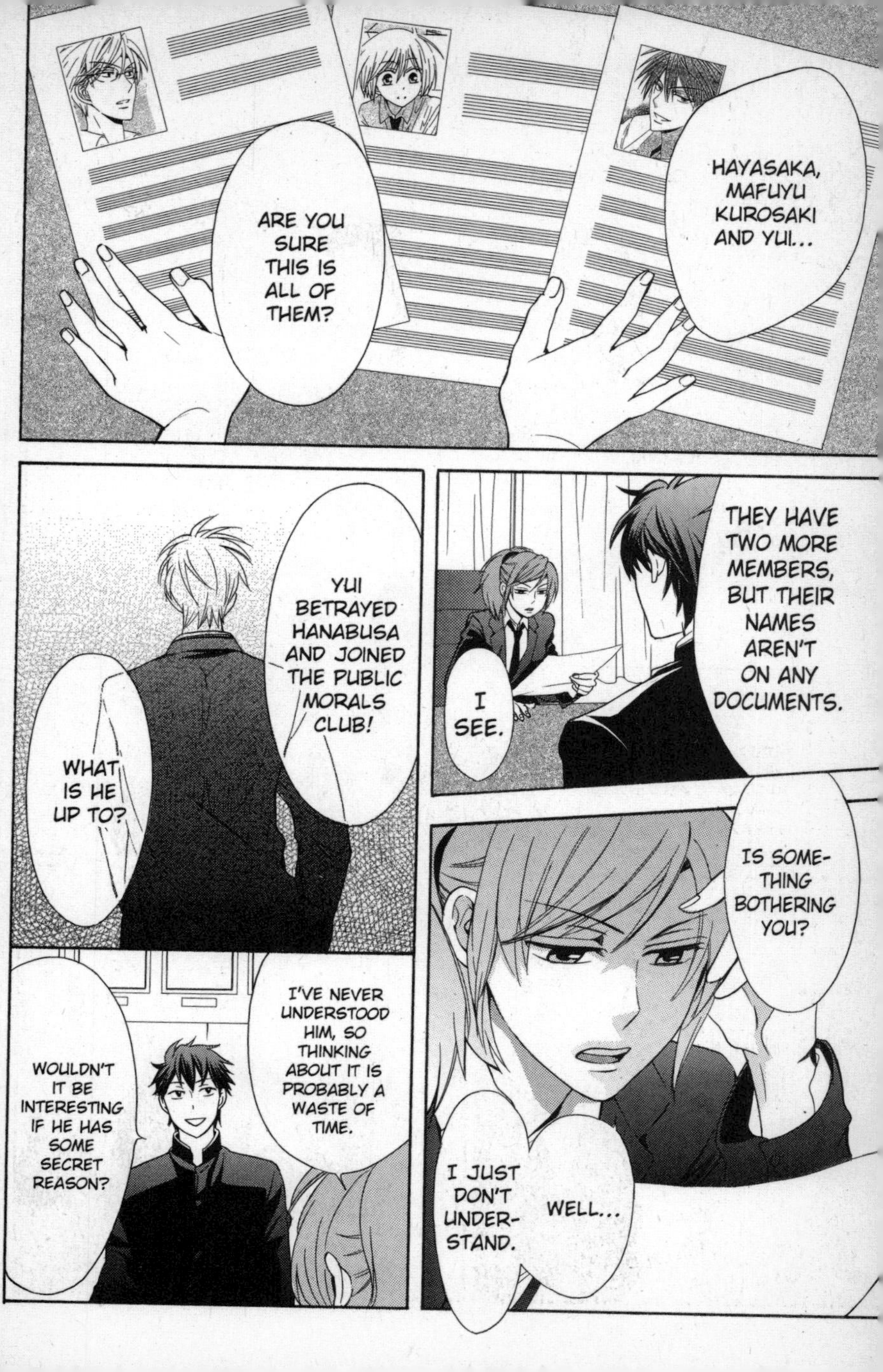
HAYASAKA, MAFUYU KUROSAKI AND YUI...
ARE YOU SURE THIS IS ALL OF THEM?
THEY HAVE TWO MORE MEMBERS, BUT THEIR NAMES AREN'T ON ANY DOCUMENTS.
I SEE.
IS SOME-THING BOTHERING YOU?
WELL...
I JUST DON'T UNDER-STAND.
YUI BETRAYED HANABUSA AND JOINED THE PUBLIC MORALS CLUB!
WHAT IS HE UP TO?
I'VE NEVER UNDERSTOOD HIM, SO THINKING ABOUT IT IS PROBABLY A WASTE OF TIME.
WOULDN'T IT BE INTERESTING IF HE HAS SOME SECRET REASON?

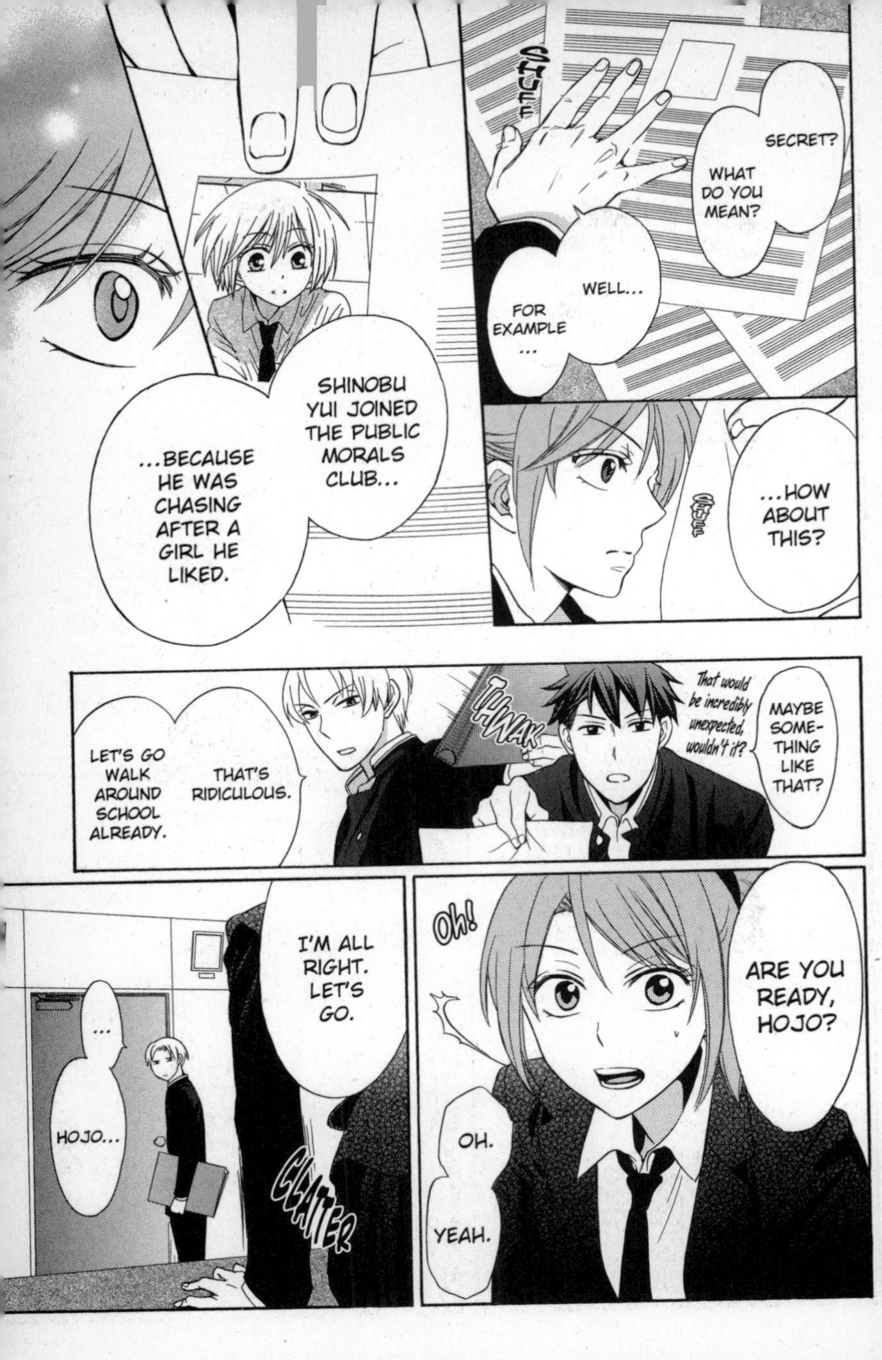
SHUFF
SECRET? WHAT DO YOU MEAN?
WELL...
FOR EXAMPLE...
SHUFF
...HOW ABOUT THIS?
SHINOBU YUI JOINED THE PUBLIC MORALS CLUB...
...BECAUSE HE WAS CHASING AFTER A GIRL HE LIKED.
MAYBE SOME-THING LIKE THAT?
That would be incredibly unexpected, wouldn't it?
THWAK
THAT'S RIDICULOUS.
LET'S GO WALK AROUND SCHOOL ALREADY.
ARE YOU READY, HOJO?
Oh!
OH.
YEAH.
I'M ALL RIGHT. LET'S GO.
...
HOJO...
CLATTER

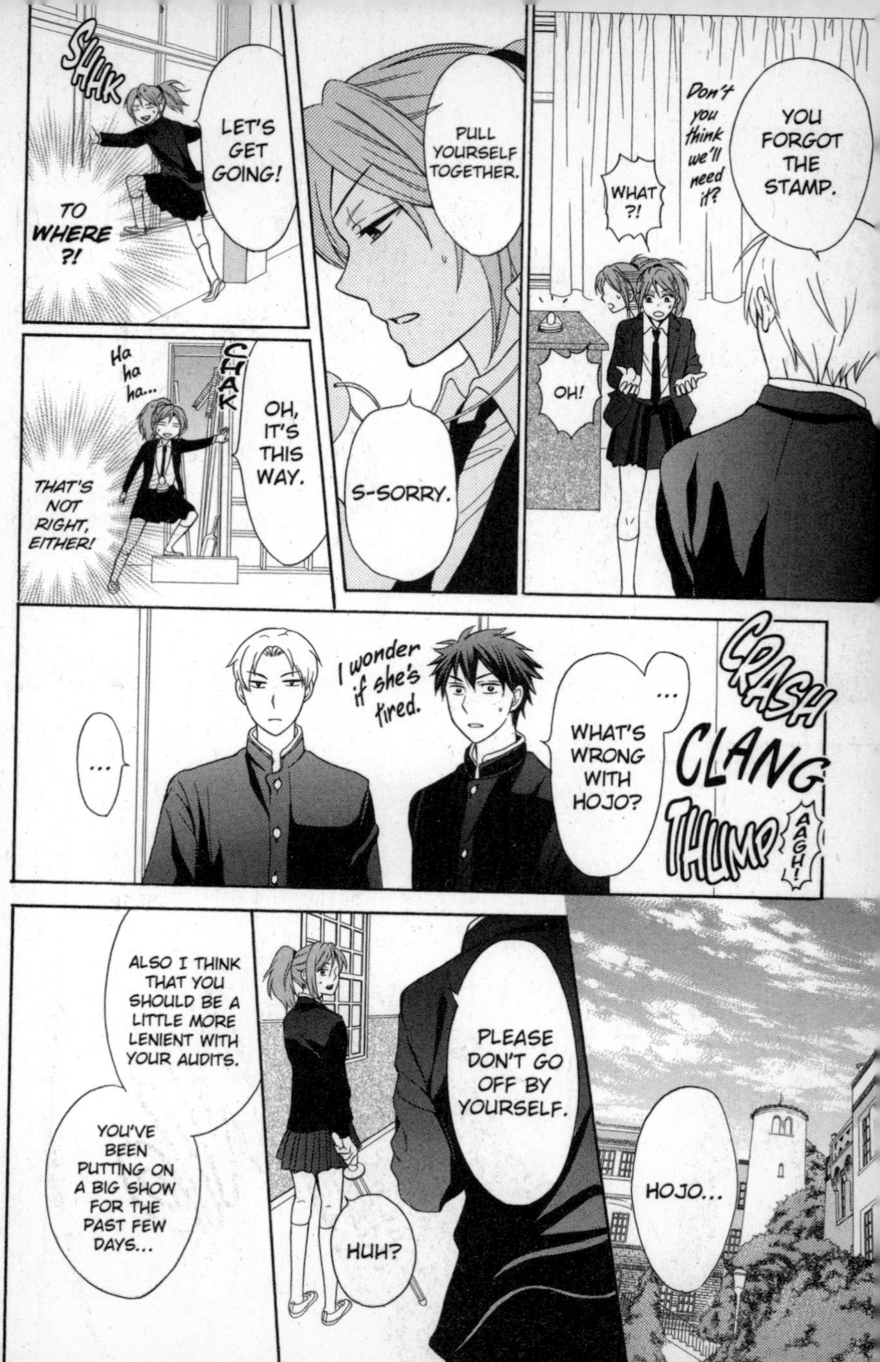
YOU FORGOT THE STAMP.
Don't you think we'll need it?
WHAT?!
OH!
PULL YOURSELF TOGETHER.
S-SORRY.
SHHK
LET'S GET GOING!
TO WHERE?!
CHAK
OH, IT'S THIS WAY.
Ha ha ha...
THAT'S NOT RIGHT, EITHER!
CRASH
CLANG
THUMP
AAGH!
...
WHAT'S WRONG WITH HOJO?
I wonder if she's tired.
...
HOJO...
PLEASE DON'T GO OFF BY YOURSELF.
HUH?
ALSO I THINK THAT YOU SHOULD BE A LITTLE MORE LENIENT WITH YOUR AUDITS.
YOU'VE BEEN PUTTING ON A BIG SHOW FOR THE PAST FEW DAYS...

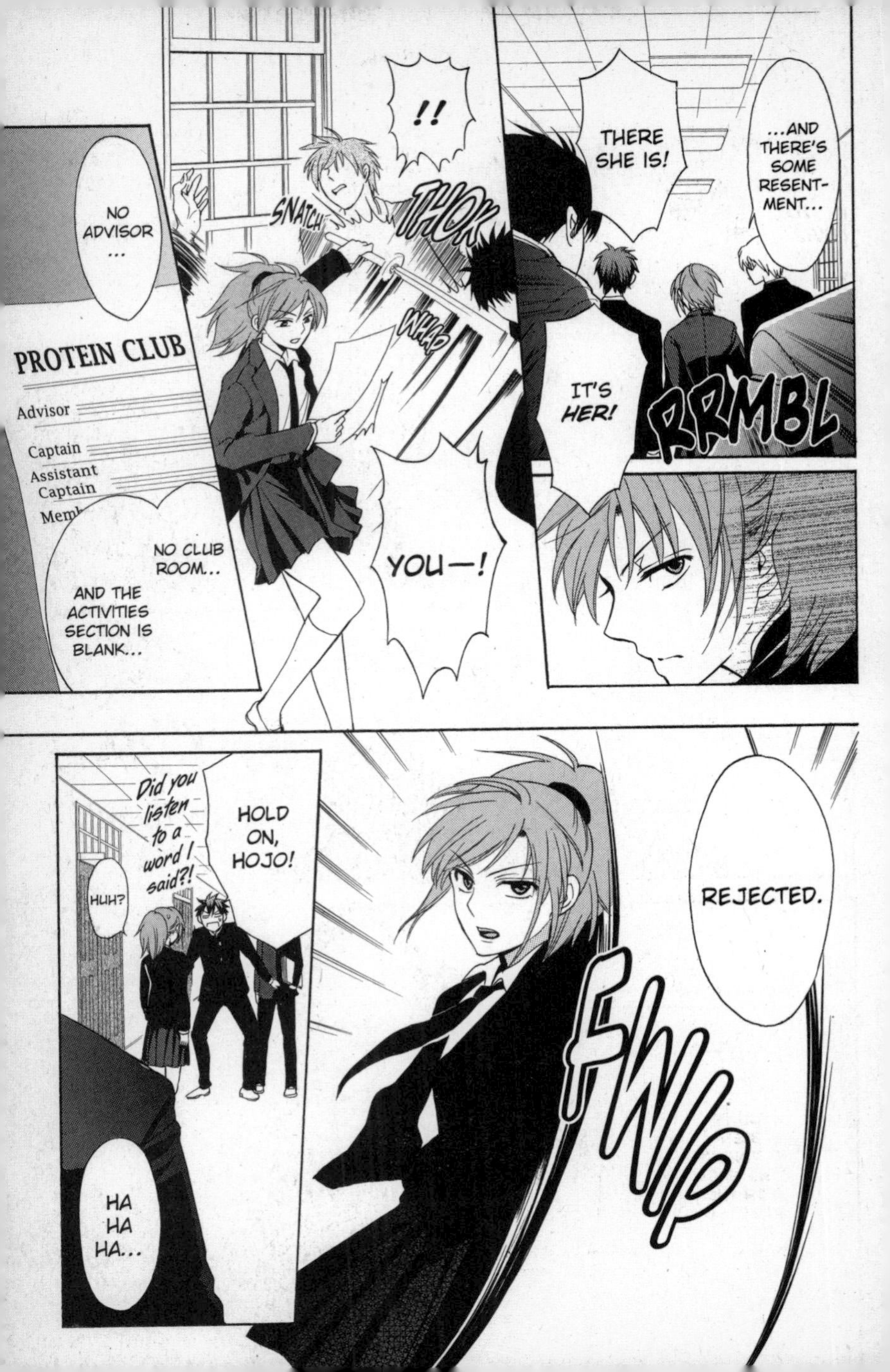
...AND THERE'S SOME RESENTMENT...
THERE SHE IS!
IT'S HER!
RRMBL
YOU—!
!!
SNATCH
THOK
WHAP
NO ADVISOR ...
PROTEIN CLUB
Advisor
Captain
Assistant Captain
Memb
NO CLUB ROOM...
AND THE ACTIVITIES SECTION IS BLANK...
REJECTED.
FWIP
HOLD ON, HOJO!
Did you listen to a word I said?!
HUH?
HA HA HA...

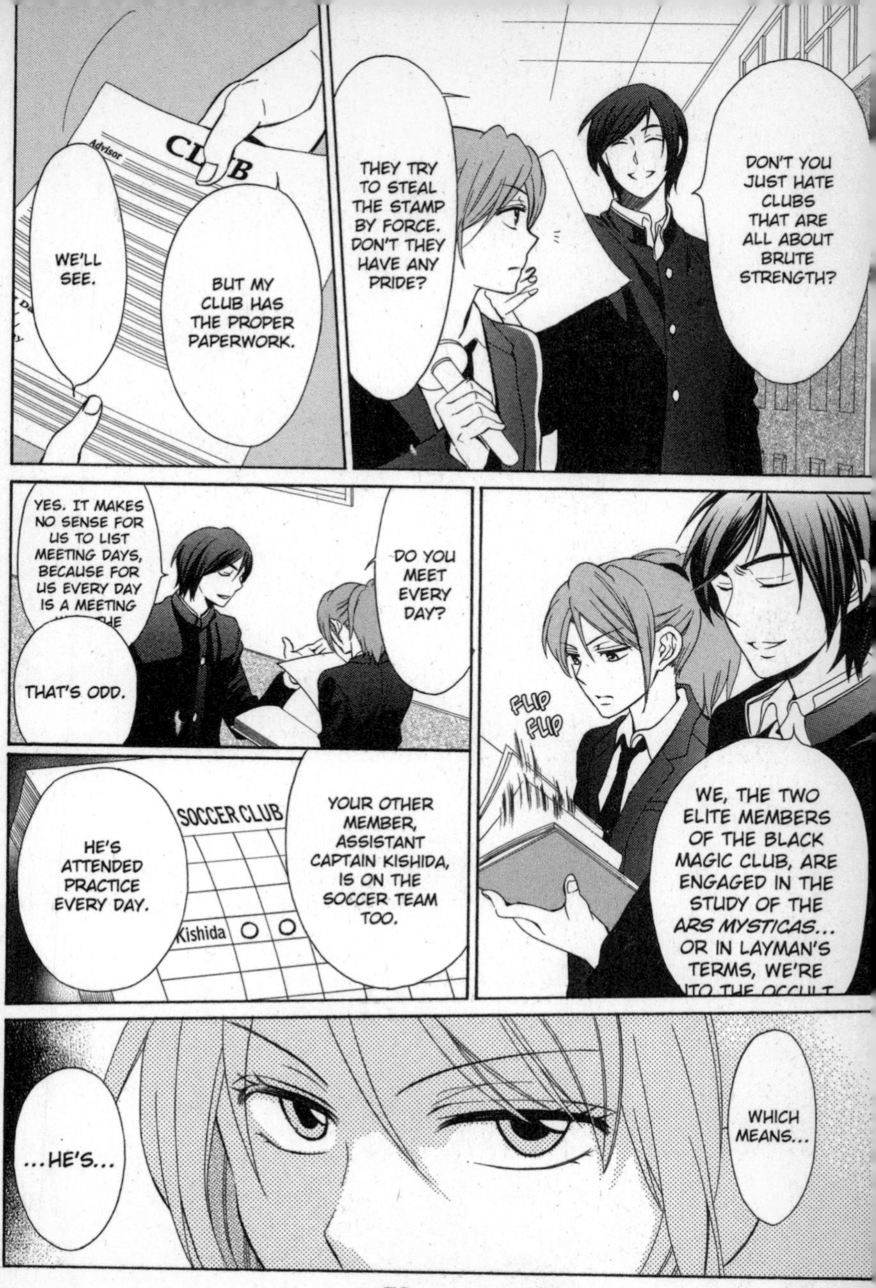
DON'T YOU JUST HATE CLUBS THAT ARE ALL ABOUT BRUTE STRENGTH?
THEY TRY TO STEAL THE STAMP BY FORCE. DON'T THEY HAVE ANY PRIDE?
CLUB
Advisor
BUT MY CLUB HAS THE PROPER PAPERWORK.
WE'LL SEE.
FLIP FLIP
WE, THE TWO ELITE MEMBERS OF THE BLACK MAGIC CLUB, ARE ENGAGED IN THE STUDY OF THE *ARS MYSTICAS*... OR IN LAYMAN'S TERMS, WE'RE
DO YOU MEET EVERY DAY?
YES. IT MAKES NO SENSE FOR US TO LIST MEETING DAYS, BECAUSE FOR US EVERY DAY IS A MEETING
THAT'S ODD.
YOUR OTHER MEMBER, ASSISTANT CAPTAIN KISHIDA, IS ON THE SOCCER TEAM TOO.
SOCCER CLUB
Kishida
HE'S ATTENDED PRACTICE EVERY DAY.
WHICH MEANS...
...HE'S...

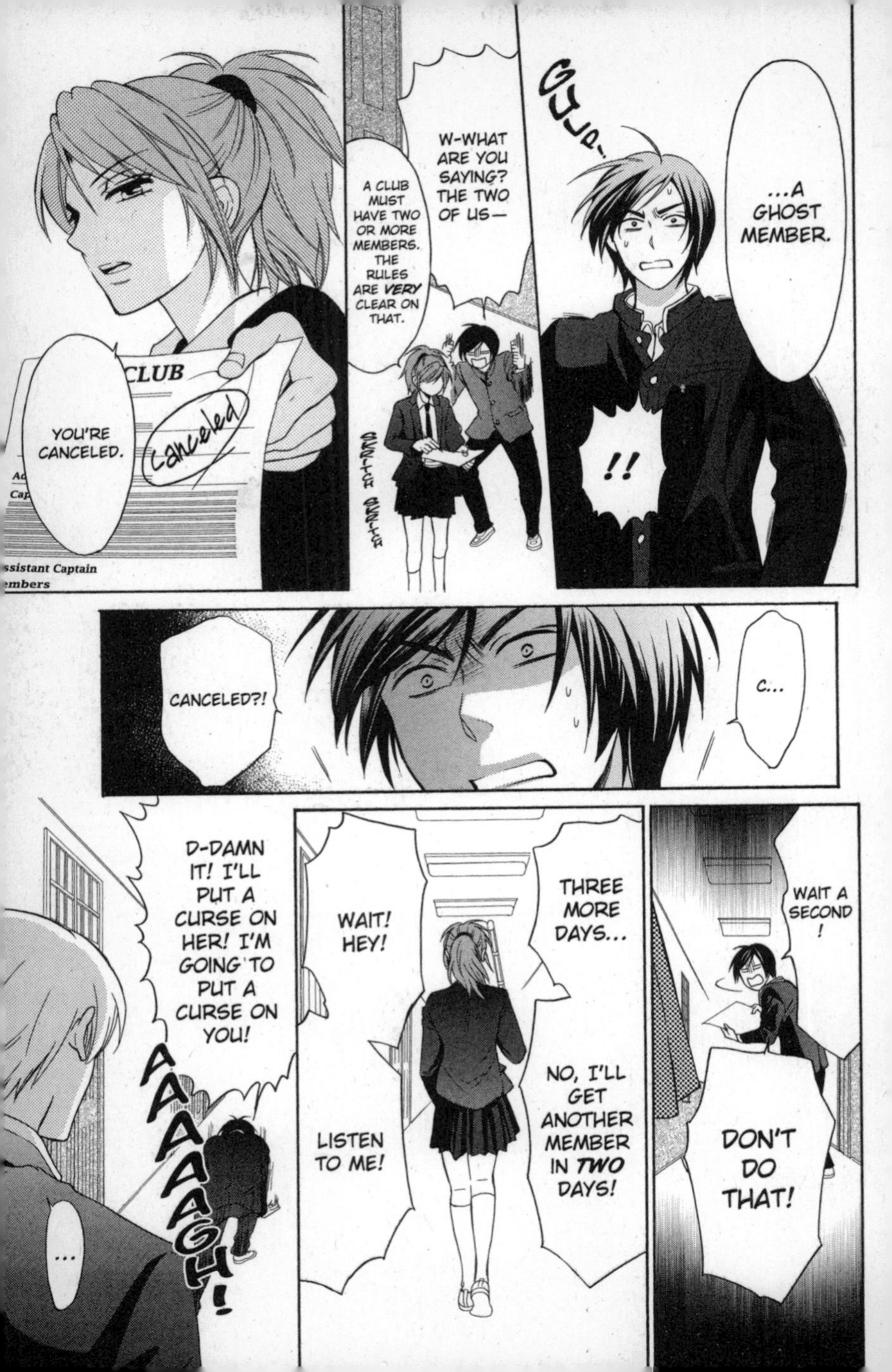
...A GHOST MEMBER.
GULP!
!!
W-WHAT ARE YOU SAYING? THE TWO OF US—
A CLUB MUST HAVE TWO OR MORE MEMBERS. THE RULES ARE *VERY* CLEAR ON THAT.
SCRITCH SCRITCH
CLUB
Canceled
YOU'RE CANCELED.
C...
CANCELED?!
WAIT A SECOND!
DON'T DO THAT!
THREE MORE DAYS...
WAIT! HEY!
NO, I'LL GET ANOTHER MEMBER IN *TWO* DAYS!
LISTEN TO ME!
D-DAMN IT! I'LL PUT A CURSE ON HER! I'M GOING TO PUT A CURSE ON YOU!
AAAAAGH!
...

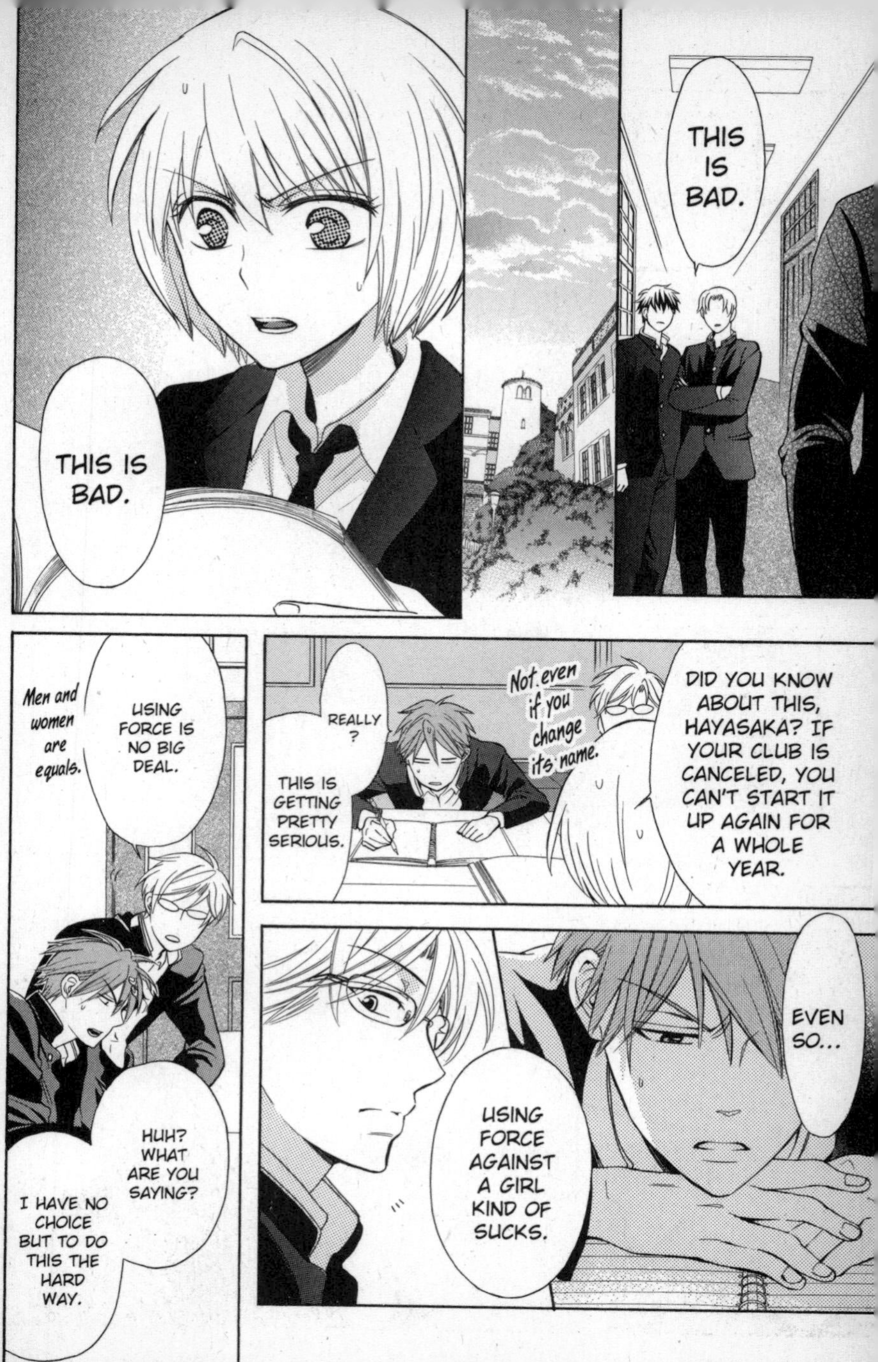
THIS IS BAD.
THIS IS BAD.
DID YOU KNOW ABOUT THIS, HAYASAKA? IF YOUR CLUB IS CANCELED, YOU CAN'T START IT UP AGAIN FOR A WHOLE YEAR.
Not even if you change its name.
REALLY?
THIS IS GETTING PRETTY SERIOUS.
EVEN SO...
USING FORCE AGAINST A GIRL KIND OF SUCKS.
USING FORCE IS NO BIG DEAL.
Men and women are equals.
HUH? WHAT ARE YOU SAYING?
I HAVE NO CHOICE BUT TO DO THIS THE HARD WAY.

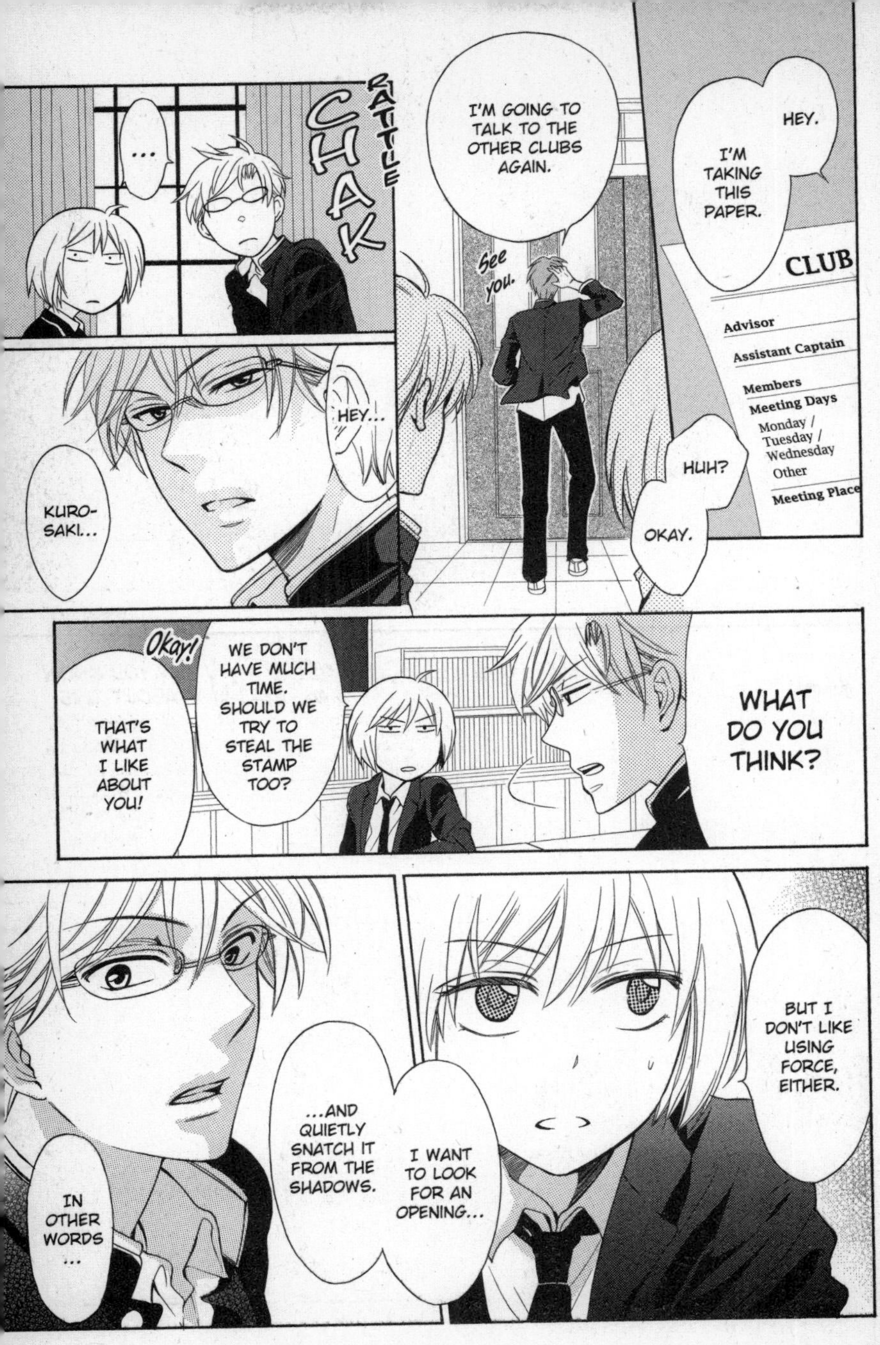
HEY.
I'M TAKING THIS PAPER.
CLUB
Advisor
Assistant Captain
Members
Meeting Days
Monday / Tuesday / Wednesday
Other
Meeting Place
HUH?
OKAY.
I'M GOING TO TALK TO THE OTHER CLUBS AGAIN.
See you.
RATTLE
CHAK
...
HEY...
KURO-SAKI...
WHAT DO YOU THINK?
WE DON'T HAVE MUCH TIME. SHOULD WE TRY TO STEAL THE STAMP TOO?
Okay!
THAT'S WHAT I LIKE ABOUT YOU!
BUT I DON'T LIKE USING FORCE, EITHER.
I WANT TO LOOK FOR AN OPENING...
...AND QUIETLY SNATCH IT FROM THE SHADOWS.
IN OTHER WORDS...

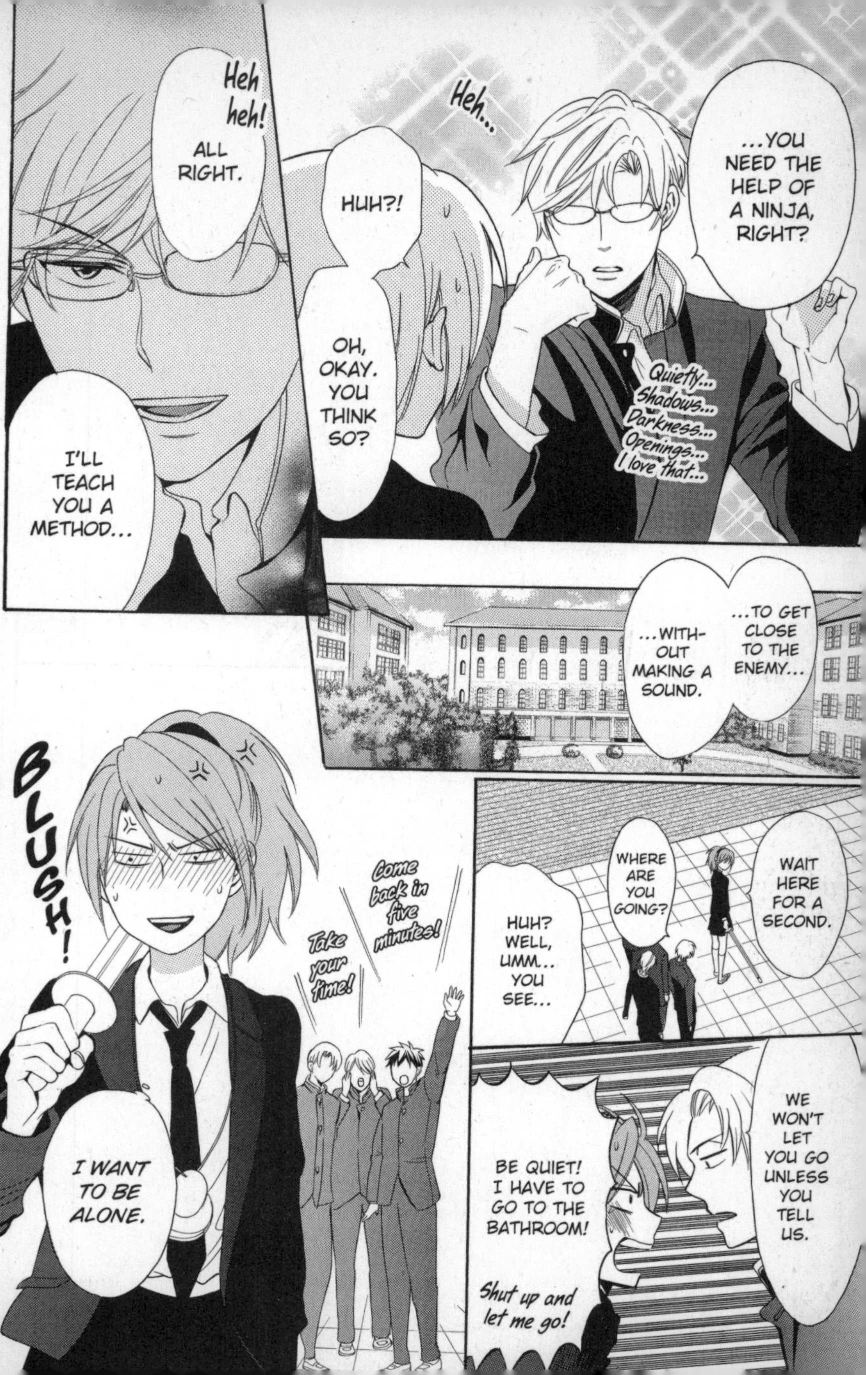
...YOU NEED THE HELP OF A NINJA, RIGHT?
Heh...
Quietly... Shadows... Darkness... Openings... I love that...
HUH?!
OH, OKAY. YOU THINK SO?
Heh heh!
ALL RIGHT.
I'LL TEACH YOU A METHOD...
...TO GET CLOSE TO THE ENEMY...
...WITH-OUT MAKING A SOUND.
WAIT HERE FOR A SECOND.
WHERE ARE YOU GOING?
HUH? WELL, UMM... YOU SEE...
WE WON'T LET YOU GO UNLESS YOU TELL US.
BE QUIET! I HAVE TO GO TO THE BATHROOM!
Shut up and let me go!
Come back in five minutes!
Take your time!
BLUSH!
I WANT TO BE ALONE.

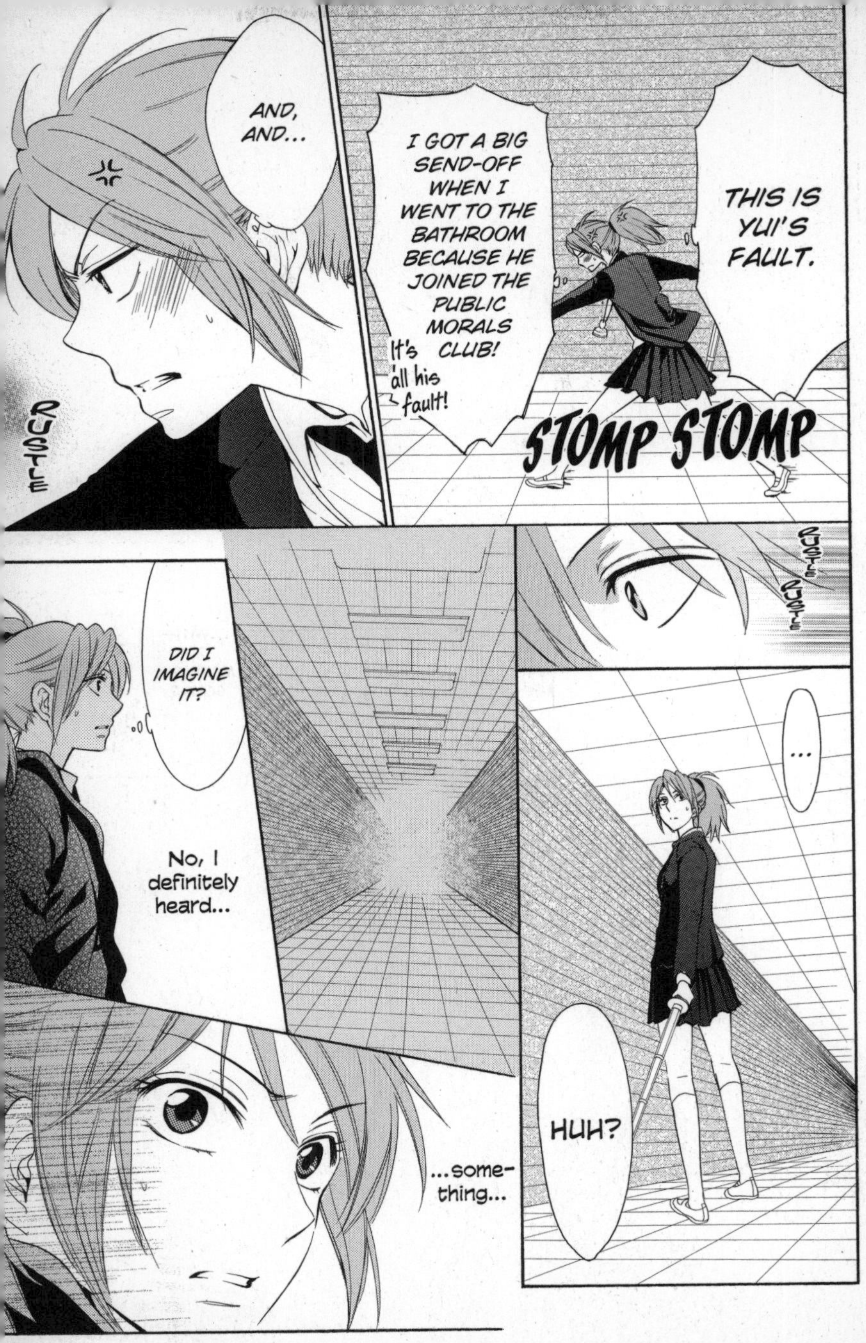
THIS IS YUI'S FAULT.
I GOT A BIG SEND-OFF WHEN I WENT TO THE BATHROOM BECAUSE HE JOINED THE PUBLIC MORALS CLUB!
It's all his fault!
STOMP STOMP
AND, AND...
RUSTLE
RUSTLE RUSTLE
...
HUH?
DID I IMAGINE IT?
No, I definitely heard...
...some-thing...

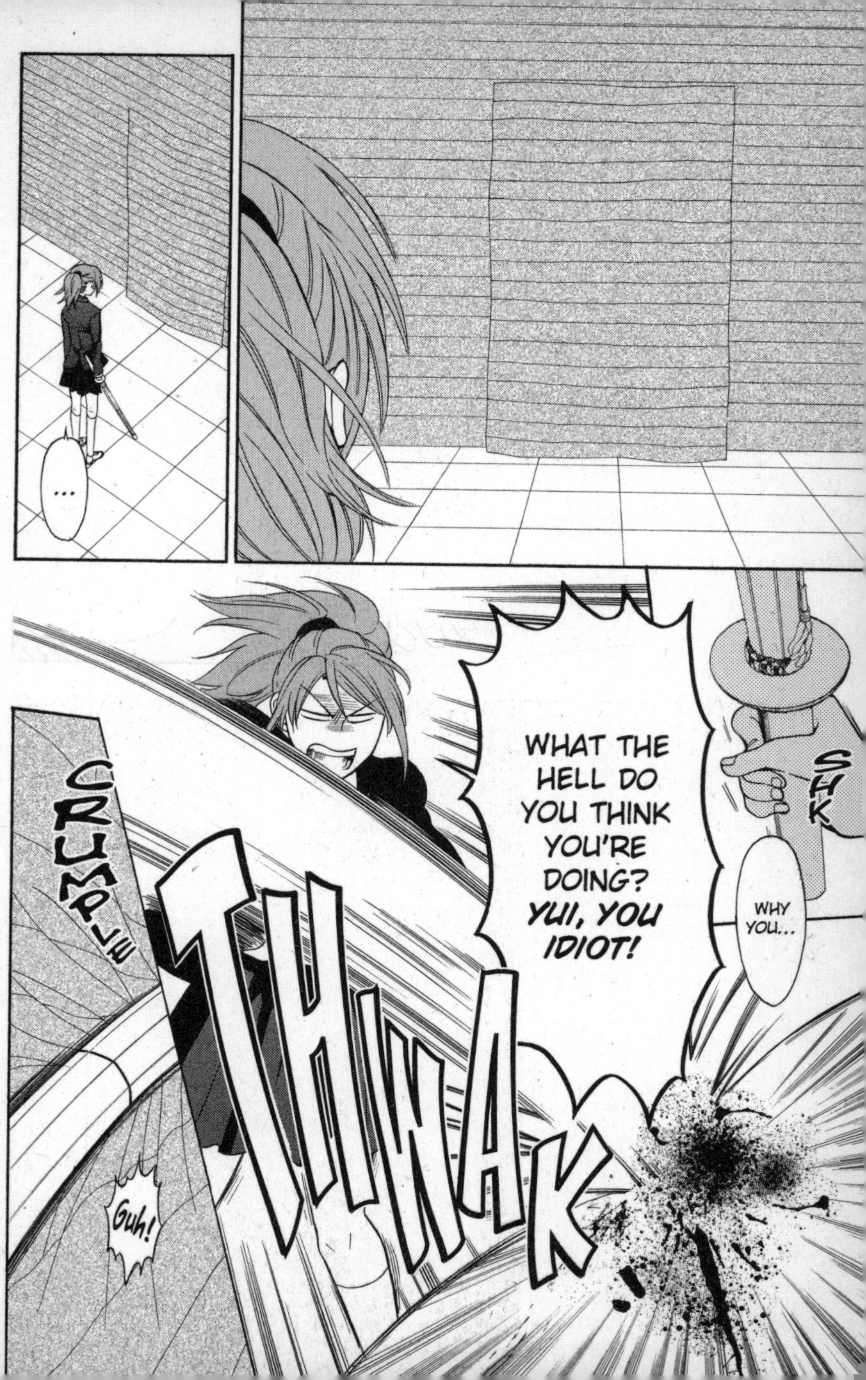
...
SHK
WHY YOU...
WHAT THE HELL DO YOU THINK YOU'RE DOING? *YUI, YOU IDIOT!*
CRUMPLE
THWAK
Guh!

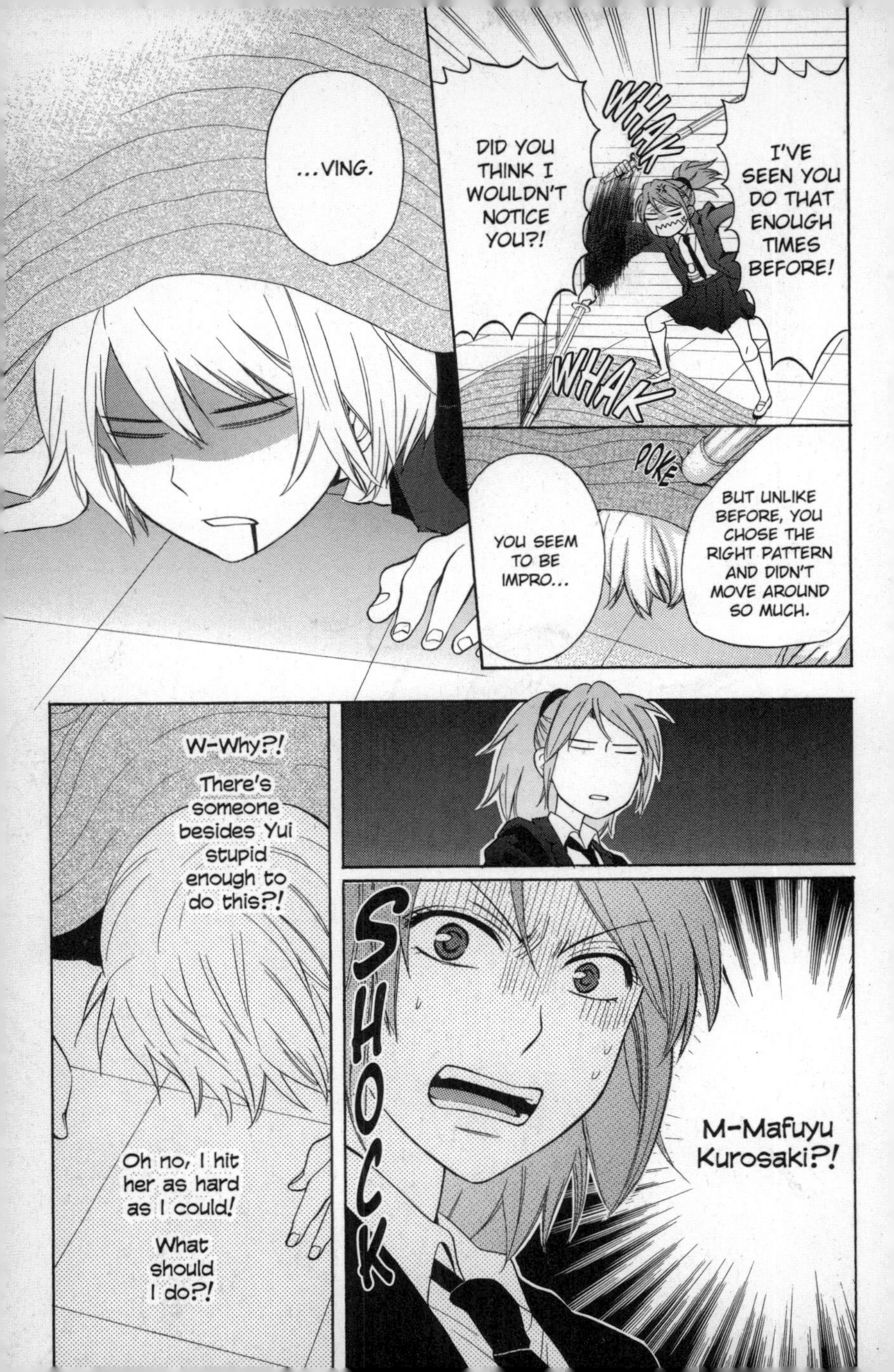
I'VE SEEN YOU DO THAT ENOUGH TIMES BEFORE!
WHAK
DID YOU THINK I WOULDN'T NOTICE YOU?!
WHAK
POKE
BUT UNLIKE BEFORE, YOU CHOSE THE RIGHT PATTERN AND DIDN'T MOVE AROUND SO MUCH.
YOU SEEM TO BE IMPRO...
...VING.
M-Mafuyu Kurosaki?!
SHOCK
W-Why?!
There's someone besides Yui stupid enough to do this?!
Oh no, I hit her as hard as I could!
What should I do?!

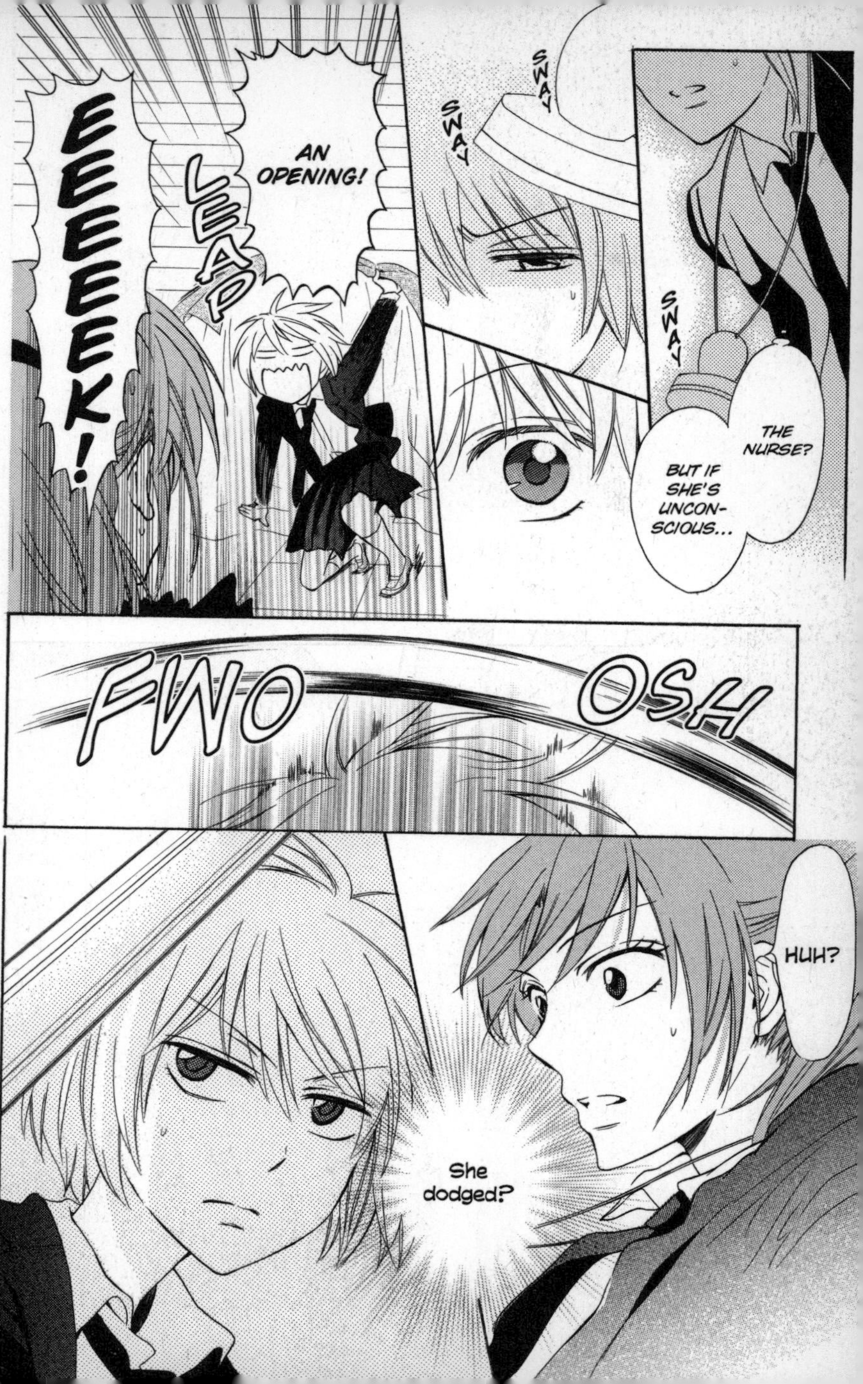

SWAY
THE NURSE?
BUT IF SHE'S UNCONSCIOUS...
SWAY
SWAY
AN OPENING!
EEEEEEK!
LEAP
FWO OSH
HUH?
She dodged?

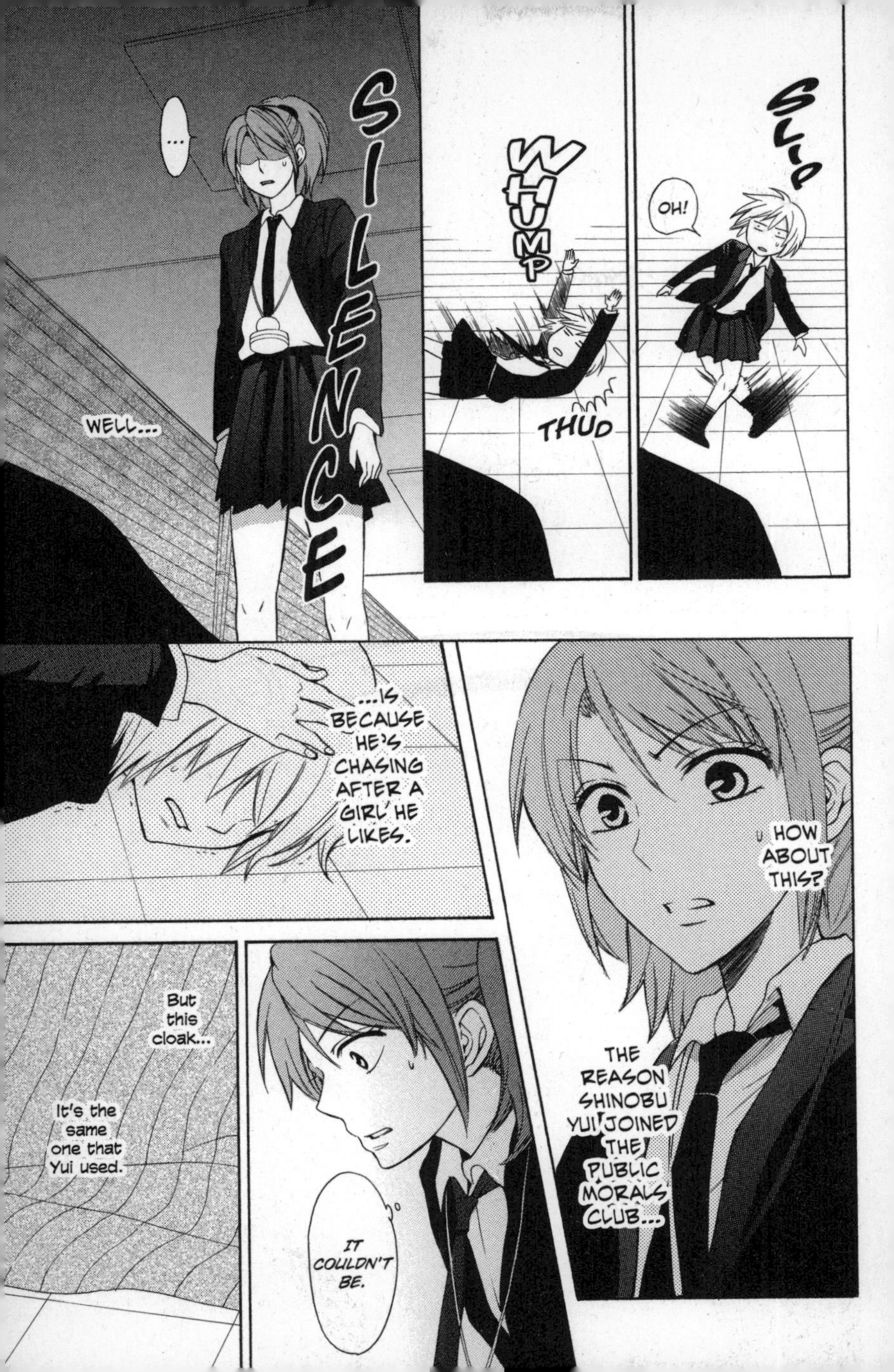
SLIP
OH!
WHUMP
THUD
...
SILENCE
WELL...
HOW ABOUT THIS?
THE REASON SHINOBU YUI JOINED THE PUBLIC MORALS CLUB...
...IS BECAUSE HE'S CHASING AFTER A GIRL HE LIKES.
IT COULDN'T BE.
But this cloak...
It's the same one that Yui used.

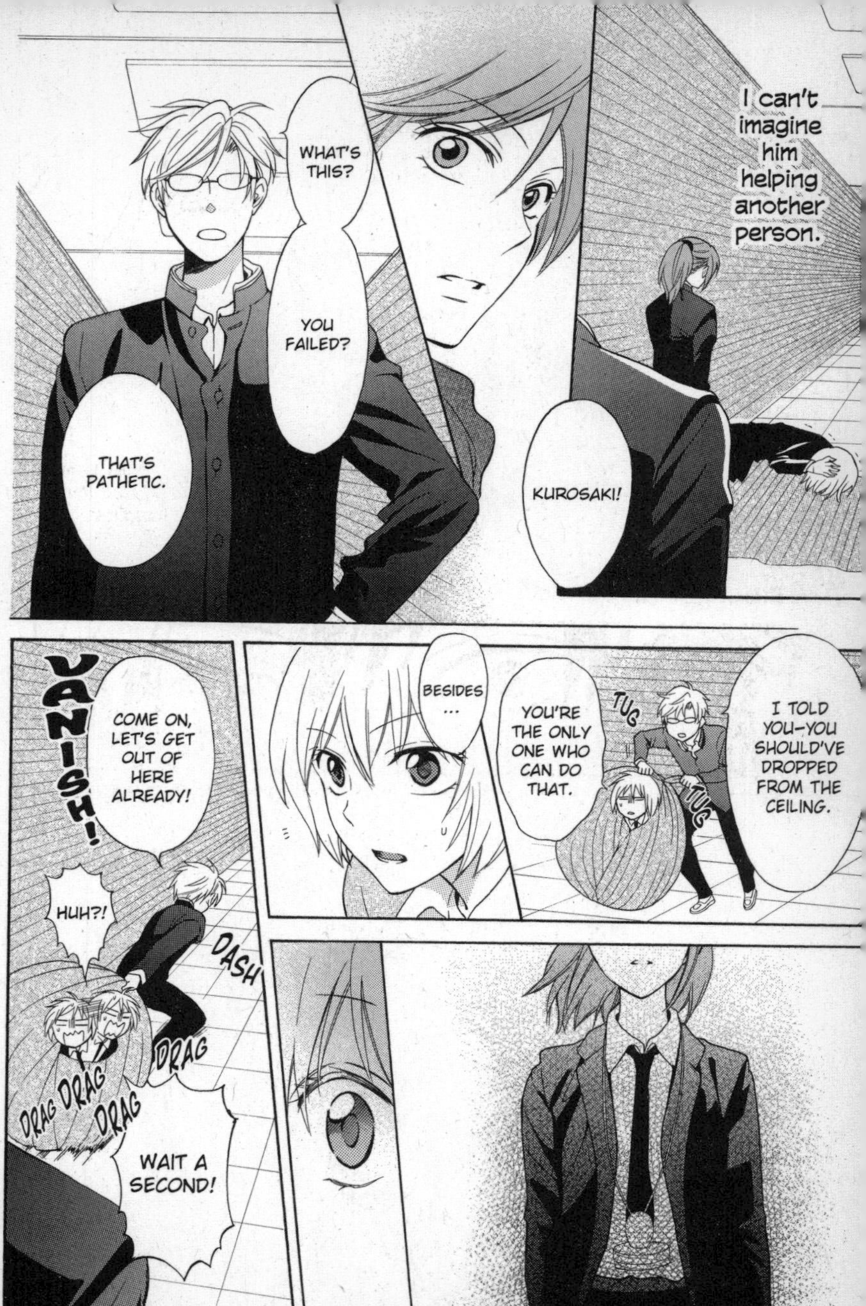
I can't imagine him helping another person.
KUROSAKI!
WHAT'S THIS?
YOU FAILED?
THAT'S PATHETIC.
I TOLD YOU—YOU SHOULD'VE DROPPED FROM THE CEILING.
TUG
TUG
YOU'RE THE ONLY ONE WHO CAN DO THAT.
BESIDES...
VANISH!
COME ON, LET'S GET OUT OF HERE ALREADY!
HUH?!
DASH
DRAG
DRAG DRAG DRAG
WAIT A SECOND!

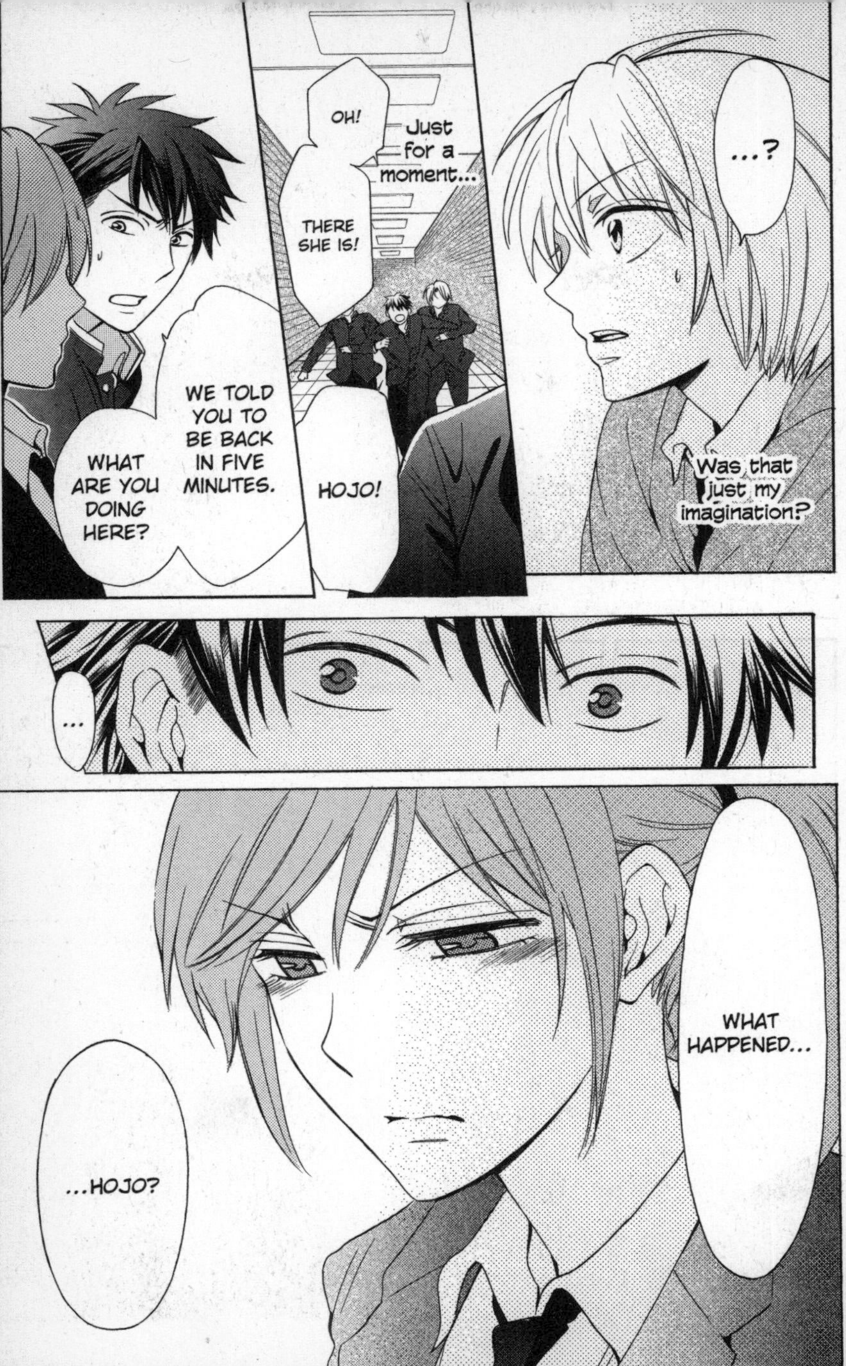
...?
Just for a moment...
Was that just my imagination?
OH!
THERE SHE IS!
HOJO!
WE TOLD YOU TO BE BACK IN FIVE MINUTES.
WHAT ARE YOU DOING HERE?
...
WHAT HAPPENED...
...HOJO?

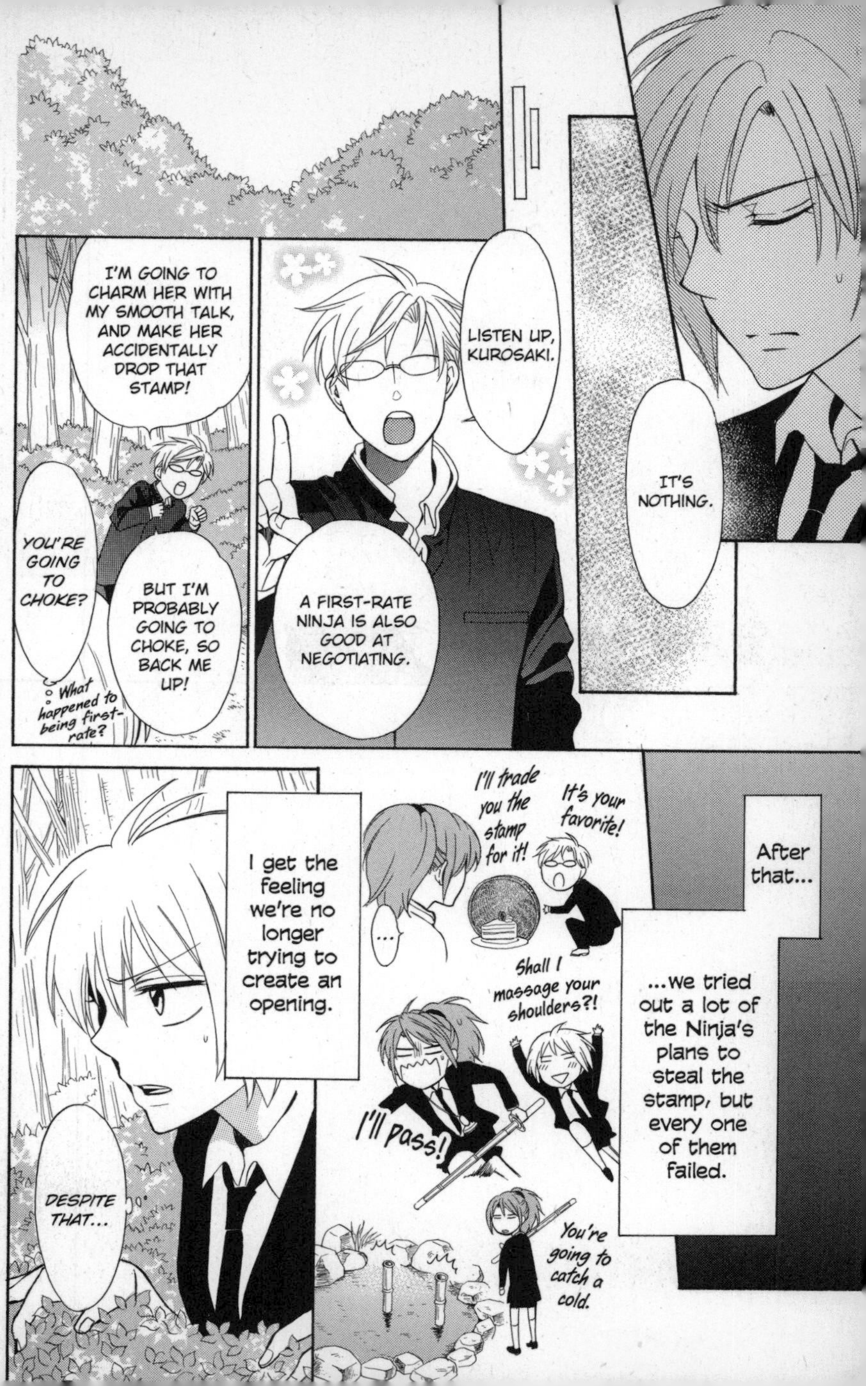
IT'S NOTHING.
LISTEN UP, KUROSAKI.
A FIRST-RATE NINJA IS ALSO GOOD AT NEGOTIATING.
I'M GOING TO CHARM HER WITH MY SMOOTH TALK, AND MAKE HER ACCIDENTALLY DROP THAT STAMP!
BUT I'M PROBABLY GOING TO CHOKE, SO BACK ME UP!
YOU'RE GOING TO CHOKE?
What happened to being first-rate?
After that...
...we tried out a lot of the Ninja's plans to steal the stamp, but every one of them failed.
It's your favorite!
I'll trade you the stamp for it!
...
Shall I massage your shoulders?!
I'll pass!
You're going to catch a cold.
I get the feeling we're no longer trying to create an opening.
DESPITE THAT...

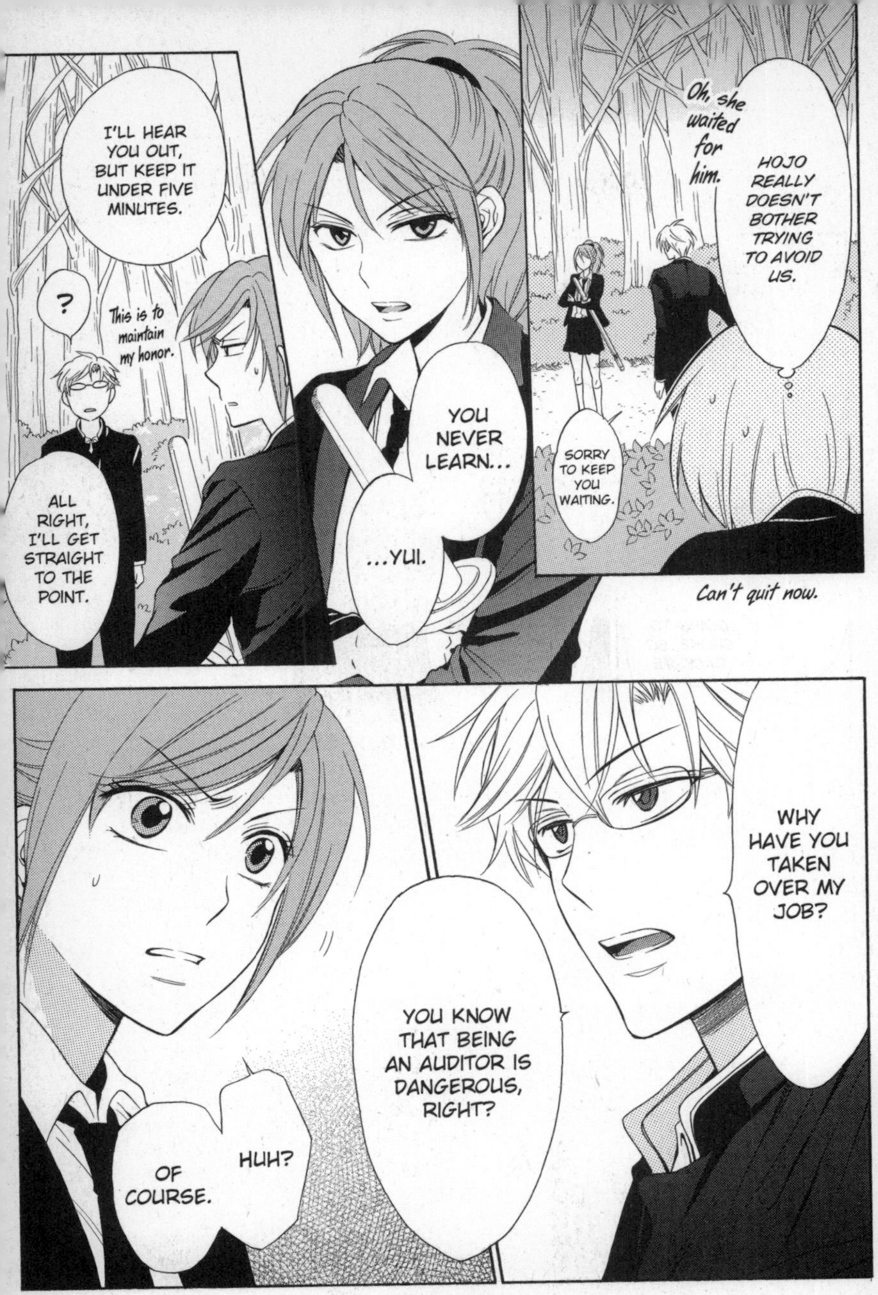
Oh, she waited for him.
HOJO REALLY DOESN'T BOTHER TRYING TO AVOID US.
SORRY TO KEEP YOU WAITING.
Can't quit now.
YOU NEVER LEARN...
...YUI.
I'LL HEAR YOU OUT, BUT KEEP IT UNDER FIVE MINUTES.
?
This is to maintain my honor.
ALL RIGHT, I'LL GET STRAIGHT TO THE POINT.
WHY HAVE YOU TAKEN OVER MY JOB?
YOU KNOW THAT BEING AN AUDITOR IS DANGEROUS, RIGHT?
HUH?
OF COURSE.

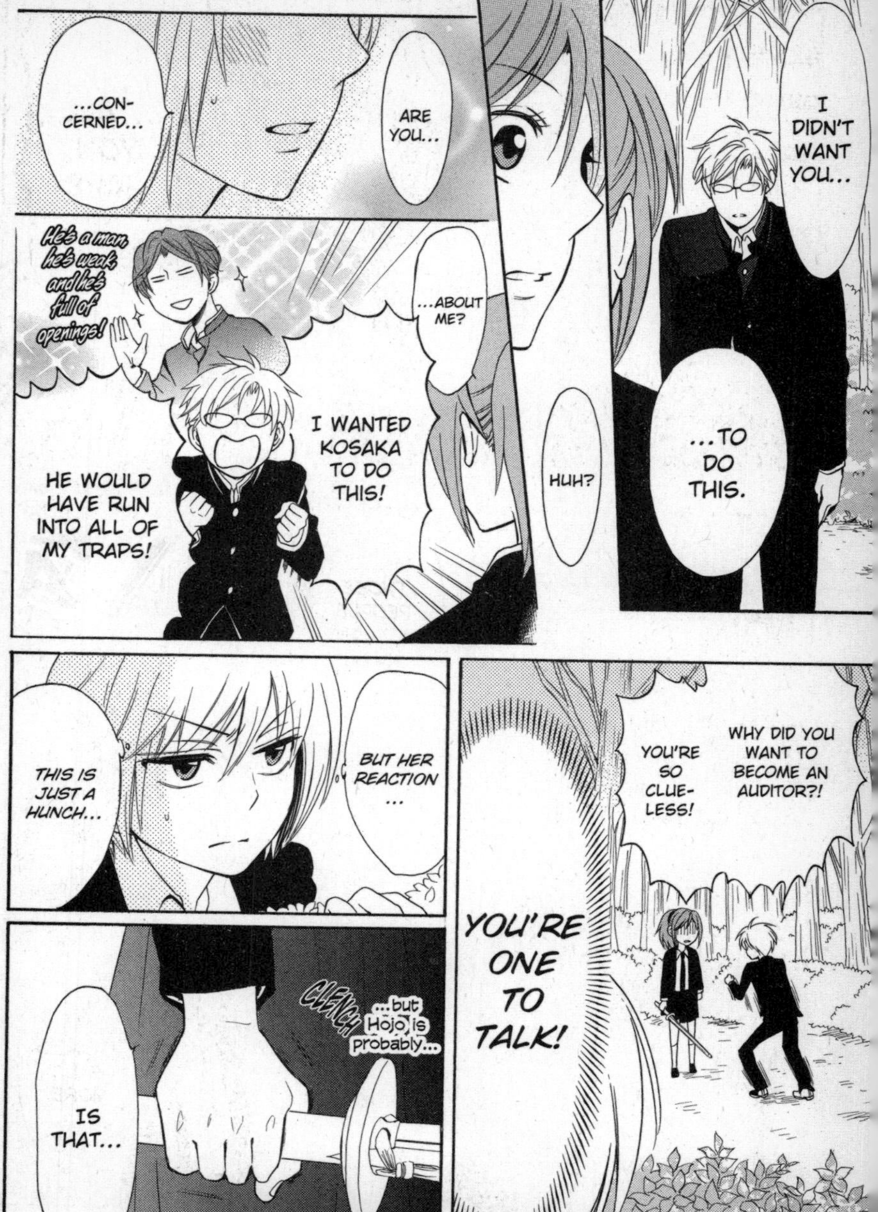
I DIDN'T WANT YOU...
...TO DO THIS.
HUH?
ARE YOU...
...CON-CERNED...
...ABOUT ME?
I WANTED KOSAKA TO DO THIS!
He's a man, he's weak and he's full of openings!
HE WOULD HAVE RUN INTO ALL OF MY TRAPS!
WHY DID YOU WANT TO BECOME AN AUDITOR?!
YOU'RE SO CLUE-LESS!
YOU'RE ONE TO TALK!
BUT HER REACTION ...
THIS IS JUST A HUNCH...
...but Hojo is probably...
CLENCH
IS THAT...

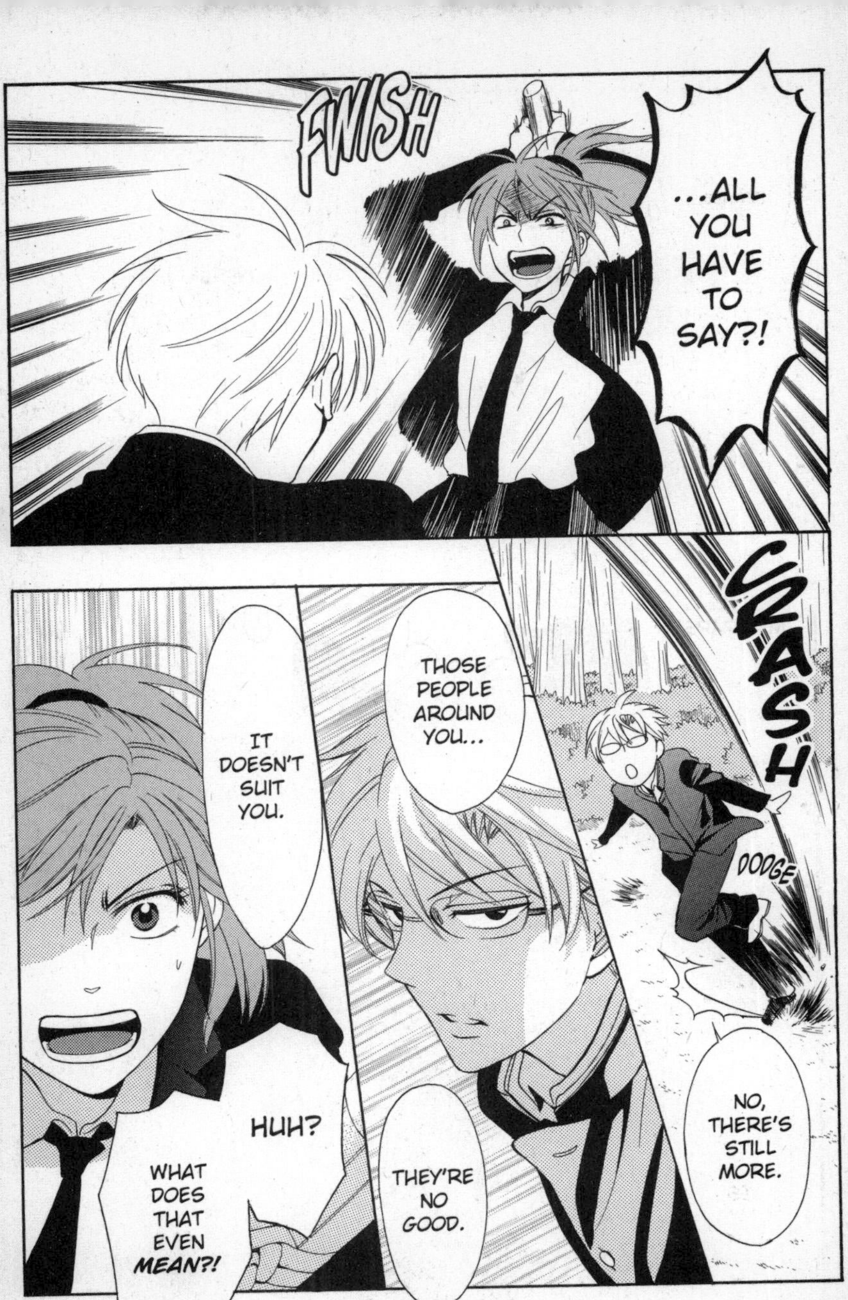
FWISH
...ALL YOU HAVE TO SAY?!
CRASH
DODGE
NO, THERE'S STILL MORE.
THOSE PEOPLE AROUND YOU...
THEY'RE NO GOOD.
IT DOESN'T SUIT YOU.
HUH?
WHAT DOES THAT EVEN *MEAN?!*

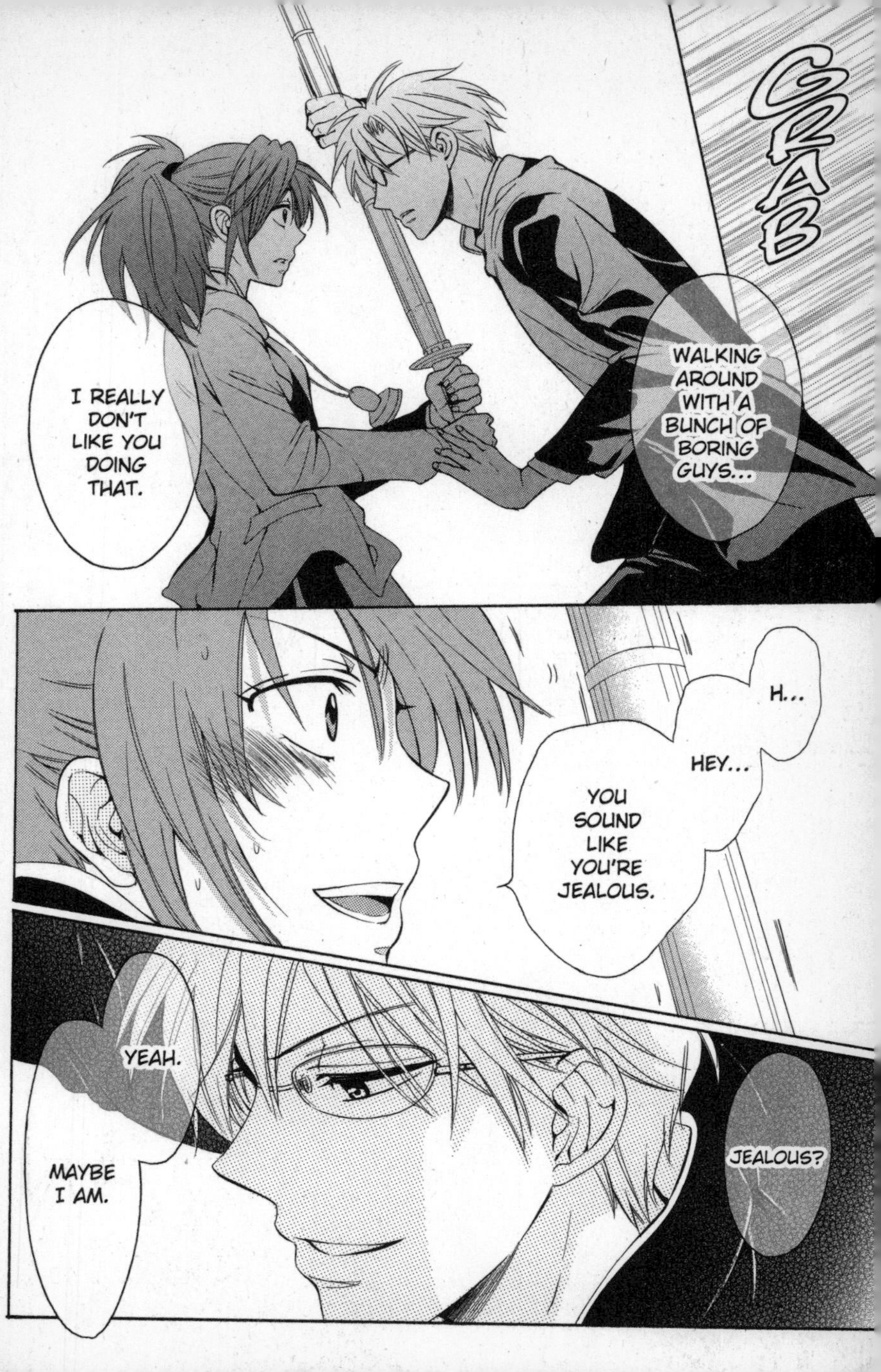
GRAB
WALKING AROUND WITH A BUNCH OF BORING GUYS...
I REALLY DON'T LIKE YOU DOING THAT.
H...
HEY...
YOU SOUND LIKE YOU'RE JEALOUS.
JEALOUS?
YEAH.
MAYBE I AM.

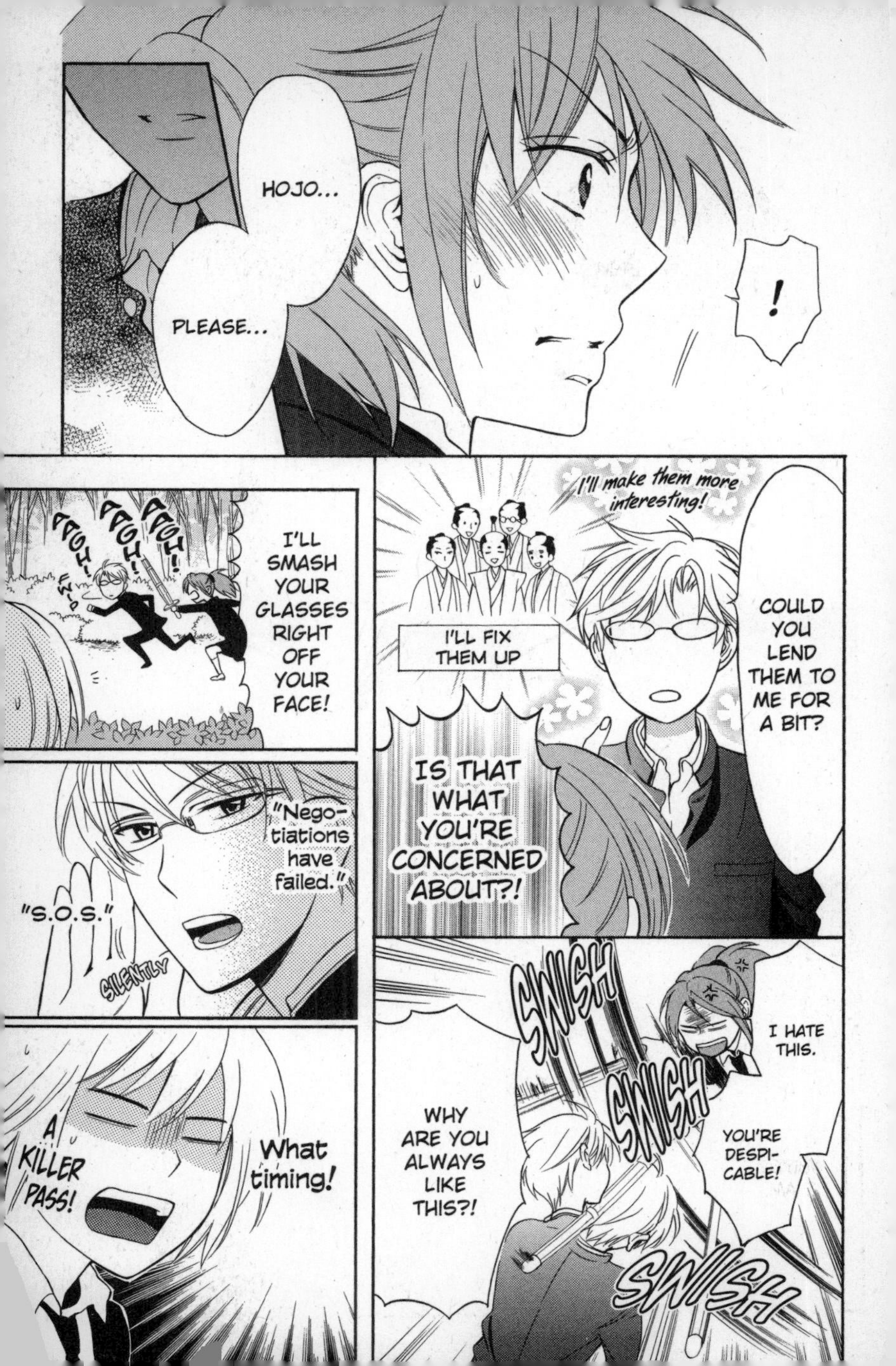
HOJO...
PLEASE...
!
COULD YOU LEND THEM TO ME FOR A BIT?
I'll make them more interesting!
I'LL FIX THEM UP
IS THAT WHAT YOU'RE CONCERNED ABOUT?!
AAGH!
AAGH!
AAGH!
FWIP
I'LL SMASH YOUR GLASSES RIGHT OFF YOUR FACE!
"Negotiations have failed."
"S.O.S."
SILENTLY
SWISH
I HATE THIS.
SWISH
YOU'RE DESPICABLE!
WHY ARE YOU ALWAYS LIKE THIS?!
SWISH
What timing!
A KILLER PASS!

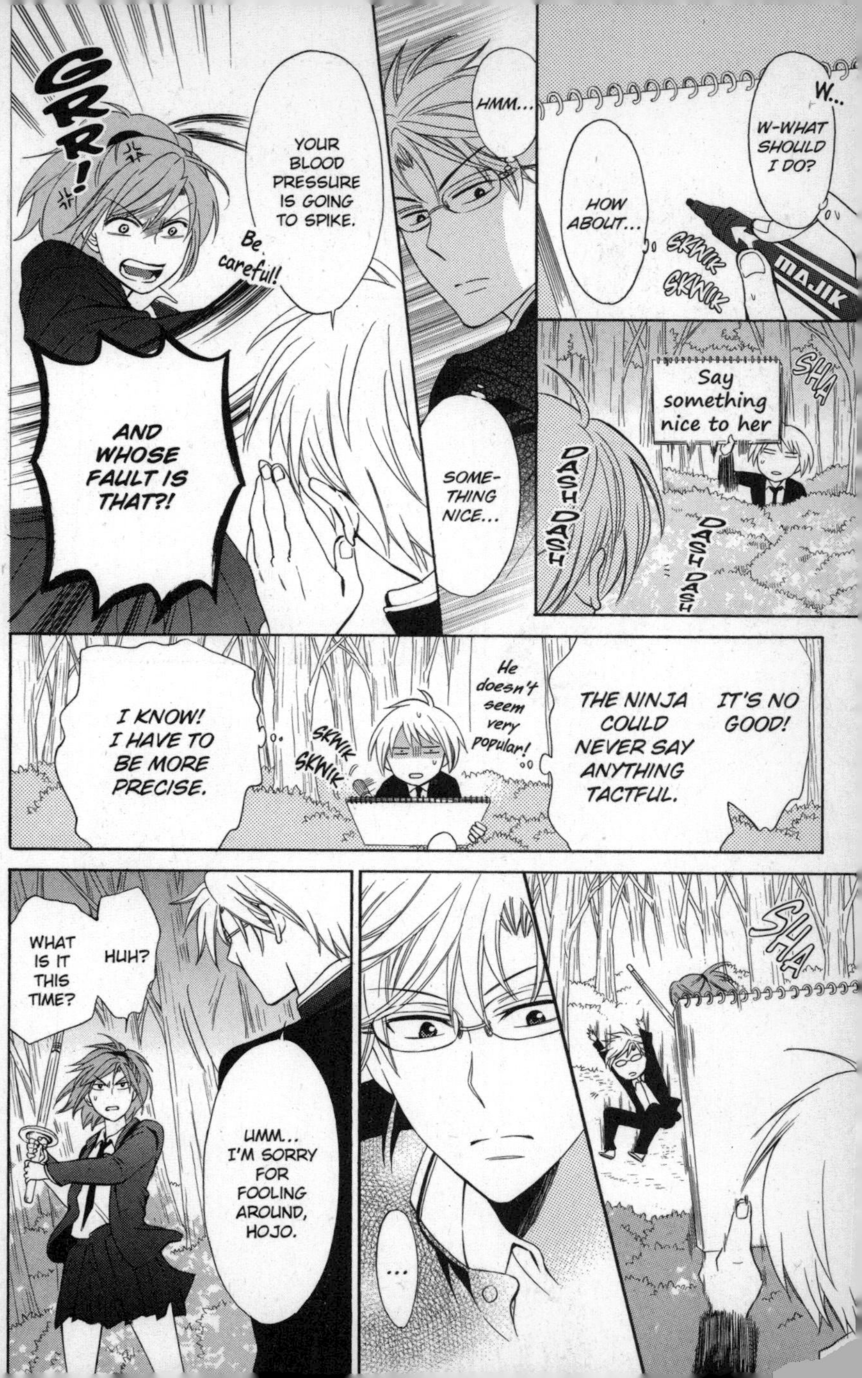
W...
W-WHAT SHOULD I DO?
HOW ABOUT...
SKWIK SKWIK
MAJIK
SHA
Say something nice to her
DASH DASH
DASH DASH
HMM...
SOME-THING NICE...
YOUR BLOOD PRESSURE IS GOING TO SPIKE.
Be careful!
GRR!
AND WHOSE FAULT IS THAT?!
IT'S NO GOOD!
THE NINJA COULD NEVER SAY ANYTHING TACTFUL.
He doesn't seem very popular!
SKWIK SKWIK
I KNOW! I HAVE TO BE MORE PRECISE.
SHA
...
UMM... I'M SORRY FOR FOOLING AROUND, HOJO.
HUH?
WHAT IS IT THIS TIME?

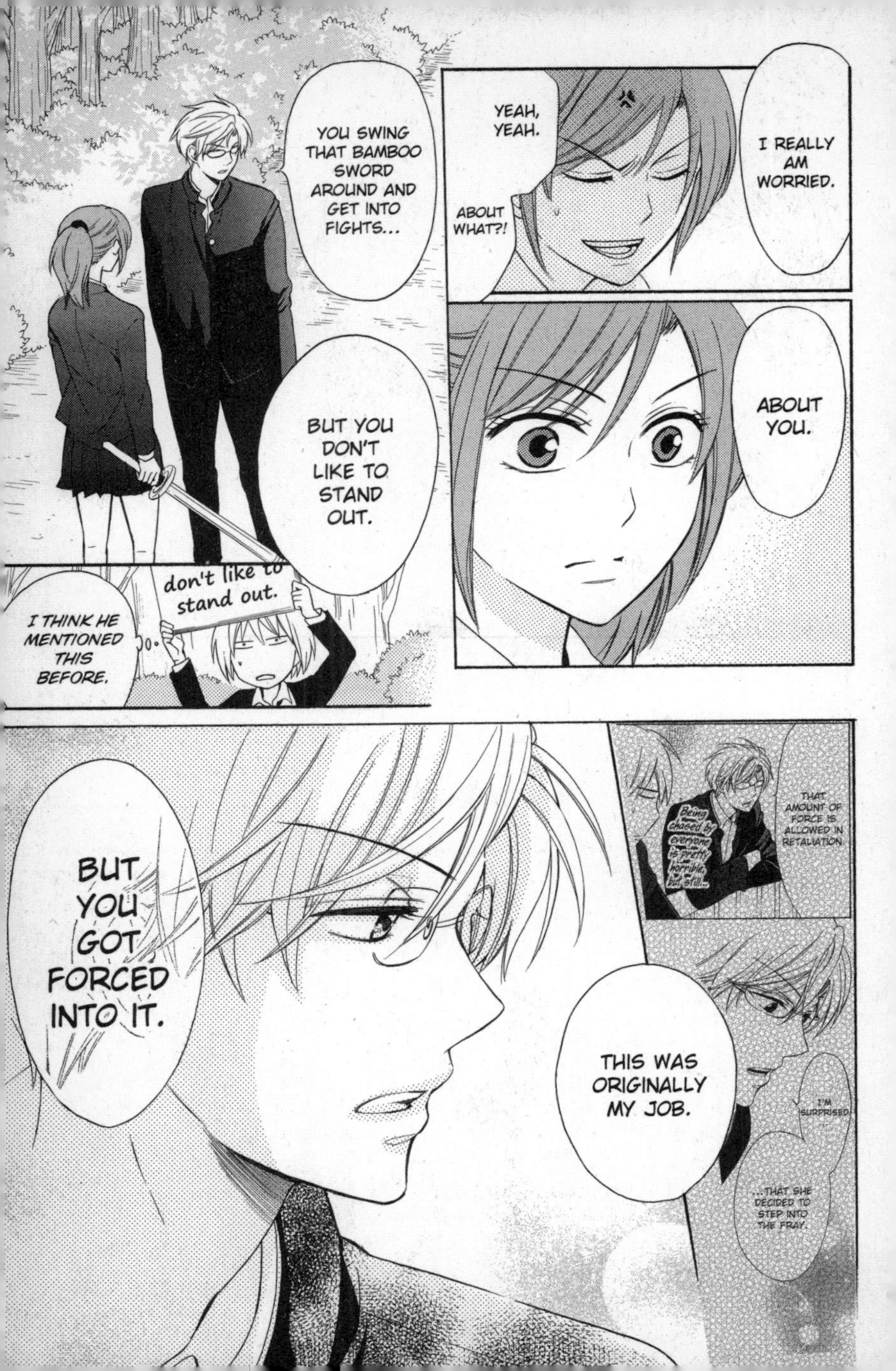
I REALLY AM WORRIED.
YEAH, YEAH.
ABOUT WHAT?!
ABOUT YOU.
YOU SWING THAT BAMBOO SWORD AROUND AND GET INTO FIGHTS...
BUT YOU DON'T LIKE TO STAND OUT.
don't like to stand out.
I THINK HE MENTIONED THIS BEFORE.
THAT AMOUNT OF FORCE IS ALLOWED IN RETALIATION.
Being chased by everyone is pretty horrible, but still...
I'M SURPRISED
...THAT SHE DECIDED TO STEP INTO THE FRAY.
THIS WAS ORIGINALLY MY JOB.
BUT YOU GOT FORCED INTO IT.

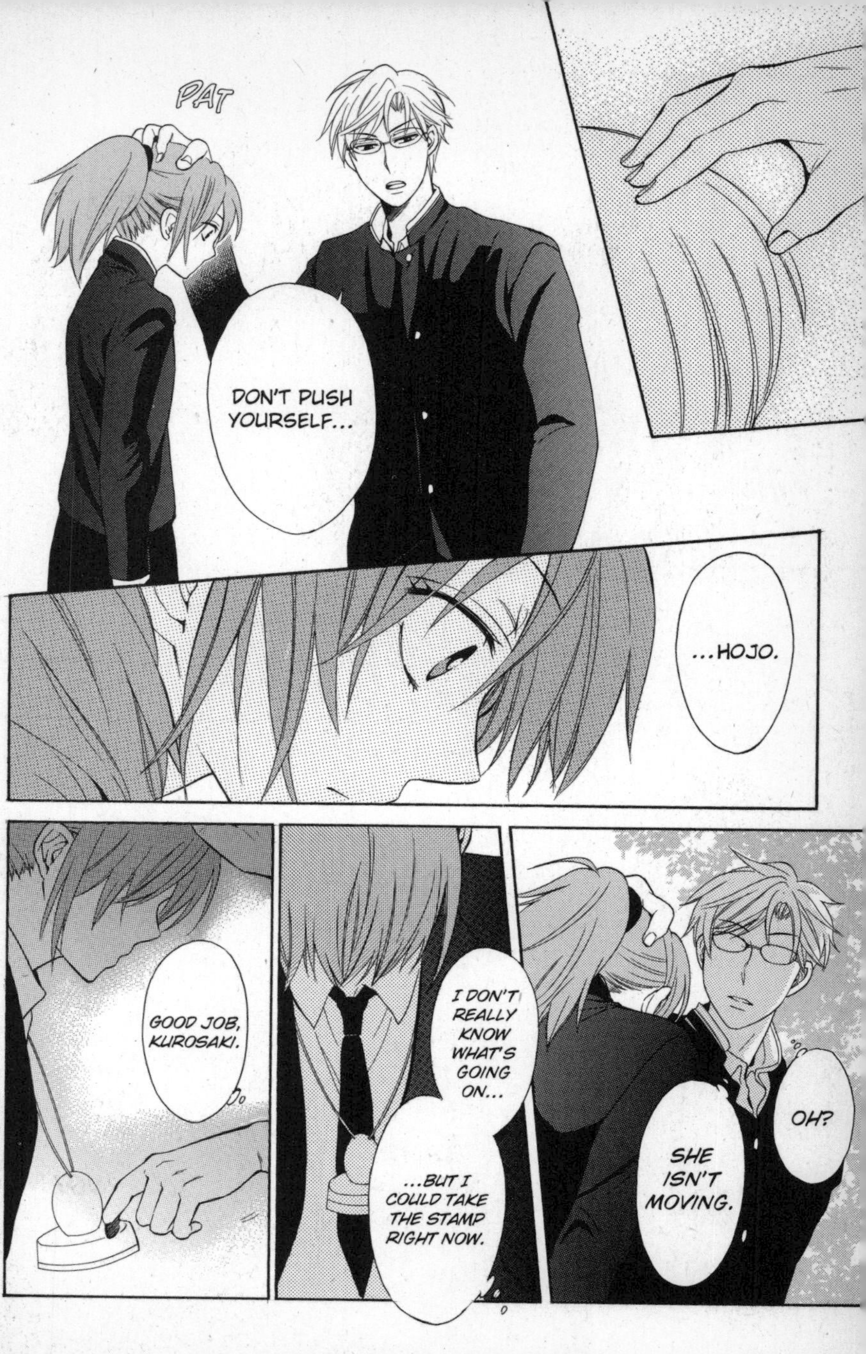
PAT
DON'T PUSH YOURSELF...
...HOJO.
OH?
SHE ISN'T MOVING.
I DON'T REALLY KNOW WHAT'S GOING ON...
...BUT I COULD TAKE THE STAMP RIGHT NOW.
GOOD JOB, KUROSAKI.

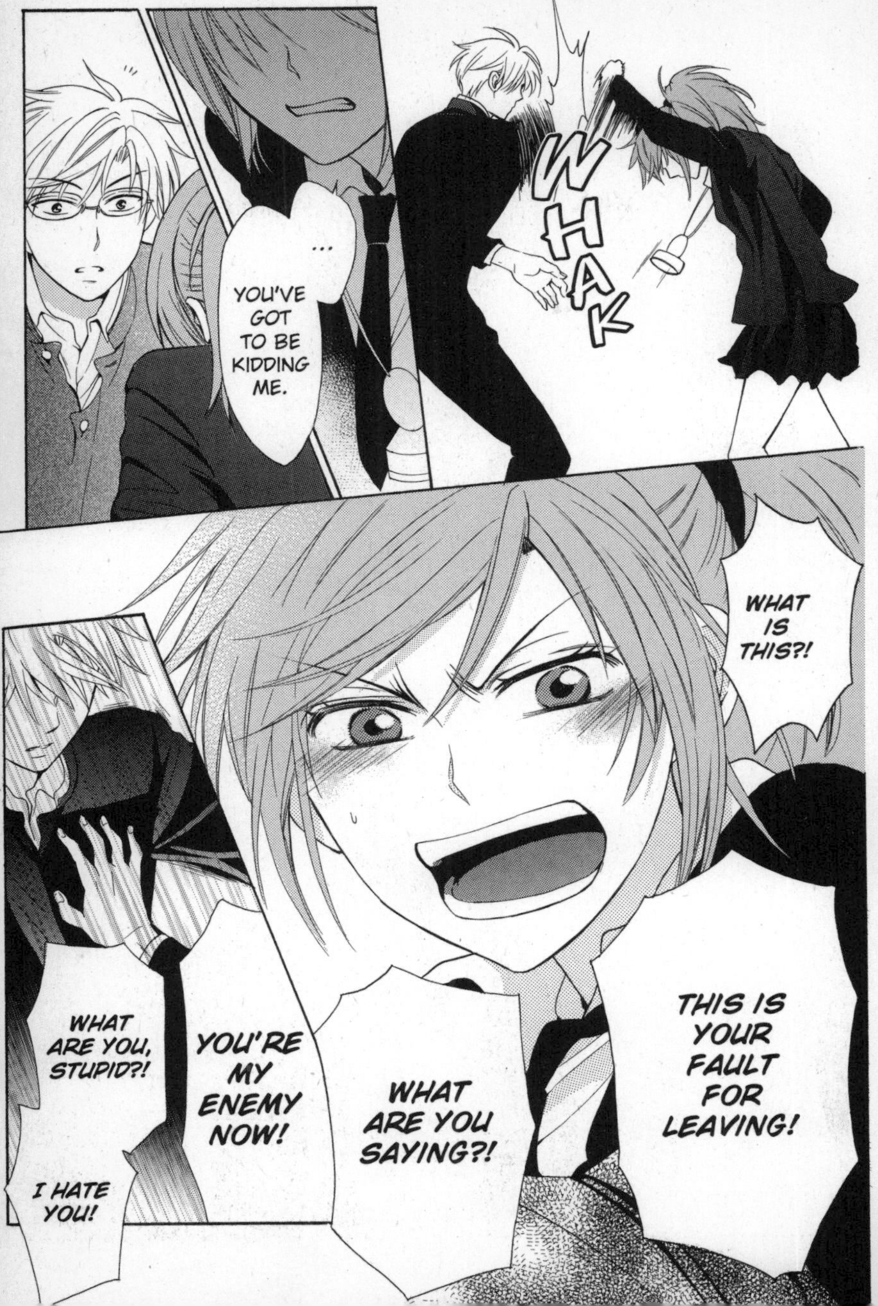
WHAK
...
YOU'VE GOT TO BE KIDDING ME.
WHAT IS THIS?!
THIS IS YOUR FAULT FOR LEAVING!
WHAT ARE YOU SAYING?!
YOU'RE MY ENEMY NOW!
WHAT ARE YOU, STUPID?!
I HATE YOU!

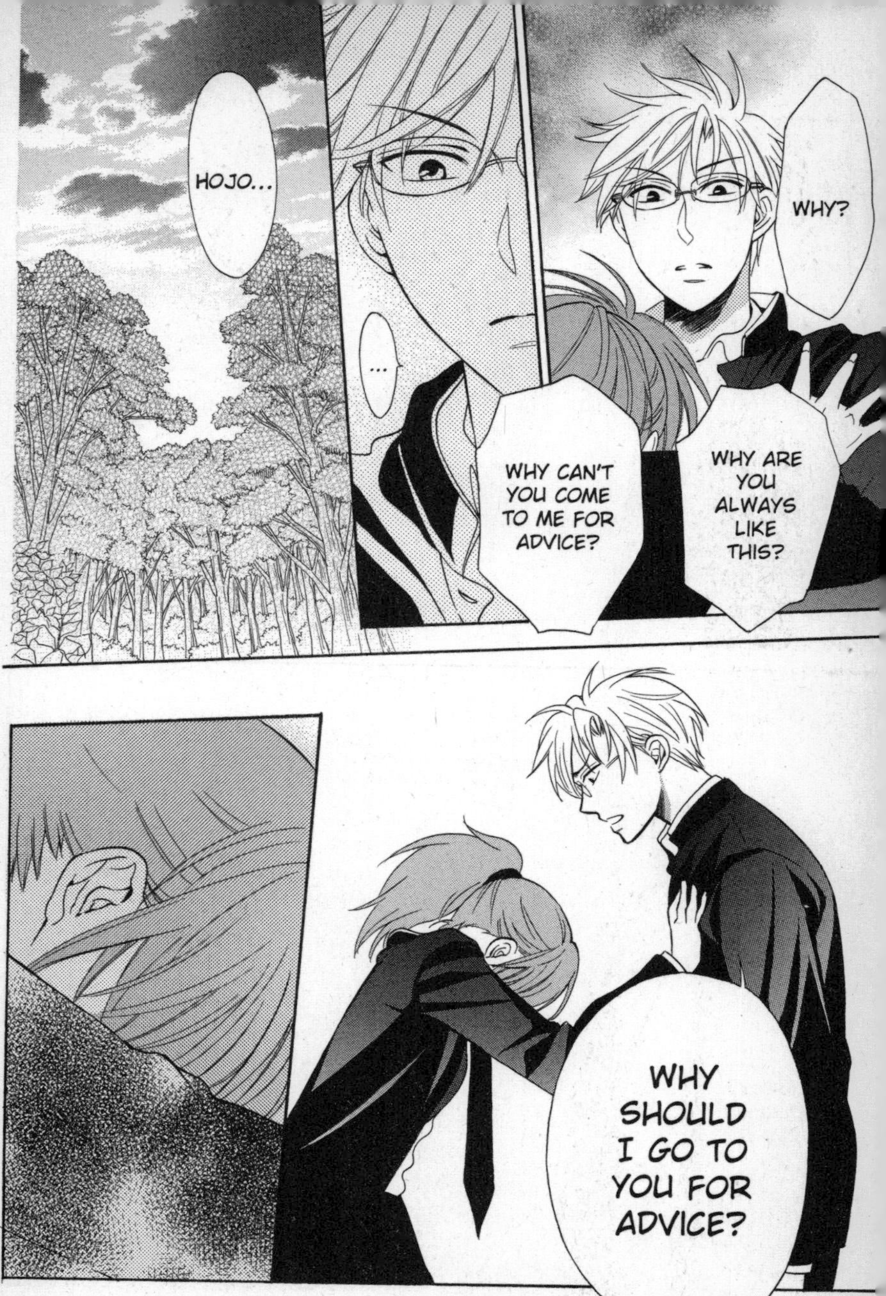
WHY?
WHY ARE YOU ALWAYS LIKE THIS?
WHY CAN'T YOU COME TO ME FOR ADVICE?
...
HOJO...
WHY SHOULD I GO TO YOU FOR ADVICE?

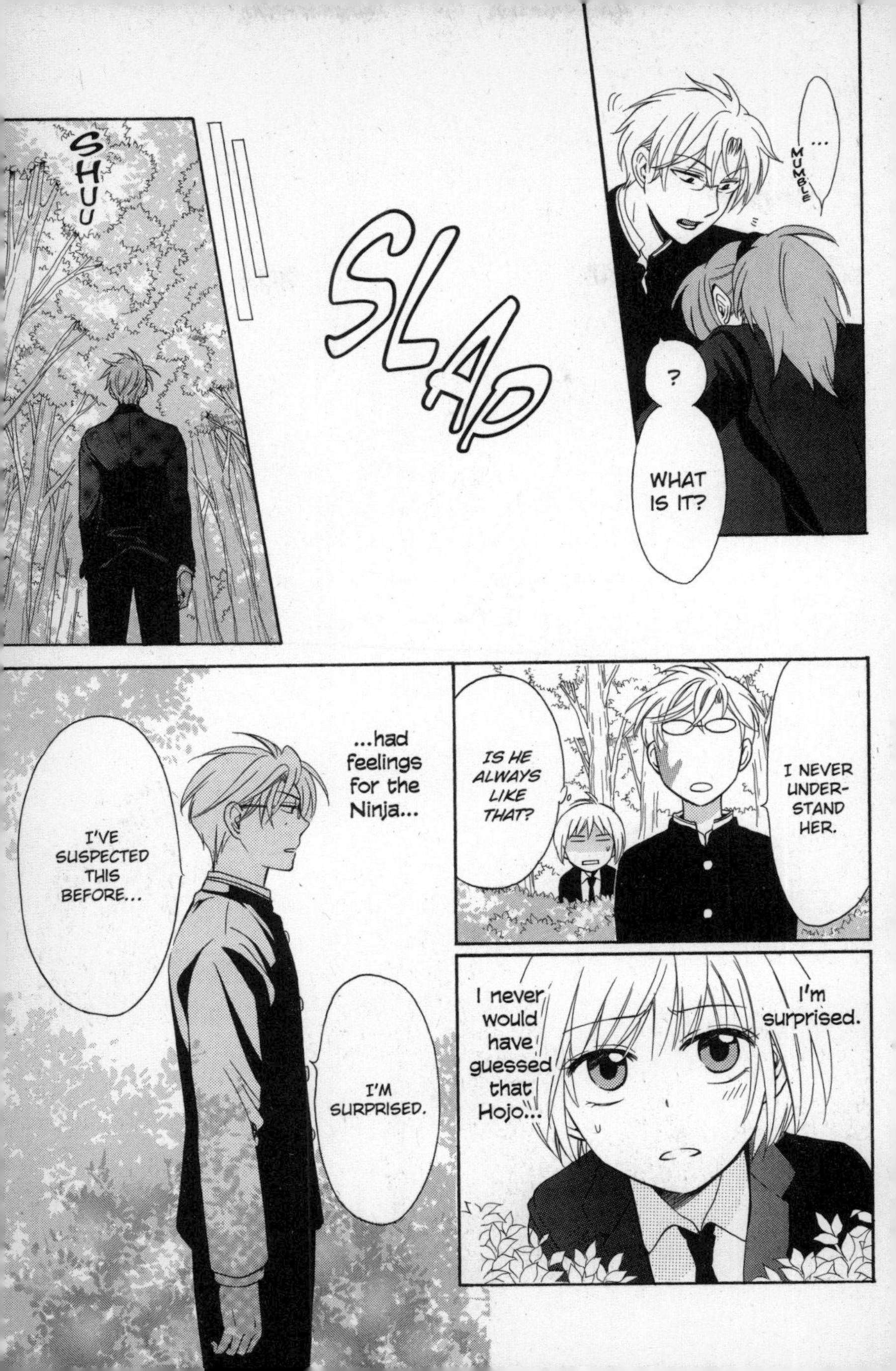
...
MUMBLE
?
WHAT IS IT?
SLAP
SHUU
I NEVER UNDER-STAND HER.
IS HE ALWAYS LIKE THAT?
I'm surprised.
I never would have guessed that Hojo...
...had feelings for the Ninja...
I'VE SUSPECTED THIS BEFORE...
I'M SURPRISED.

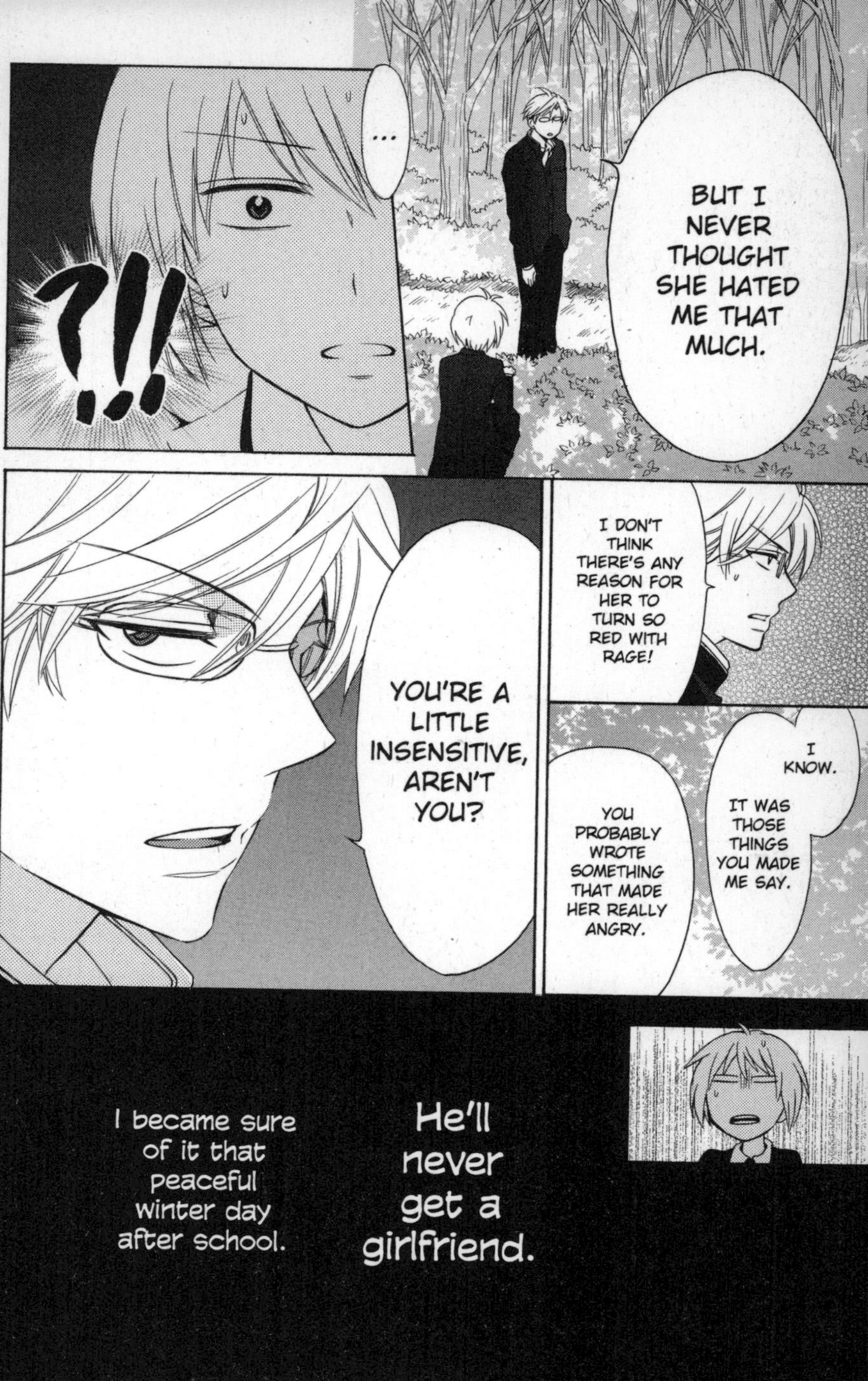
BUT I NEVER THOUGHT SHE HATED ME THAT MUCH.
...
?!!
I DON'T THINK THERE'S ANY REASON FOR HER TO TURN SO RED WITH RAGE!
I KNOW.
IT WAS THOSE THINGS YOU MADE ME SAY.
YOU PROBABLY WROTE SOMETHING THAT MADE HER REALLY ANGRY.
YOU'RE A LITTLE INSENSITIVE, AREN'T YOU?
He'll never get a girlfriend.
I became sure of it that peaceful winter day after school.

Chapter 55

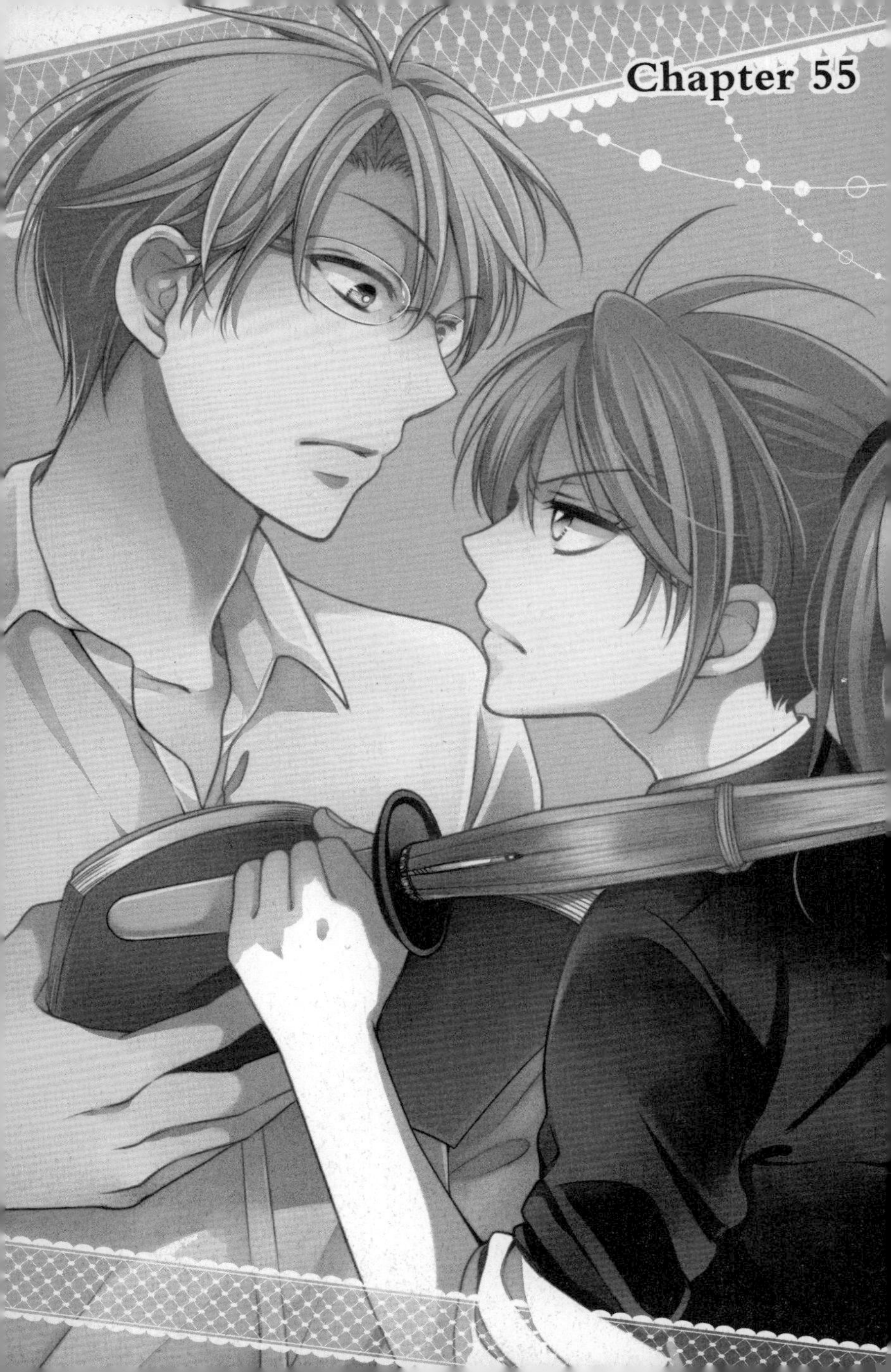

THIS YEAR'S REPRESENTATIVE

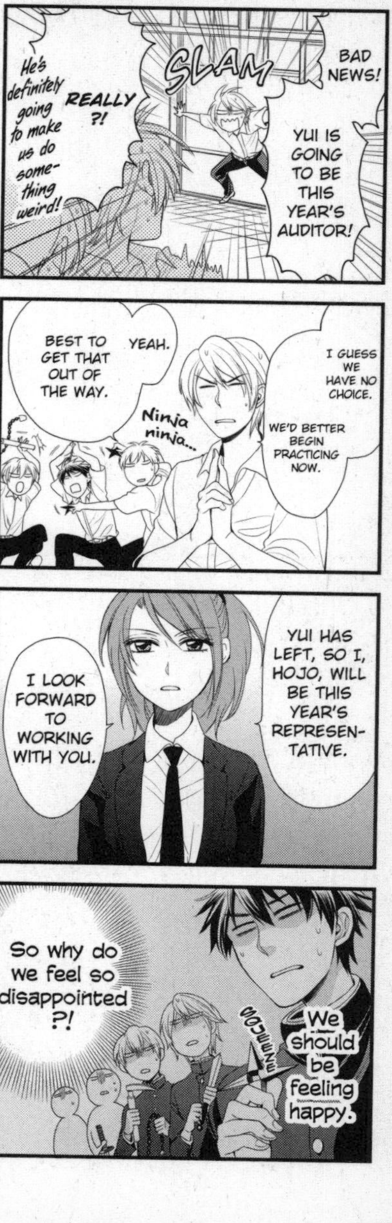
BAD NEWS!
SLAM
YUI IS GOING TO BE THIS YEAR'S AUDITOR!
REALLY ?!
He's definitely going to make us do something weird!
I GUESS WE HAVE NO CHOICE.
WE'D BETTER BEGIN PRACTICING NOW.
YEAH.
BEST TO GET THAT OUT OF THE WAY.
Ninja ninja...
YUI HAS LEFT, SO I, HOJO, WILL BE THIS YEAR'S REPRESEN-TATIVE.
I LOOK FORWARD TO WORKING WITH YOU.
We should be feeling happy.
SQUEEZE
So why do we feel so disappointed ?!

THE IDEAL REPRESENTATIVE

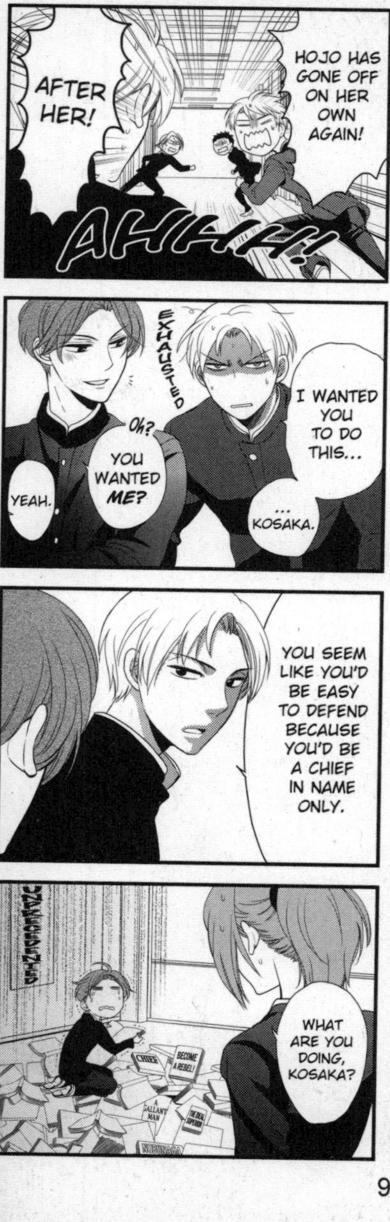
HOJO HAS GONE OFF ON HER OWN AGAIN!
AFTER HER!
AHHHH!!
I WANTED YOU TO DO THIS...
EXHAUSTED
... KOSAKA.
Oh?
YOU WANTED ME?
YEAH.
YOU SEEM LIKE YOU'D BE EASY TO DEFEND BECAUSE YOU'D BE A CHIEF IN NAME ONLY.
WHAT ARE YOU DOING, KOSAKA?
UNDESERVED
CHIEF
BECOME A REBEL!
A GALLANT MAN
THE IDEAL SUPERIOR
NOBUNAGA

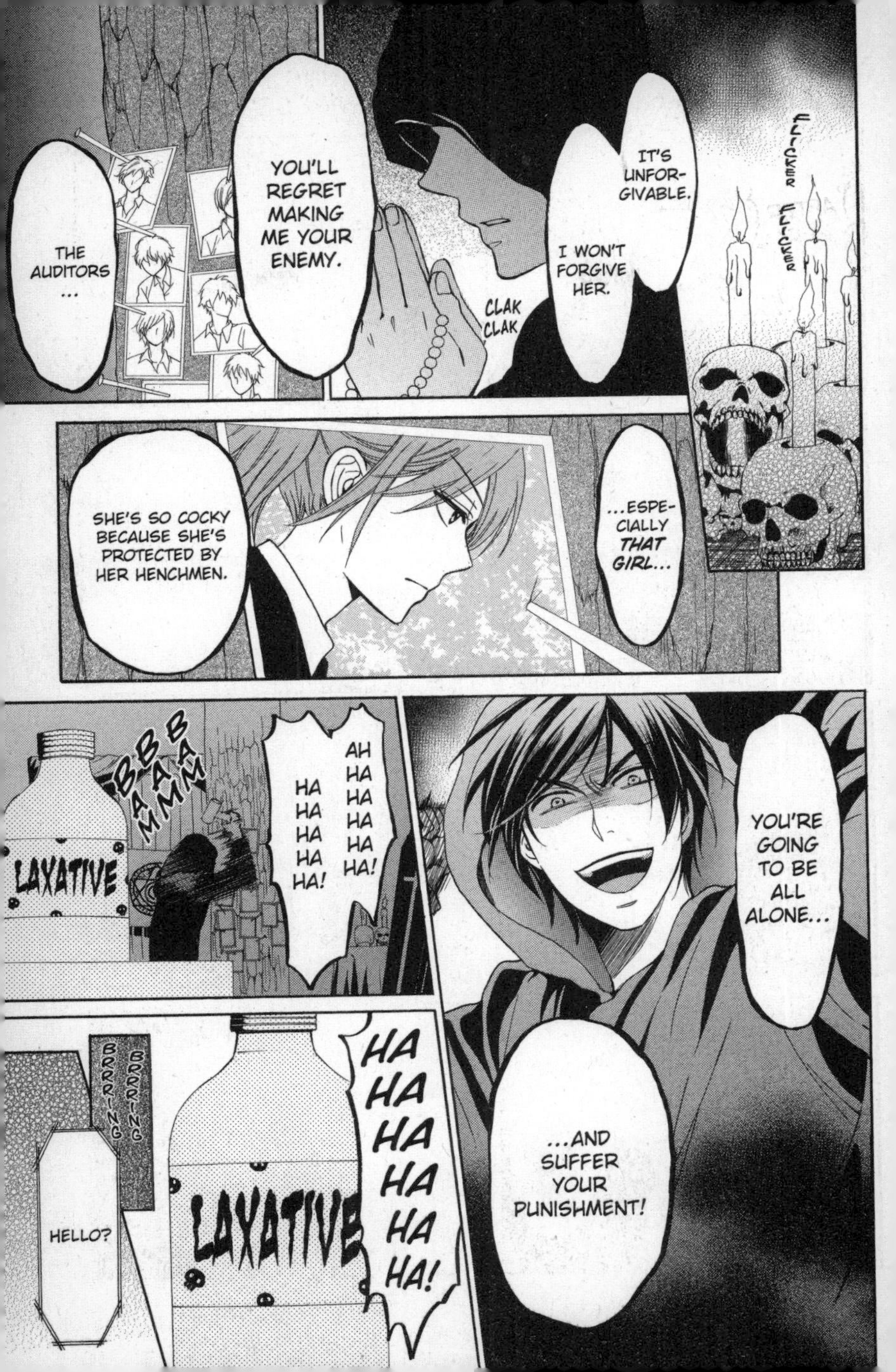
FLICKER FLICKER
IT'S UNFORGIVABLE.
I WON'T FORGIVE HER.
CLAK CLAK
YOU'LL REGRET MAKING ME YOUR ENEMY.
THE AUDITORS ...
...ESPE-CIALLY THAT GIRL...
SHE'S SO COCKY BECAUSE SHE'S PROTECTED BY HER HENCHMEN.
YOU'RE GOING TO BE ALL ALONE...
...AND SUFFER YOUR PUNISHMENT!
AH HA HA HA HA HA HA!
HA HA HA HA HA HA!
BBB AAA MMM
LAXATIVE
HAHAHAHAHAHAHAHA!
LAXATIVE
BRRRING BRRRING
HELLO?

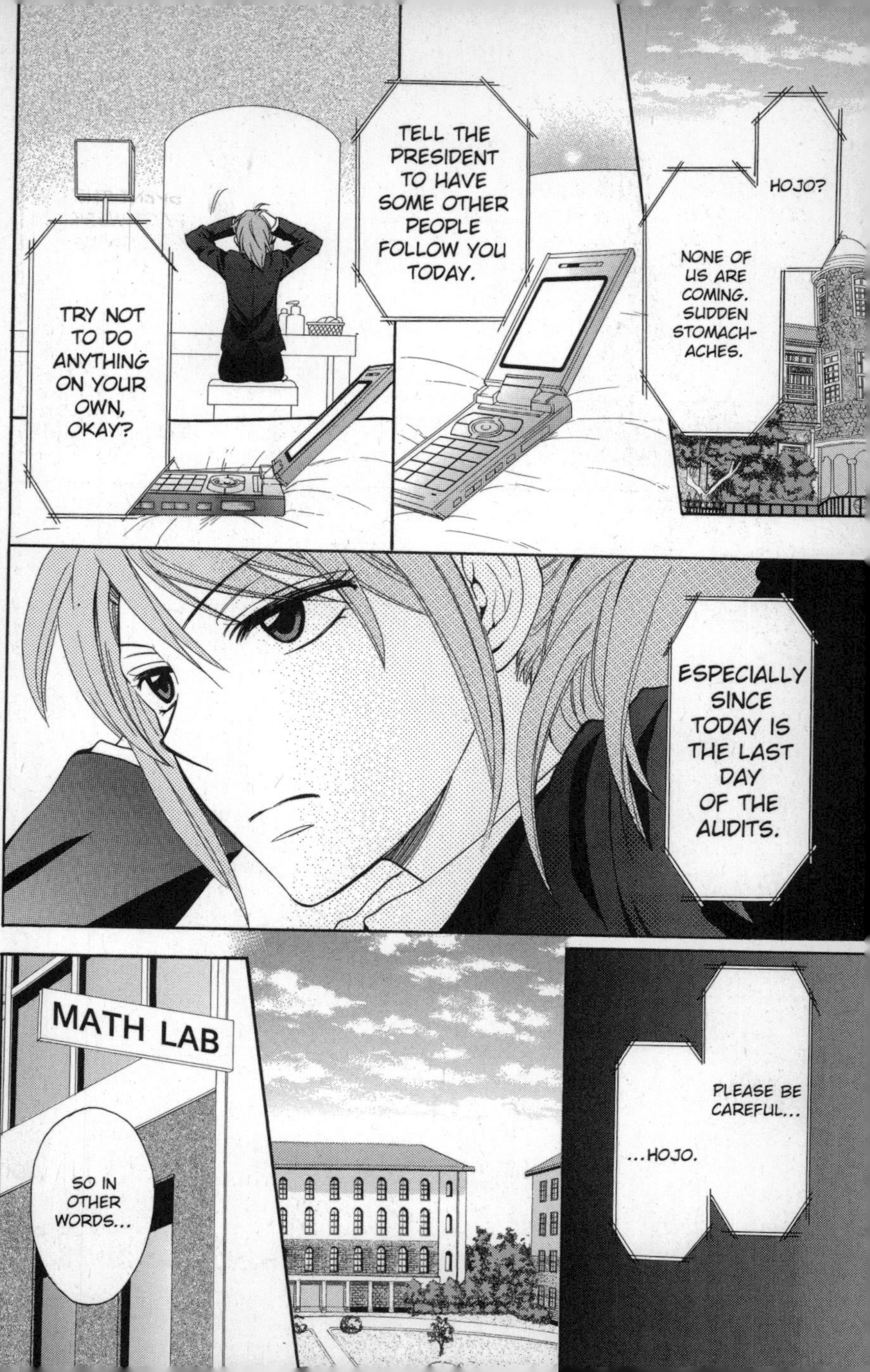
HOJO?
NONE OF US ARE COMING. SUDDEN STOMACH-ACHES.
TELL THE PRESIDENT TO HAVE SOME OTHER PEOPLE FOLLOW YOU TODAY.
TRY NOT TO DO ANYTHING ON YOUR OWN, OKAY?
ESPECIALLY SINCE TODAY IS THE LAST DAY OF THE AUDITS.
PLEASE BE CAREFUL...
...HOJO.
MATH LAB
SO IN OTHER WORDS...

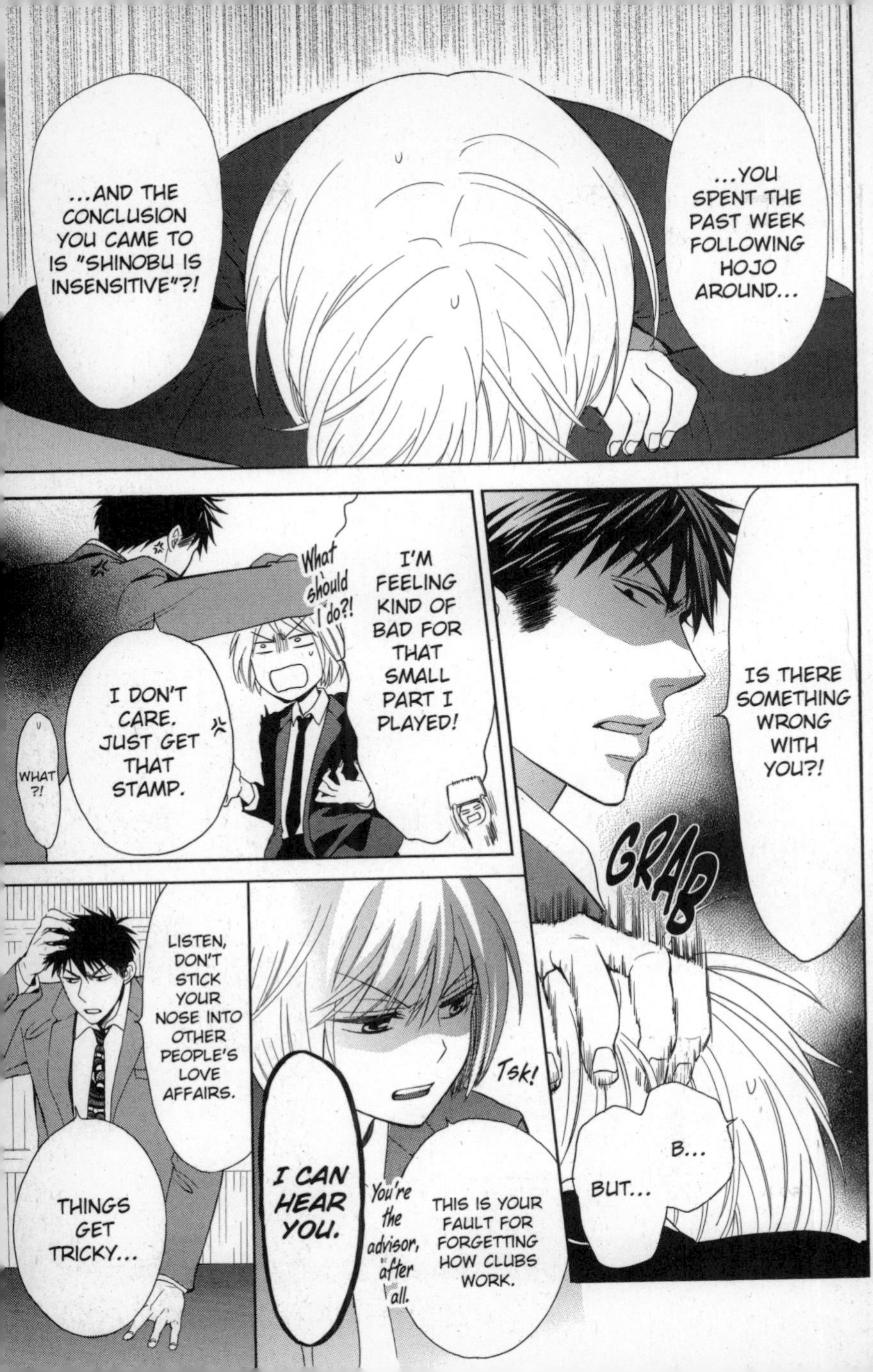
...YOU SPENT THE PAST WEEK FOLLOWING HOJO AROUND...
...AND THE CONCLUSION YOU CAME TO IS "SHINOBU IS INSENSITIVE"?!
IS THERE SOMETHING WRONG WITH YOU?!
GRAB
B...
BUT...
I'M FEELING KIND OF BAD FOR THAT SMALL PART I PLAYED!
What should I do?!
I DON'T CARE. JUST GET THAT STAMP.
WHAT?!
Tsk!
THIS IS YOUR FAULT FOR FORGETTING HOW CLUBS WORK.
You're the advisor, after all.
I CAN HEAR YOU.
LISTEN, DON'T STICK YOUR NOSE INTO OTHER PEOPLE'S LOVE AFFAIRS.
THINGS GET TRICKY...

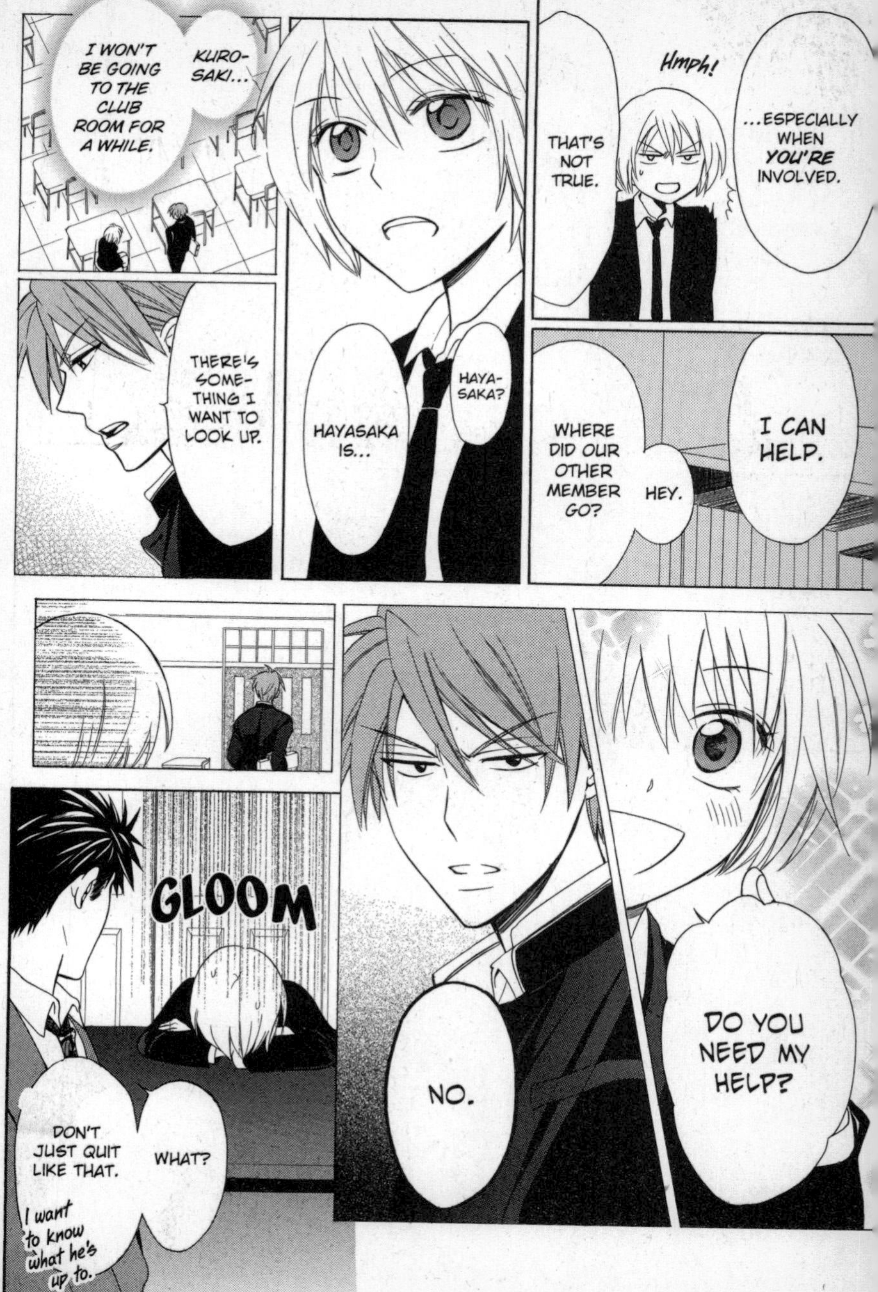
Hmph!
...ESPECIALLY WHEN YOU'RE INVOLVED.
THAT'S NOT TRUE.
I CAN HELP.
HEY.
WHERE DID OUR OTHER MEMBER GO?
HAYA-SAKA?
HAYASAKA IS...
KURO-SAKI...
I WON'T BE GOING TO THE CLUB ROOM FOR A WHILE.
THERE'S SOME-THING I WANT TO LOOK UP.
DO YOU NEED MY HELP?
NO.
GLOOM
WHAT?
DON'T JUST QUIT LIKE THAT.
I want to know what he's up to.

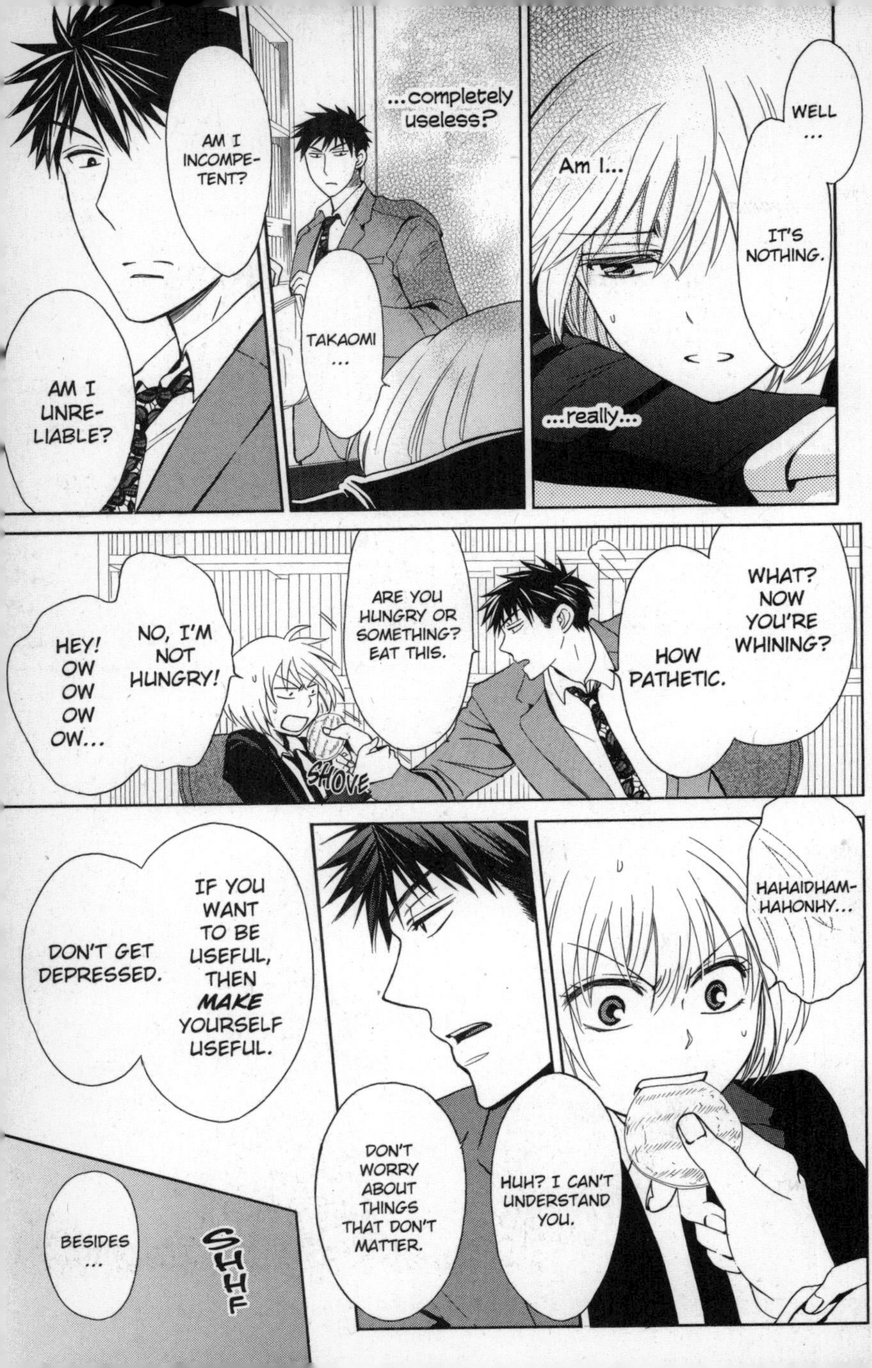
WELL ...
IT'S NOTHING.
Am I...
...really...
...completely useless?
TAKAOMI ...
AM I INCOMPETENT?
AM I UNRELIABLE?
WHAT? NOW YOU'RE WHINING?
HOW PATHETIC.
ARE YOU HUNGRY OR SOMETHING? EAT THIS.
SHOVE
NO, I'M NOT HUNGRY!
HEY! OW OW OW OW...
HAHAIDHAM-HAHONHY...
HUH? I CAN'T UNDERSTAND YOU.
DON'T WORRY ABOUT THINGS THAT DON'T MATTER.
IF YOU WANT TO BE USEFUL, THEN *MAKE* YOURSELF USEFUL.
DON'T GET DEPRESSED.
SHHF
BESIDES ...

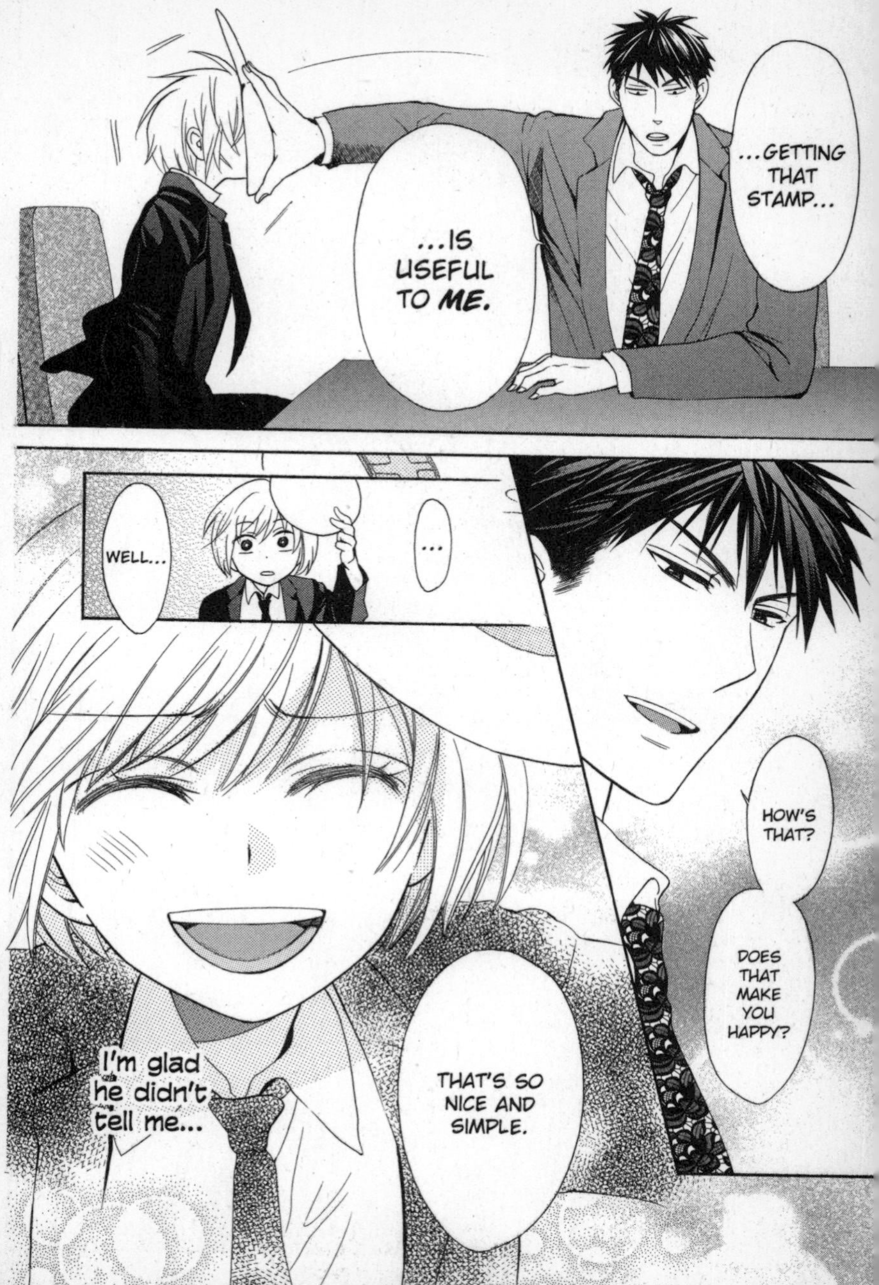
...GETTING THAT STAMP...
...IS USEFUL TO ME.
HOW'S THAT?
DOES THAT MAKE YOU HAPPY?
...
WELL...
THAT'S SO NICE AND SIMPLE.
I'm glad he didn't tell me...

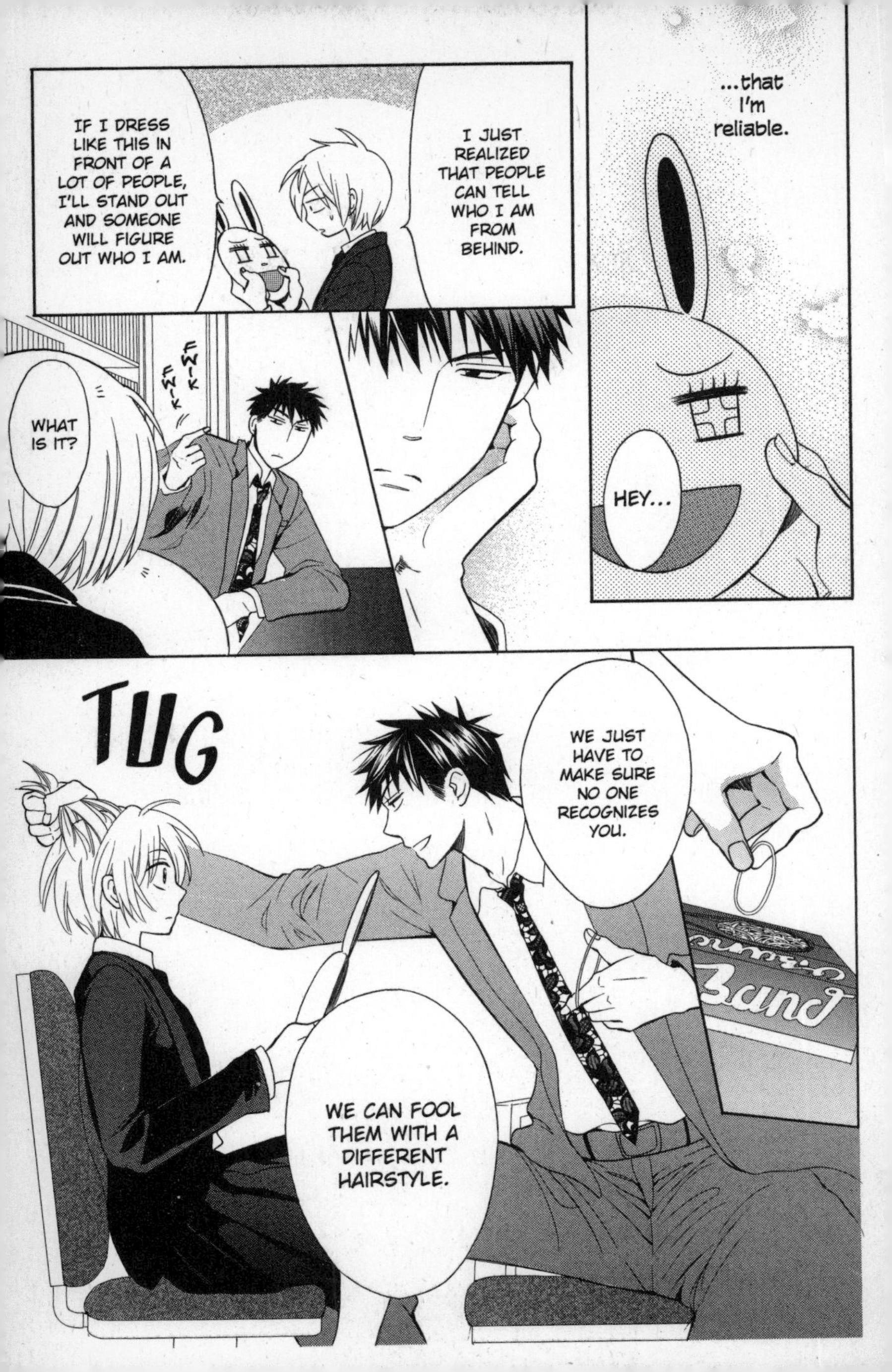
...that I'm reliable.
HEY...
I JUST REALIZED THAT PEOPLE CAN TELL WHO I AM FROM BEHIND.
IF I DRESS LIKE THIS IN FRONT OF A LOT OF PEOPLE, I'LL STAND OUT AND SOMEONE WILL FIGURE OUT WHO I AM.
FWIK FWIK
WHAT IS IT?
WE JUST HAVE TO MAKE SURE NO ONE RECOGNIZES YOU.
TUG
Band
WE CAN FOOL THEM WITH A DIFFERENT HAIRSTYLE.

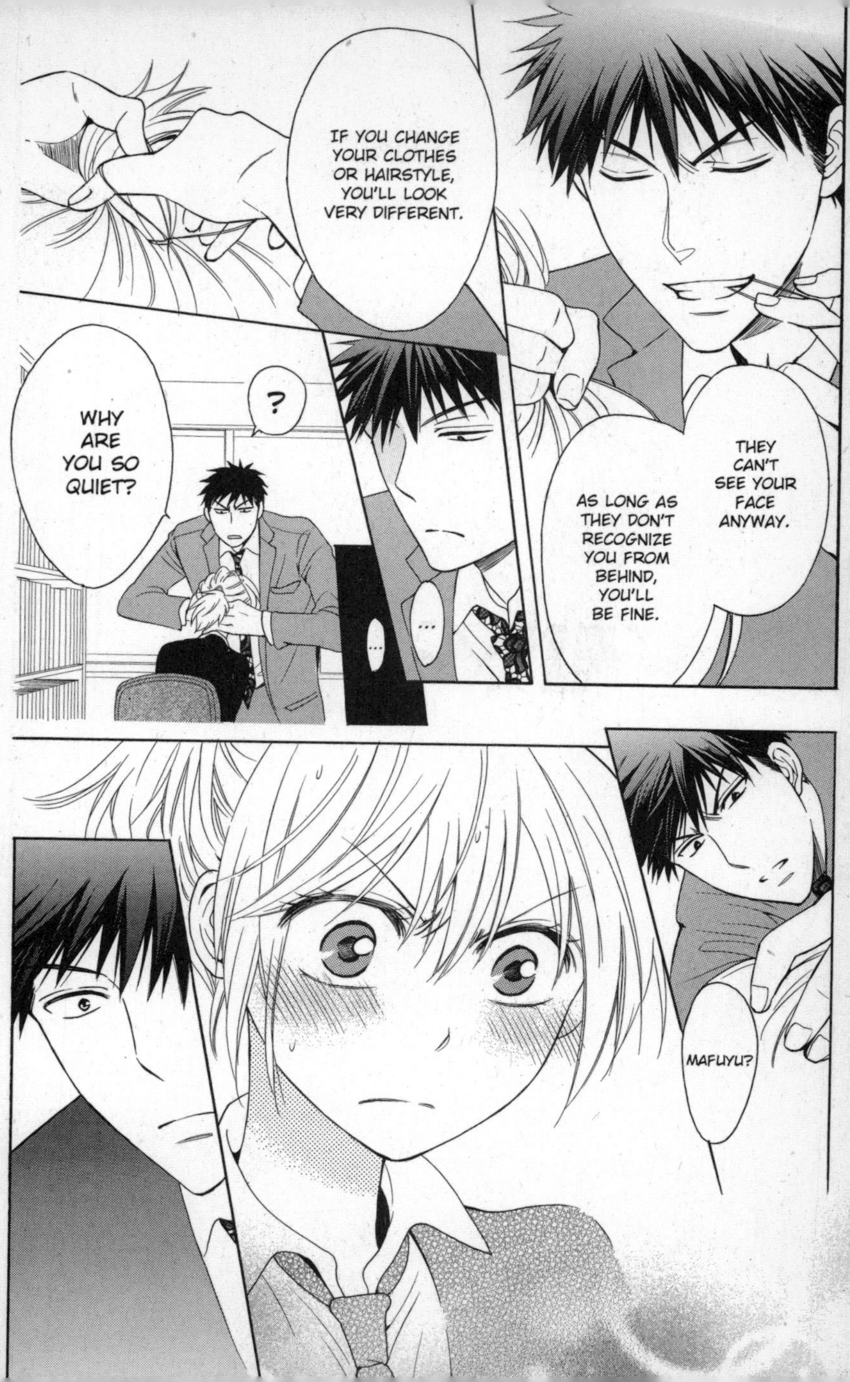
IF YOU CHANGE YOUR CLOTHES OR HAIRSTYLE, YOU'LL LOOK VERY DIFFERENT.
THEY CAN'T SEE YOUR FACE ANYWAY.
AS LONG AS THEY DON'T RECOGNIZE YOU FROM BEHIND, YOU'LL BE FINE.
...
...
?
WHY ARE YOU SO QUIET?
MAFUYU?

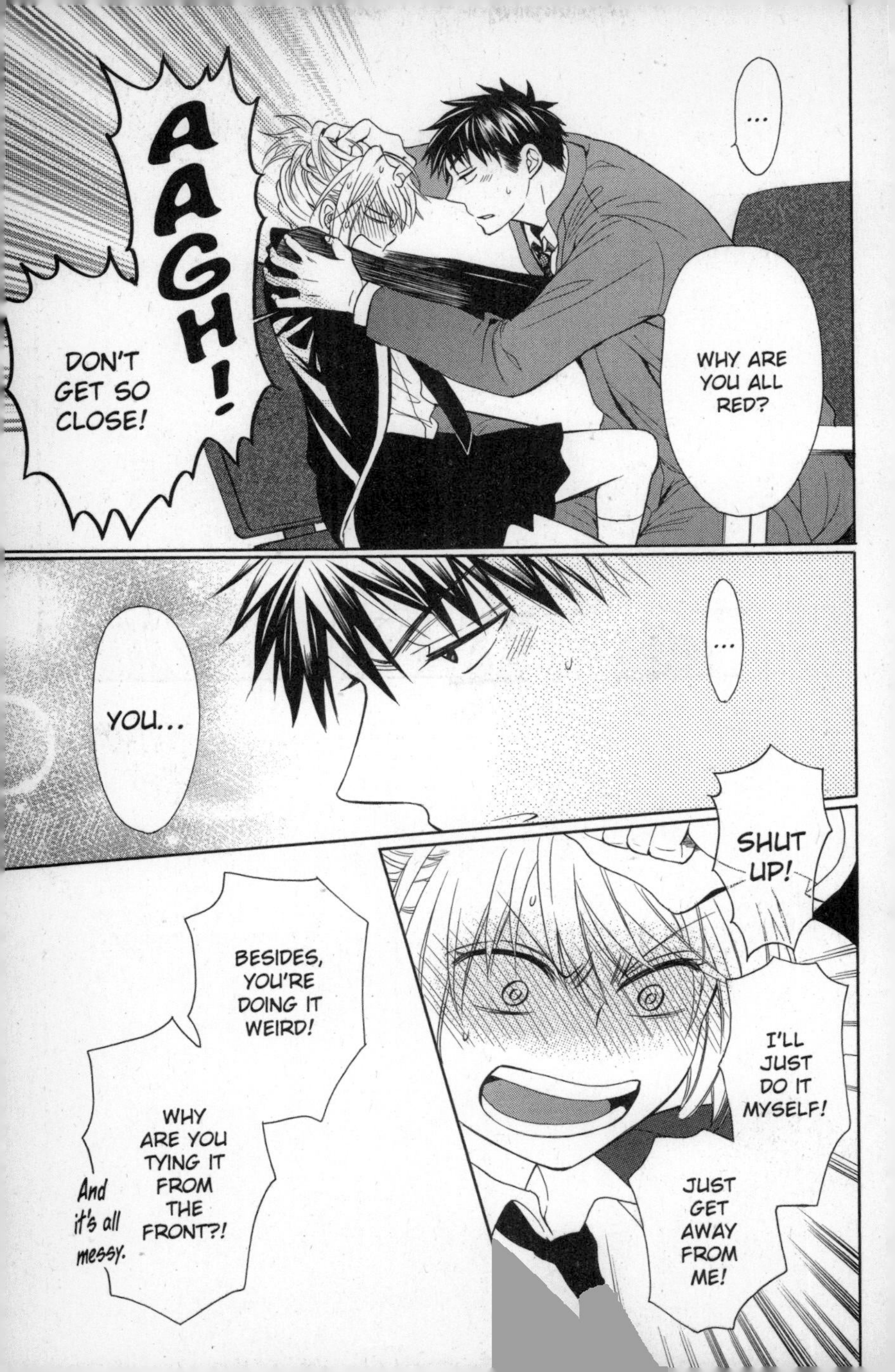
...
WHY ARE YOU ALL RED?
AAGH!
DON'T GET SO CLOSE!
...
YOU...
SHUT UP!
I'LL JUST DO IT MYSELF!
JUST GET AWAY FROM ME!
BESIDES, YOU'RE DOING IT WEIRD!
WHY ARE YOU TYING IT FROM THE FRONT?!
And it's all messy.

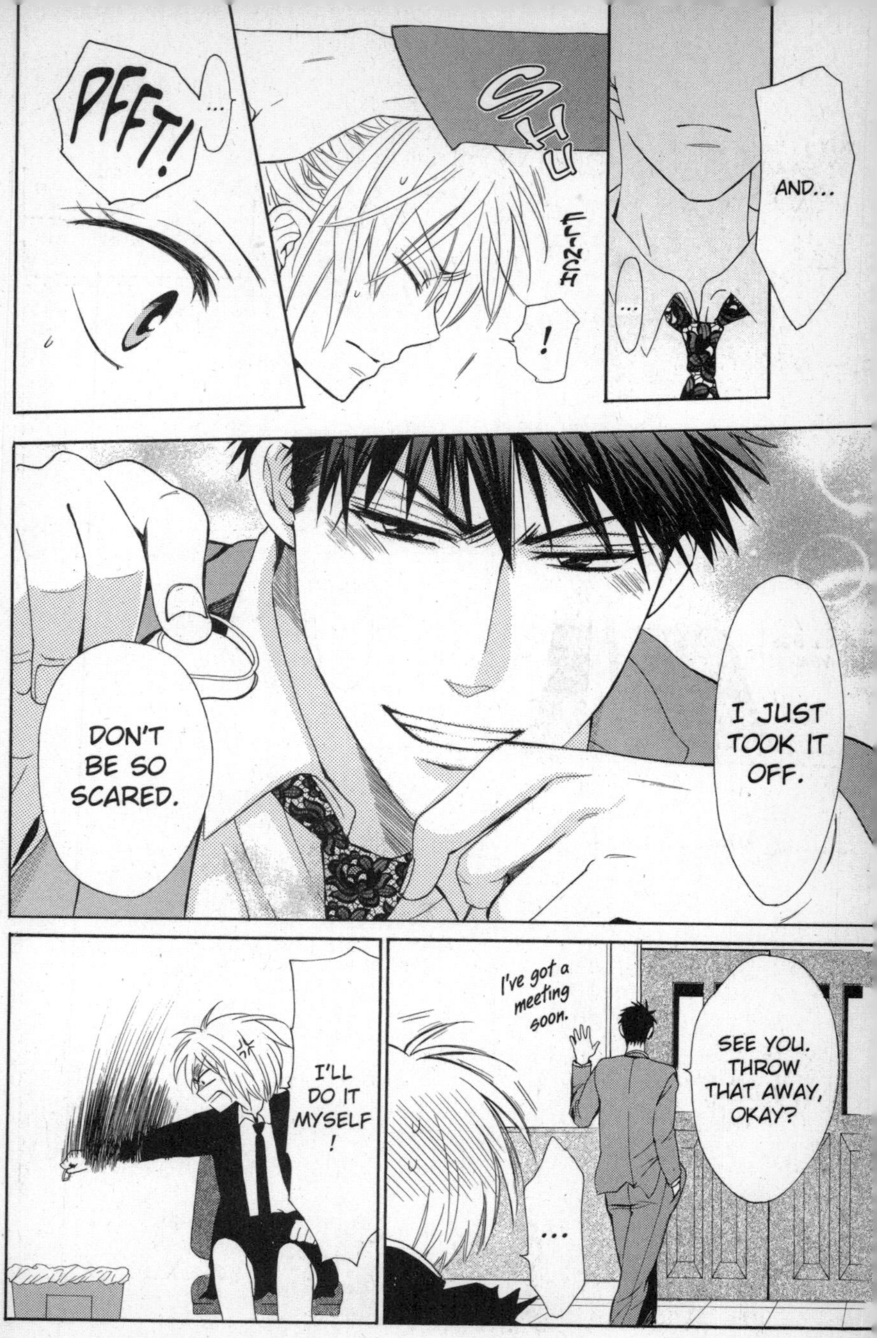
AND...
...
SHU
FLINCH
!
PFFT!
...
I JUST TOOK IT OFF.
DON'T BE SO SCARED.
SEE YOU. THROW THAT AWAY, OKAY?
I've got a meeting soon.
...
I'LL DO IT MYSELF!

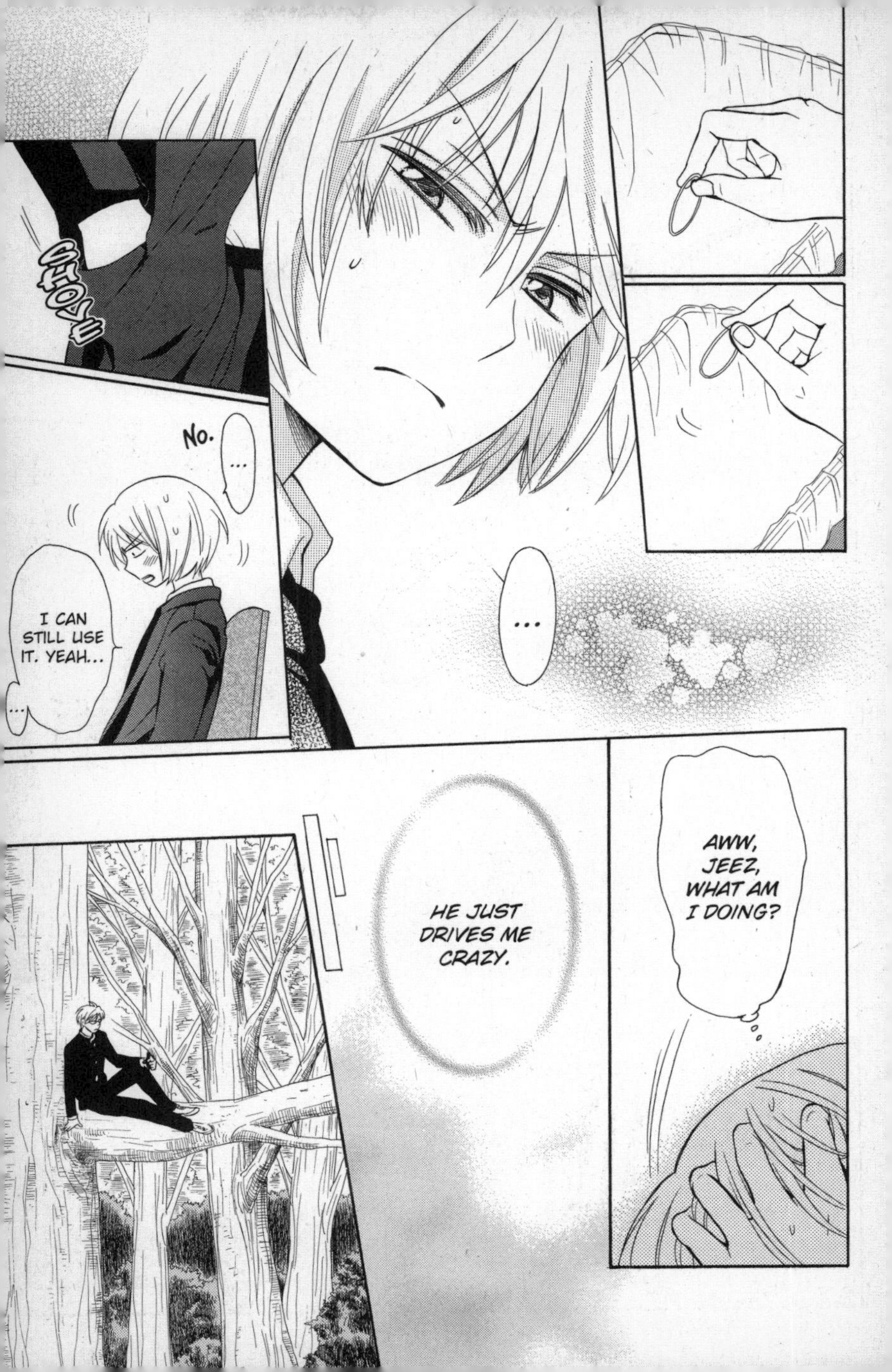
...
SHOVE
...
No.
I CAN STILL USE IT. YEAH...
...
AWW, JEEZ, WHAT AM I DOING?
HE JUST DRIVES ME CRAZY.

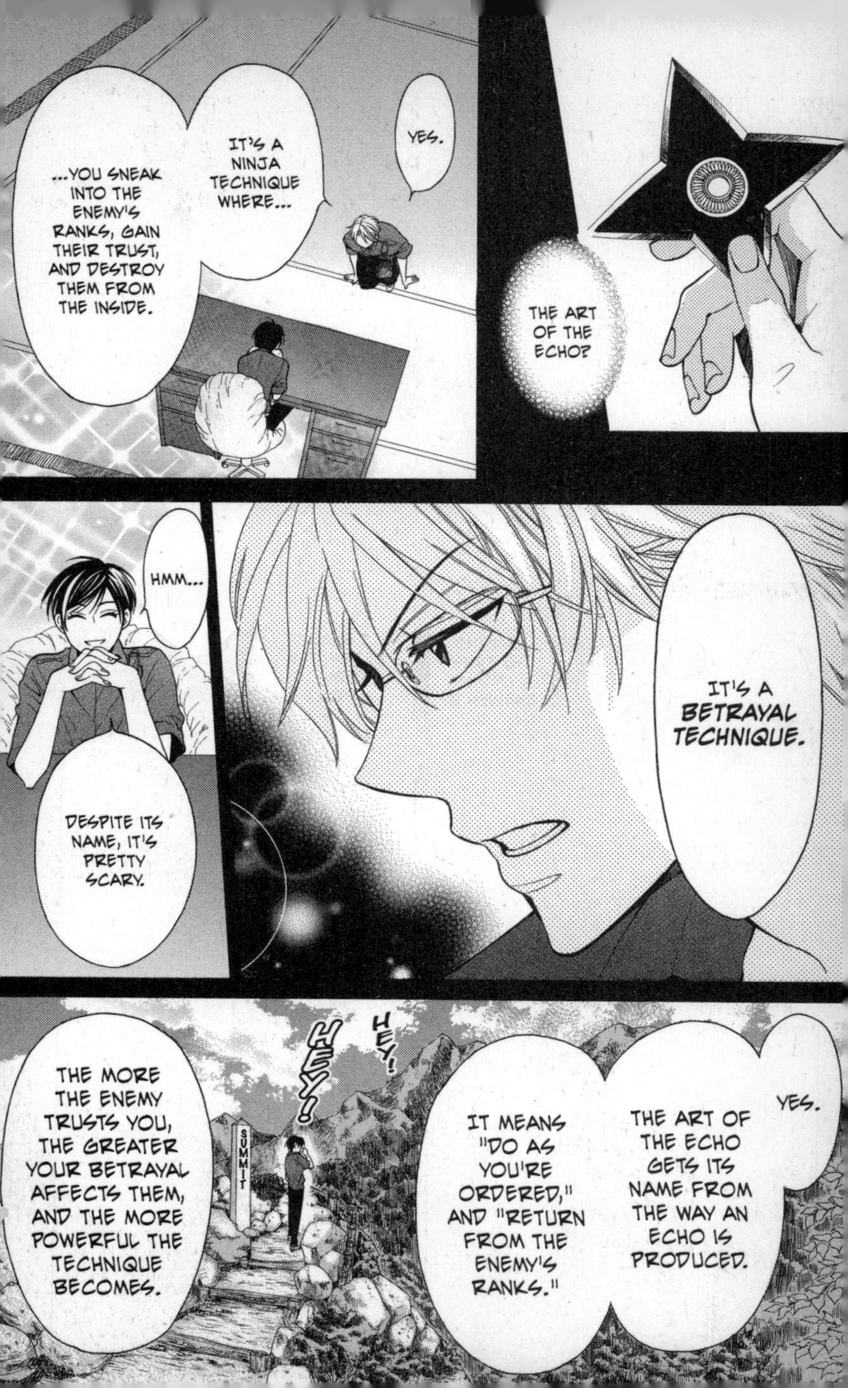
THE ART OF THE ECHO?
YES.
IT'S A NINJA TECHNIQUE WHERE...
...YOU SNEAK INTO THE ENEMY'S RANKS, GAIN THEIR TRUST, AND DESTROY THEM FROM THE INSIDE.
IT'S A BETRAYAL TECHNIQUE.
HMM...
DESPITE ITS NAME, IT'S PRETTY SCARY.
YES.
THE ART OF THE ECHO GETS ITS NAME FROM THE WAY AN ECHO IS PRODUCED.
IT MEANS "DO AS YOU'RE ORDERED," AND "RETURN FROM THE ENEMY'S RANKS."
HEY!
HEY!
SUMMIT
THE MORE THE ENEMY TRUSTS YOU, THE GREATER YOUR BETRAYAL AFFECTS THEM, AND THE MORE POWERFUL THE TECHNIQUE BECOMES.

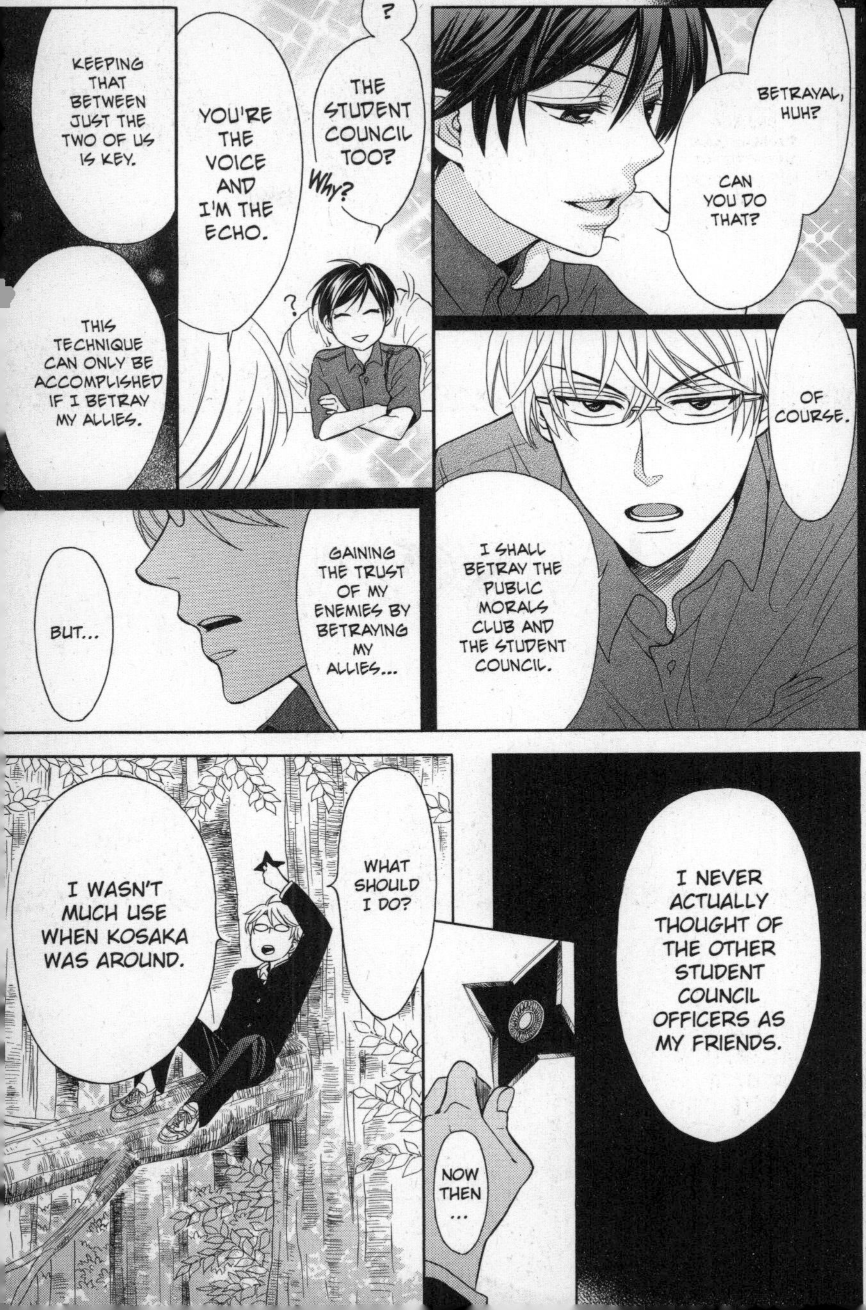
BETRAYAL, HUH?
CAN YOU DO THAT?
OF COURSE.
I SHALL BETRAY THE PUBLIC MORALS CLUB AND THE STUDENT COUNCIL.
?
THE STUDENT COUNCIL TOO?
Why?
YOU'RE THE VOICE AND I'M THE ECHO.
KEEPING THAT BETWEEN JUST THE TWO OF US IS KEY.
THIS TECHNIQUE CAN ONLY BE ACCOMPLISHED IF I BETRAY MY ALLIES.
GAINING THE TRUST OF MY ENEMIES BY BETRAYING MY ALLIES...
BUT...
I NEVER ACTUALLY THOUGHT OF THE OTHER STUDENT COUNCIL OFFICERS AS MY FRIENDS.
NOW THEN...
WHAT SHOULD I DO?
I WASN'T MUCH USE WHEN KOSAKA WAS AROUND.

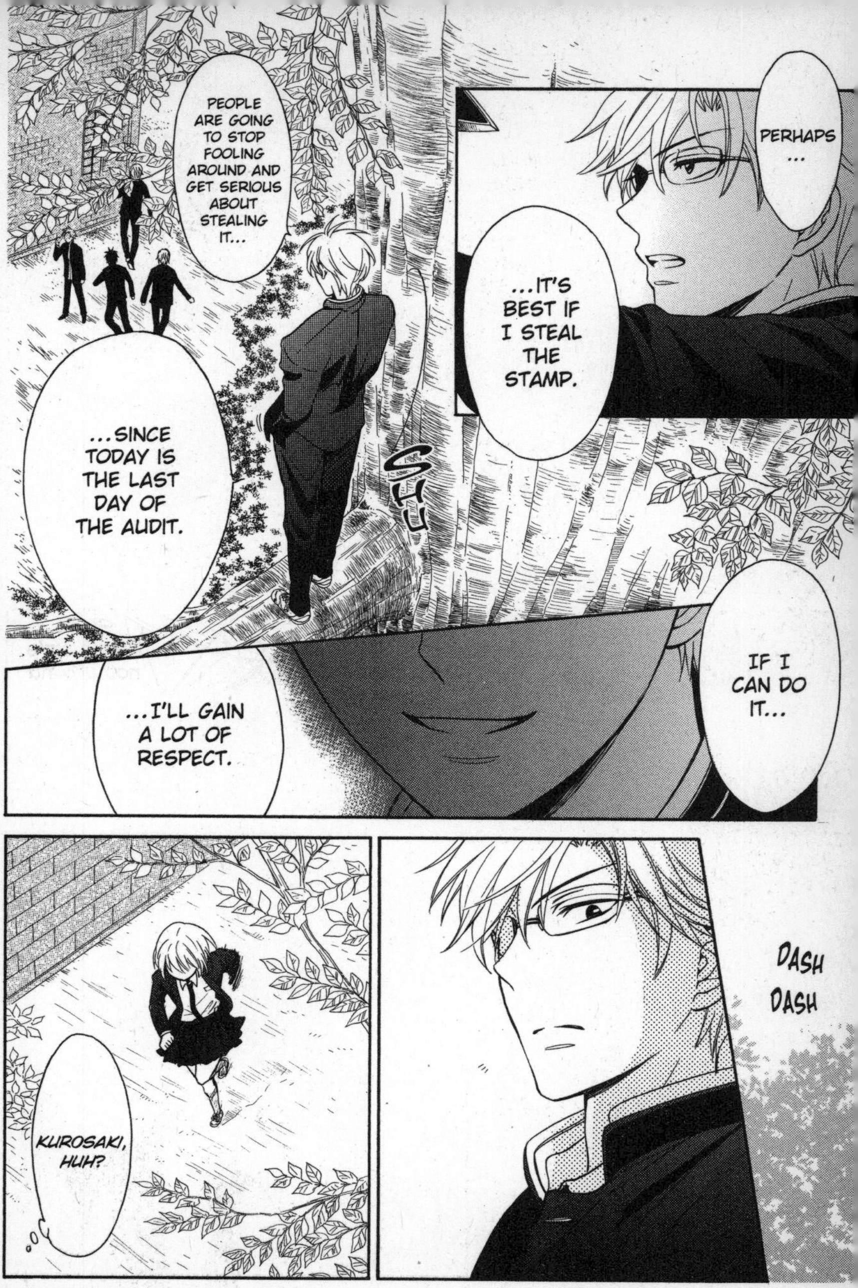
PERHAPS...
...IT'S BEST IF I STEAL THE STAMP.
PEOPLE ARE GOING TO STOP FOOLING AROUND AND GET SERIOUS ABOUT STEALING IT...
...SINCE TODAY IS THE LAST DAY OF THE AUDIT.
SHU
IF I CAN DO IT...
...I'LL GAIN A LOT OF RESPECT.
DASH DASH
KUROSAKI, HUH?

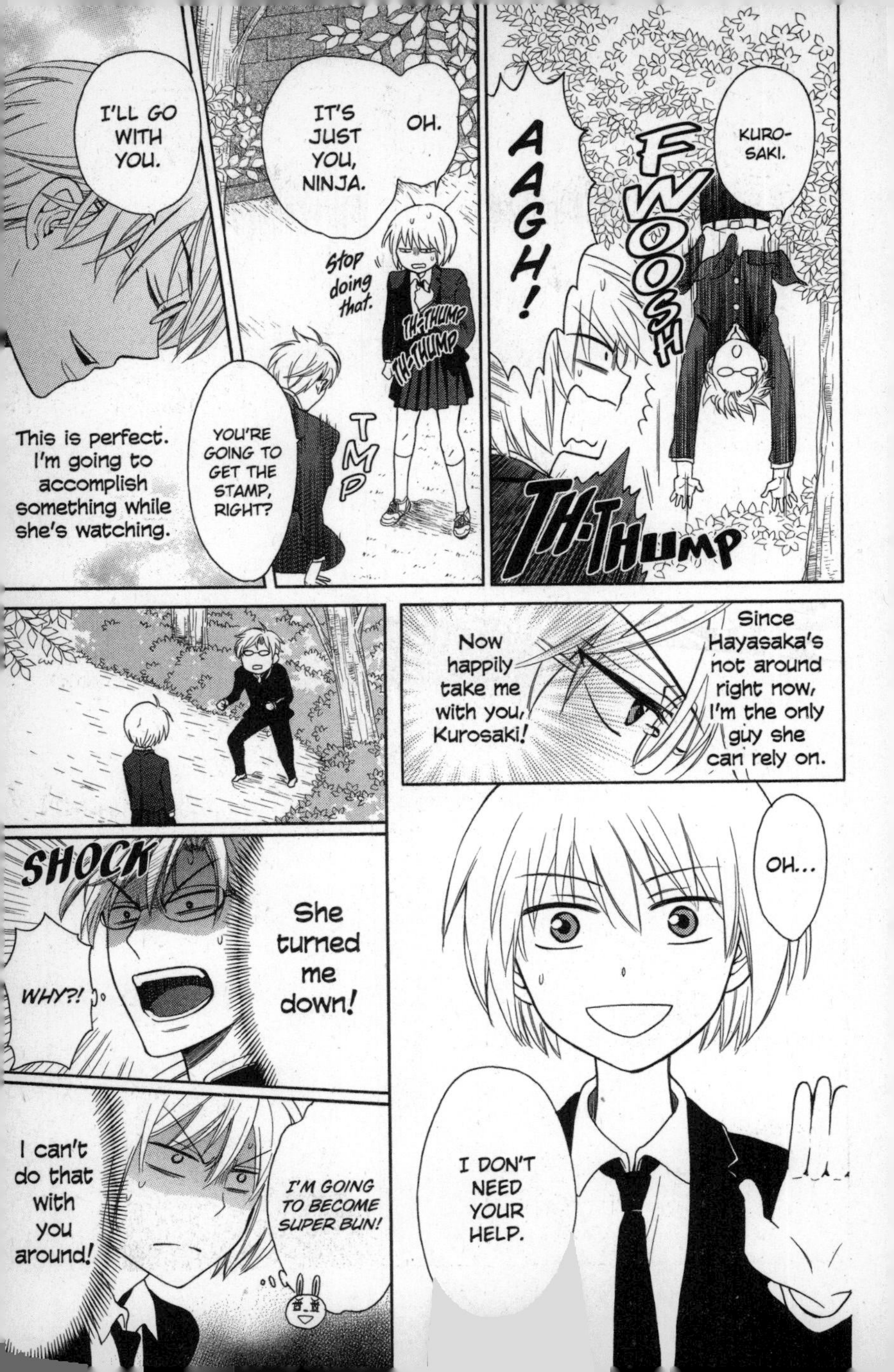
KURO-SAKI.
FWOOSH
AAGH!
TH-THUMP
OH.
IT'S JUST YOU, NINJA.
Stop doing that.
TH-THUMP TH-THUMP
TMP
YOU'RE GOING TO GET THE STAMP, RIGHT?
I'LL GO WITH YOU.
This is perfect. I'm going to accomplish something while she's watching.
Since Hayasaka's not around right now, I'm the only guy she can rely on.
Now happily take me with you, Kurosaki!
OH...
I DON'T NEED YOUR HELP.
SHOCK
She turned me down!
WHY?!
I'M GOING TO BECOME SUPER BUN!
I can't do that with you around!

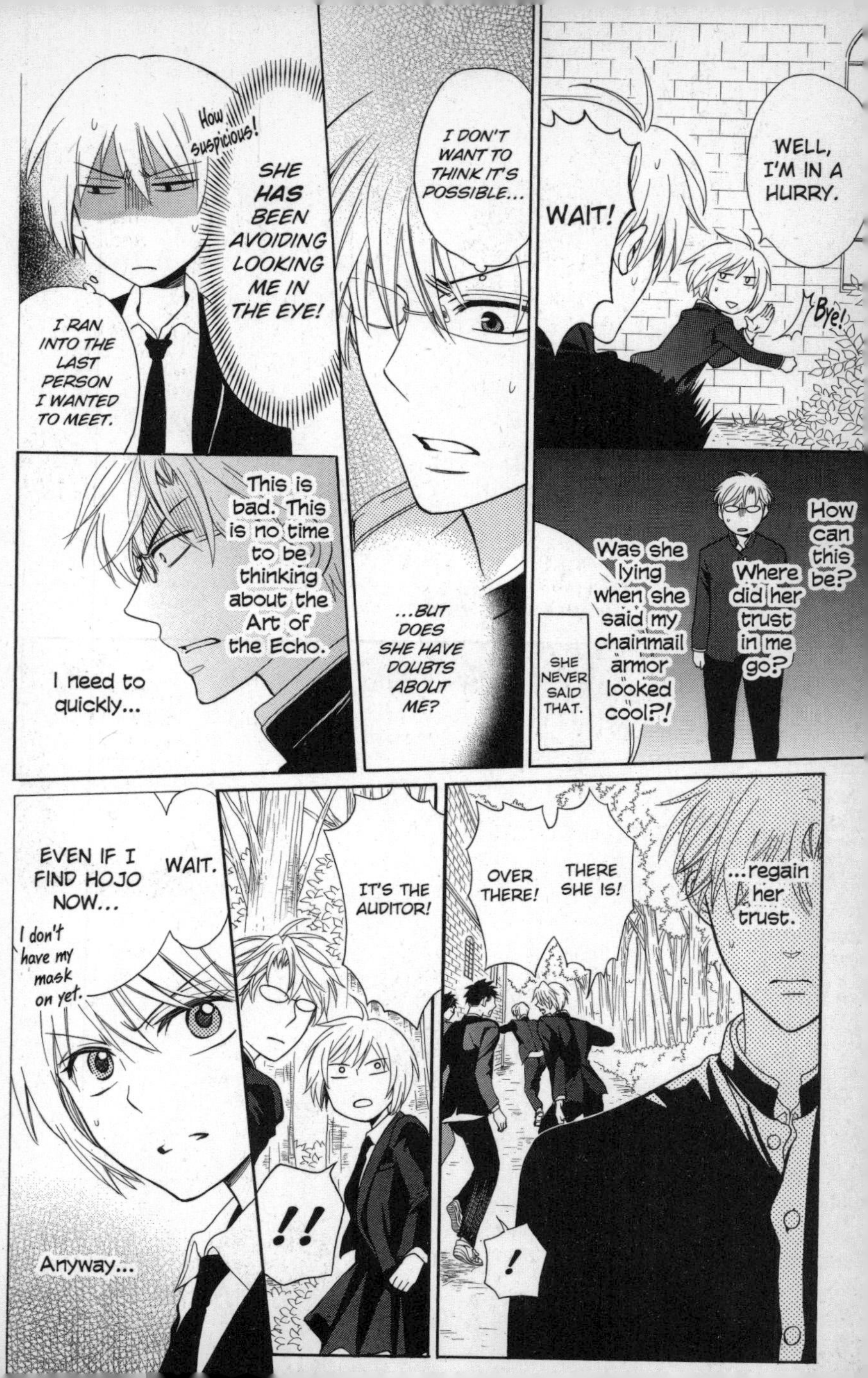
WELL, I'M IN A HURRY.
Bye!
WAIT!
How can this be?
Where did her trust in me go?
Was she lying when she said my chainmail armor looked cool?!
SHE NEVER SAID THAT.
I DON'T WANT TO THINK IT'S POSSIBLE...
...BUT DOES SHE HAVE DOUBTS ABOUT ME?
How suspicious!
SHE HAS BEEN AVOIDING LOOKING ME IN THE EYE!
I RAN INTO THE LAST PERSON I WANTED TO MEET.
This is bad. This is no time to be thinking about the Art of the Echo.
I need to quickly...
...regain her trust.
THERE SHE IS!
OVER THERE!
!
IT'S THE AUDITOR!
!!
WAIT.
EVEN IF I FIND HOJO NOW...
I don't have my mask on yet.
Anyway...

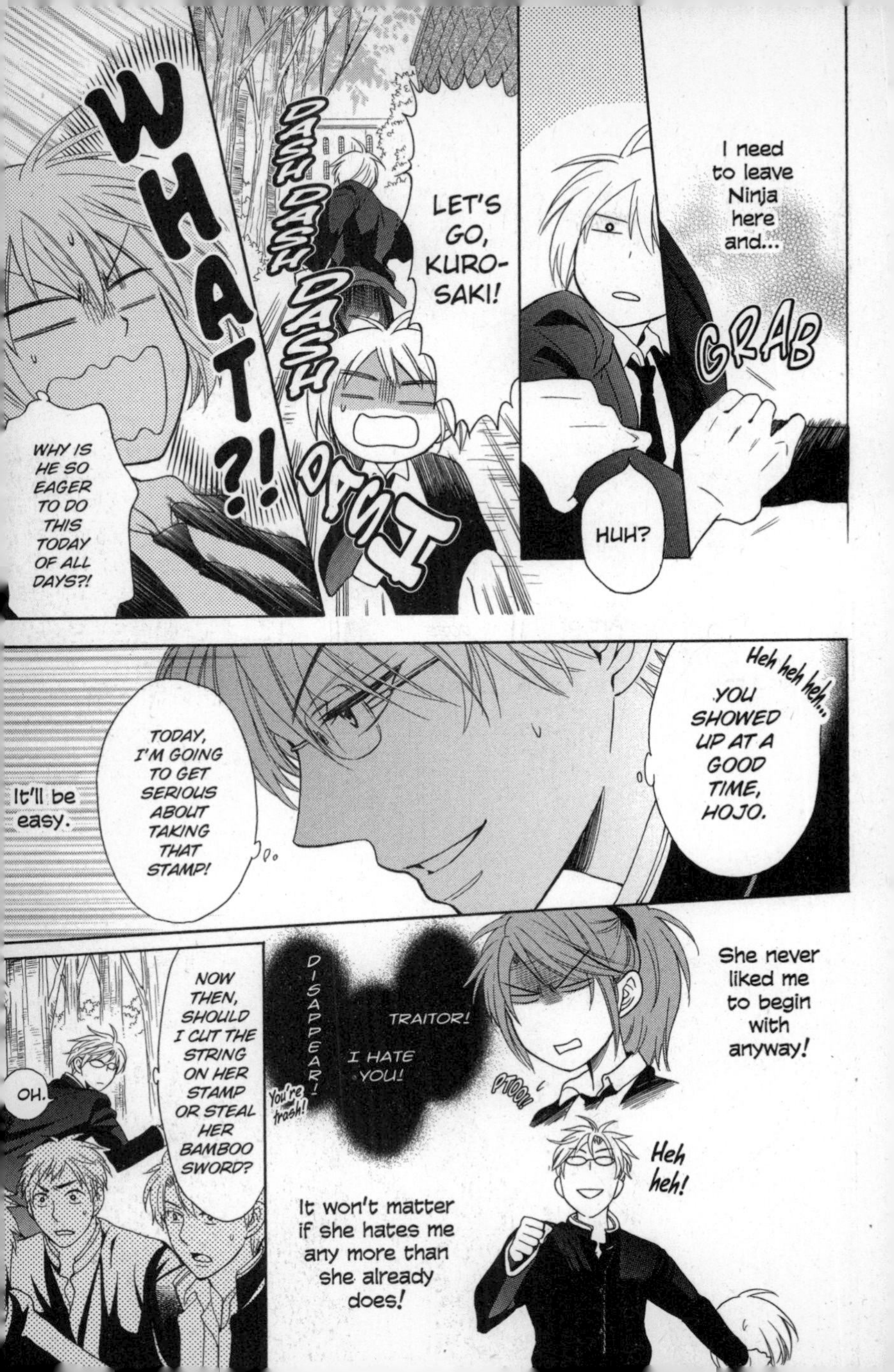
I need to leave Ninja here and...
GRAB
HUH?
LET'S GO, KURO-SAKI!
DASH DASH DASH
DASH
WHAT?!
WHY IS HE SO EAGER TO DO THIS TODAY OF ALL DAYS?!
Heh heh heh...
YOU SHOWED UP AT A GOOD TIME, HOJO.
TODAY, I'M GOING TO GET SERIOUS ABOUT TAKING THAT STAMP!
It'll be easy.
She never liked me to begin with anyway!
PTOOY!
DISAPPEAR!
TRAITOR!
I HATE YOU!
You're trash!
Heh heh!
It won't matter if she hates me any more than she already does!
NOW THEN, SHOULD I CUT THE STRING ON HER STAMP OR STEAL HER BAMBOO SWORD?
OH.

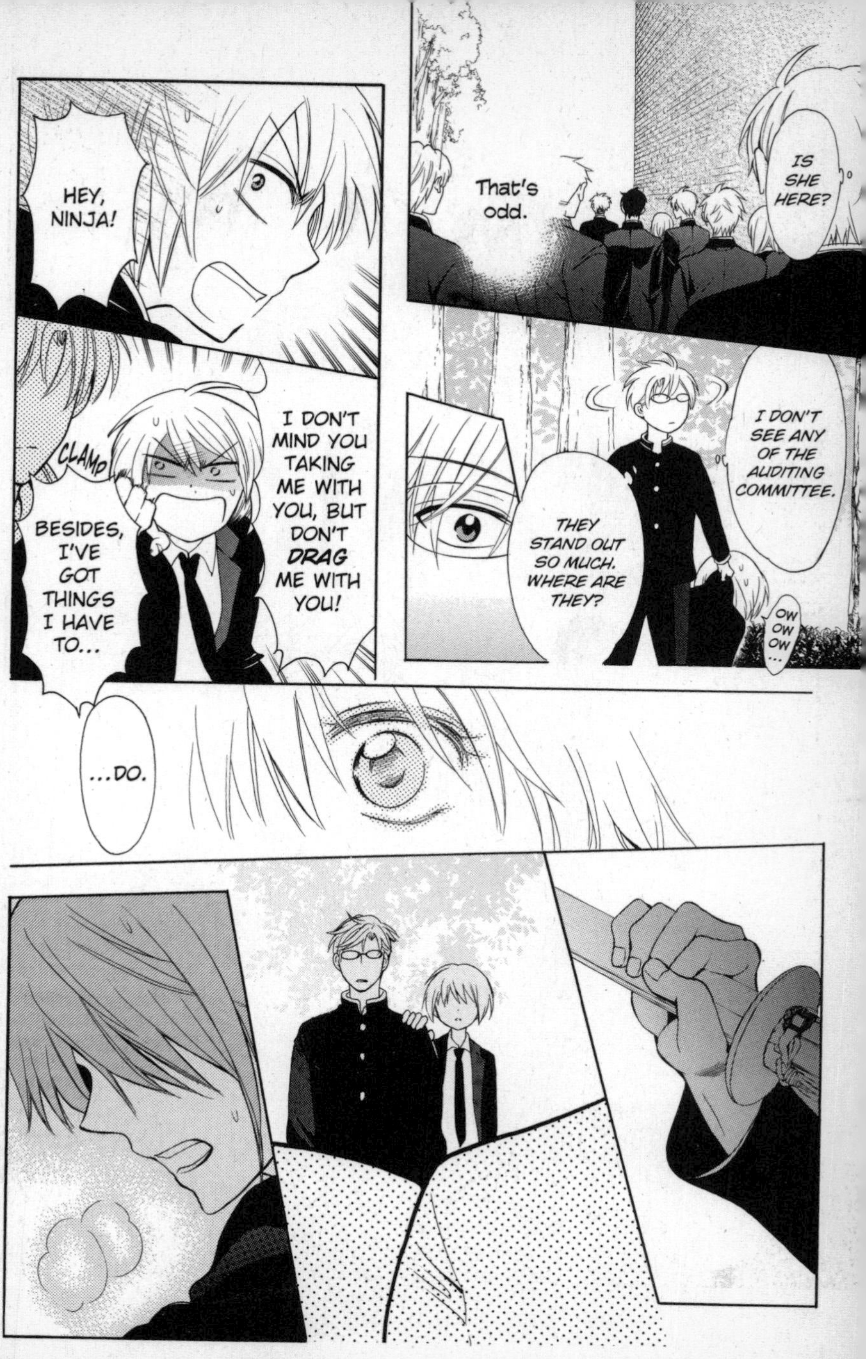
IS SHE HERE?
That's odd.
HEY, NINJA!
I DON'T SEE ANY OF THE AUDITING COMMITTEE.
OW OW OW...
THEY STAND OUT SO MUCH. WHERE ARE THEY?
I DON'T MIND YOU TAKING ME WITH YOU, BUT DON'T DRAG ME WITH YOU!
CLAMP
BESIDES, I'VE GOT THINGS I HAVE TO...
...DO.

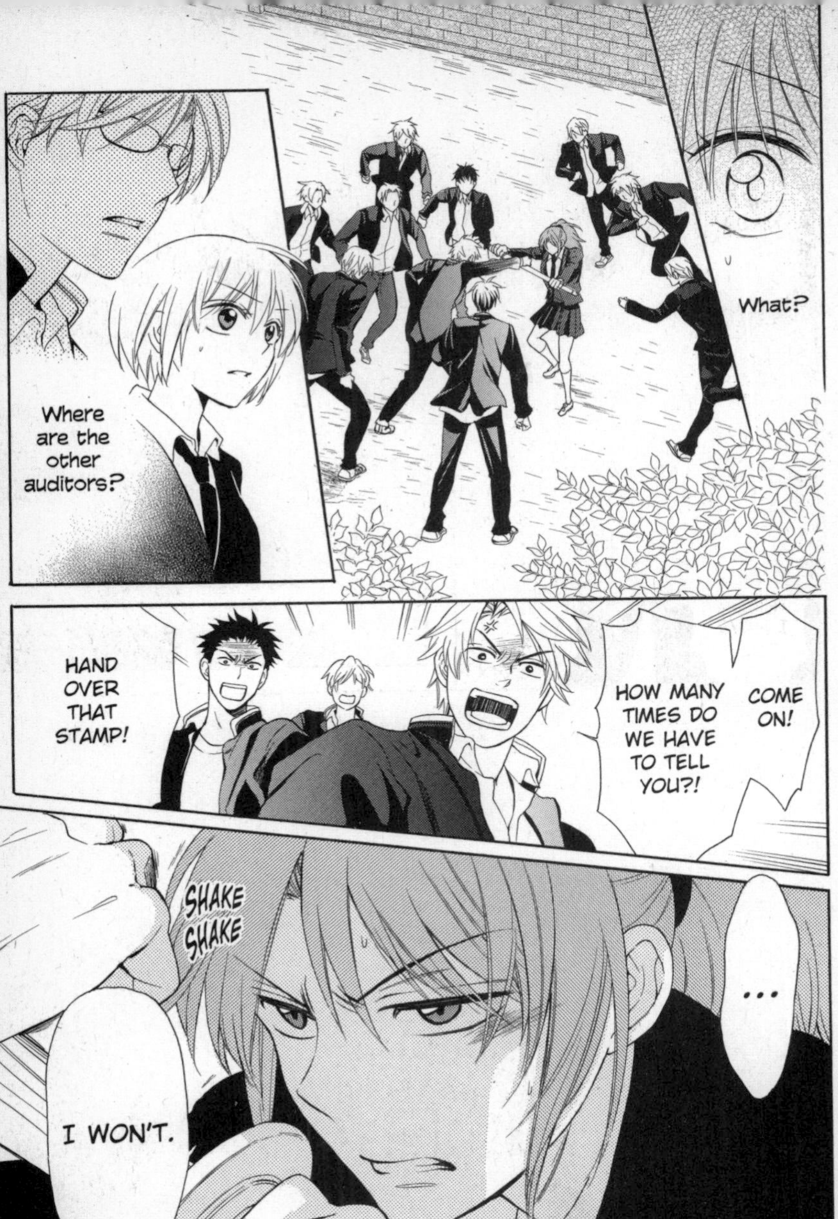
What?
Where are the other auditors?
COME ON!
HOW MANY TIMES DO WE HAVE TO TELL YOU?!
HAND OVER THAT STAMP!
...
SHAKE SHAKE
I WON'T.

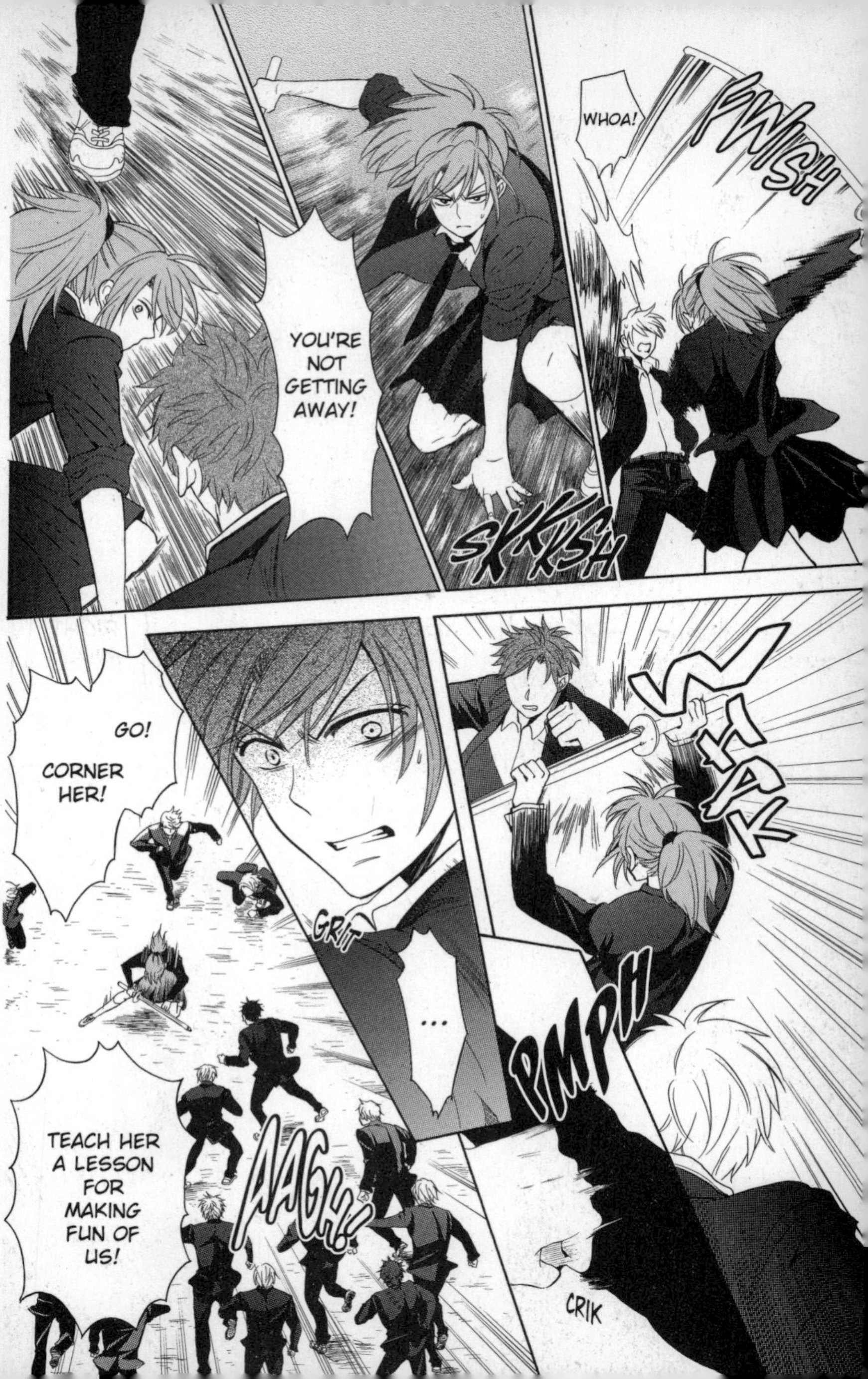
WHOA!
PWISH
YOU'RE NOT GETTING AWAY!
SKKKSH
WHAK
PMPH
CRIK
GRIT
...
GO!
CORNER HER!
TEACH HER A LESSON FOR MAKING FUN OF US!
AAGH!!

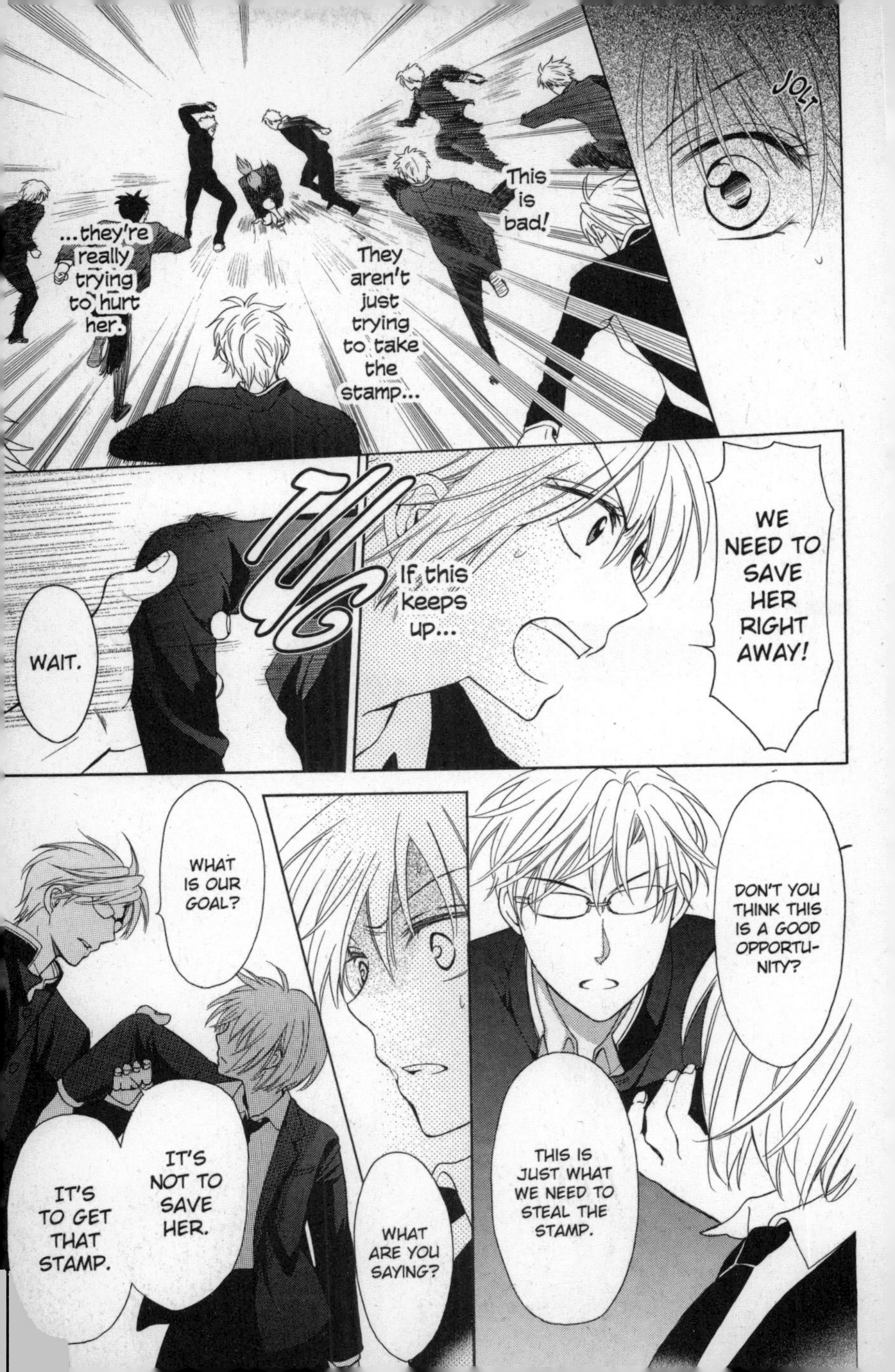
JOLT
This is bad!
They aren't just trying to take the stamp...
...they're really trying to hurt her.
WE NEED TO SAVE HER RIGHT AWAY!
If this keeps up...
THUG
WAIT.
DON'T YOU THINK THIS IS A GOOD OPPORTUNITY?
THIS IS JUST WHAT WE NEED TO STEAL THE STAMP.
WHAT ARE YOU SAYING?
WHAT IS OUR GOAL?
IT'S NOT TO SAVE HER.
IT'S TO GET THAT STAMP.

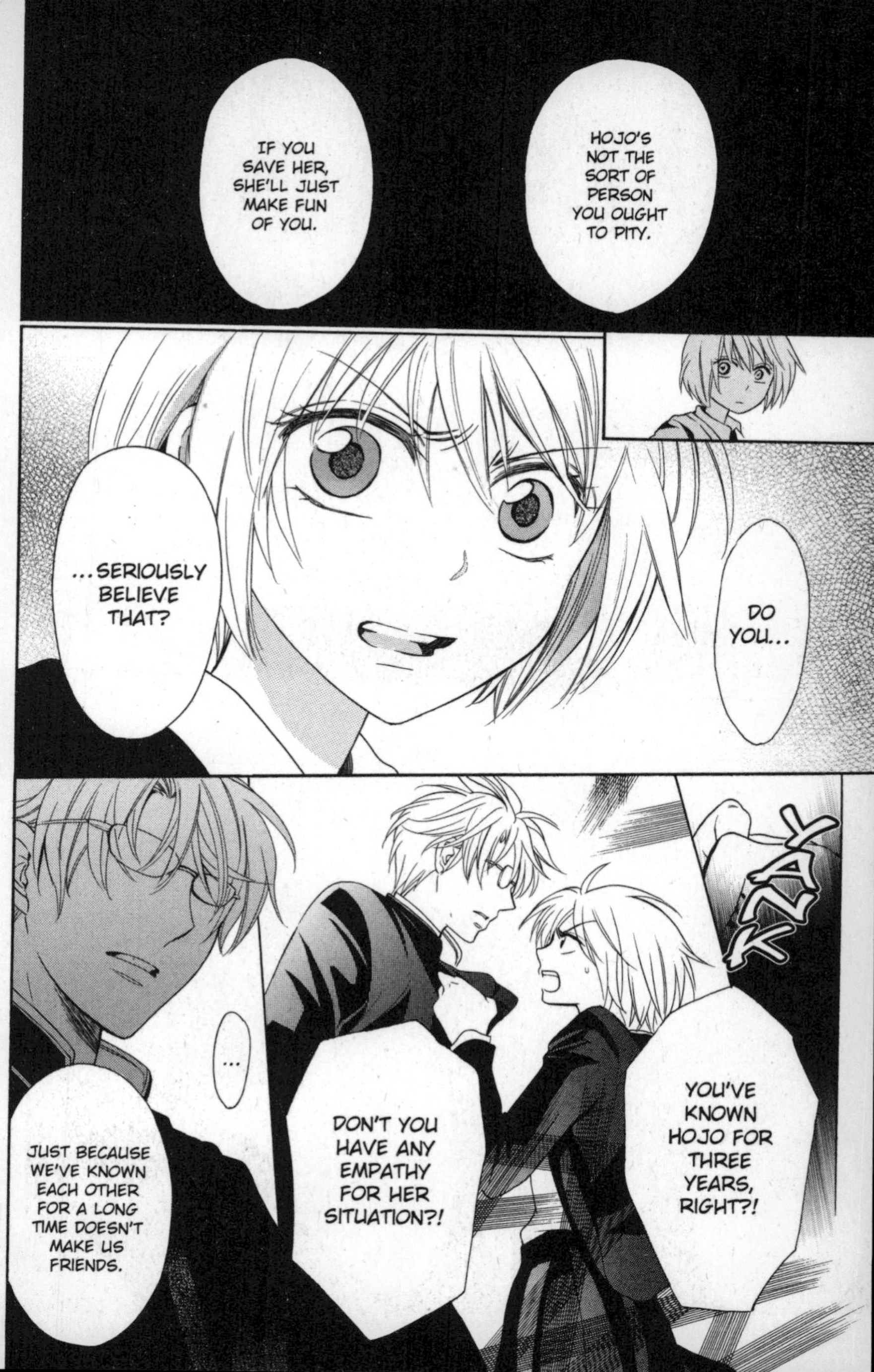
HOJO'S NOT THE SORT OF PERSON YOU OUGHT TO PITY.
IF YOU SAVE HER, SHE'LL JUST MAKE FUN OF YOU.
DO YOU...
...SERIOUSLY BELIEVE THAT?
YANK
YOU'VE KNOWN HOJO FOR THREE YEARS, RIGHT?!
DON'T YOU HAVE ANY EMPATHY FOR HER SITUATION?!
...
JUST BECAUSE WE'VE KNOWN EACH OTHER FOR A LONG TIME DOESN'T MAKE US FRIENDS.

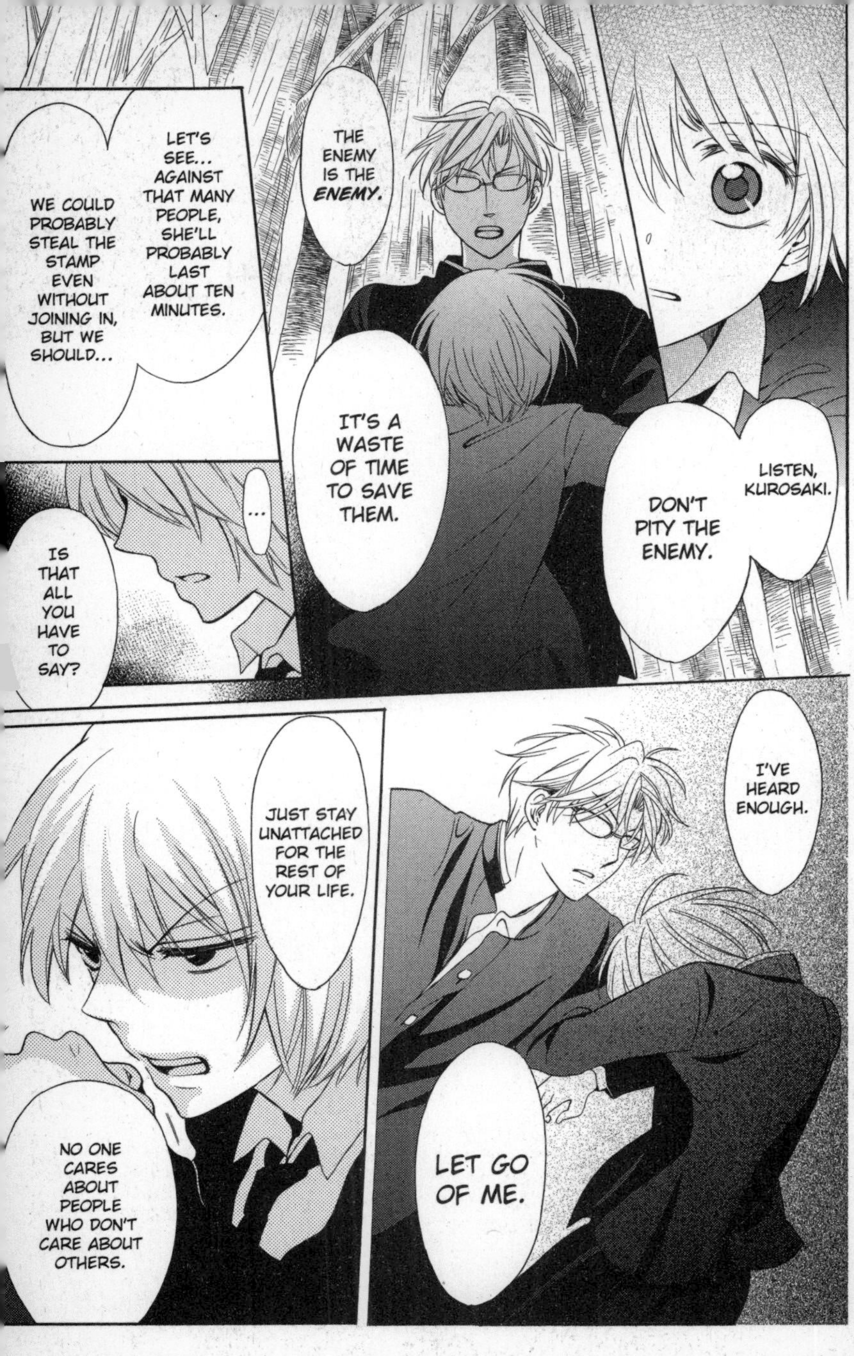
LISTEN, KUROSAKI.
DON'T PITY THE ENEMY.
THE ENEMY IS THE *ENEMY.*
IT'S A WASTE OF TIME TO SAVE THEM.
LET'S SEE... AGAINST THAT MANY PEOPLE, SHE'LL PROBABLY LAST ABOUT TEN MINUTES.
WE COULD PROBABLY STEAL THE STAMP EVEN WITHOUT JOINING IN, BUT WE SHOULD...
...
IS THAT ALL YOU HAVE TO SAY?
I'VE HEARD ENOUGH.
LET GO OF ME.
JUST STAY UNATTACHED FOR THE REST OF YOUR LIFE.
NO ONE CARES ABOUT PEOPLE WHO DON'T CARE ABOUT OTHERS.

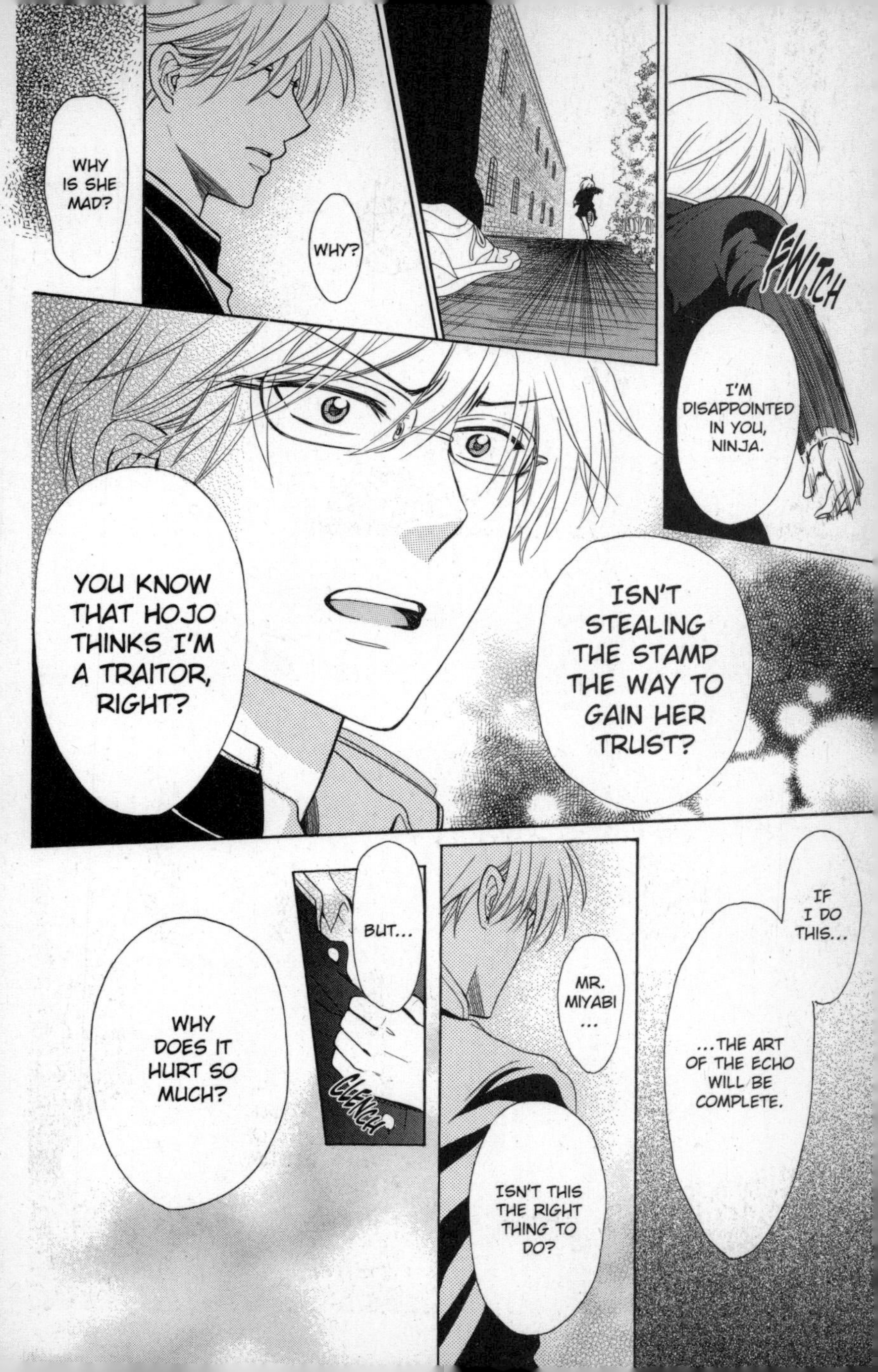
FWITCH
I'M DISAPPOINTED IN YOU, NINJA.
WHY?
WHY IS SHE MAD?
ISN'T STEALING THE STAMP THE WAY TO GAIN HER TRUST?
YOU KNOW THAT HOJO THINKS I'M A TRAITOR, RIGHT?
IF I DO THIS...
...THE ART OF THE ECHO WILL BE COMPLETE.
MR. MIYABI...
ISN'T THIS THE RIGHT THING TO DO?
BUT...
CLENCH
WHY DOES IT HURT SO MUCH?

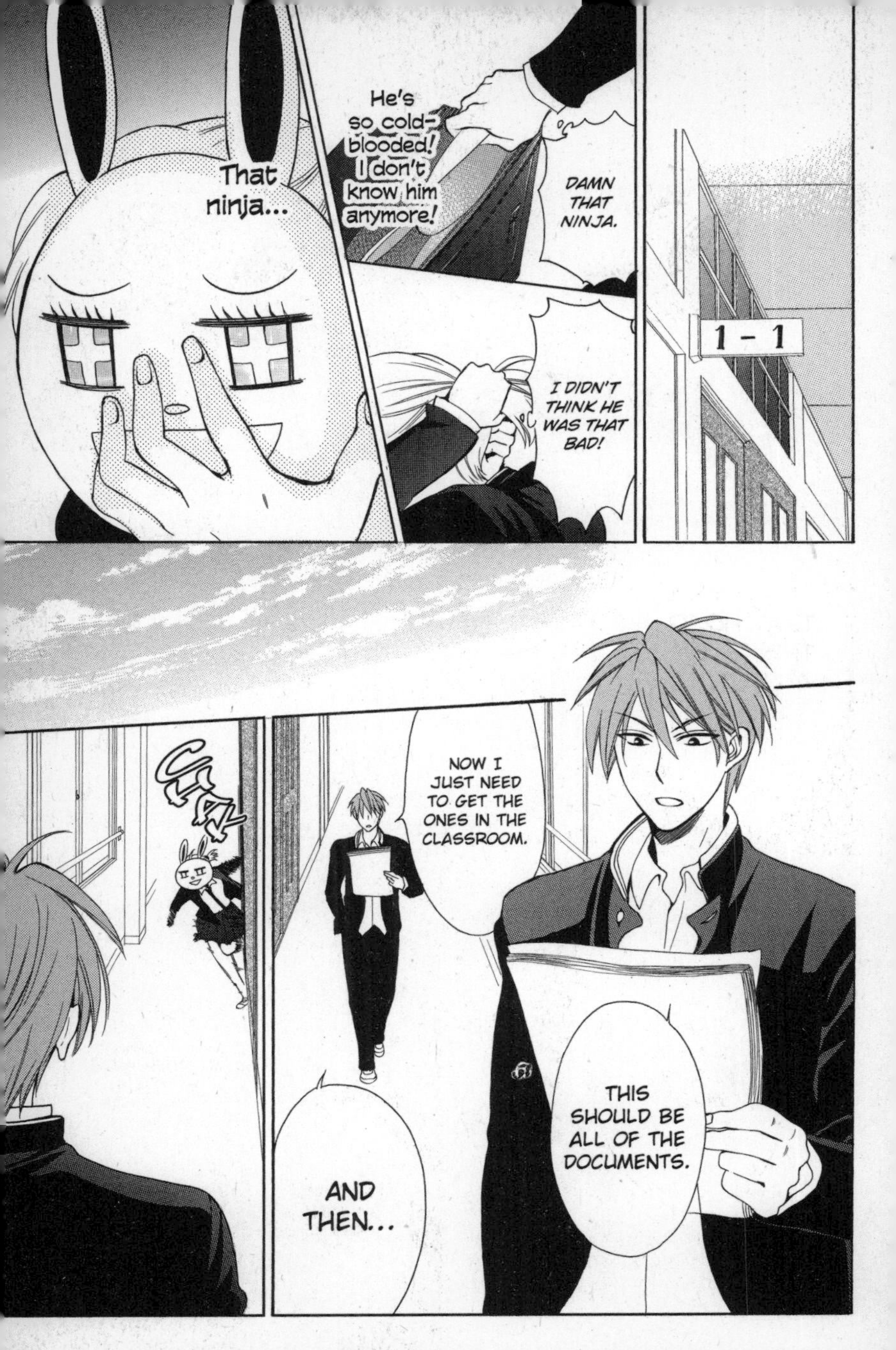
DAMN THAT NINJA.
He's so cold-blooded! I don't know him anymore!
I DIDN'T THINK HE WAS THAT BAD!
That ninja...
1 - 1
NOW I JUST NEED TO GET THE ONES IN THE CLASSROOM.
THIS SHOULD BE ALL OF THE DOCUMENTS.
AND THEN...

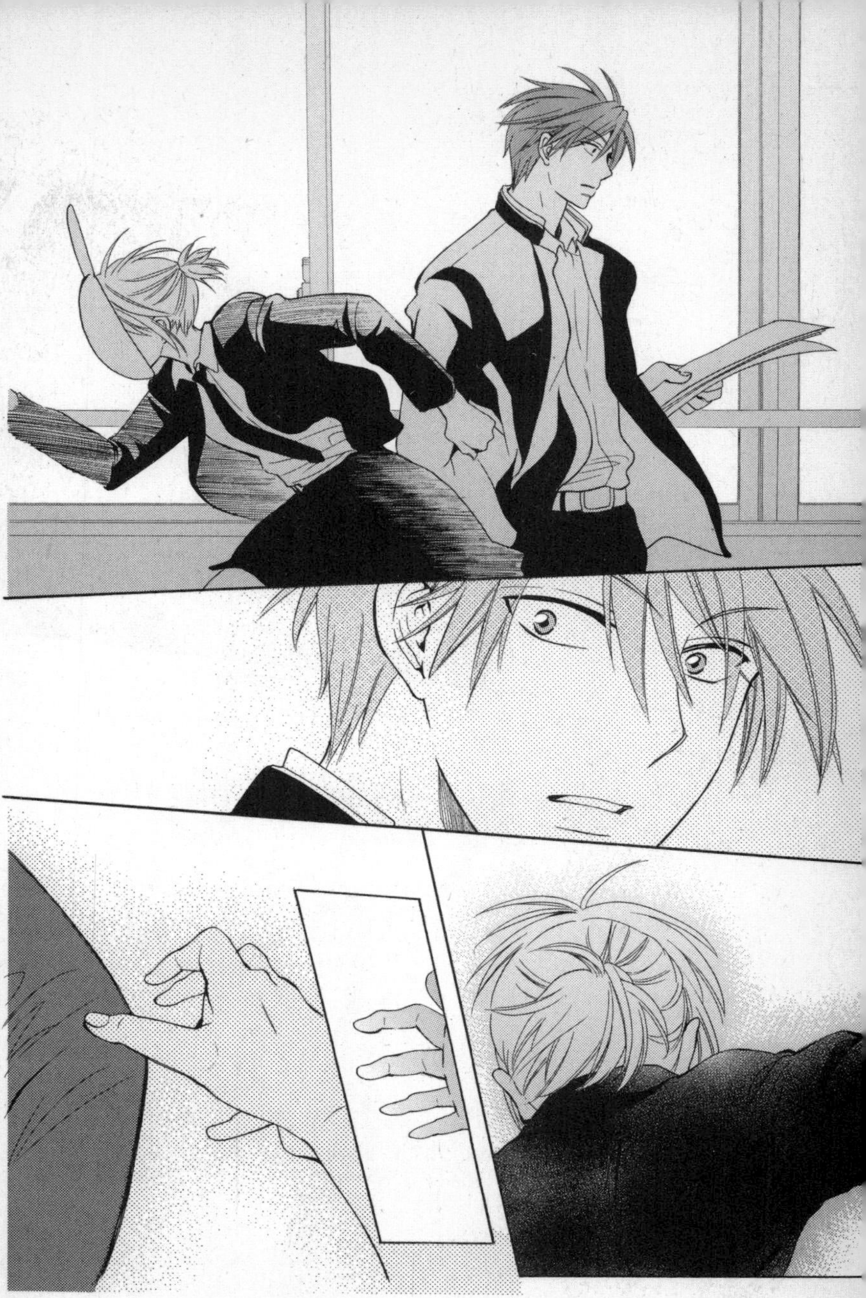

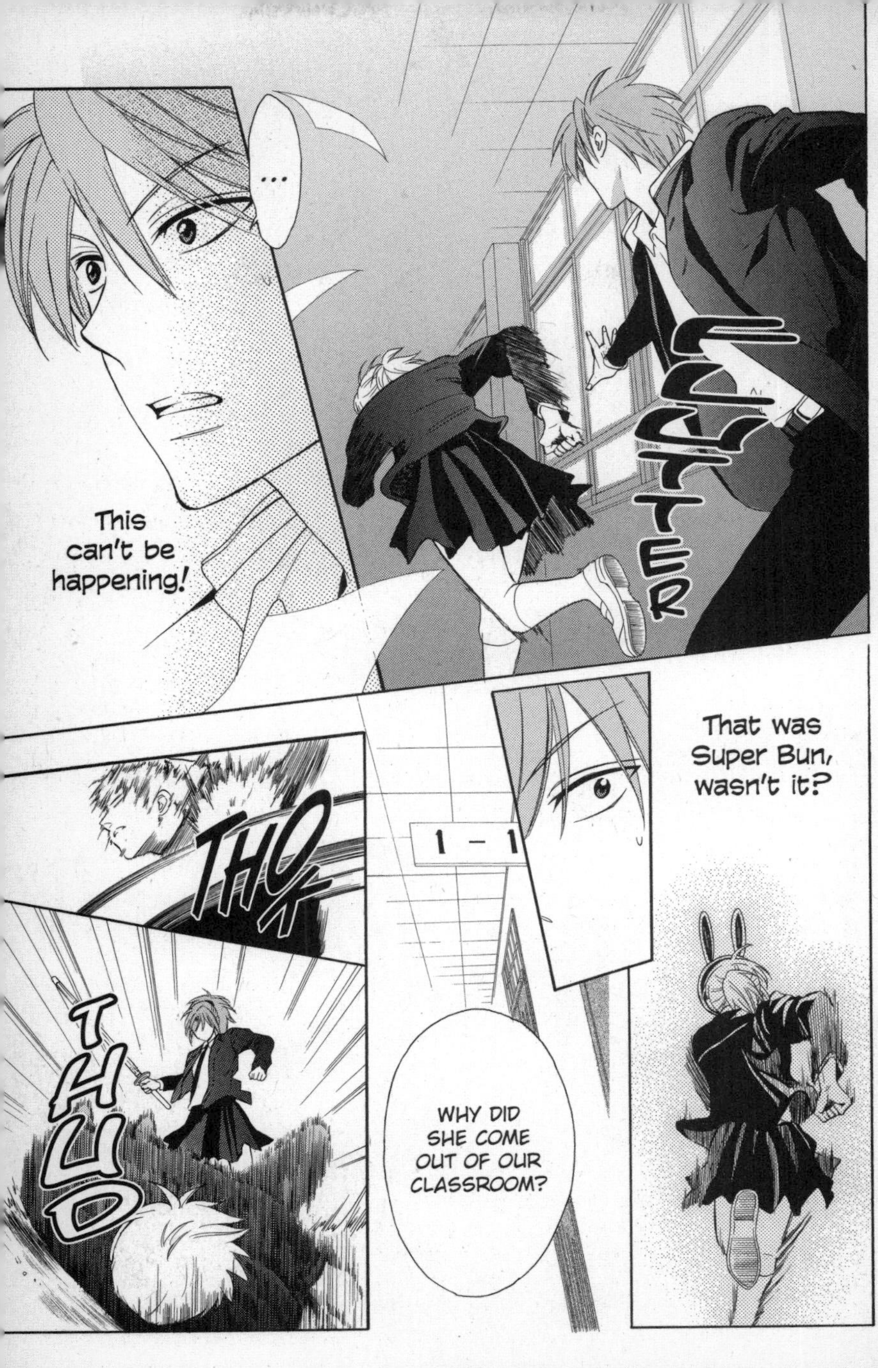
SCUTTER
...
This can't be happening!
That was Super Bun, wasn't it?
1 - 1
WHY DID SHE COME OUT OF OUR CLASSROOM?
THOK
THUD

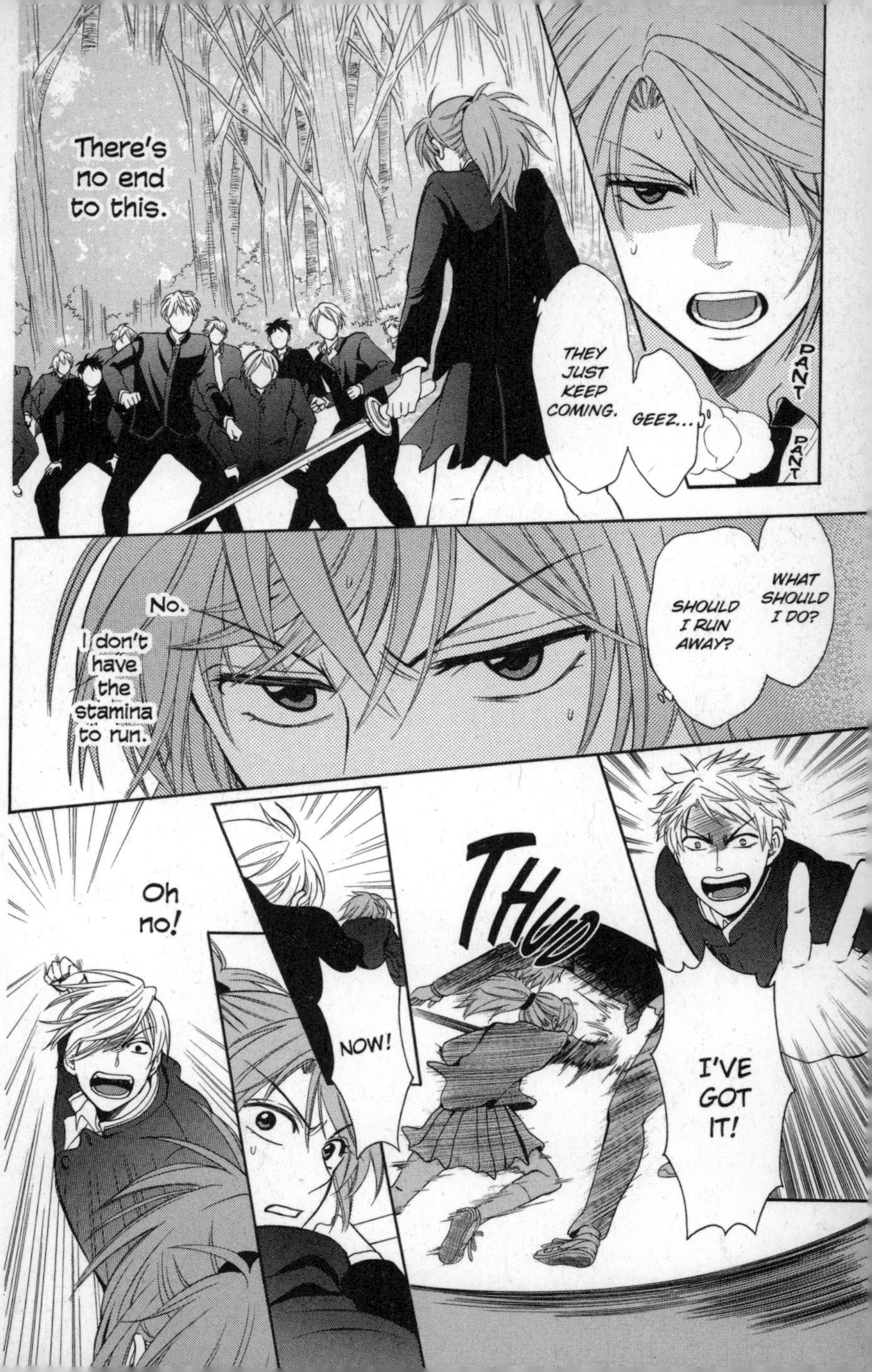
PANT
PANT
GEEZ...
THEY JUST KEEP COMING.
There's no end to this.
WHAT SHOULD I DO?
SHOULD I RUN AWAY?
No.
I don't have the stamina to run.
I'VE GOT IT!
THUD
NOW!
Oh no!

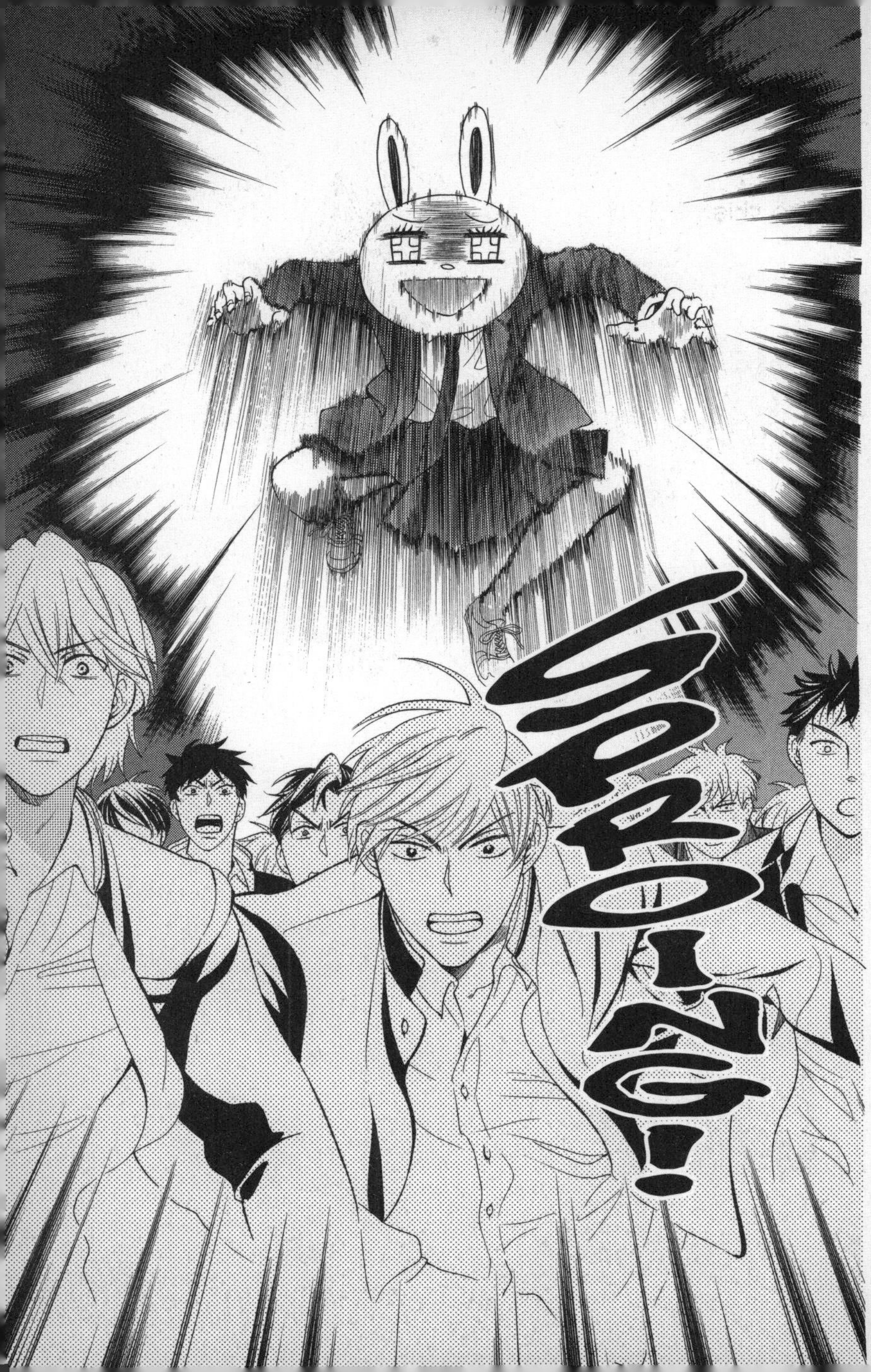
SPRING!

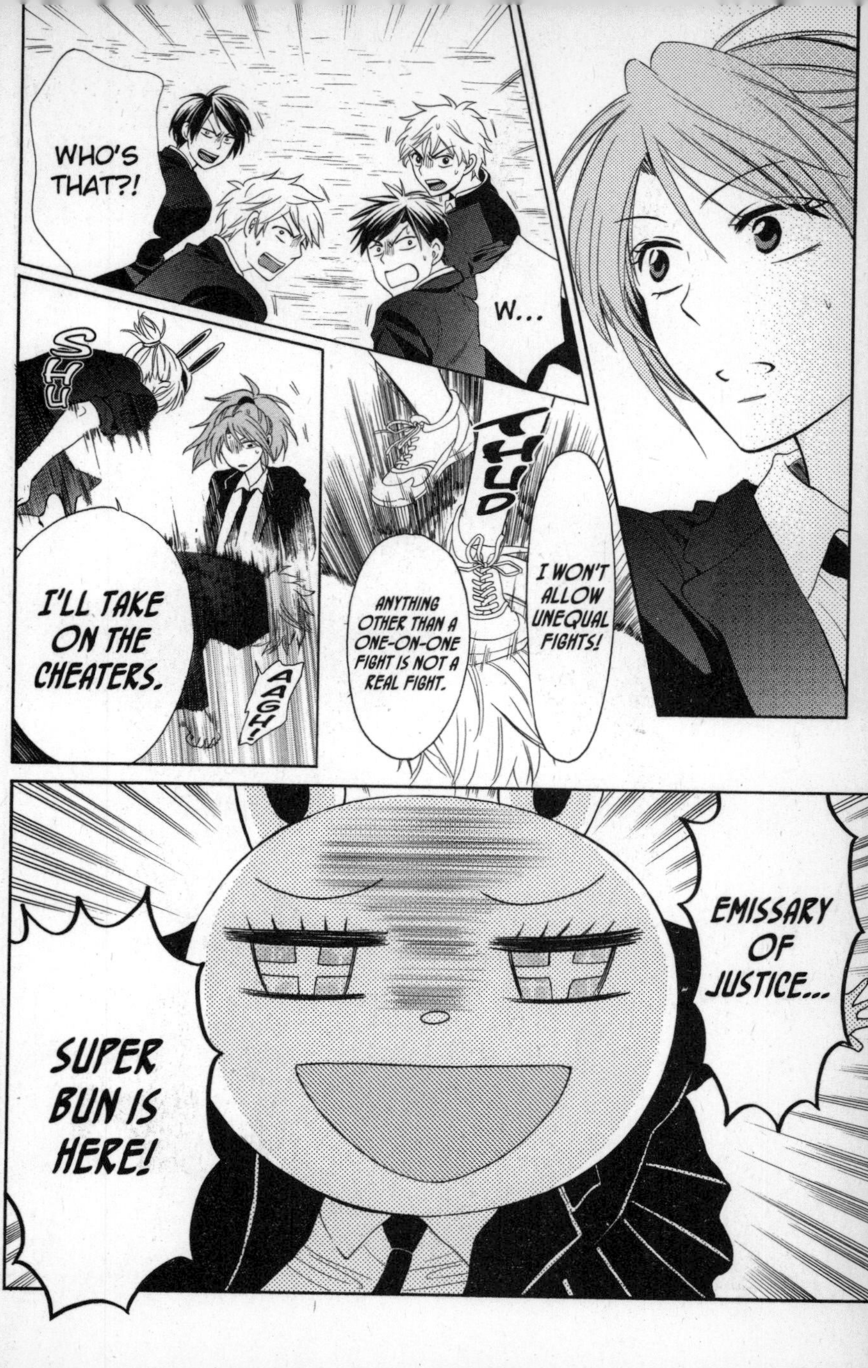
W...
WHO'S THAT?!
I WON'T ALLOW UNEQUAL FIGHTS!
THUD
ANYTHING OTHER THAN A ONE-ON-ONE FIGHT IS NOT A REAL FIGHT.
AAGH!
I'LL TAKE ON THE CHEATERS.
EMISSARY OF JUSTICE...
SUPER BUN IS HERE!

Chapter 56

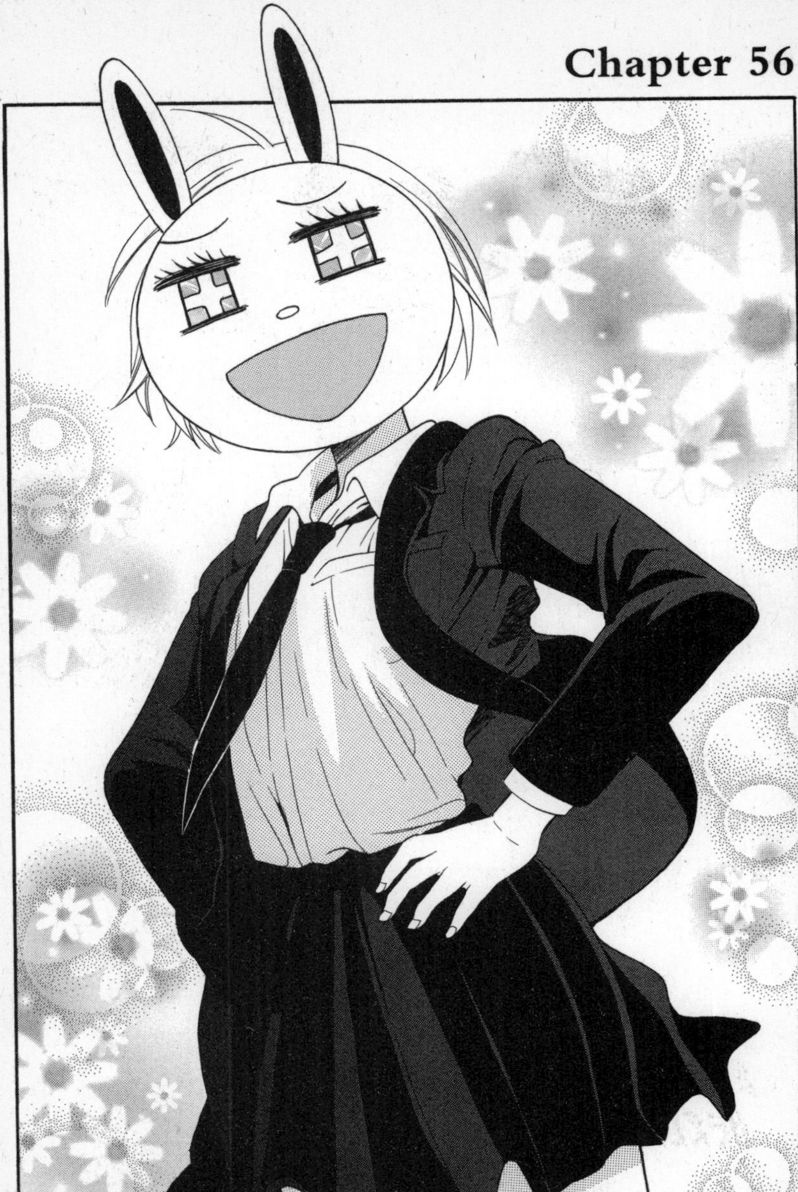

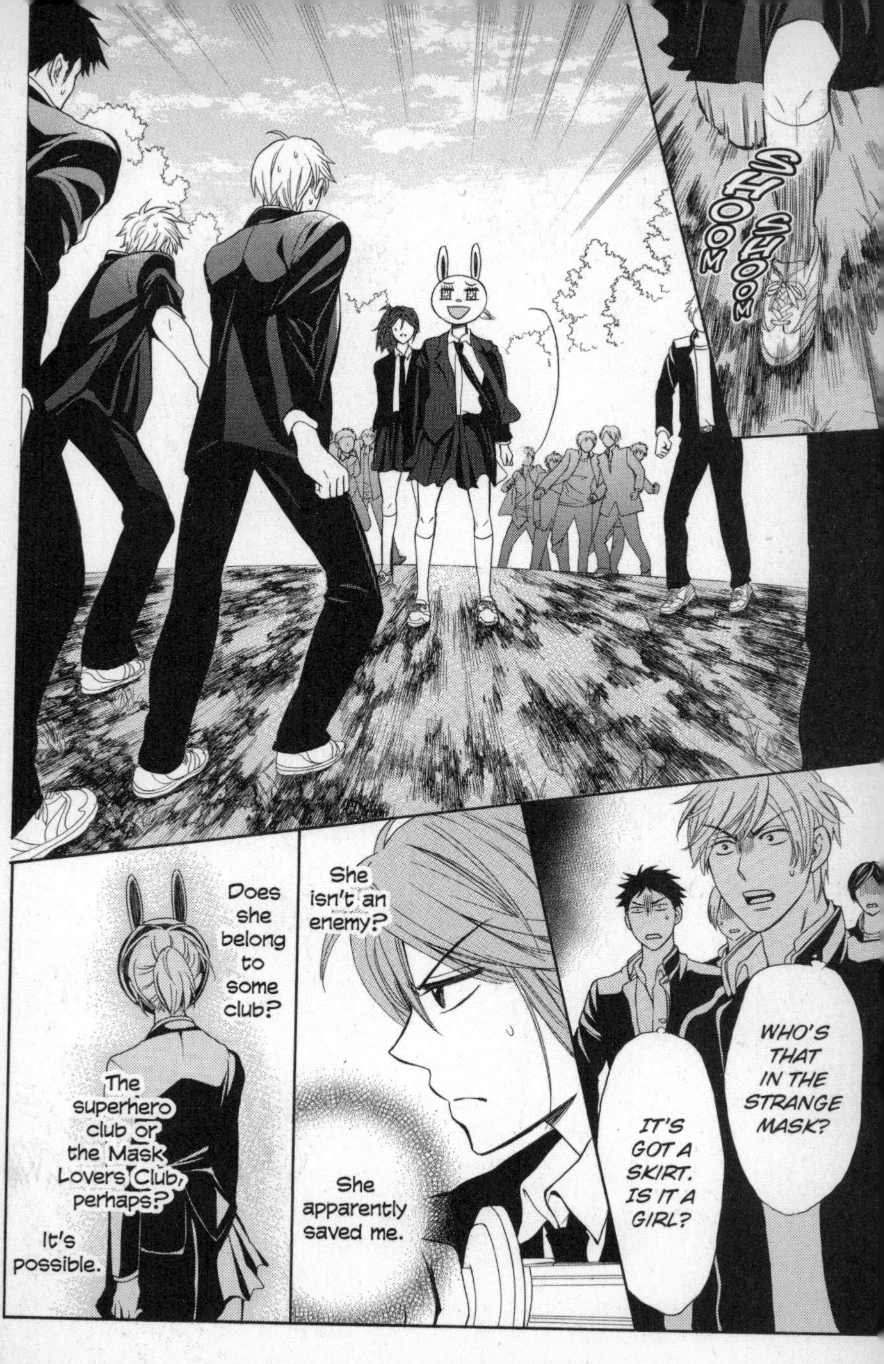
SHOOM SHOOM
WHO'S THAT IN THE STRANGE MASK?
IT'S GOT A SKIRT. IS IT A GIRL?
She isn't an enemy?
She apparently saved me.
Does she belong to some club?
The superhero club or the Mask Lovers Club, perhaps?
It's possible.

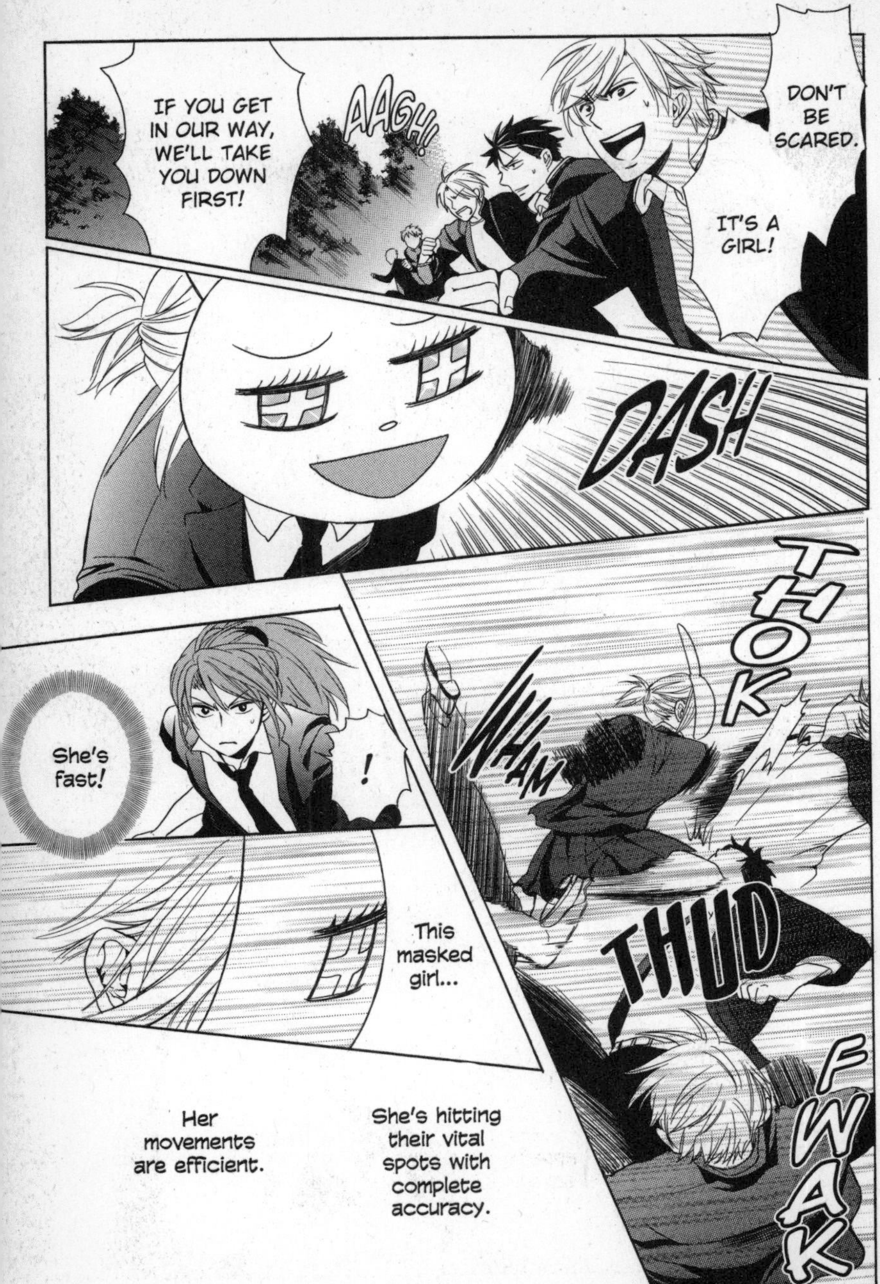

DON'T BE SCARED.
IT'S A GIRL!
AAGH!!
IF YOU GET IN OUR WAY, WE'LL TAKE YOU DOWN FIRST!
DASH
THOK
WHAM
THUD
FWAK
!
She's fast!
This masked girl...
She's hitting their vital spots with complete accuracy.
Her movements are efficient.

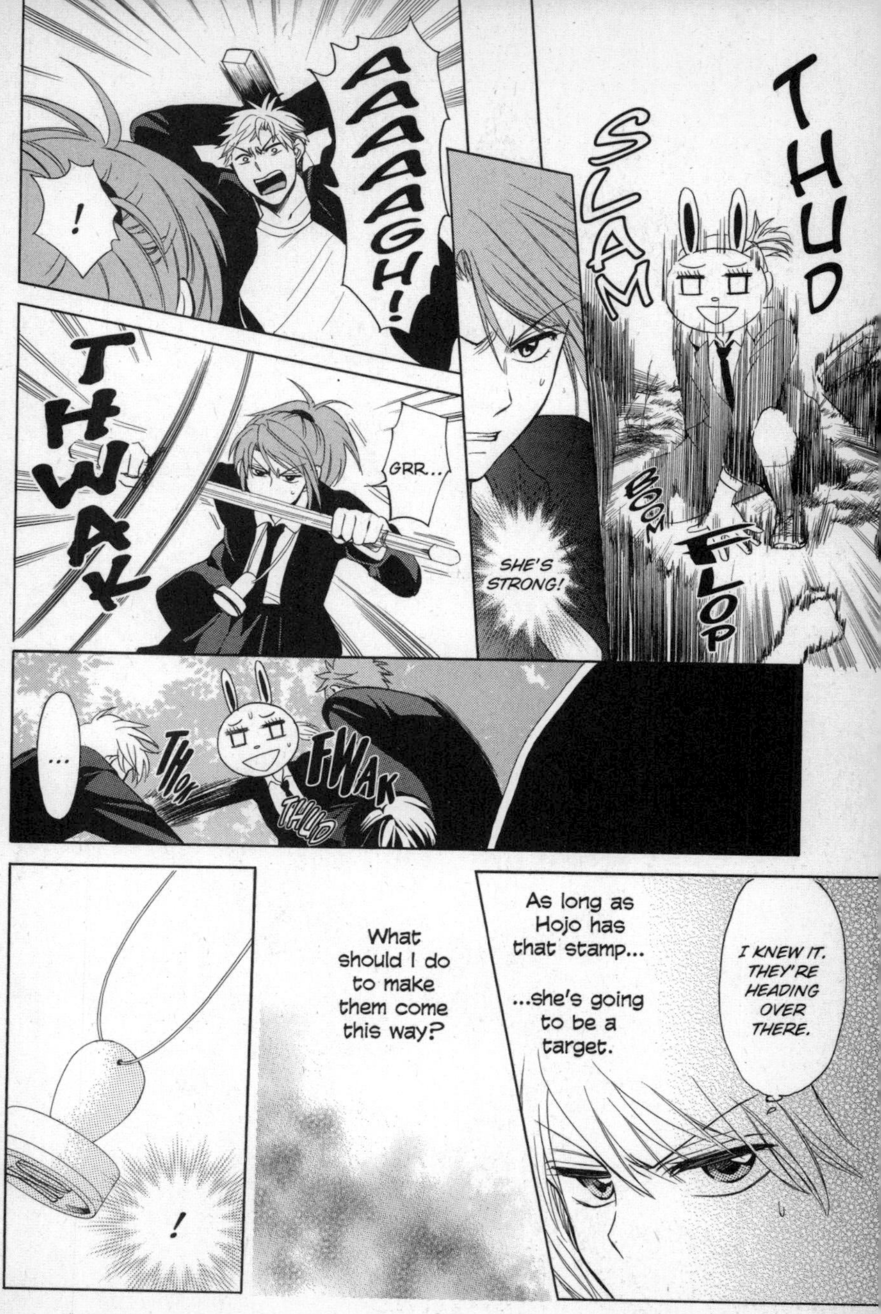

THUD
SLAM
BOOM
FLOP
SHE'S STRONG!
AAAAAAGH!
!
GRR...
THWAK
...
FWAK
THOK
THUD
I KNEW IT. THEY'RE HEADING OVER THERE.
As long as Hojo has that stamp...
...she's going to be a target.
What should I do to make them come this way?
!

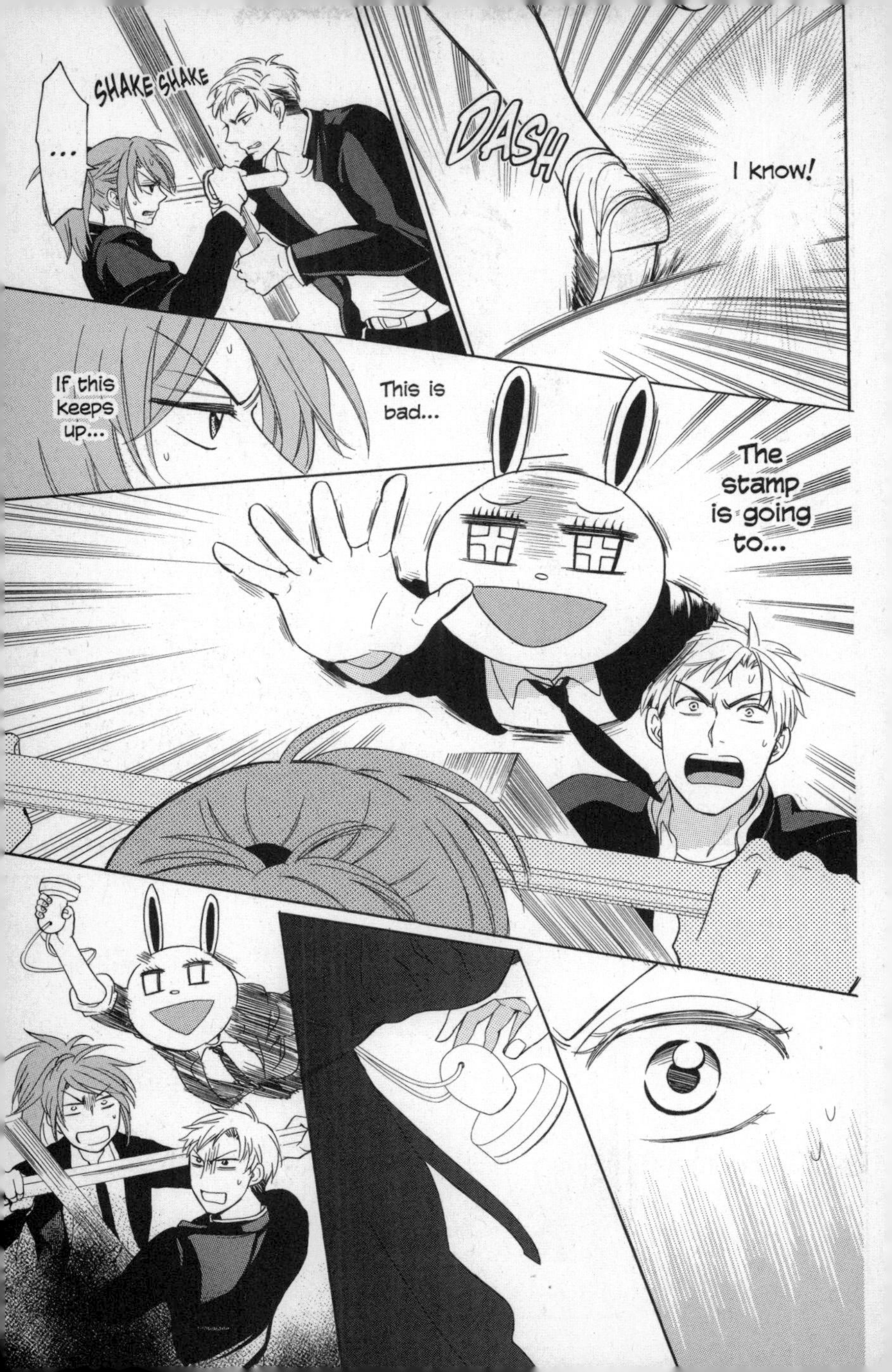

I know!
DASH
SHAKE SHAKE
...
This is bad...
If this keeps up...
The stamp is going to...

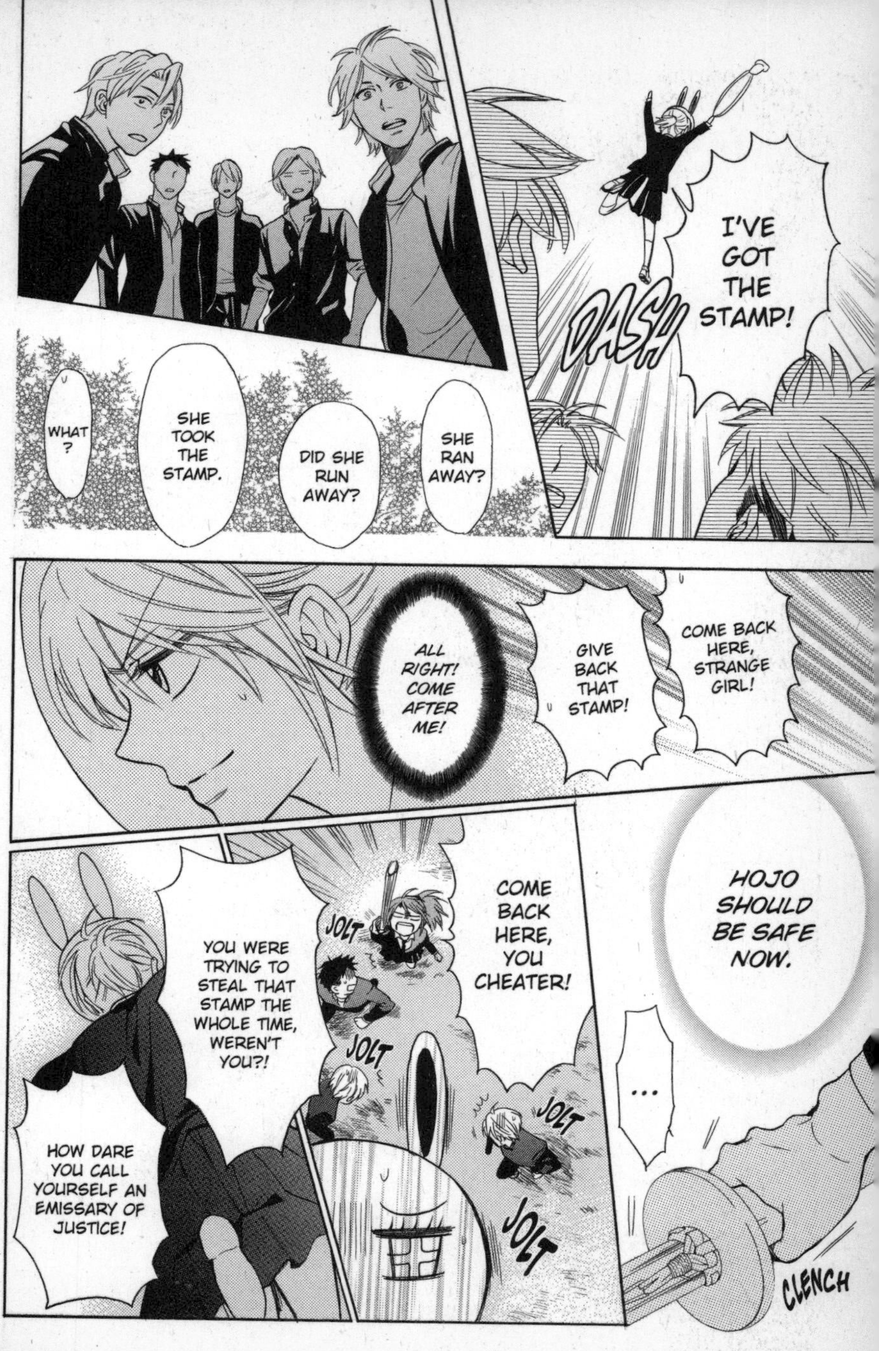
I'VE GOT THE STAMP!
DASH
SHE RAN AWAY?
DID SHE RUN AWAY?
SHE TOOK THE STAMP.
WHAT?
COME BACK HERE, STRANGE GIRL!
GIVE BACK THAT STAMP!
ALL RIGHT! COME AFTER ME!
HOJO SHOULD BE SAFE NOW.
...
CLENCH
COME BACK HERE, YOU CHEATER!
JOLT
JOLT
JOLT
JOLT
YOU WERE TRYING TO STEAL THAT STAMP THE WHOLE TIME, WEREN'T YOU?!
HOW DARE YOU CALL YOURSELF AN EMISSARY OF JUSTICE!

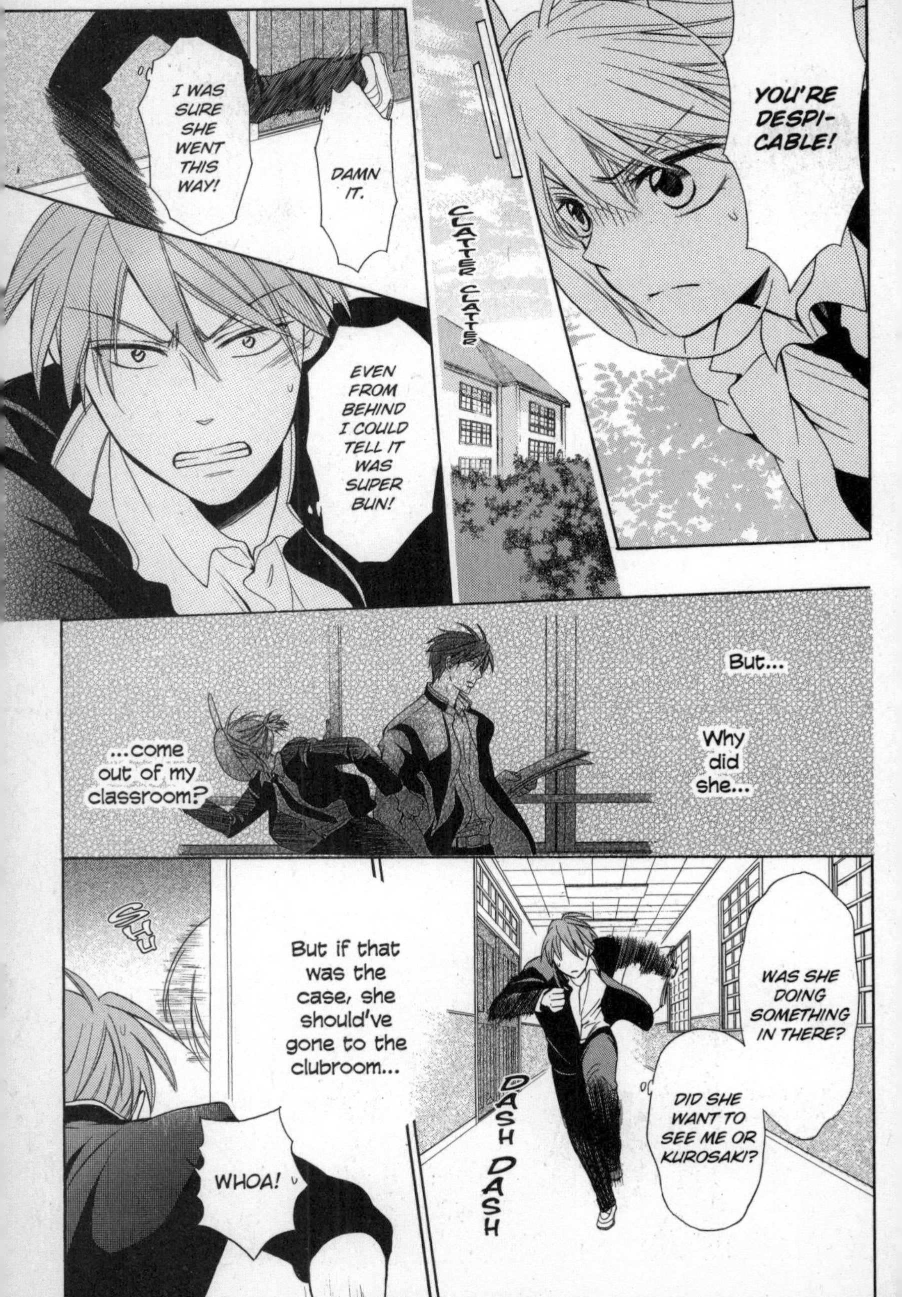
YOU'RE DESPICABLE!
CLATTER CLATTER
I WAS SURE SHE WENT THIS WAY!
DAMN IT.
EVEN FROM BEHIND I COULD TELL IT WAS SUPER BUN!
But...
Why did she...
...come out of my classroom?
WAS SHE DOING SOMETHING IN THERE?
DID SHE WANT TO SEE ME OR KUROSAKI?
DASH DASH
But if that was the case, she should've gone to the clubroom...
SHU
WHOA!

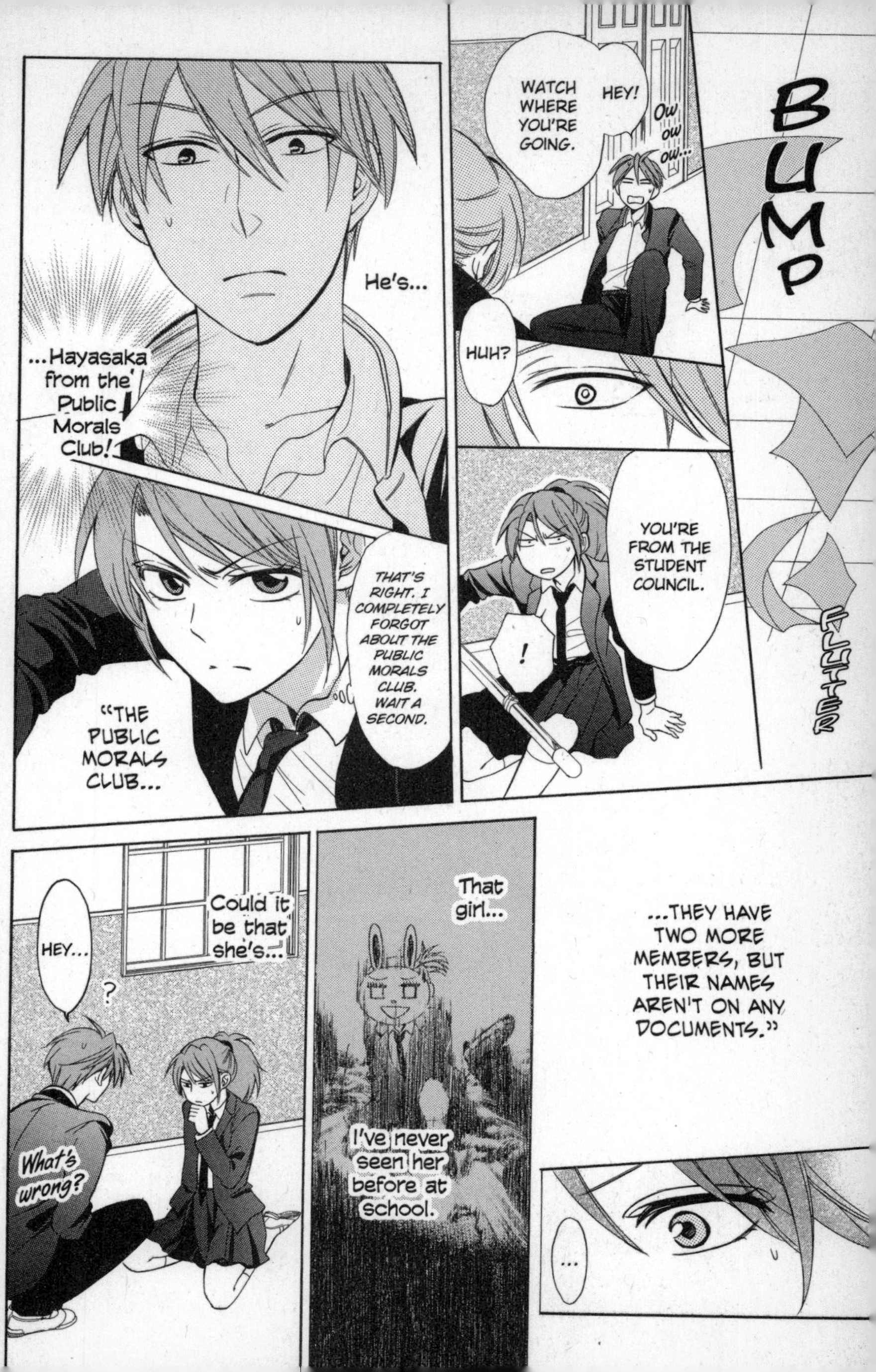
BUMP
HEY! WATCH WHERE YOU'RE GOING.
Ow ow ow...
HUH?
YOU'RE FROM THE STUDENT COUNCIL.
FLUTTER
!
He's...
...Hayasaka from the Public Morals Club!
THAT'S RIGHT. I COMPLETELY FORGOT ABOUT THE PUBLIC MORALS CLUB. WAIT A SECOND.
"THE PUBLIC MORALS CLUB...
...THEY HAVE TWO MORE MEMBERS, BUT THEIR NAMES AREN'T ON ANY DOCUMENTS."
...
That girl...
I've never seen her before at school.
Could it be that she's...
HEY...
?
What's wrong?

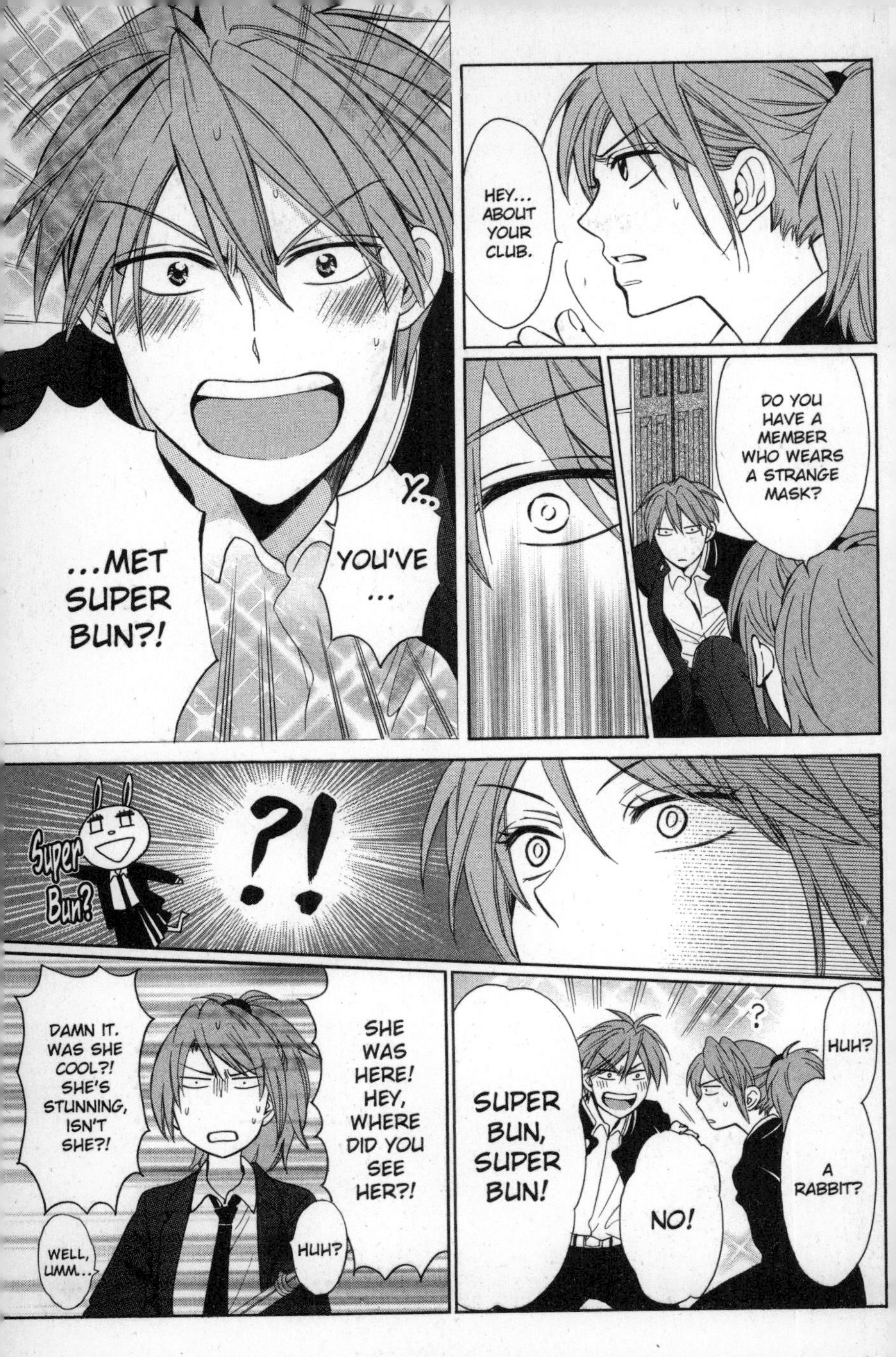
HEY... ABOUT YOUR CLUB.
DO YOU HAVE A MEMBER WHO WEARS A STRANGE MASK?
Y...
YOU'VE ...
...MET SUPER BUN?!
?!
Super Bun?
?
HUH?
A RABBIT?
SUPER BUN, SUPER BUN!
NO!
SHE WAS HERE! HEY, WHERE DID YOU SEE HER?!
HUH?
DAMN IT. WAS SHE COOL?! SHE'S STUNNING, ISN'T SHE?!
WELL, UMM...

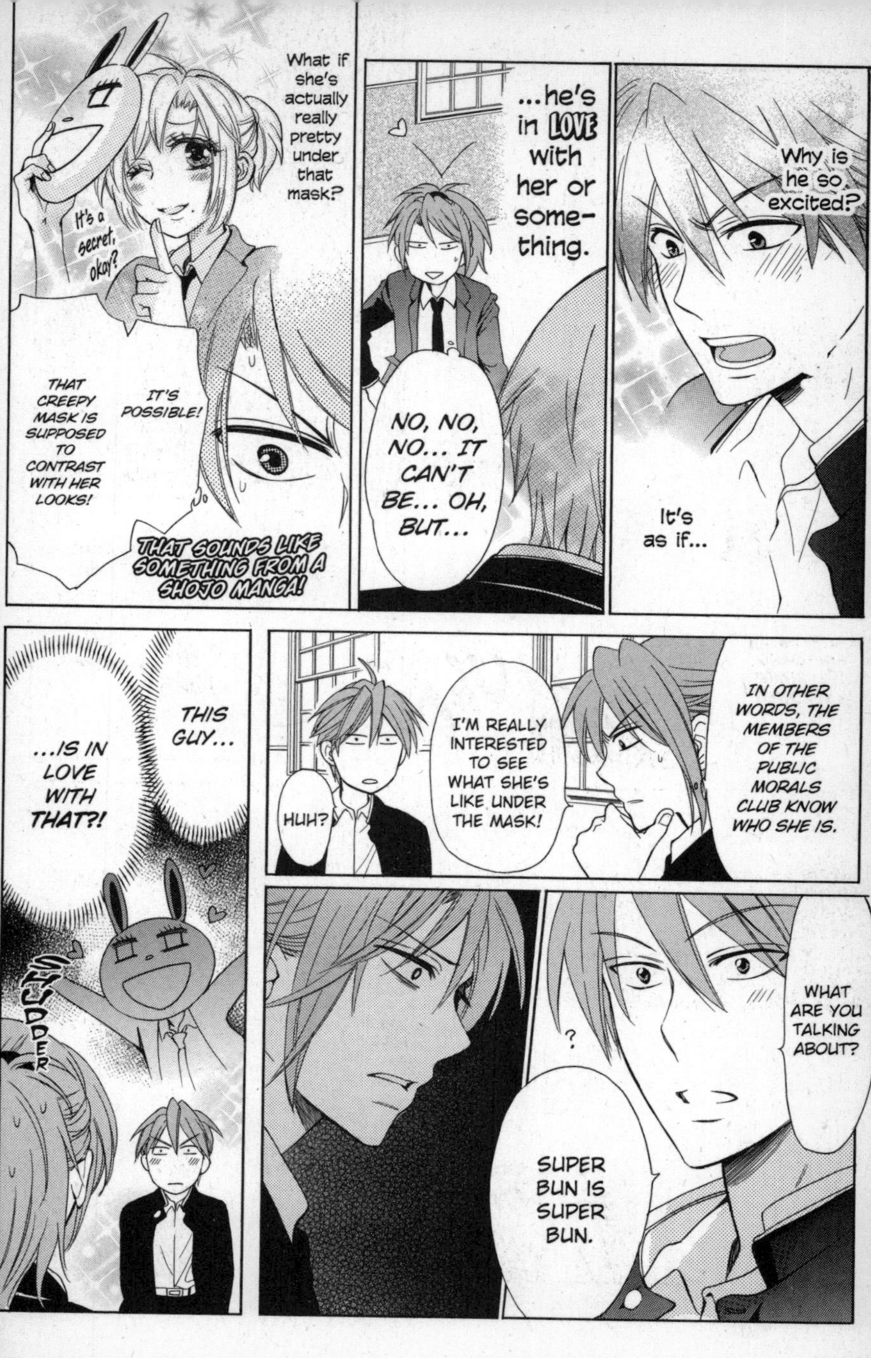
Why is he so excited?
It's as if...
...he's in LOVE with her or something.
NO, NO, NO... IT CAN'T BE... OH, BUT...
What if she's actually really pretty under that mask?
It's a secret, okay?
IT'S POSSIBLE!
THAT CREEPY MASK IS SUPPOSED TO CONTRAST WITH HER LOOKS!
THAT SOUNDS LIKE SOMETHING FROM A SHOJO MANGA!
IN OTHER WORDS, THE MEMBERS OF THE PUBLIC MORALS CLUB KNOW WHO SHE IS.
I'M REALLY INTERESTED TO SEE WHAT SHE'S LIKE UNDER THE MASK!
HUH?
WHAT ARE YOU TALKING ABOUT?
SUPER BUN IS SUPER BUN.
?
THIS GUY...
...IS IN LOVE WITH THAT?!
SHUDDER

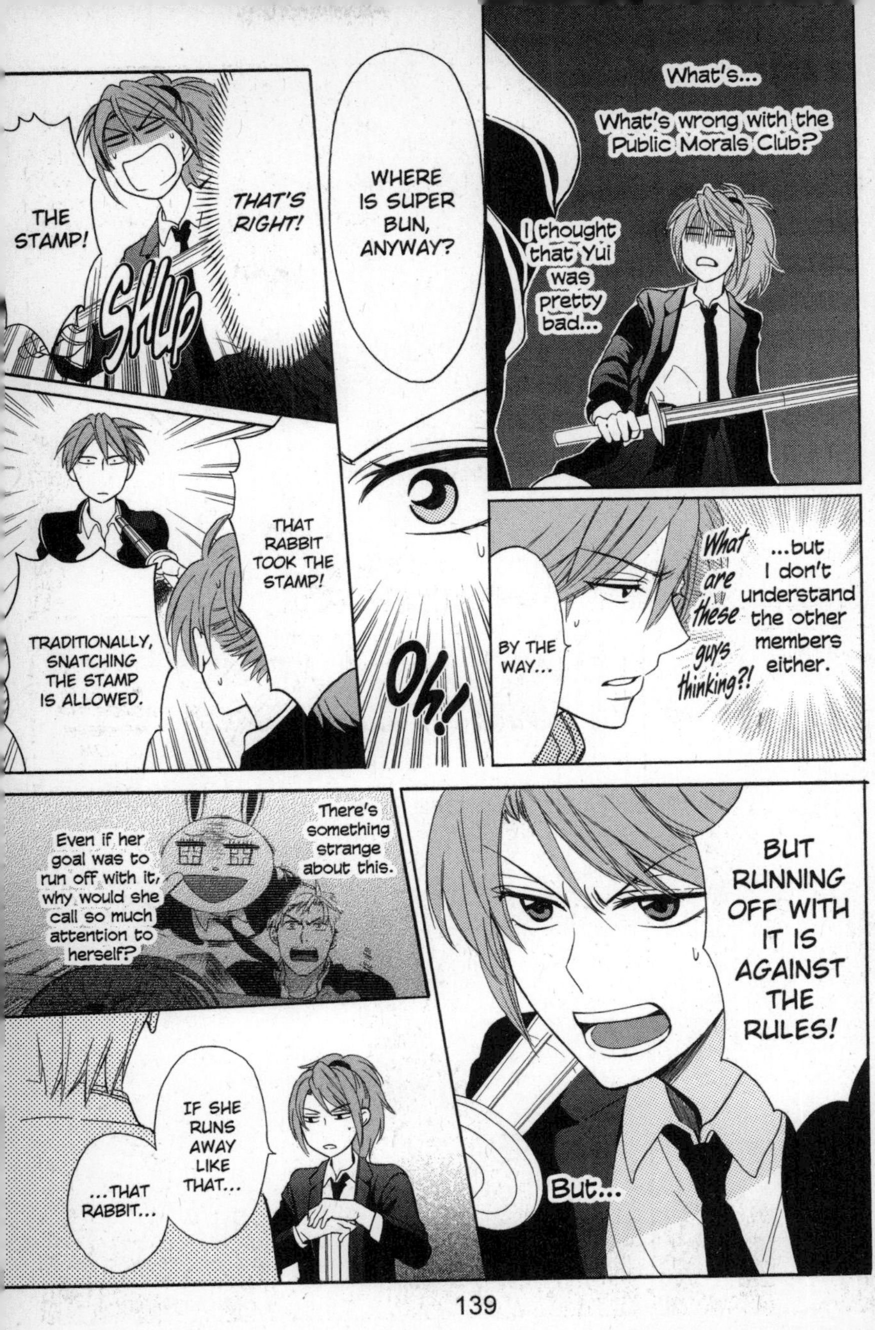
What's...
What's wrong with the Public Morals Club?
I thought that Yui was pretty bad...
...but I don't understand the other members either.
What are these guys thinking?!
BY THE WAY...
WHERE IS SUPER BUN, ANYWAY?
THAT'S RIGHT!
THE STAMP!
SHUP
THAT RABBIT TOOK THE STAMP!
Oh!
TRADITIONALLY, SNATCHING THE STAMP IS ALLOWED.
BUT RUNNING OFF WITH IT IS AGAINST THE RULES!
But...
There's something strange about this.
Even if her goal was to run off with it, why would she call so much attention to herself?
IF SHE RUNS AWAY LIKE THAT...
...THAT RABBIT...

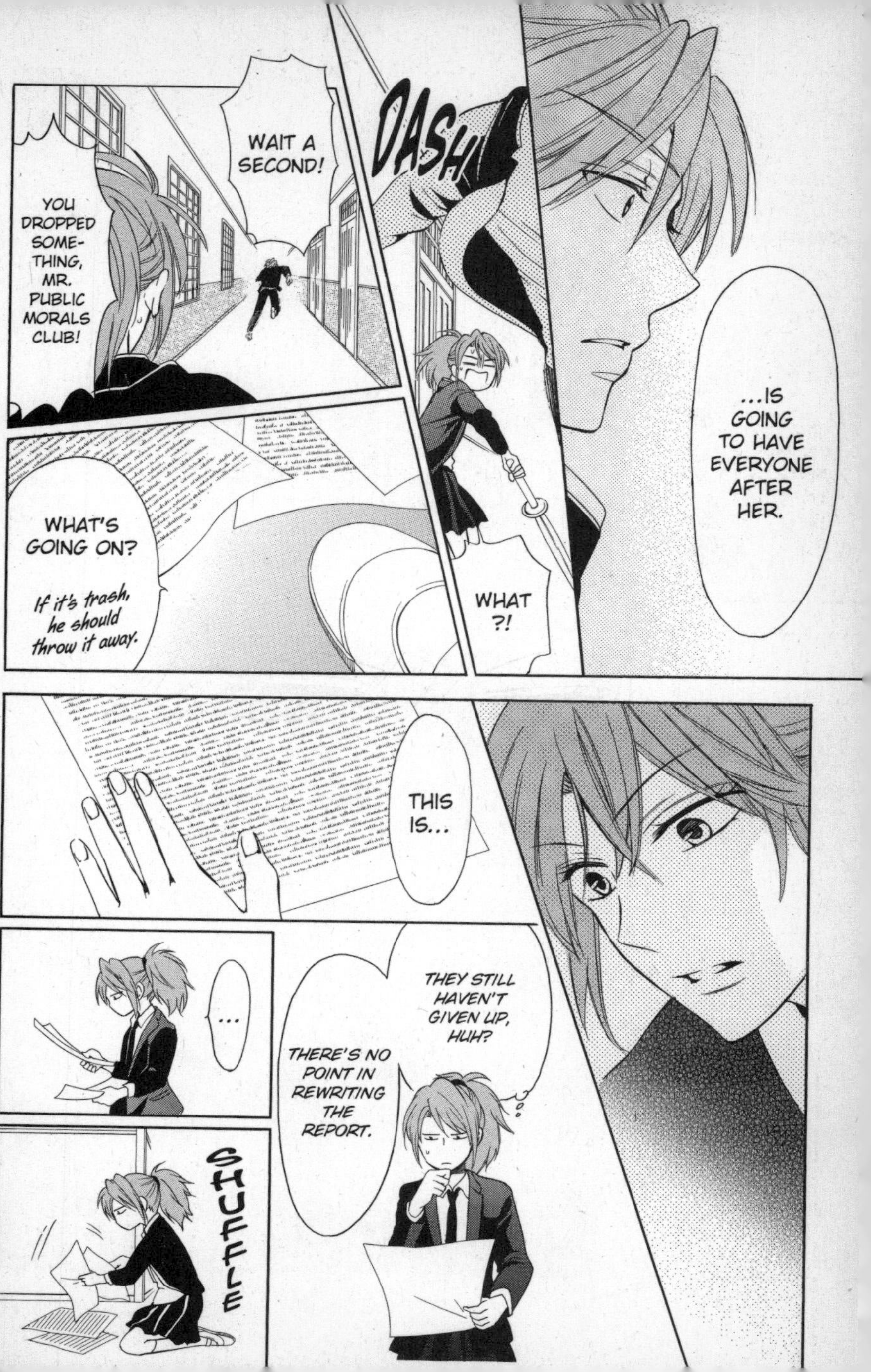

...IS GOING TO HAVE EVERYONE AFTER HER.
DASH
WHAT?!
WAIT A SECOND!
YOU DROPPED SOME-THING, MR. PUBLIC MORALS CLUB!
WHAT'S GOING ON?
If it's trash, he should throw it away.
THIS IS...
THEY STILL HAVEN'T GIVEN UP, HUH?
THERE'S NO POINT IN REWRITING THE REPORT.
...
SHUFFLE

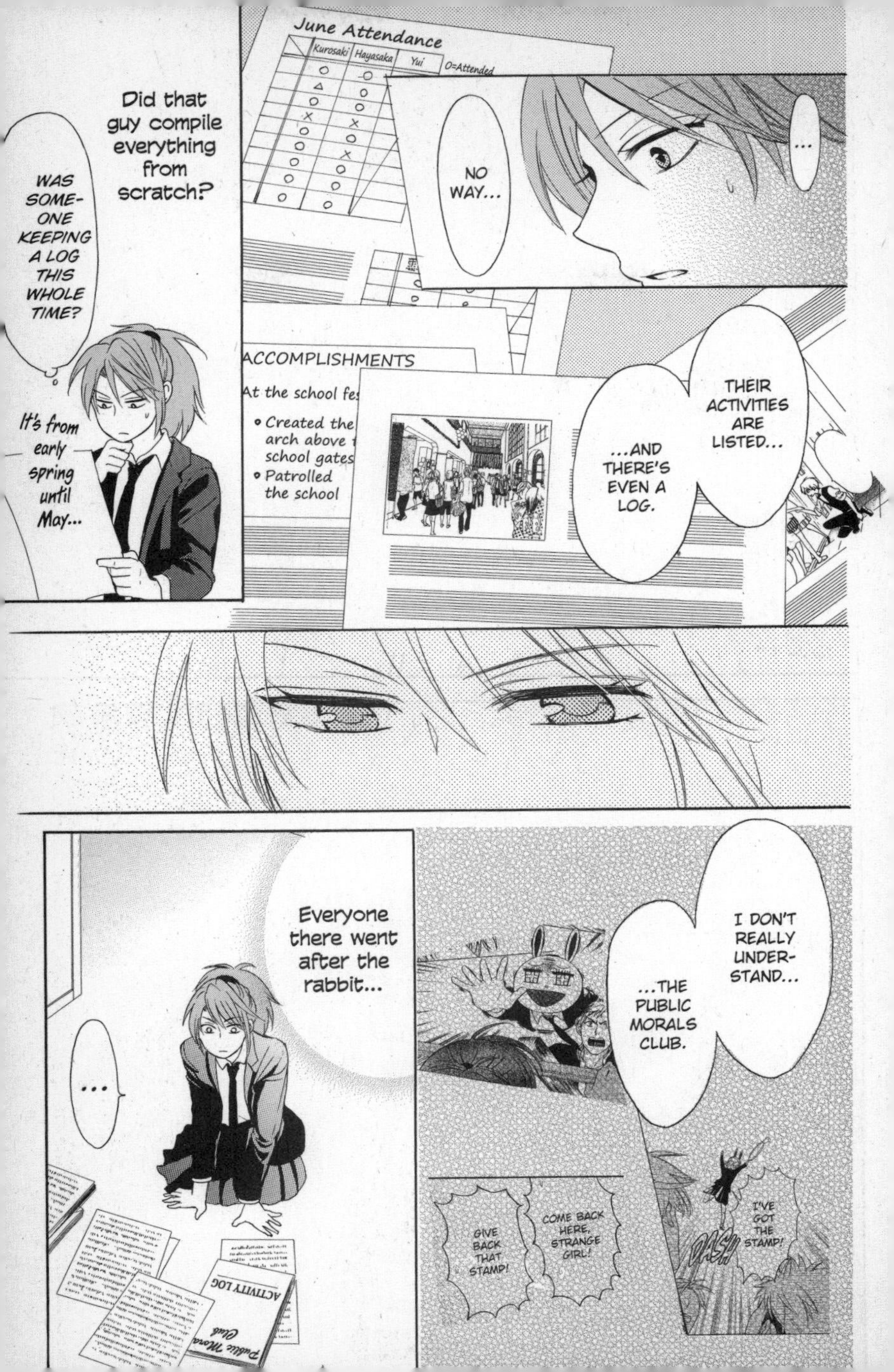
...
NO WAY...
June Attendance
Kurosaki
Hayasaka
Yui
O=Attended
ACCOMPLISHMENTS
At the school fes
• Created the arch above t school gates
• Patrolled the school
THEIR ACTIVITIES ARE LISTED...
...AND THERE'S EVEN A LOG.
Did that guy compile everything from scratch?
WAS SOMEONE KEEPING A LOG THIS WHOLE TIME?
It's from early spring until May...
I DON'T REALLY UNDERSTAND...
...THE PUBLIC MORALS CLUB.
I'VE GOT THE STAMP!
COME BACK HERE, STRANGE GIRL!
GIVE BACK THAT STAMP!
Everyone there went after the rabbit...
...
ACTIVITY LOG
Public Morals Club

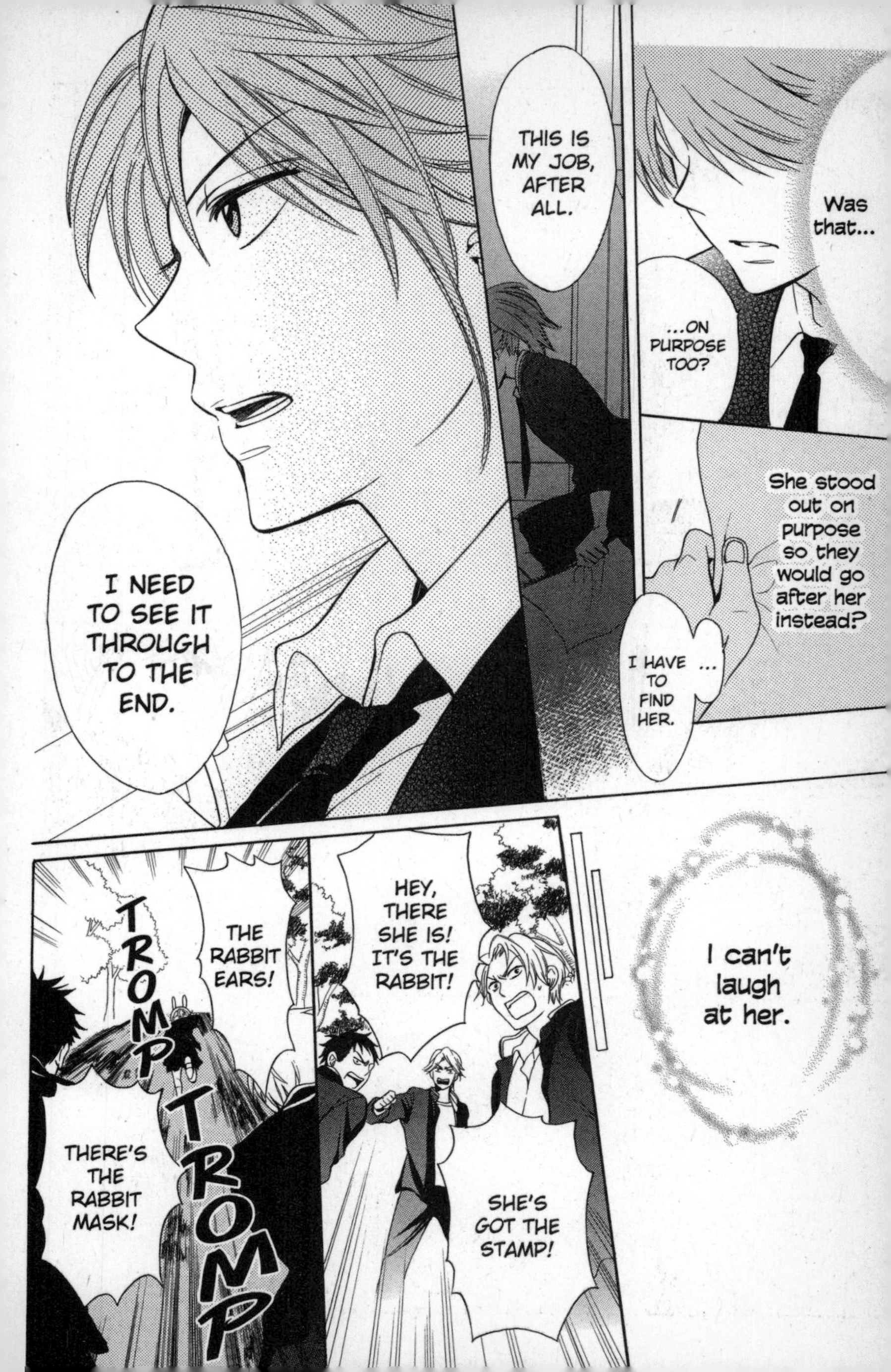

Was that...
...ON PURPOSE TOO?
She stood out on purpose so they would go after her instead?
I HAVE TO FIND HER...
THIS IS MY JOB, AFTER ALL.
I NEED TO SEE IT THROUGH TO THE END.
I can't laugh at her.
HEY, THERE SHE IS! IT'S THE RABBIT!
SHE'S GOT THE STAMP!
THE RABBIT EARS!
TROMP
TROMP
THERE'S THE RABBIT MASK!

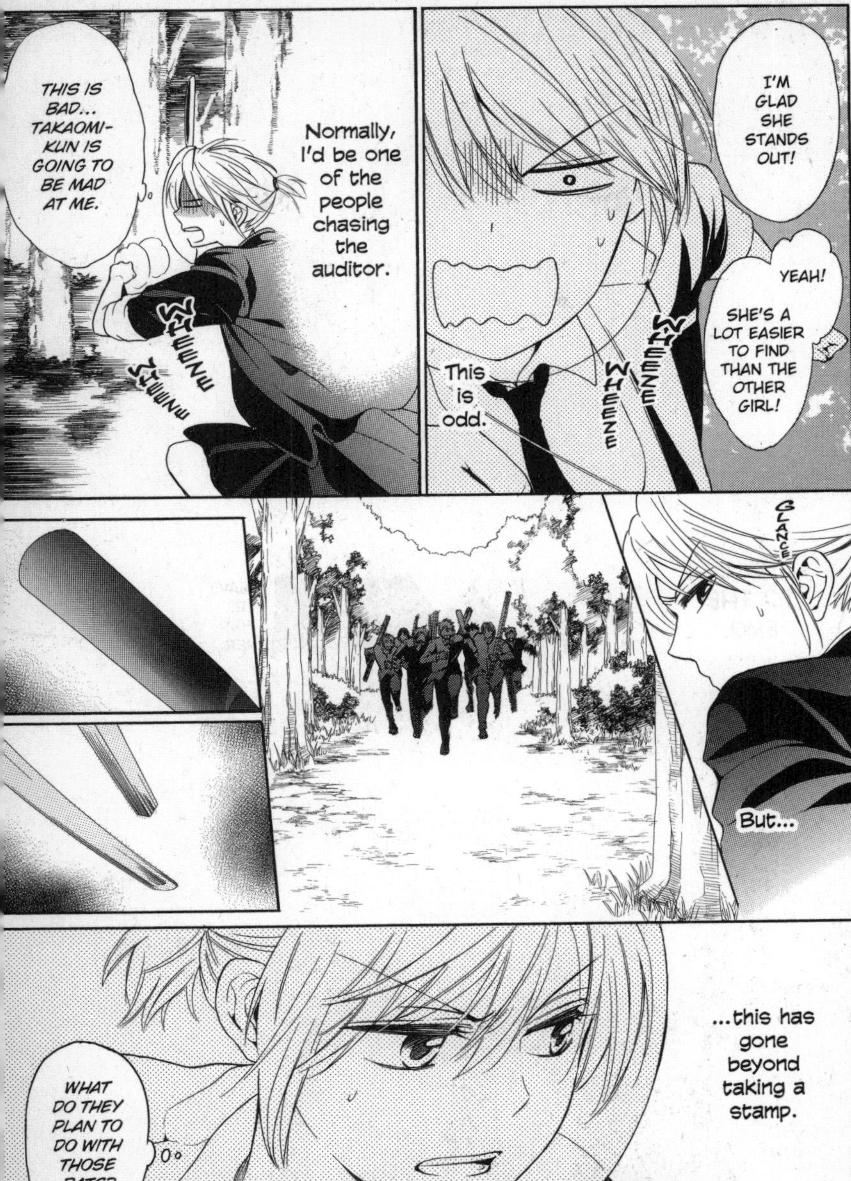

I'M GLAD SHE STANDS OUT!
YEAH! SHE'S A LOT EASIER TO FIND THAN THE OTHER GIRL!
WHEEZE
WHEEZE
This is odd.
Normally, I'd be one of the people chasing the auditor.
THIS IS BAD... TAKAOMI-KUN IS GOING TO BE MAD AT ME.
WHEEZE
WHEEZE
GLANCE
But...
...this has gone beyond taking a stamp.
WHAT DO THEY PLAN TO DO WITH THOSE BATS?

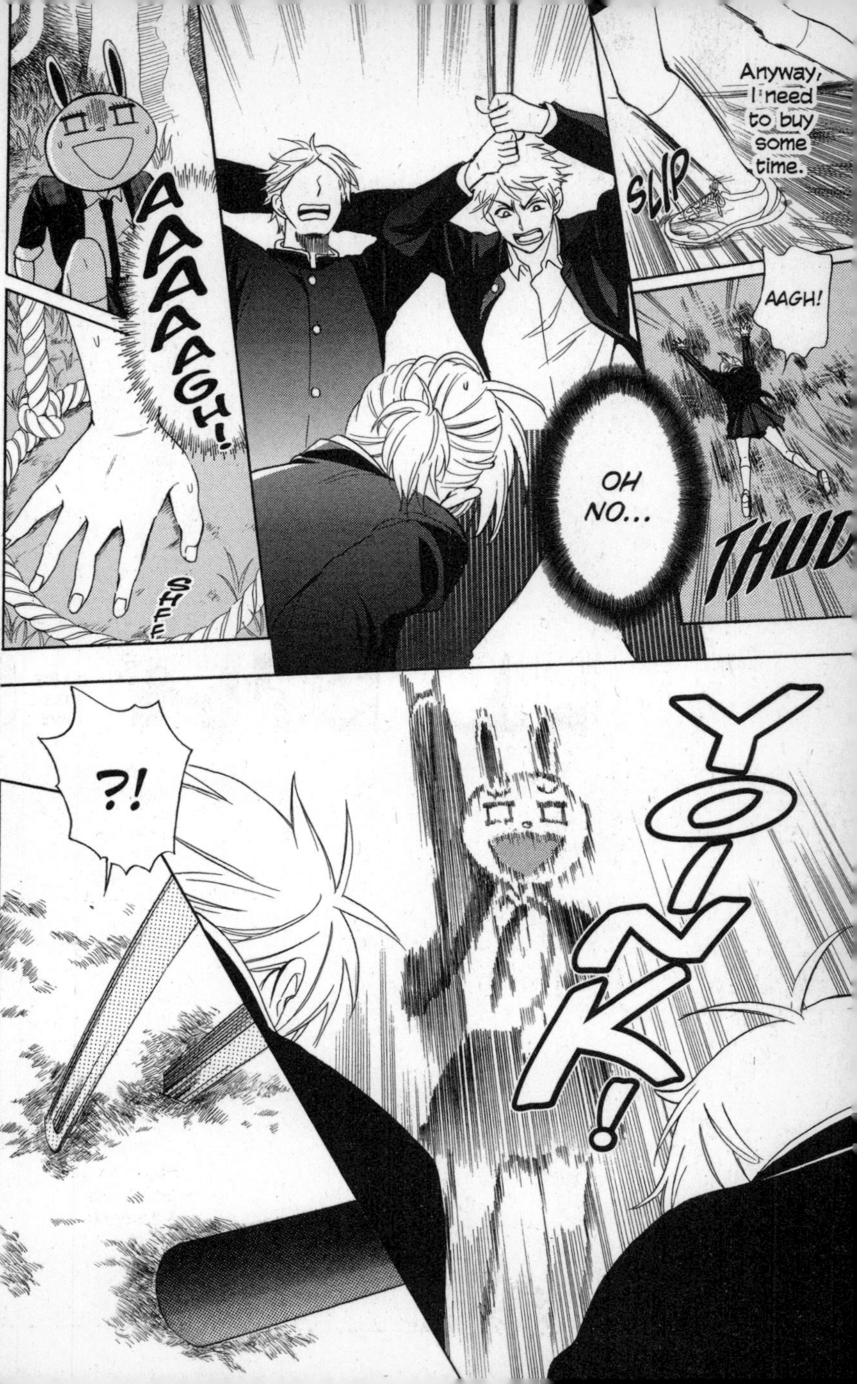
Anyway, I need to buy some time.
SLIP
AAGH!
THUD
OH NO...
AAAAAGH!
SHFF
YOINK!
?!

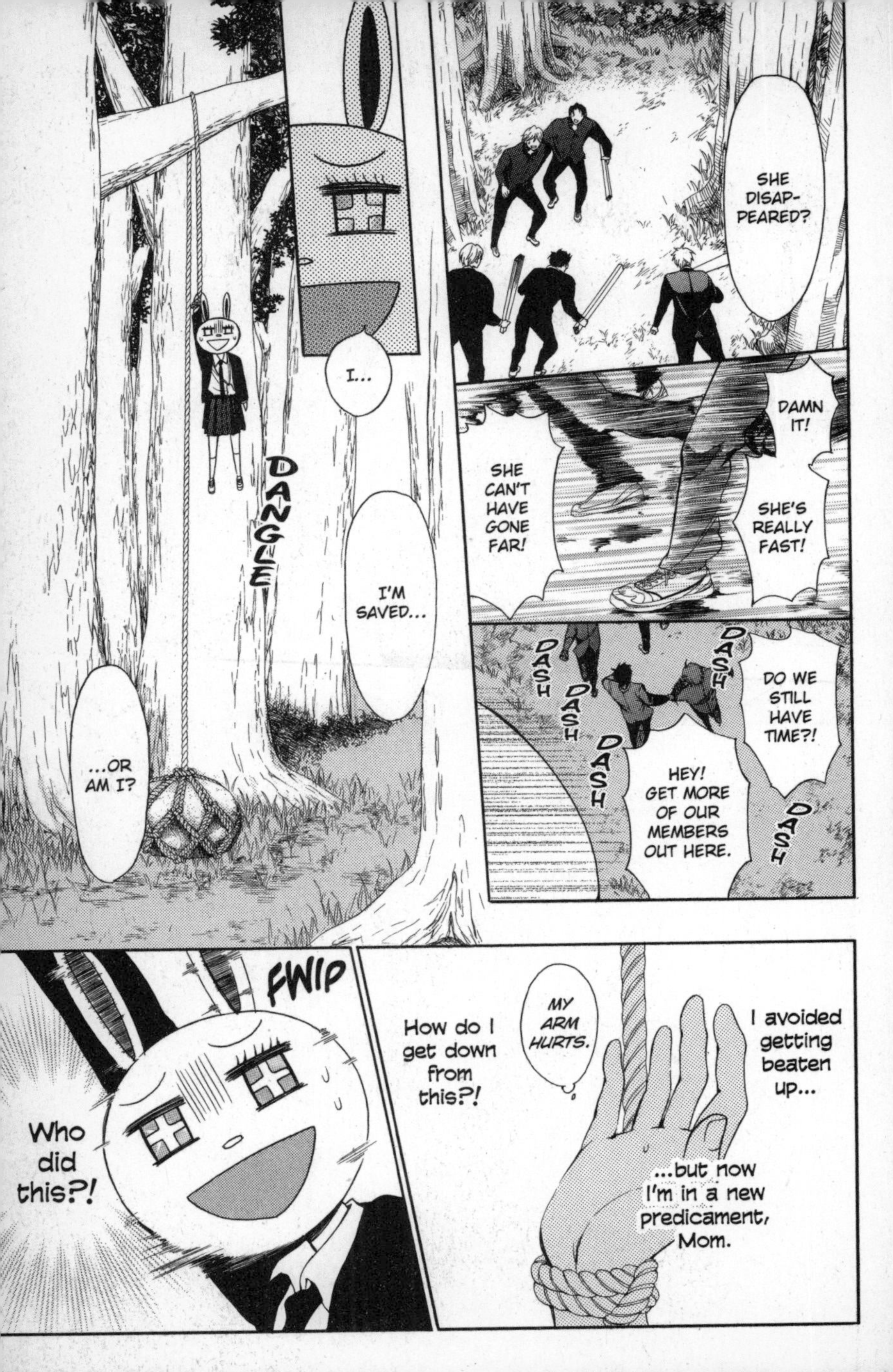
SHE DISAP-PEARED?
DAMN IT!
SHE'S REALLY FAST!
SHE CAN'T HAVE GONE FAR!
DASH
DASH
DO WE STILL HAVE TIME?!
DASH
DASH
HEY! GET MORE OF OUR MEMBERS OUT HERE.
DASH
I...
DANGLE
I'M SAVED...
...OR AM I?
I avoided getting beaten up...
MY ARM HURTS.
How do I get down from this?!
...but now I'm in a new predicament, Mom.
FWIP
Who did this?!

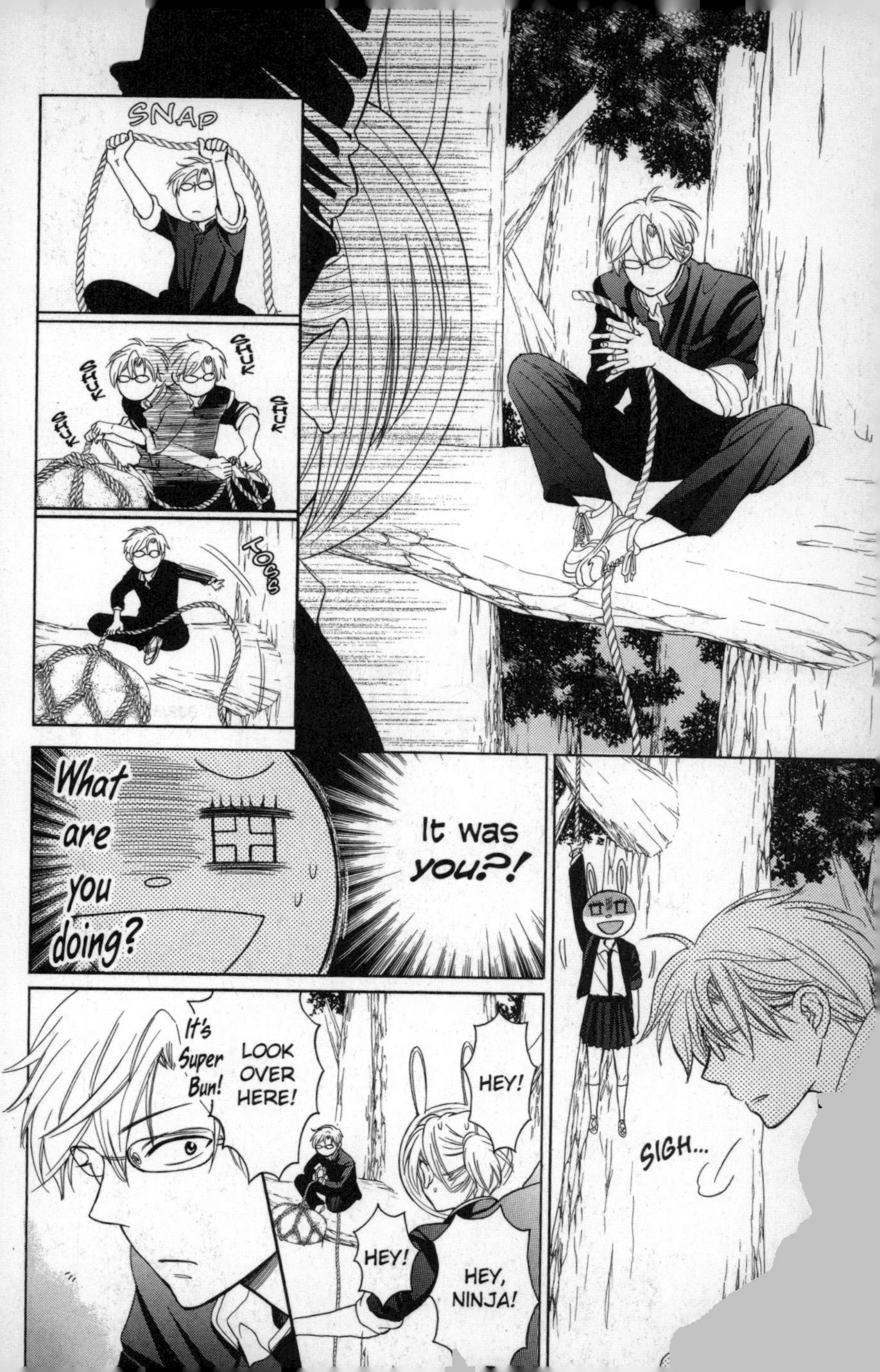
SNAP
SHUK SHUK
SHUK SHUK
TOSS
SIGH...
It was you?!
What are you doing?
HEY!
LOOK OVER HERE!
It's Super Bun!
HEY, NINJA!
HEY!

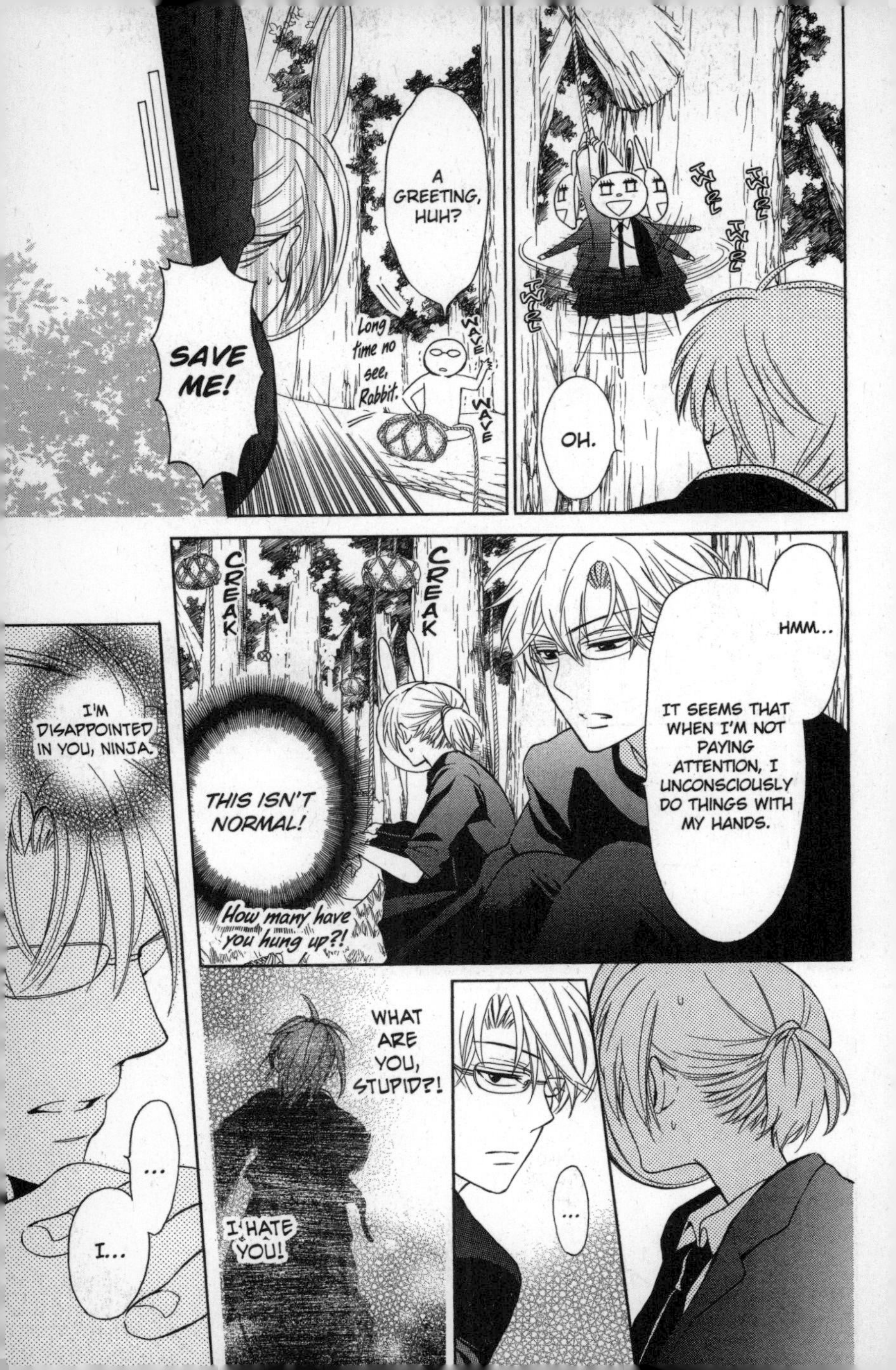
TWIRL
TWIRL
TWIRL
TWIRL
OH.
A GREETING, HUH?
Long time no see, Rabbit.
WAVE
WAVE
SAVE ME!
HMM...
IT SEEMS THAT WHEN I'M NOT PAYING ATTENTION, I UNCONSCIOUSLY DO THINGS WITH MY HANDS.
CREAK
CREAK
THIS ISN'T NORMAL!
How many have you hung up?!
...
WHAT ARE YOU, STUPID?!
I HATE YOU!
I'M DISAPPOINTED IN YOU, NINJA.
...
I...

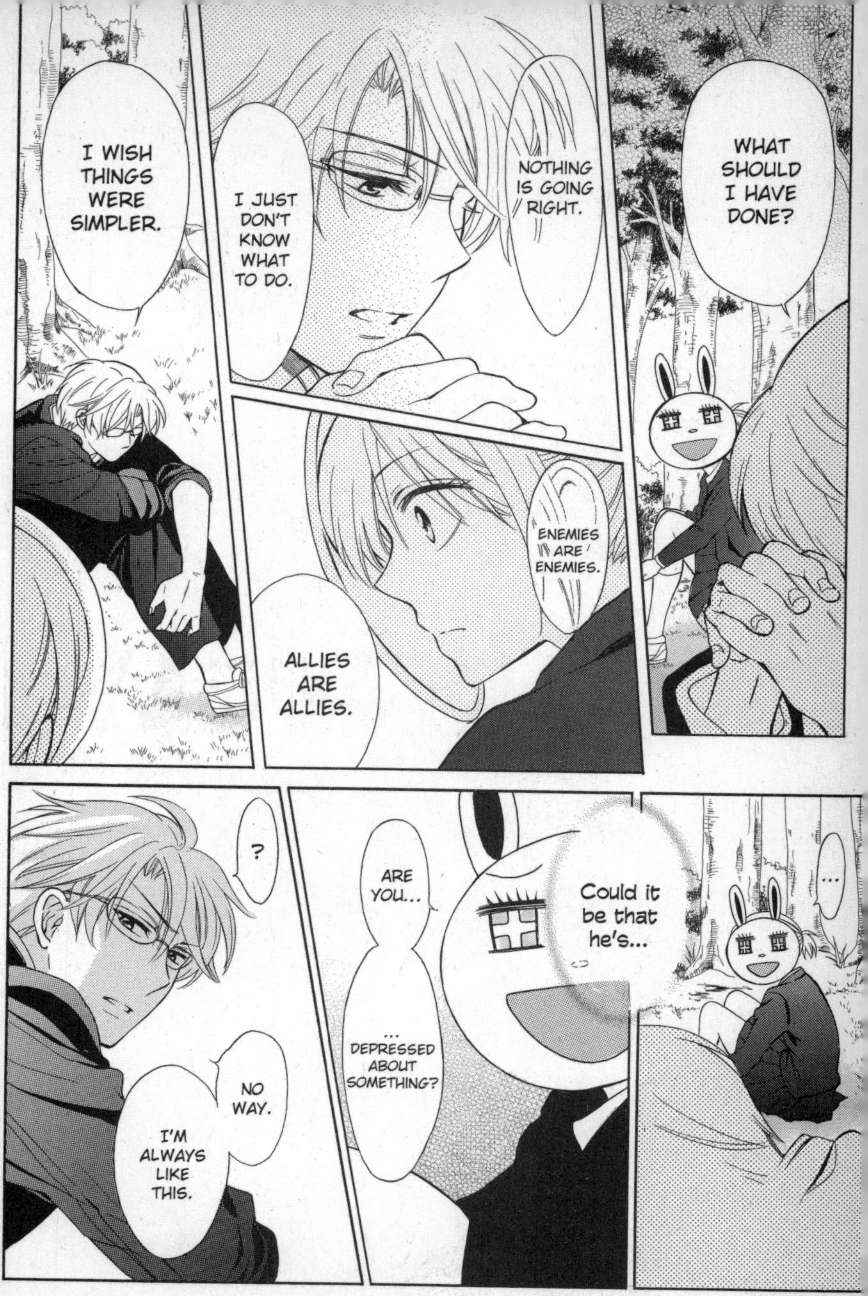
WHAT SHOULD I HAVE DONE?
NOTHING IS GOING RIGHT.
I JUST DON'T KNOW WHAT TO DO.
ENEMIES ARE ENEMIES.
ALLIES ARE ALLIES.
I WISH THINGS WERE SIMPLER.
...
Could it be that he's...
ARE YOU...
... DEPRESSED ABOUT SOMETHING?
?
NO WAY.
I'M ALWAYS LIKE THIS.

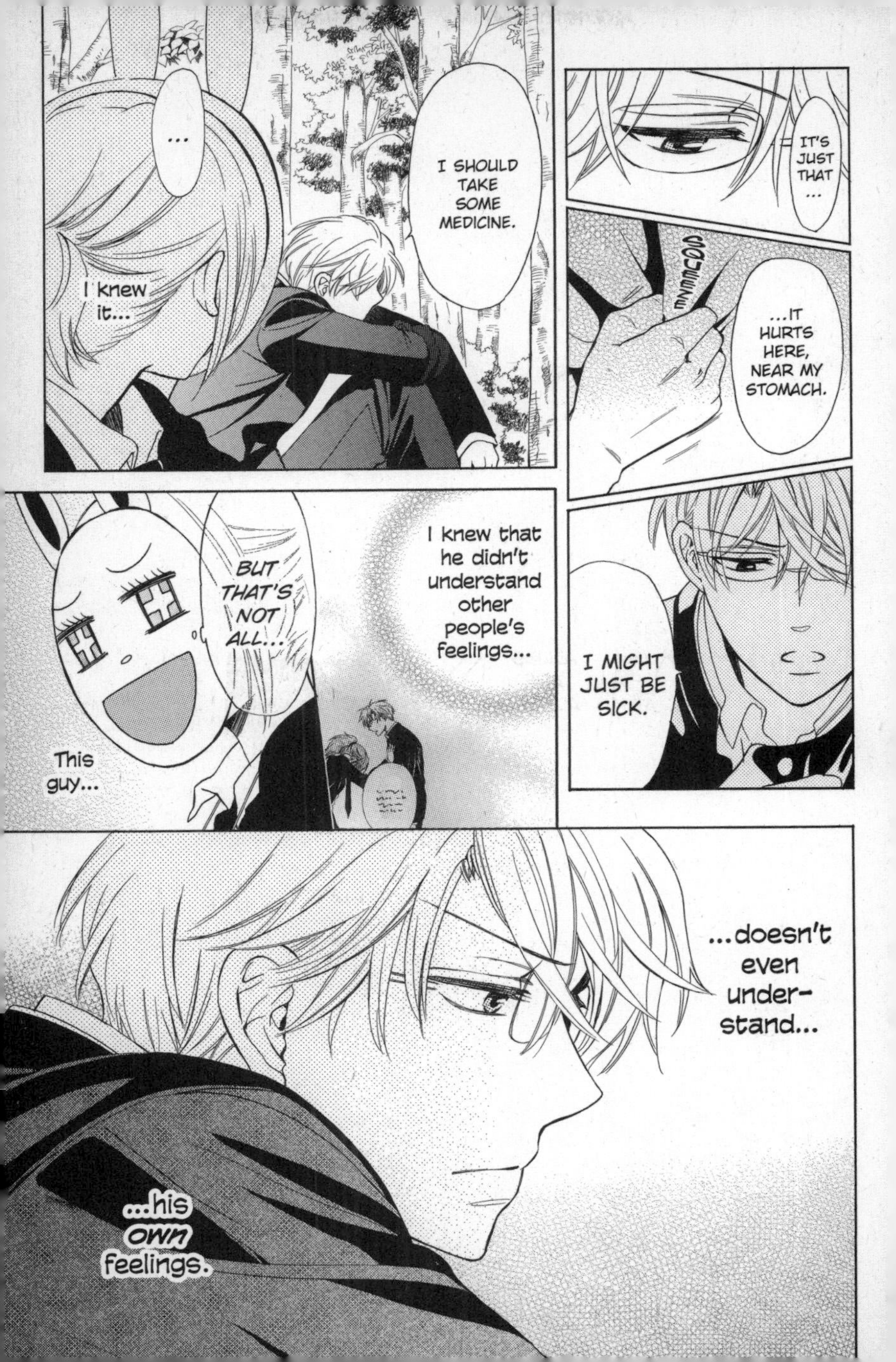
IT'S JUST THAT ...
SQUEEZE
...IT HURTS HERE, NEAR MY STOMACH.
I MIGHT JUST BE SICK.
I SHOULD TAKE SOME MEDICINE.
...
I knew it...
I knew that he didn't understand other people's feelings...
BUT THAT'S NOT ALL...
This guy...
...doesn't even under-stand...
...his own feelings.

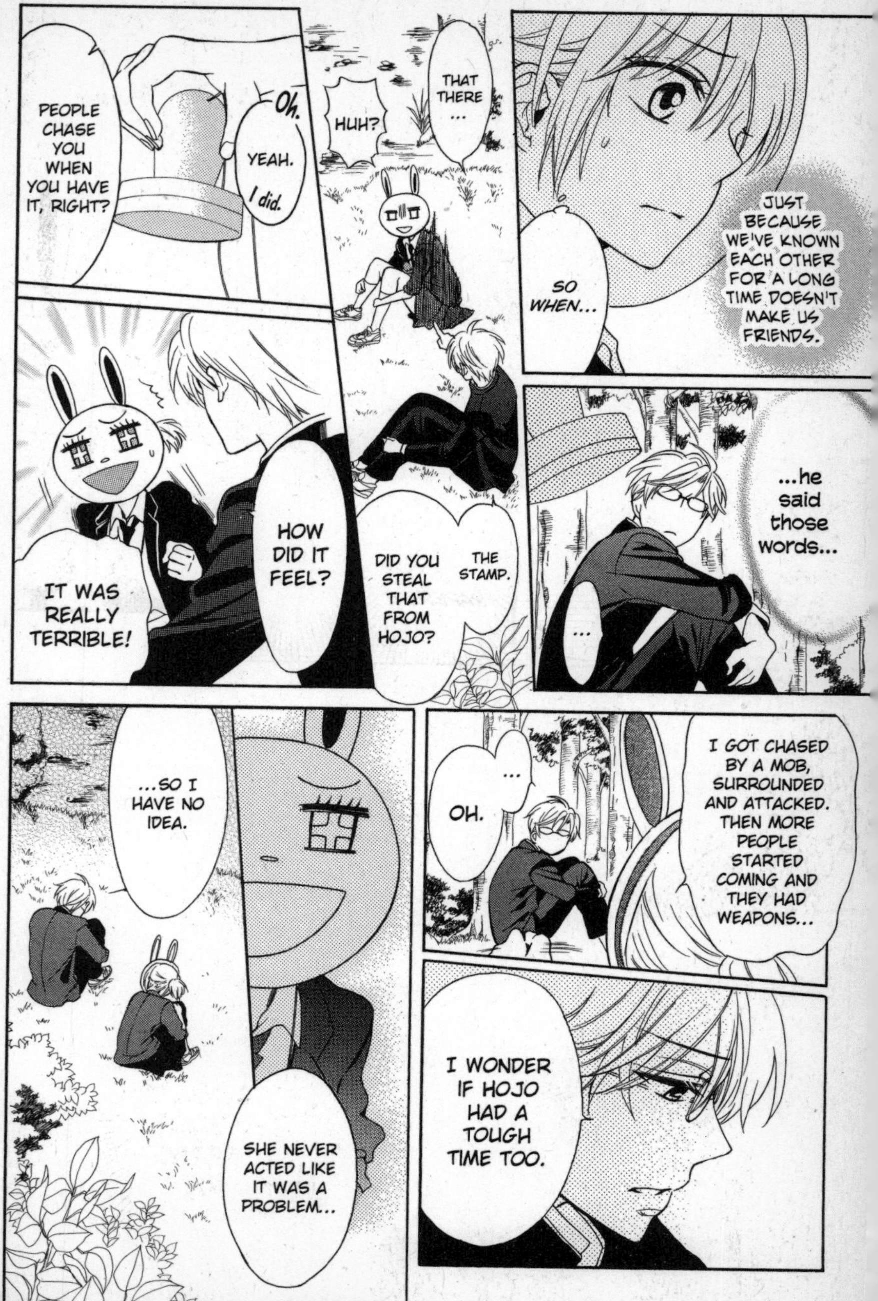
JUST BECAUSE WE'VE KNOWN EACH OTHER FOR A LONG TIME DOESN'T MAKE US FRIENDS.
SO WHEN...
...he said those words...
...
THAT THERE ...
HUH?
THE STAMP.
DID YOU STEAL THAT FROM HOJO?
Oh.
YEAH.
I did.
PEOPLE CHASE YOU WHEN YOU HAVE IT, RIGHT?
HOW DID IT FEEL?
IT WAS REALLY TERRIBLE!
I GOT CHASED BY A MOB, SURROUNDED AND ATTACKED. THEN MORE PEOPLE STARTED COMING AND THEY HAD WEAPONS...
...
OH.
I WONDER IF HOJO HAD A TOUGH TIME TOO.
...SO I HAVE NO IDEA.
SHE NEVER ACTED LIKE IT WAS A PROBLEM...

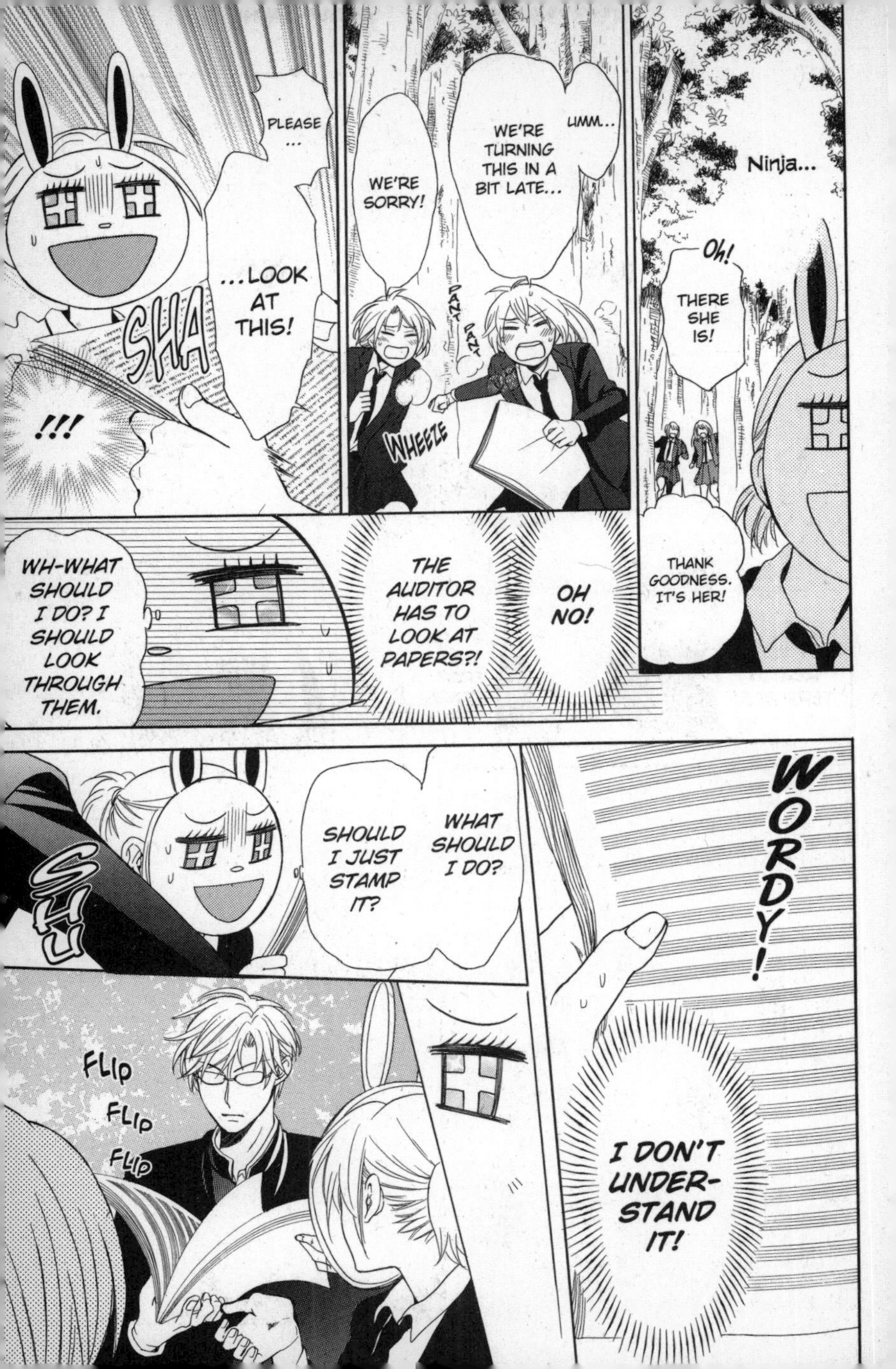
Ninja...
Oh!
THERE SHE IS!
THANK GOODNESS. IT'S HER!
UMM...
WE'RE TURNING THIS IN A BIT LATE...
WE'RE SORRY!
PANT PANT
WHEEZE
PLEASE...
...LOOK AT THIS!
SHA
!!!
OH NO!
THE AUDITOR HAS TO LOOK AT PAPERS?!
WH-WHAT SHOULD I DO? I SHOULD LOOK THROUGH THEM.
WORDY!
I DON'T UNDER-STAND IT!
WHAT SHOULD I DO?
SHOULD I JUST STAMP IT?
SHU
FLIP
FLIP
FLIP

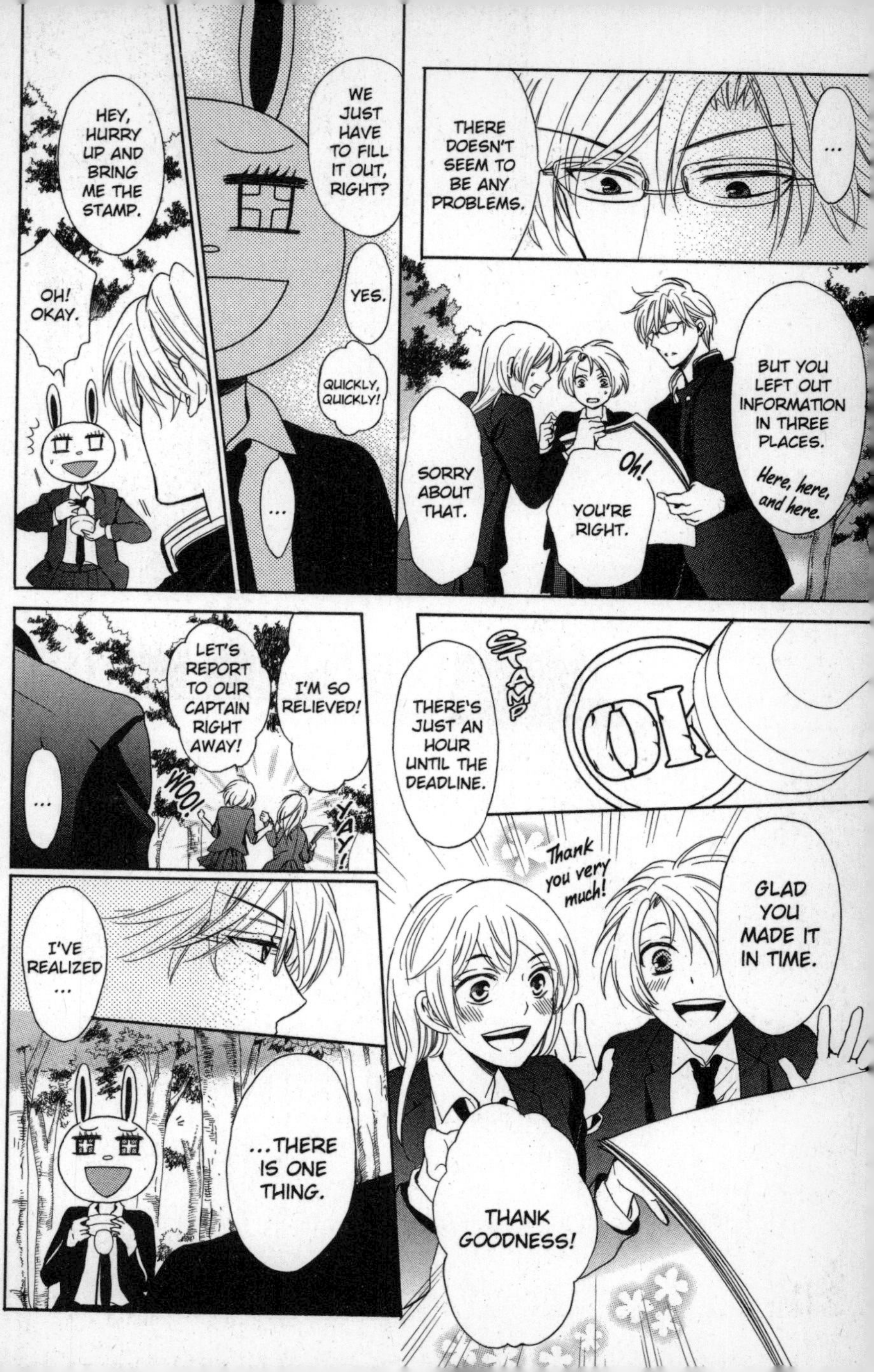
...
THERE DOESN'T SEEM TO BE ANY PROBLEMS.
BUT YOU LEFT OUT INFORMATION IN THREE PLACES.
Here, here, and here.
Oh!
YOU'RE RIGHT.
SORRY ABOUT THAT.
WE JUST HAVE TO FILL IT OUT, RIGHT?
YES.
QUICKLY, QUICKLY!
...
HEY, HURRY UP AND BRING ME THE STAMP.
OH! OKAY.
STAMP
OK
THERE'S JUST AN HOUR UNTIL THE DEADLINE.
I'M SO RELIEVED!
LET'S REPORT TO OUR CAPTAIN RIGHT AWAY!
YAY!
WOO!
...
GLAD YOU MADE IT IN TIME.
Thank you very much!
THANK GOODNESS!
I'VE REALIZED ...
...THERE IS ONE THING.

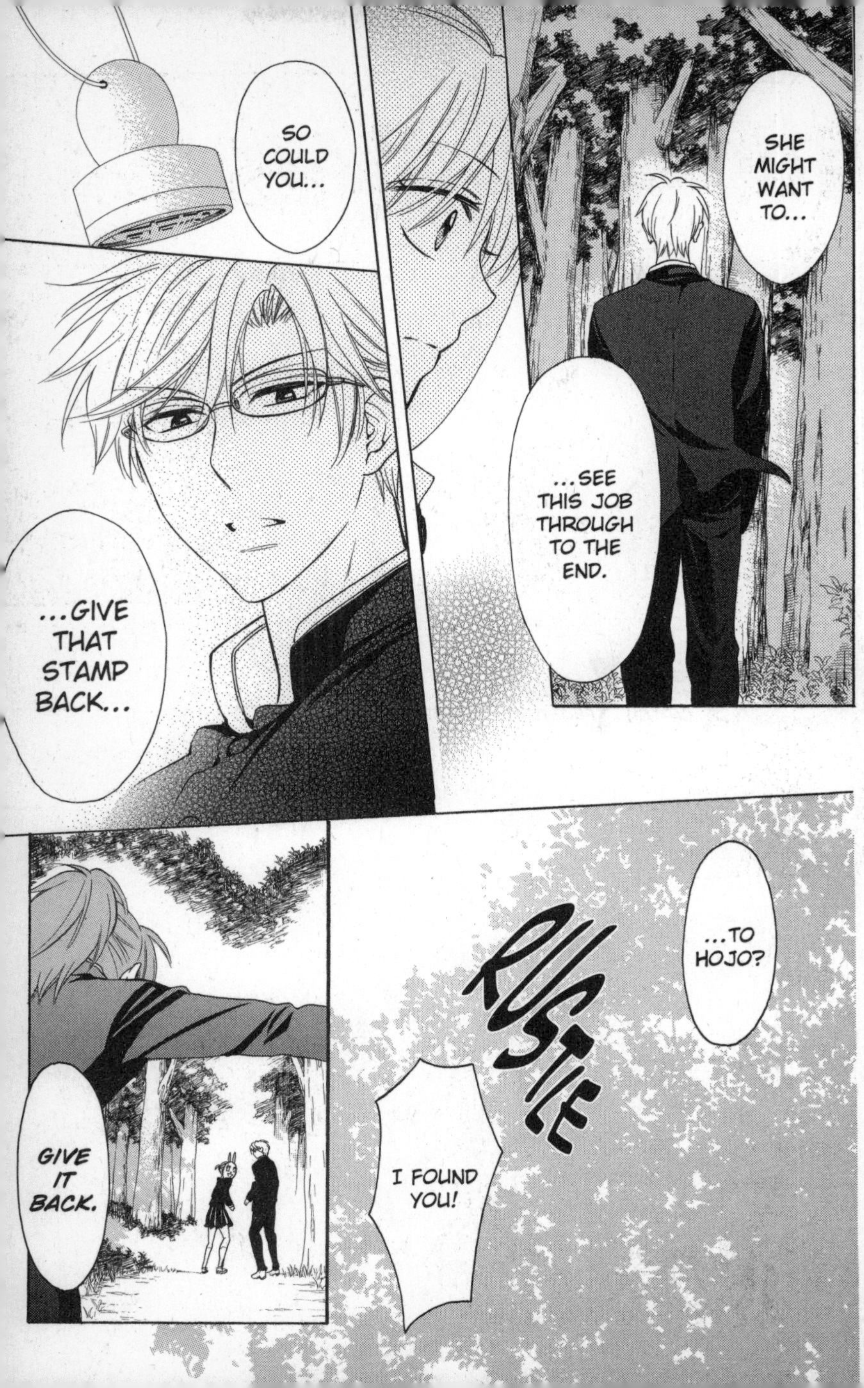
SHE MIGHT WANT TO...
...SEE THIS JOB THROUGH TO THE END.
SO COULD YOU...
...GIVE THAT STAMP BACK...
...TO HOJO?
RUSTLE
I FOUND YOU!
GIVE IT BACK.

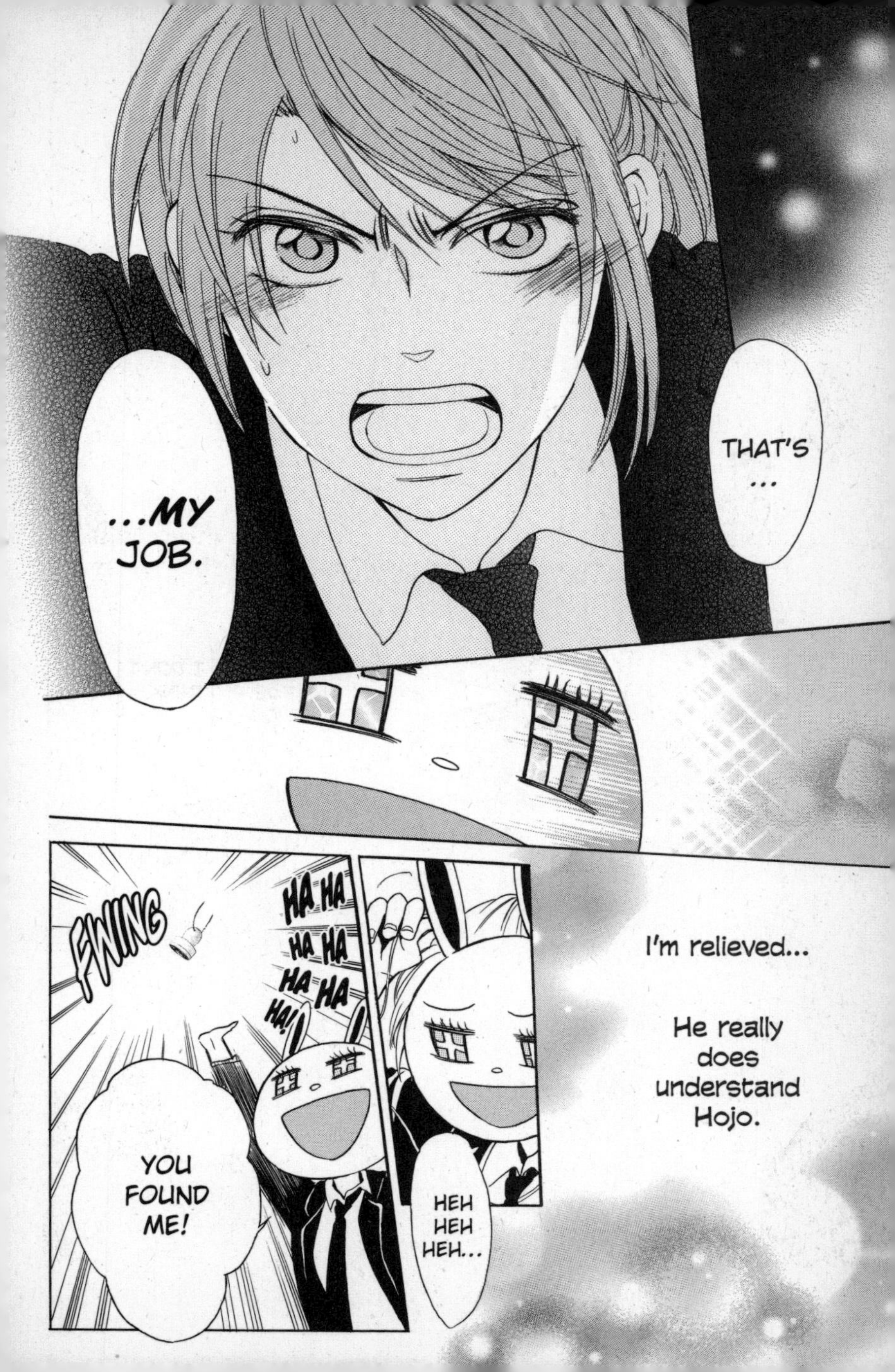
THAT'S ...
...MY JOB.
I'm relieved...
He really does understand Hojo.
HEH HEH HEH...
FWING
HA HA HA HA HA HA HA!
YOU FOUND ME!

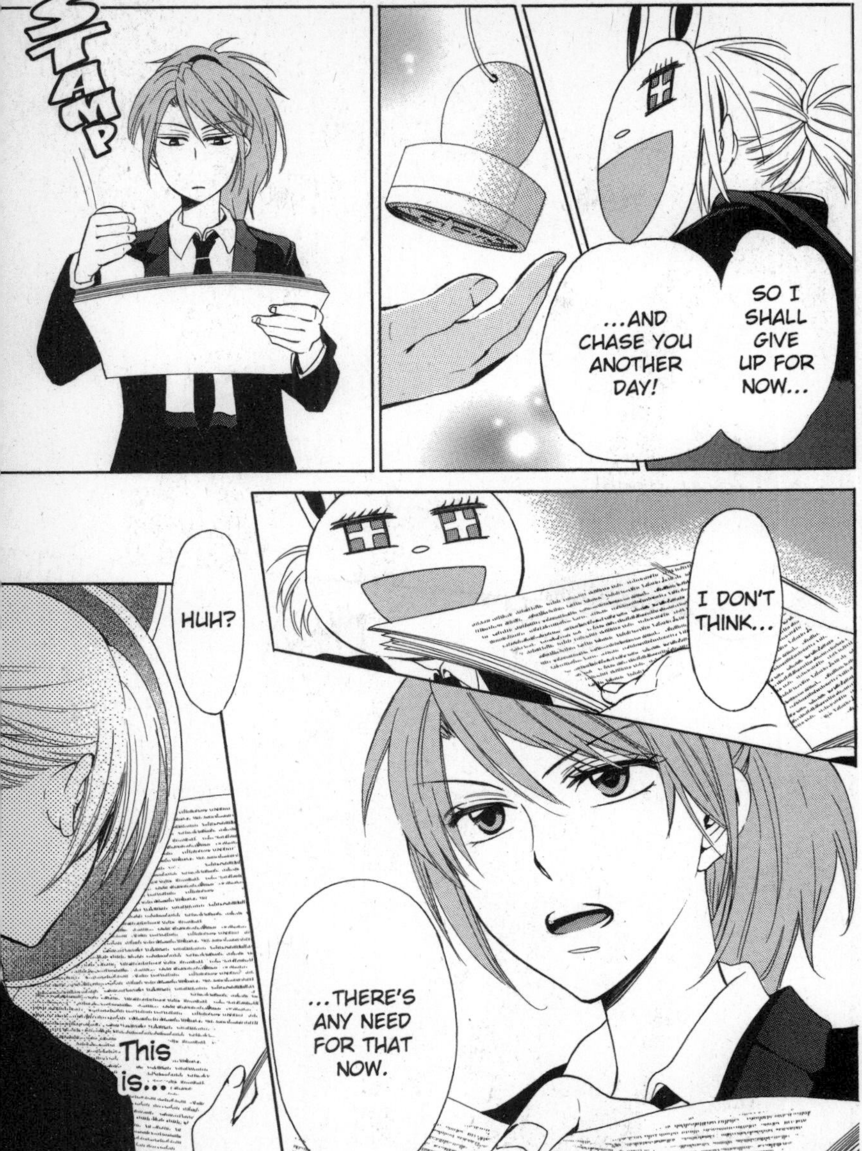
SO I SHALL GIVE UP FOR NOW...
...AND CHASE YOU ANOTHER DAY!
STAMP
I DON'T THINK...
...THERE'S ANY NEED FOR THAT NOW.
HUH?
This is...

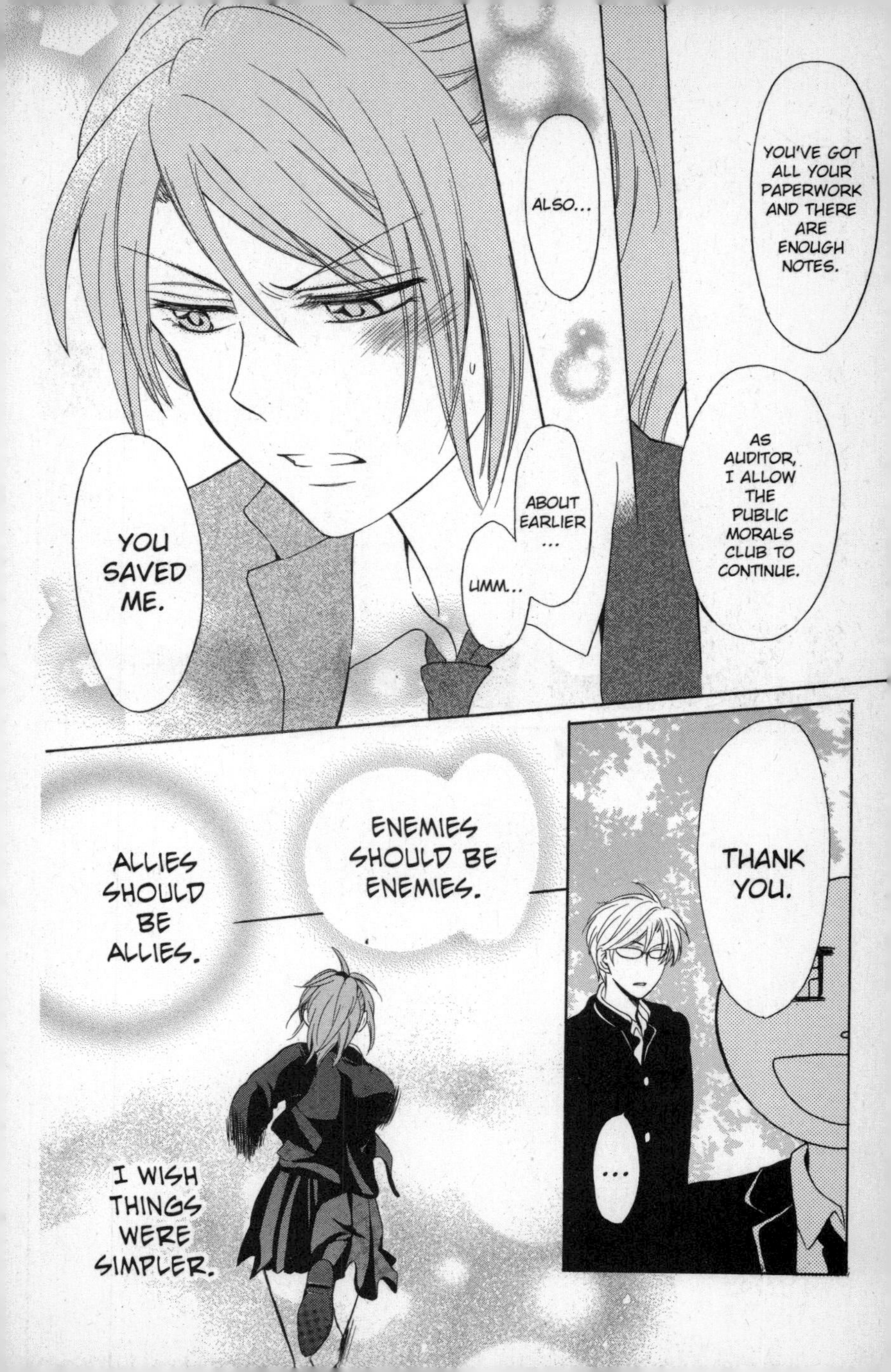
YOU'VE GOT ALL YOUR PAPERWORK AND THERE ARE ENOUGH NOTES.
AS AUDITOR, I ALLOW THE PUBLIC MORALS CLUB TO CONTINUE.
ALSO...
ABOUT EARLIER...
UMM...
YOU SAVED ME.
THANK YOU.
...
ENEMIES SHOULD BE ENEMIES.
ALLIES SHOULD BE ALLIES.
I WISH THINGS WERE SIMPLER.

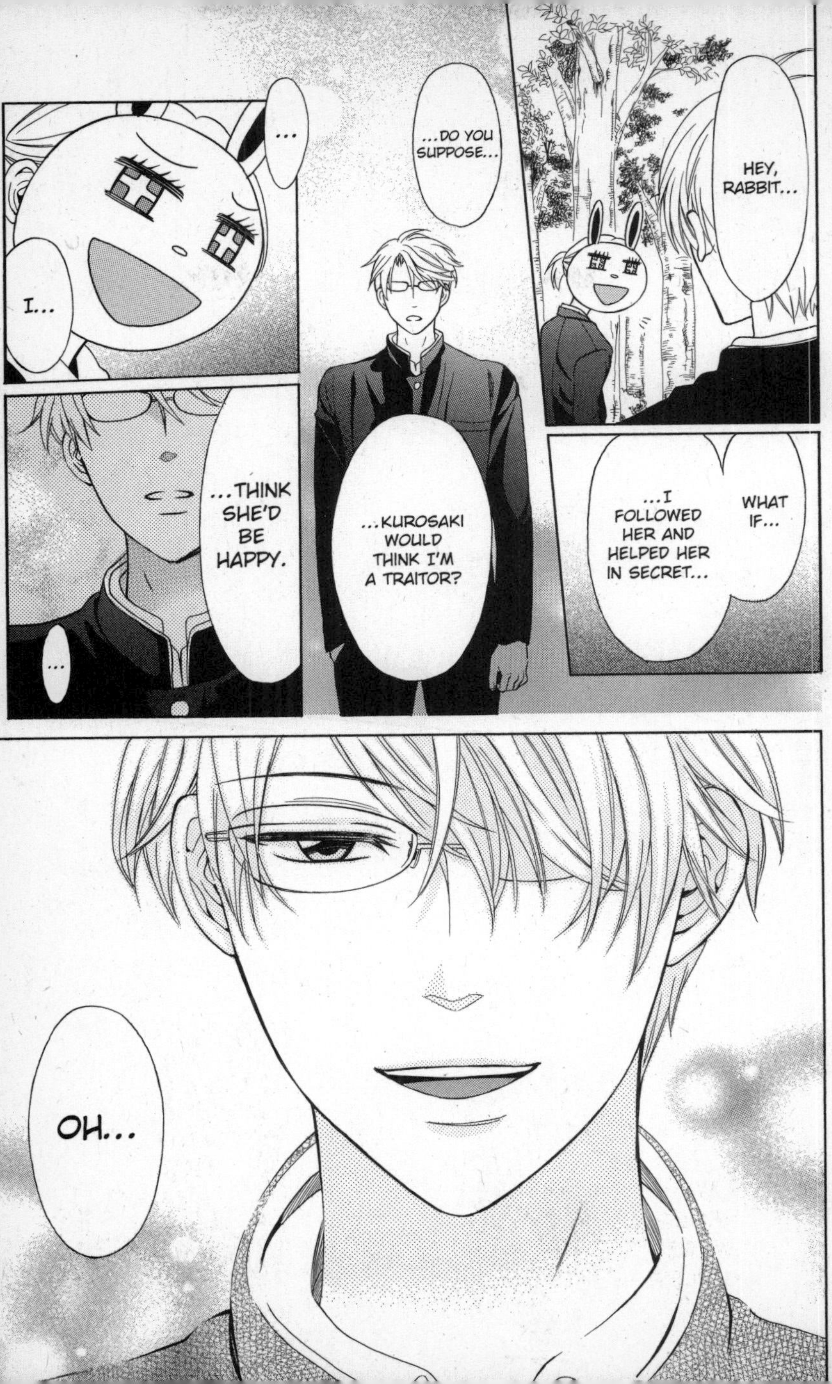
HEY, RABBIT...
WHAT IF...
...I FOLLOWED HER AND HELPED HER IN SECRET...
...DO YOU SUPPOSE...
...KUROSAKI WOULD THINK I'M A TRAITOR?
...
I...
...THINK SHE'D BE HAPPY.
...
OH...

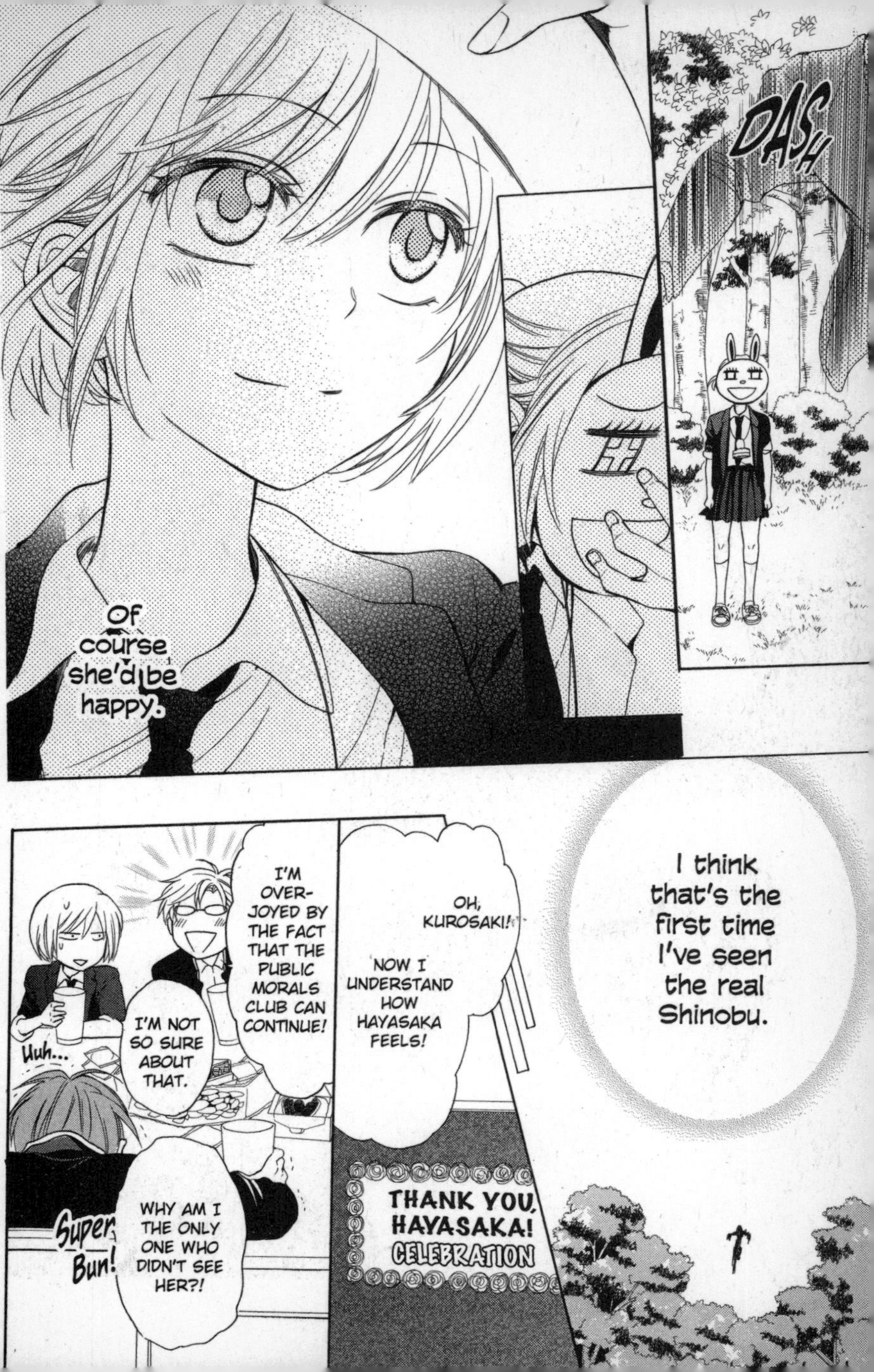
DASH
Of course she'd be happy.
I think that's the first time I've seen the real Shinobu.
OH, KUROSAKI! NOW I UNDERSTAND HOW HAYASAKA FEELS!
THANK YOU, HAYASAKA! CELEBRATION
I'M OVER-JOYED BY THE FACT THAT THE PUBLIC MORALS CLUB CAN CONTINUE!
I'M NOT SO SURE ABOUT THAT.
Uuh...
WHY AM I THE ONLY ONE WHO DIDN'T SEE HER?!
Super Bun!

Chapter 57

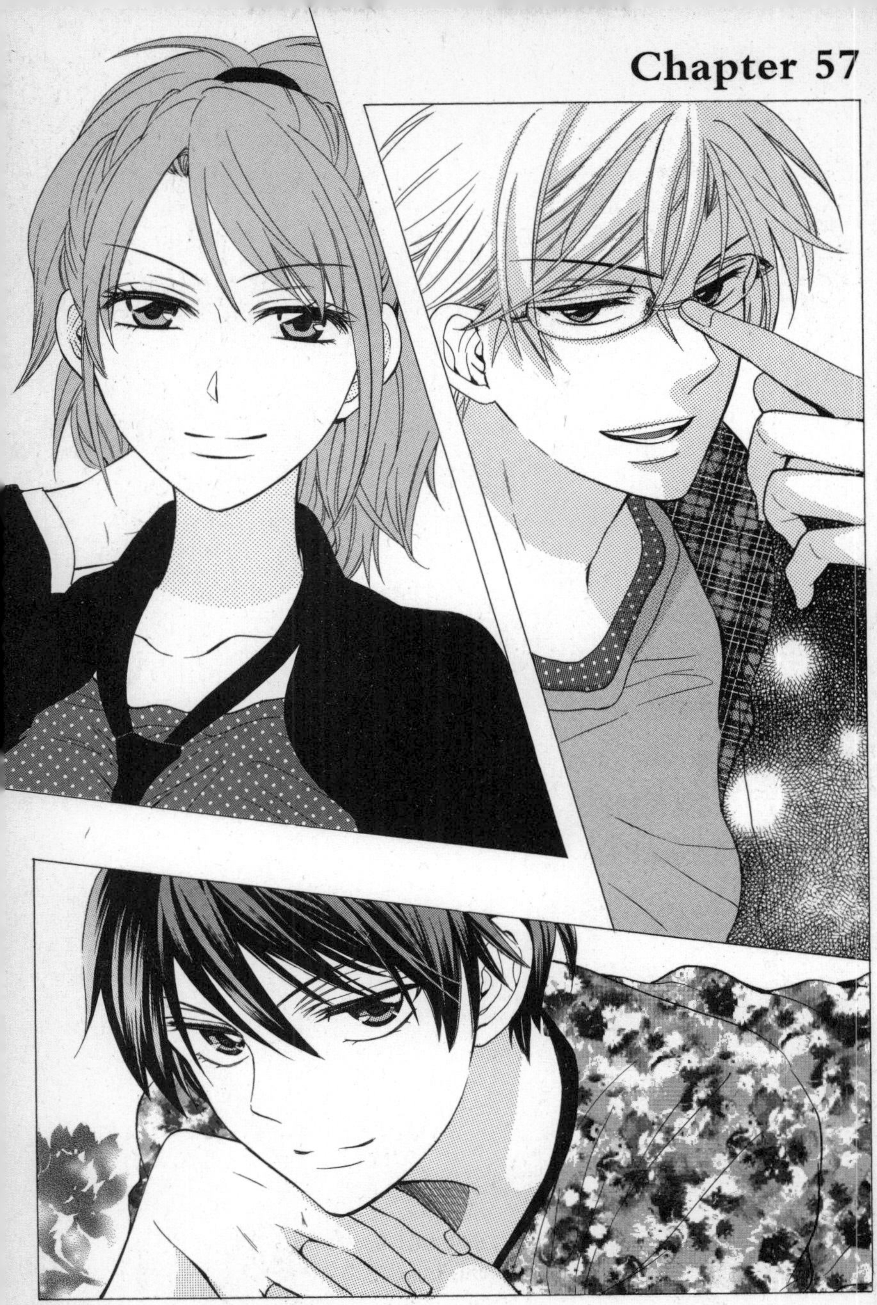

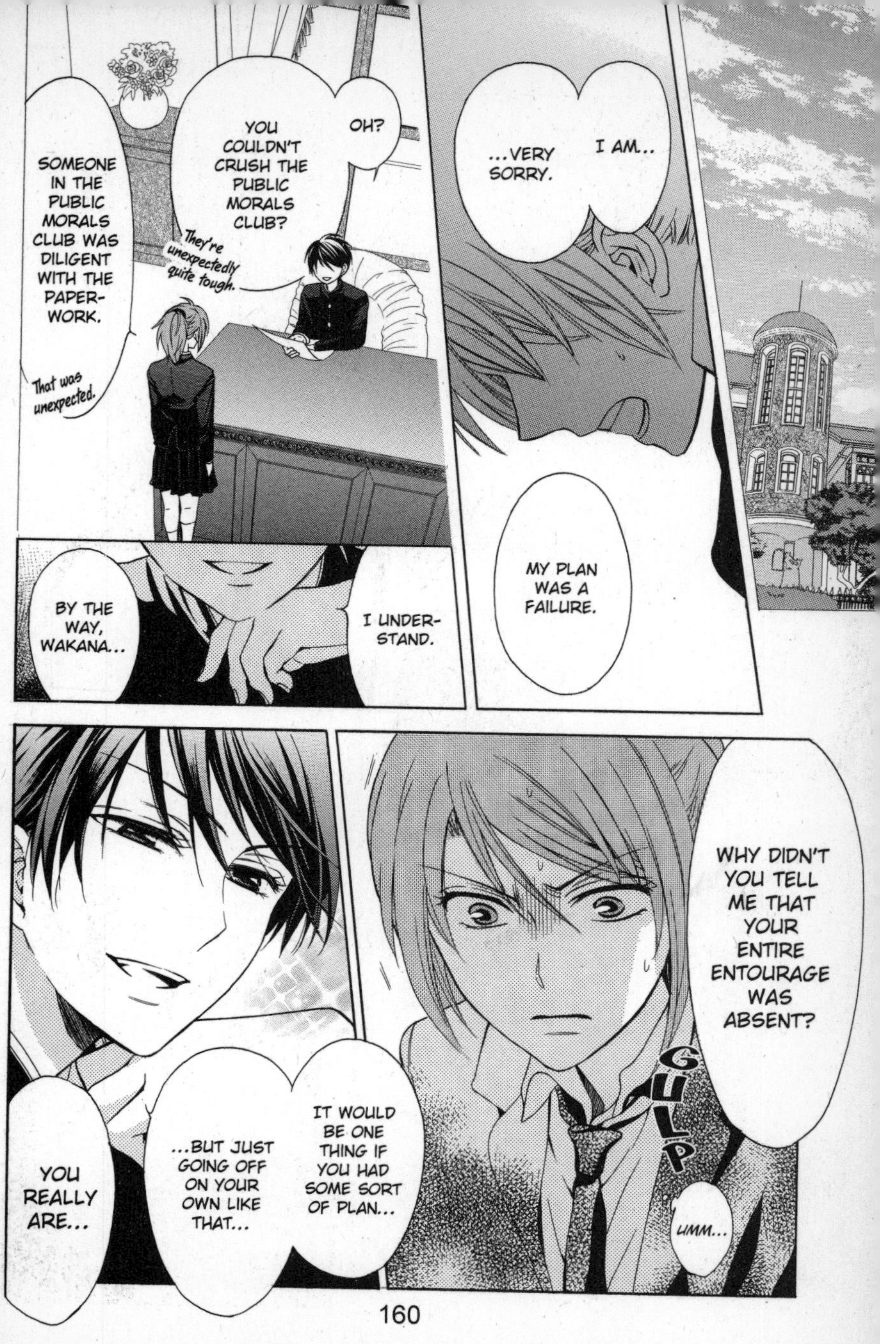
I AM...
...VERY SORRY.
MY PLAN WAS A FAILURE.
OH?
YOU COULDN'T CRUSH THE PUBLIC MORALS CLUB?
They're unexpectedly quite tough.
SOMEONE IN THE PUBLIC MORALS CLUB WAS DILIGENT WITH THE PAPER-WORK.
That was unexpected.
I UNDER-STAND.
BY THE WAY, WAKANA...
WHY DIDN'T YOU TELL ME THAT YOUR ENTIRE ENTOURAGE WAS ABSENT?
GULP
UMM...
IT WOULD BE ONE THING IF YOU HAD SOME SORT OF PLAN...
...BUT JUST GOING OFF ON YOUR OWN LIKE THAT...
YOU REALLY ARE...

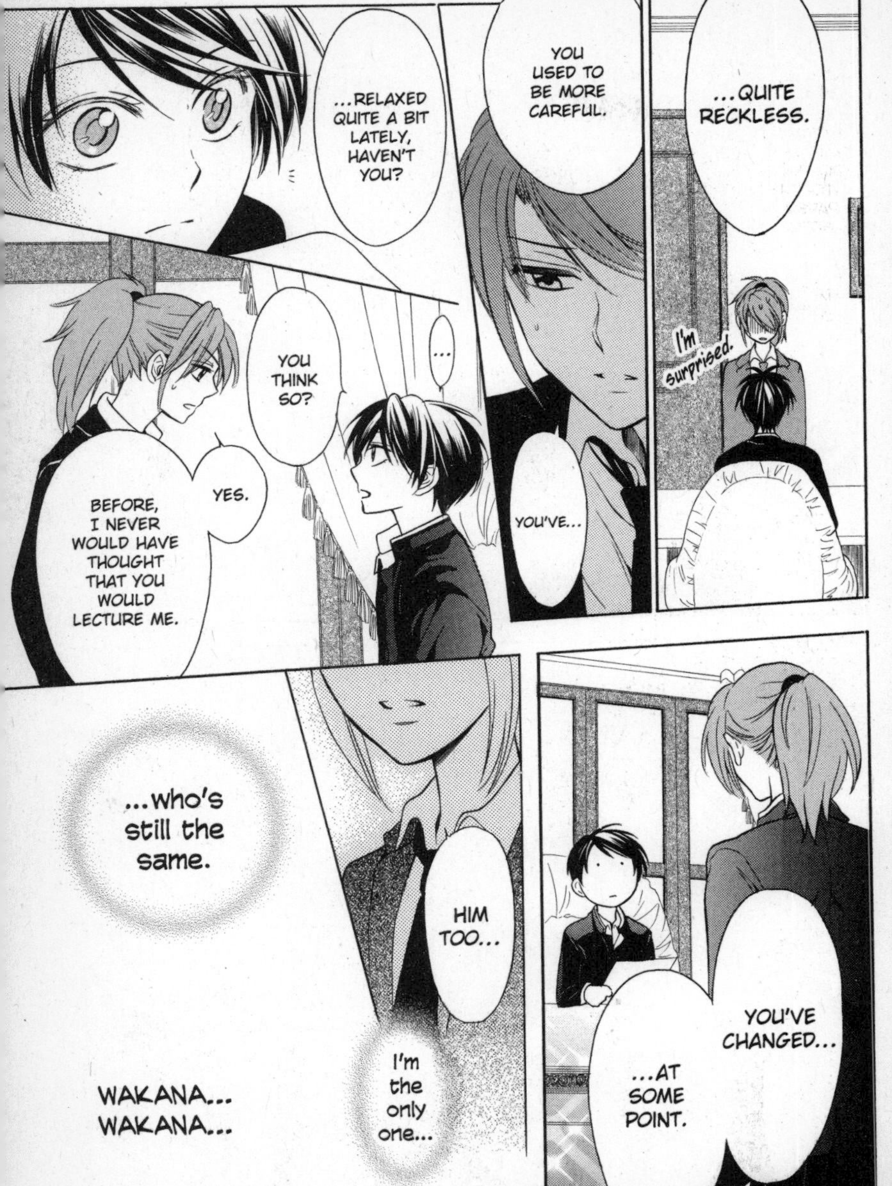
...QUITE RECKLESS.
I'm surprised.
YOU USED TO BE MORE CAREFUL.
YOU'VE...
...RELAXED QUITE A BIT LATELY, HAVEN'T YOU?
...
YOU THINK SO?
YES.
BEFORE, I NEVER WOULD HAVE THOUGHT THAT YOU WOULD LECTURE ME.
YOU'VE CHANGED...
...AT SOME POINT.
HIM TOO...
I'm the only one...
...who's still the same.
WAKANA... WAKANA...

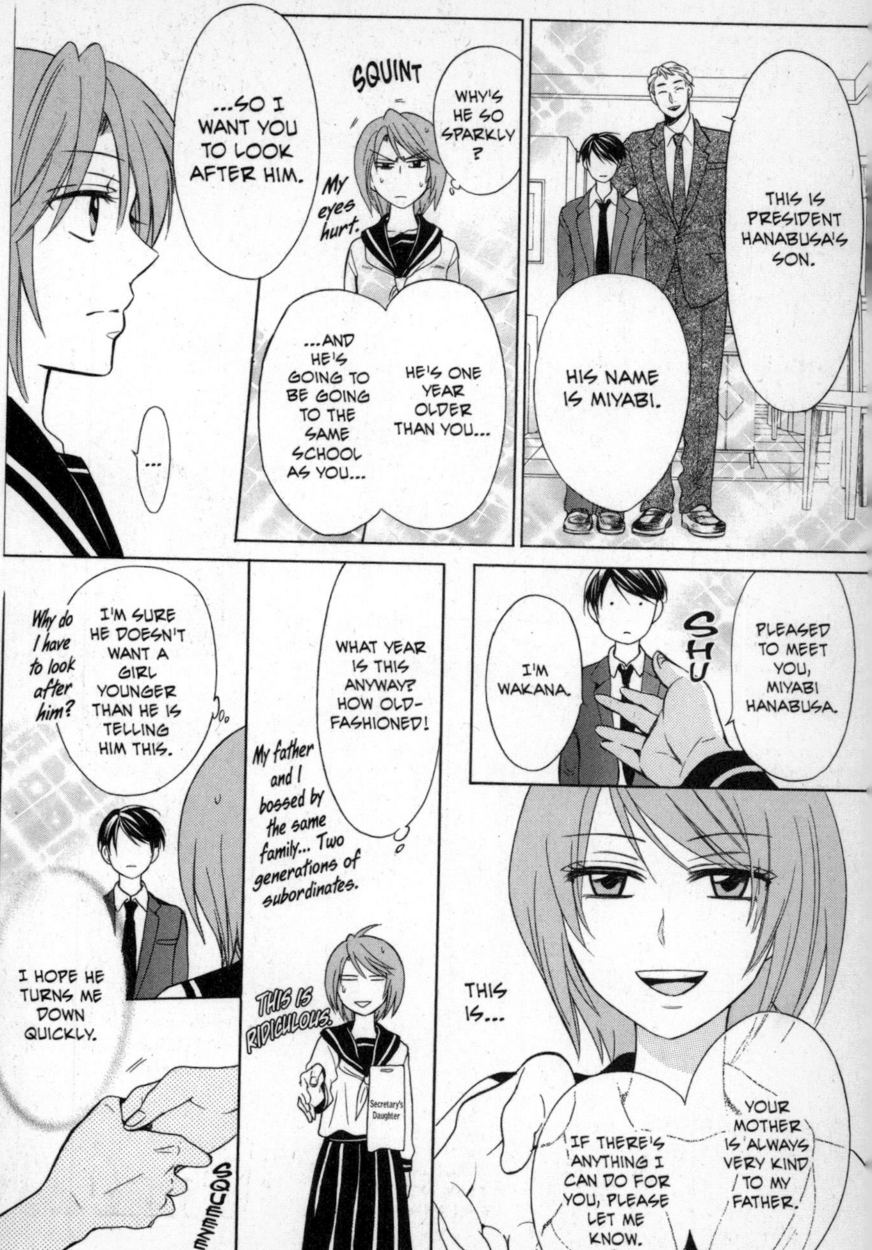
THIS IS PRESIDENT HANABUSA'S SON.
HIS NAME IS MIYABI.
SQUINT
WHY'S HE SO SPARKLY?
My eyes hurt.
HE'S ONE YEAR OLDER THAN YOU...
...AND HE'S GOING TO BE GOING TO THE SAME SCHOOL AS YOU...
...SO I WANT YOU TO LOOK AFTER HIM.
...
PLEASED TO MEET YOU, MIYABI HANABUSA.
SHU
I'M WAKANA.
THIS IS...
YOUR MOTHER IS ALWAYS VERY KIND TO MY FATHER.
IF THERE'S ANYTHING I CAN DO FOR YOU, PLEASE LET ME KNOW.
WHAT YEAR IS THIS ANYWAY? HOW OLD-FASHIONED!
My father and I bossed by the same family... Two generations of subordinates.
THIS IS RIDICULOUS.
Secretary's Daughter
I'M SURE HE DOESN'T WANT A GIRL YOUNGER THAN HE IS TELLING HIM THIS.
Why do I have to look after him?
I HOPE HE TURNS ME DOWN QUICKLY.
SQUEEEEE

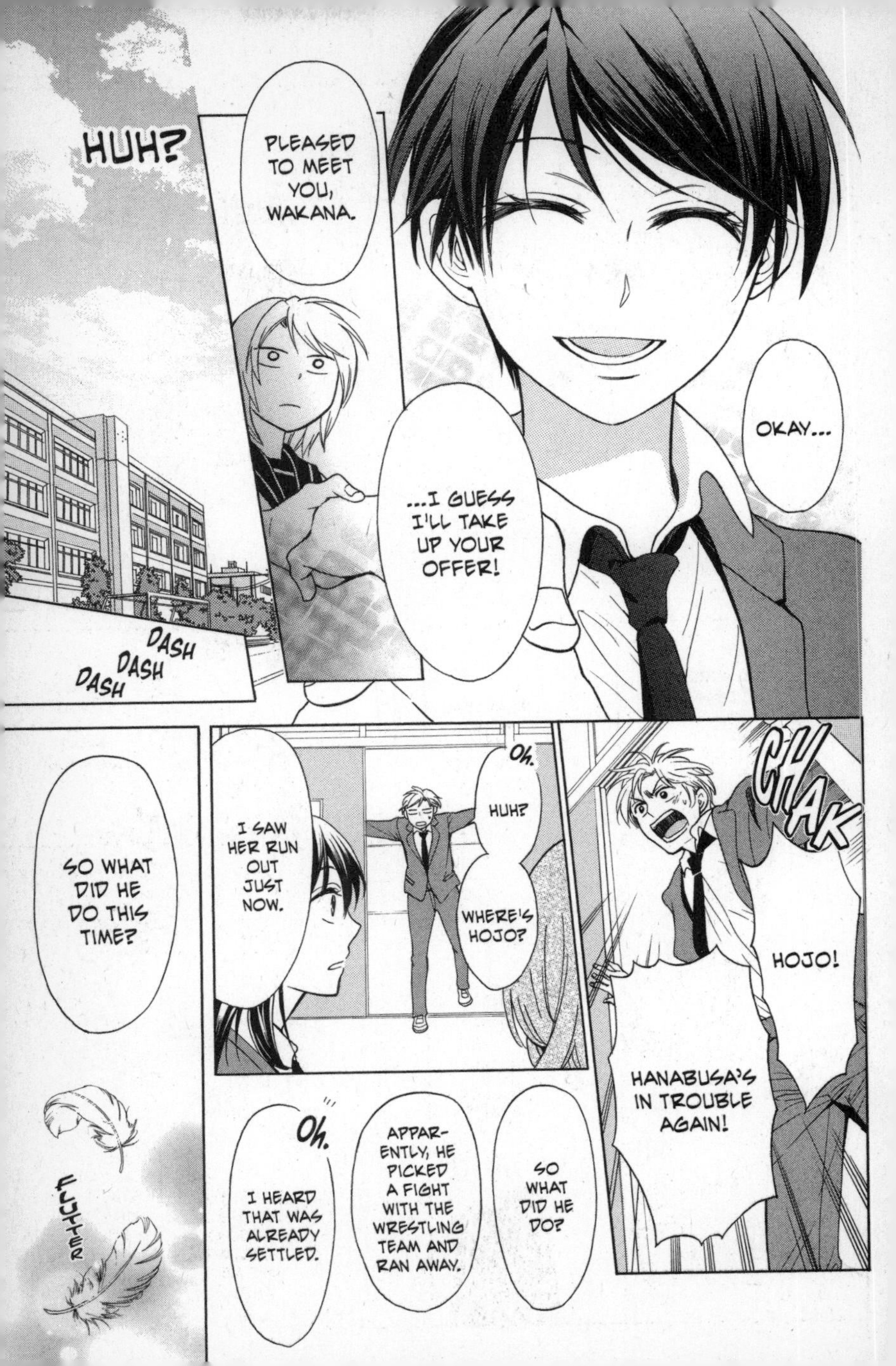
OKAY...
...I GUESS I'LL TAKE UP YOUR OFFER!
PLEASED TO MEET YOU, WAKANA.
HUH?
DASH DASH DASH
CHAK
HOJO!
HANABUSA'S IN TROUBLE AGAIN!
Oh.
HUH?
WHERE'S HOJO?
I SAW HER RUN OUT JUST NOW.
SO WHAT DID HE DO THIS TIME?
SO WHAT DID HE DO?
APPAR-ENTLY, HE PICKED A FIGHT WITH THE WRESTLING TEAM AND RAN AWAY.
Oh.
I HEARD THAT WAS ALREADY SETTLED.
FLUTTER

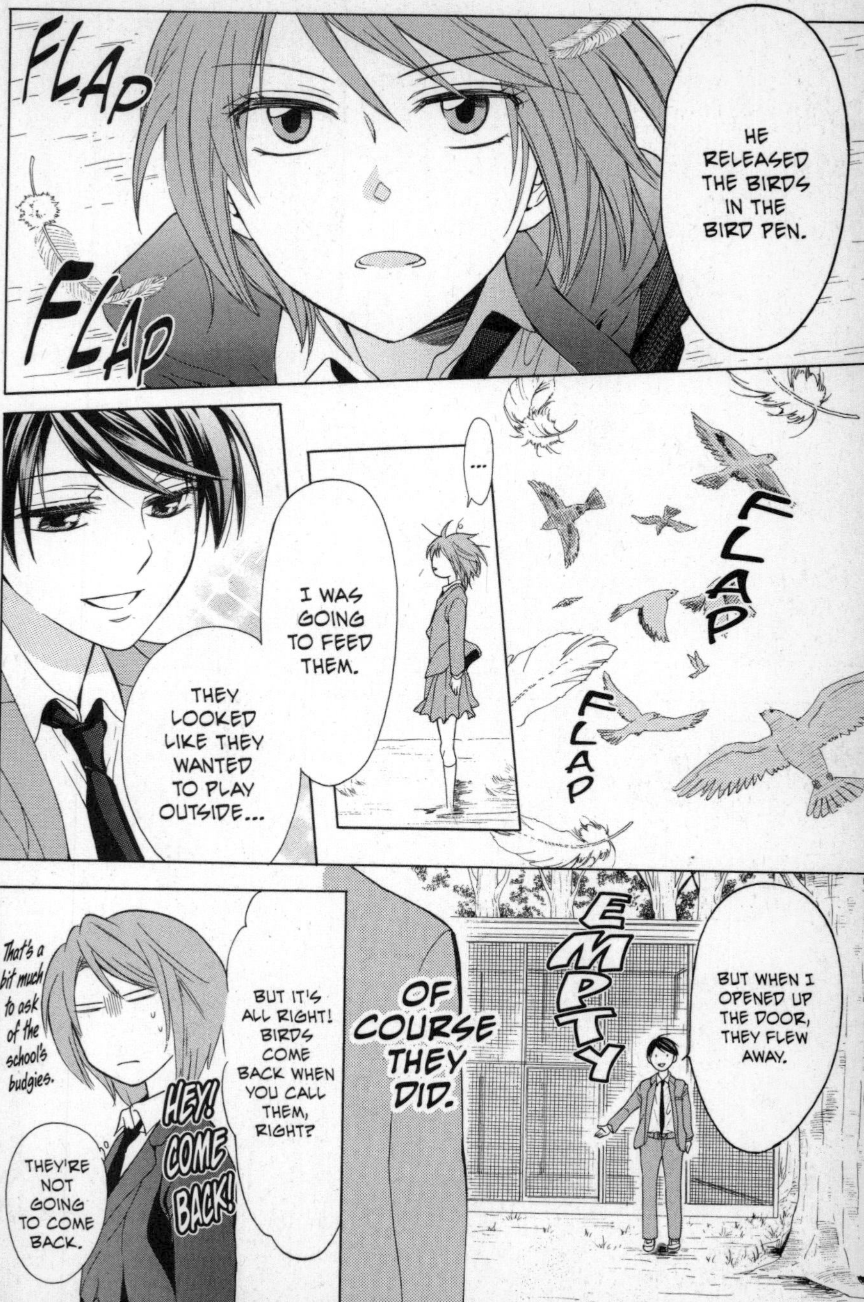
HE RELEASED THE BIRDS IN THE BIRD PEN.
FLAP
FLAP
FLAP
FLAP
...
I WAS GOING TO FEED THEM.
THEY LOOKED LIKE THEY WANTED TO PLAY OUTSIDE...
BUT WHEN I OPENED UP THE DOOR, THEY FLEW AWAY.
EMPTY
OF COURSE THEY DID.
BUT IT'S ALL RIGHT! BIRDS COME BACK WHEN YOU CALL THEM, RIGHT?
HEY! COME BACK!
That's a bit much to ask of the school's budgies.
THEY'RE NOT GOING TO COME BACK.

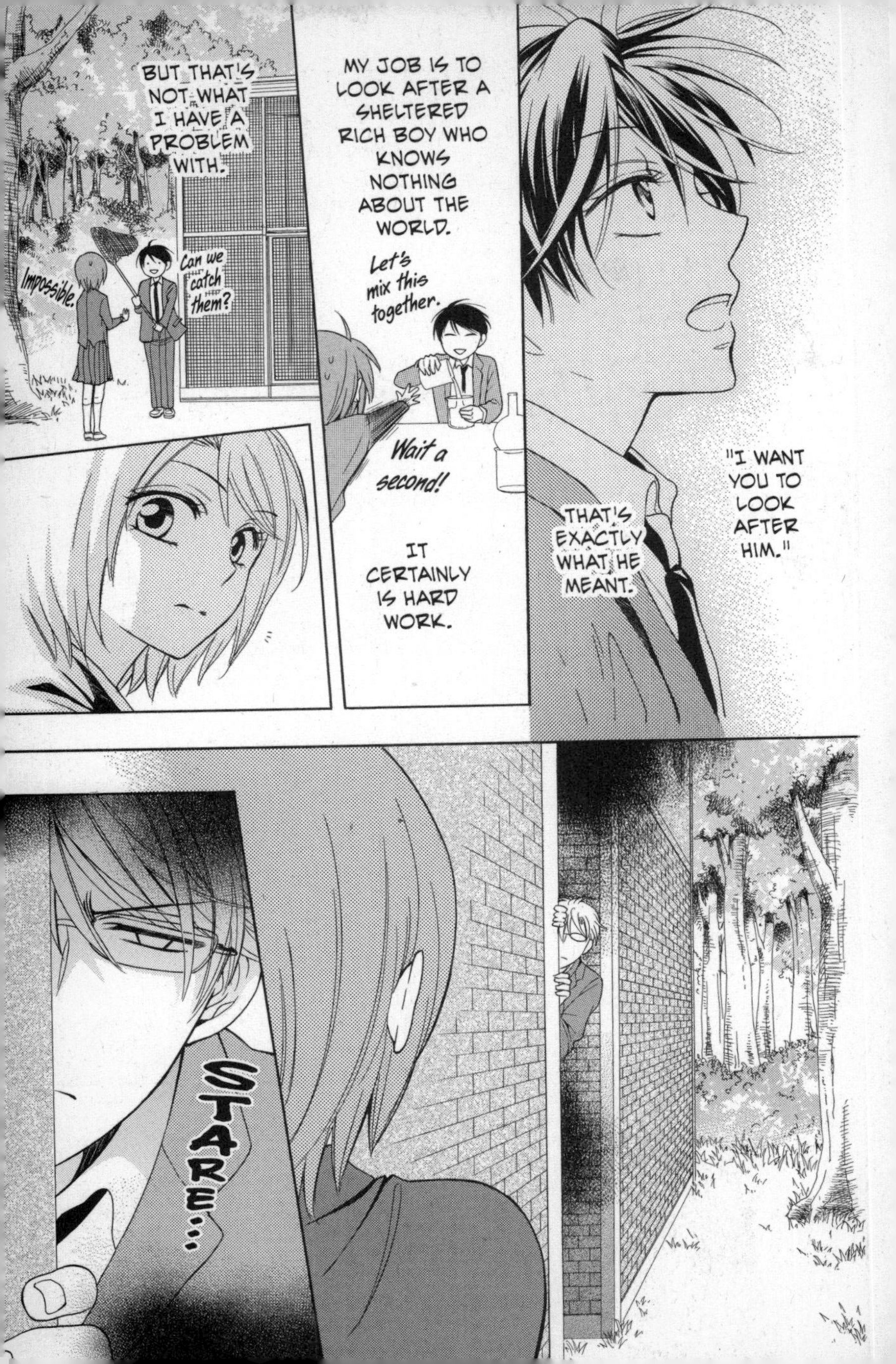
"I WANT YOU TO LOOK AFTER HIM."
THAT'S EXACTLY WHAT HE MEANT.
MY JOB IS TO LOOK AFTER A SHELTERED RICH BOY WHO KNOWS NOTHING ABOUT THE WORLD.
Let's mix this together.
Wait a second!
IT CERTAINLY IS HARD WORK.
BUT THAT'S NOT WHAT I HAVE A PROBLEM WITH.
Can we catch them?
Impossible.
STARE...

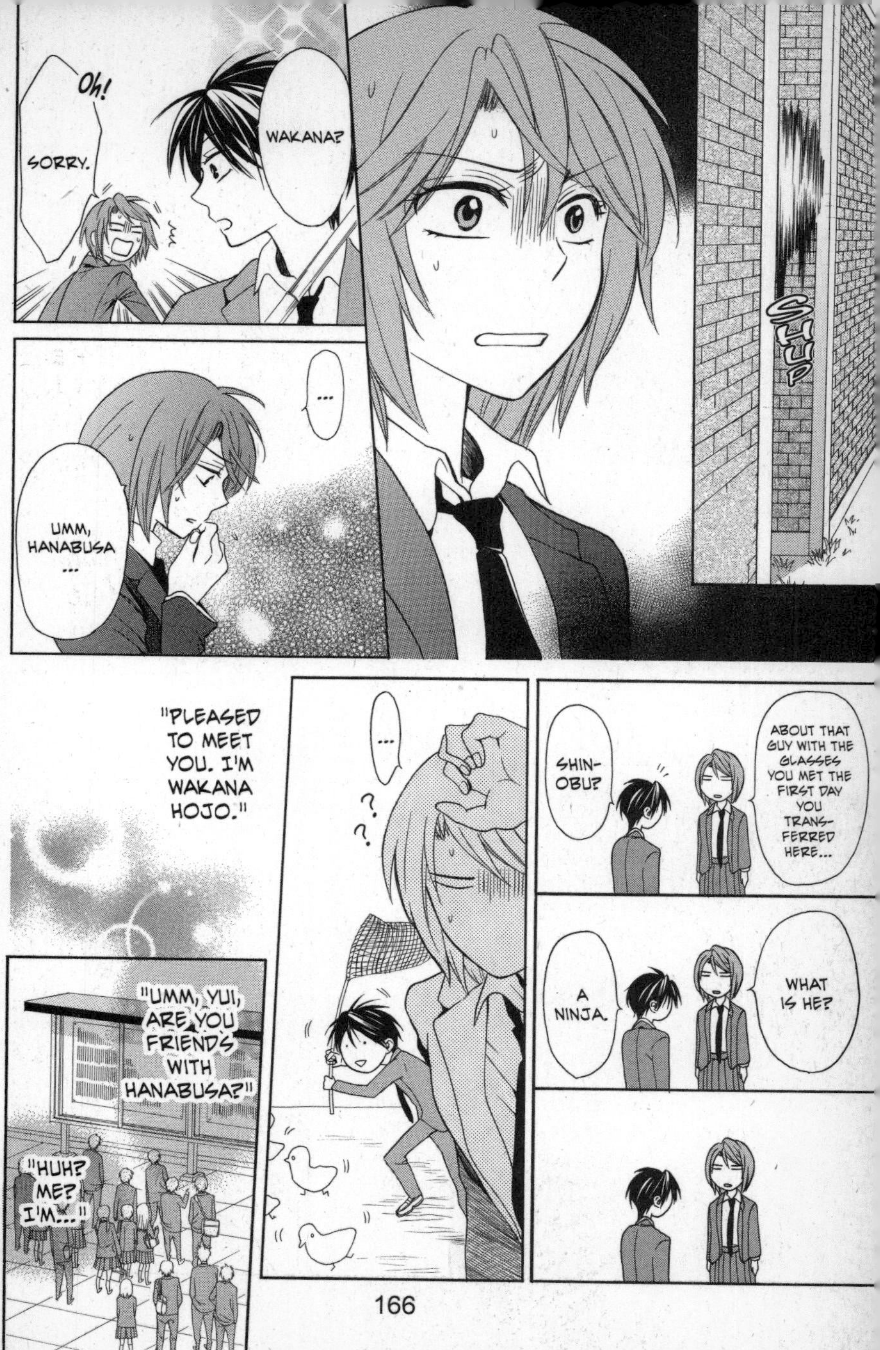
SHUP
WAKANA?
Oh!
SORRY.
...
UMM, HANABUSA ...
ABOUT THAT GUY WITH THE GLASSES YOU MET THE FIRST DAY YOU TRANS-FERRED HERE...
SHIN-OBU?
WHAT IS HE?
A NINJA.
...
"PLEASED TO MEET YOU. I'M WAKANA HOJO."
"UMM, YUI, ARE YOU FRIENDS WITH HANABUSA?"
"HUH? ME? I'M..."

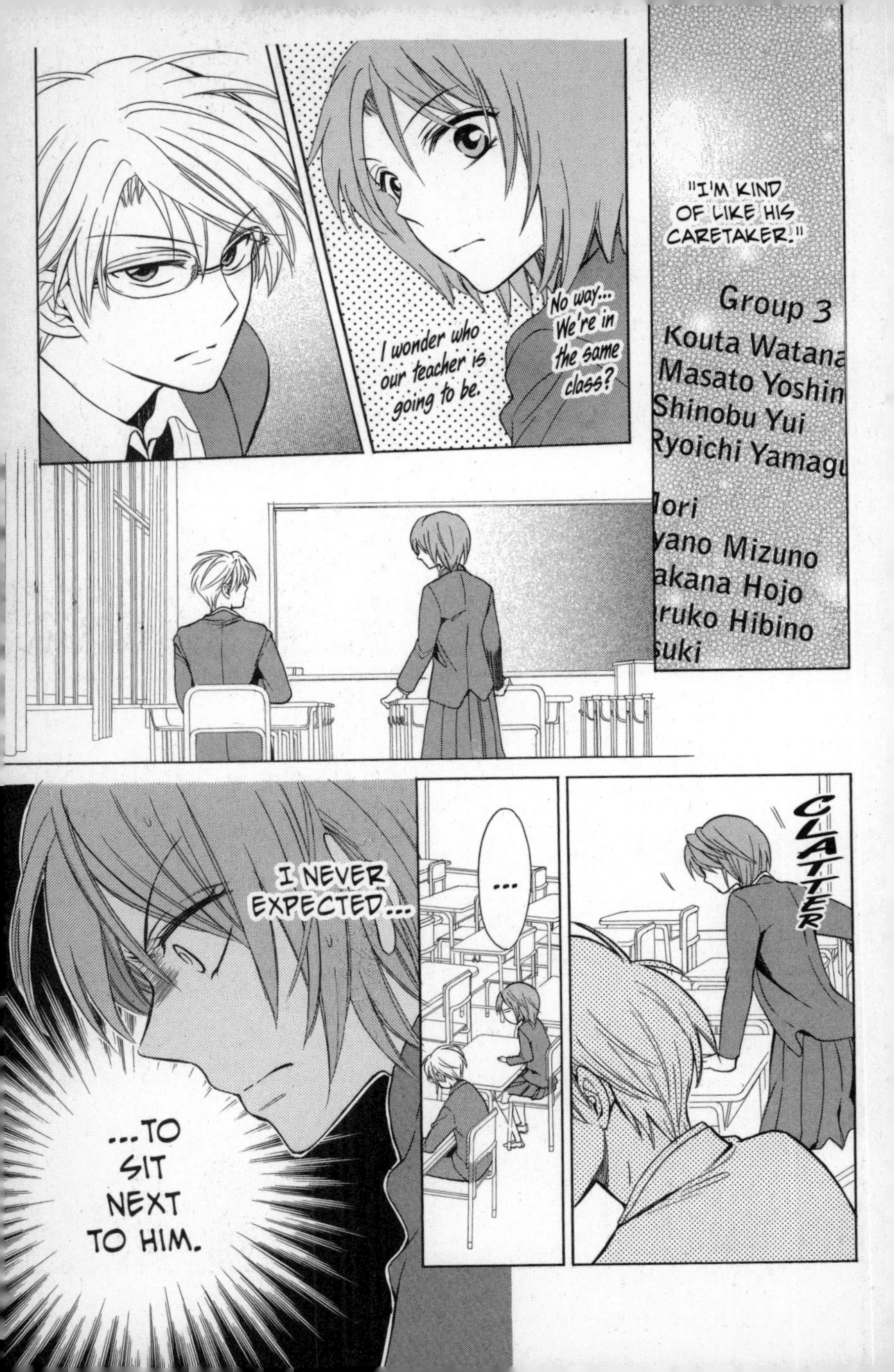

"I'M KIND OF LIKE HIS CARETAKER."
Group 3
Kouta Watana
Masato Yoshin
Shinobu Yui
Ryoichi Yamagu
lori
yano Mizuno
akana Hojo
aruko Hibino
suki
No way... We're in the same class?
I wonder who our teacher is going to be.
CLATTER
...
I NEVER EXPECTED...
...TO SIT NEXT TO HIM.

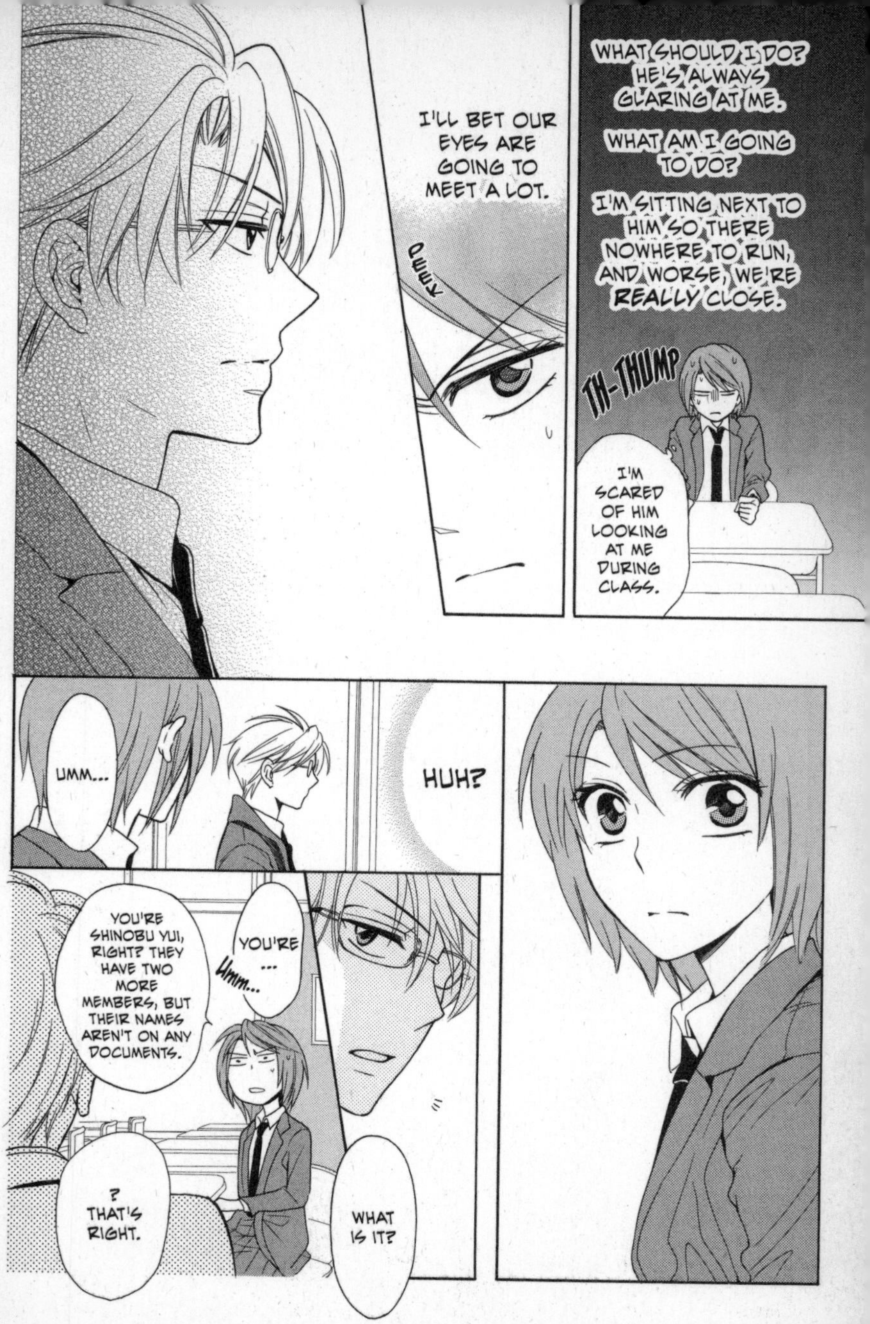
WHAT SHOULD I DO? HE'S ALWAYS GLARING AT ME.
WHAT AM I GOING TO DO?
I'M SITTING NEXT TO HIM SO THERE NOWHERE TO RUN, AND WORSE, WE'RE REALLY CLOSE.
TH-THUMP
I'M SCARED OF HIM LOOKING AT ME DURING CLASS.
I'LL BET OUR EYES ARE GOING TO MEET A LOT.
PEEK
HUH?
UMM...
YOU'RE ...
Umm...
WHAT IS IT?
YOU'RE SHINOBU YUI, RIGHT? THEY HAVE TWO MORE MEMBERS, BUT THEIR NAMES AREN'T ON ANY DOCUMENTS.
? THAT'S RIGHT.

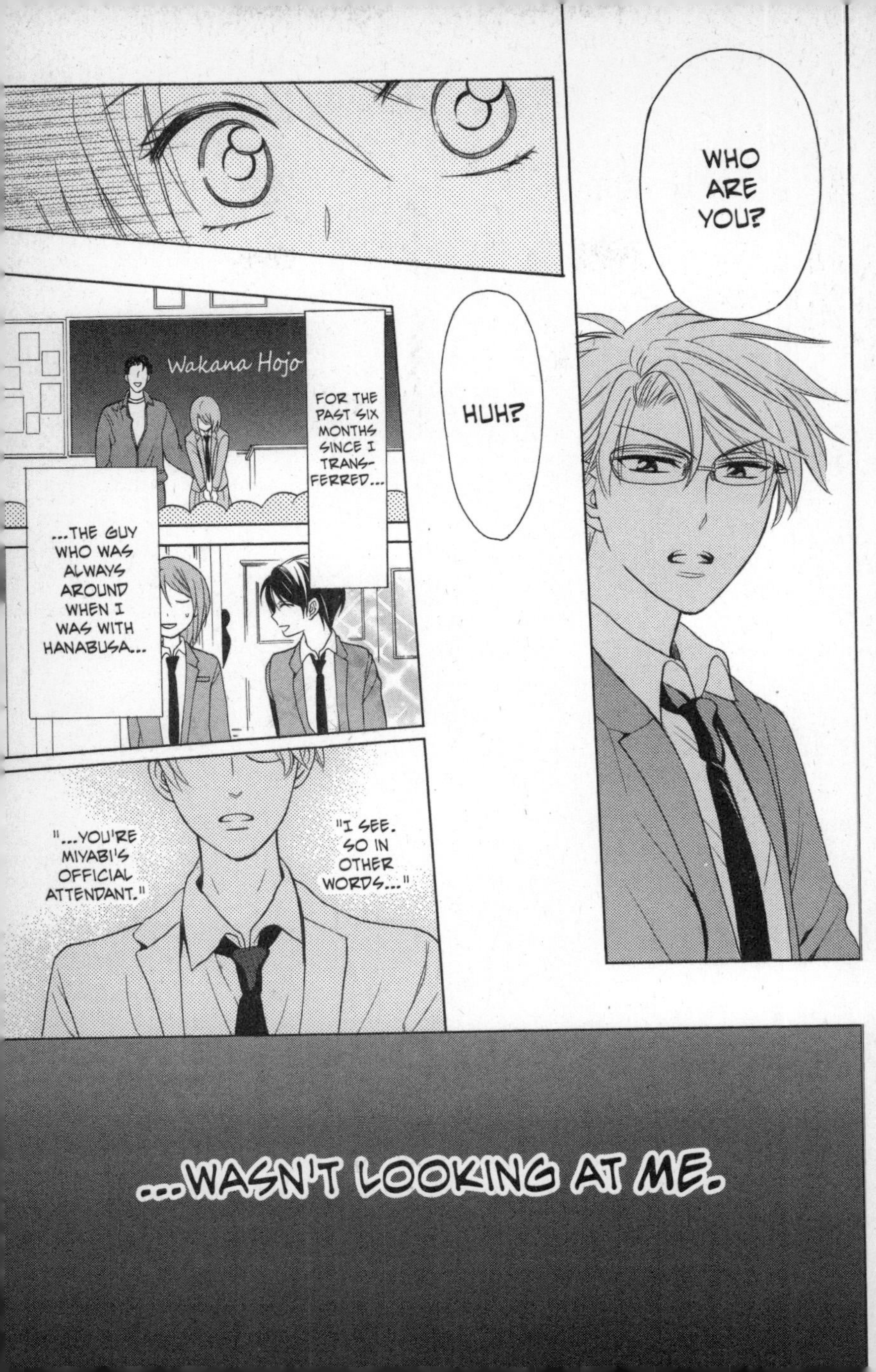
WHO ARE YOU?
HUH?
FOR THE PAST SIX MONTHS SINCE I TRANSFERRED...
Wakana Hojo
...THE GUY WHO WAS ALWAYS AROUND WHEN I WAS WITH HANABUSA...
"I SEE. SO IN OTHER WORDS..."
"...YOU'RE MIYABI'S OFFICIAL ATTENDANT."
...WASN'T LOOKING AT ME.

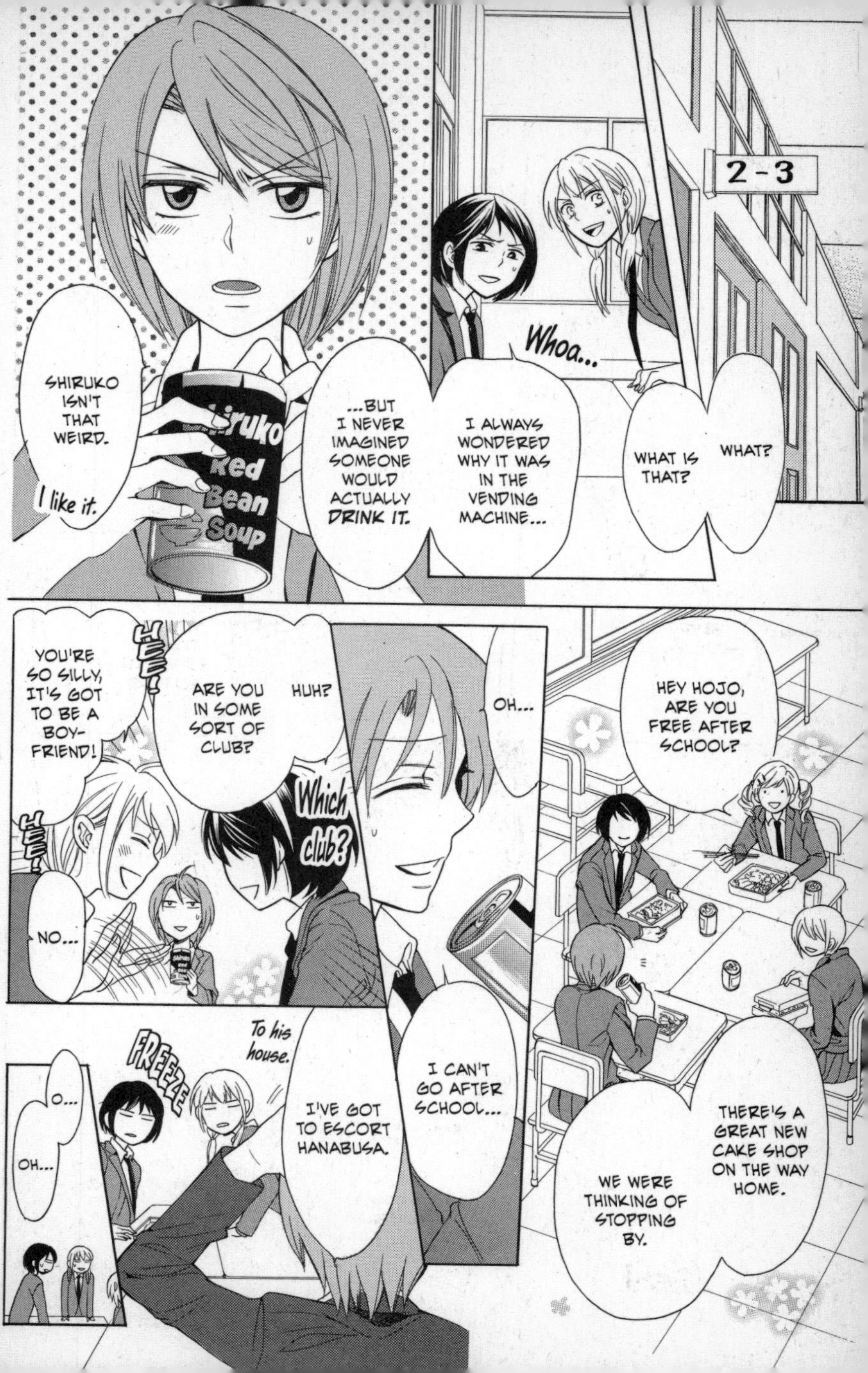
2-3
Whoa...
WHAT?
WHAT IS THAT?
I ALWAYS WONDERED WHY IT WAS IN THE VENDING MACHINE...
...BUT I NEVER IMAGINED SOMEONE WOULD ACTUALLY DRINK IT.
Red Bean Soup
SHIRUKO ISN'T THAT WEIRD.
I like it.
HEY HOJO, ARE YOU FREE AFTER SCHOOL?
THERE'S A GREAT NEW CAKE SHOP ON THE WAY HOME.
WE WERE THINKING OF STOPPING BY.
OH...
HUH?
ARE YOU IN SOME SORT OF CLUB?
Which club?
HEE!
YOU'RE SO SILLY, IT'S GOT TO BE A BOY-FRIEND!
HEE!
NO...
I CAN'T GO AFTER SCHOOL...
I'VE GOT TO ESCORT HANABUSA.
To his house.
FREEZE
O...
OH...

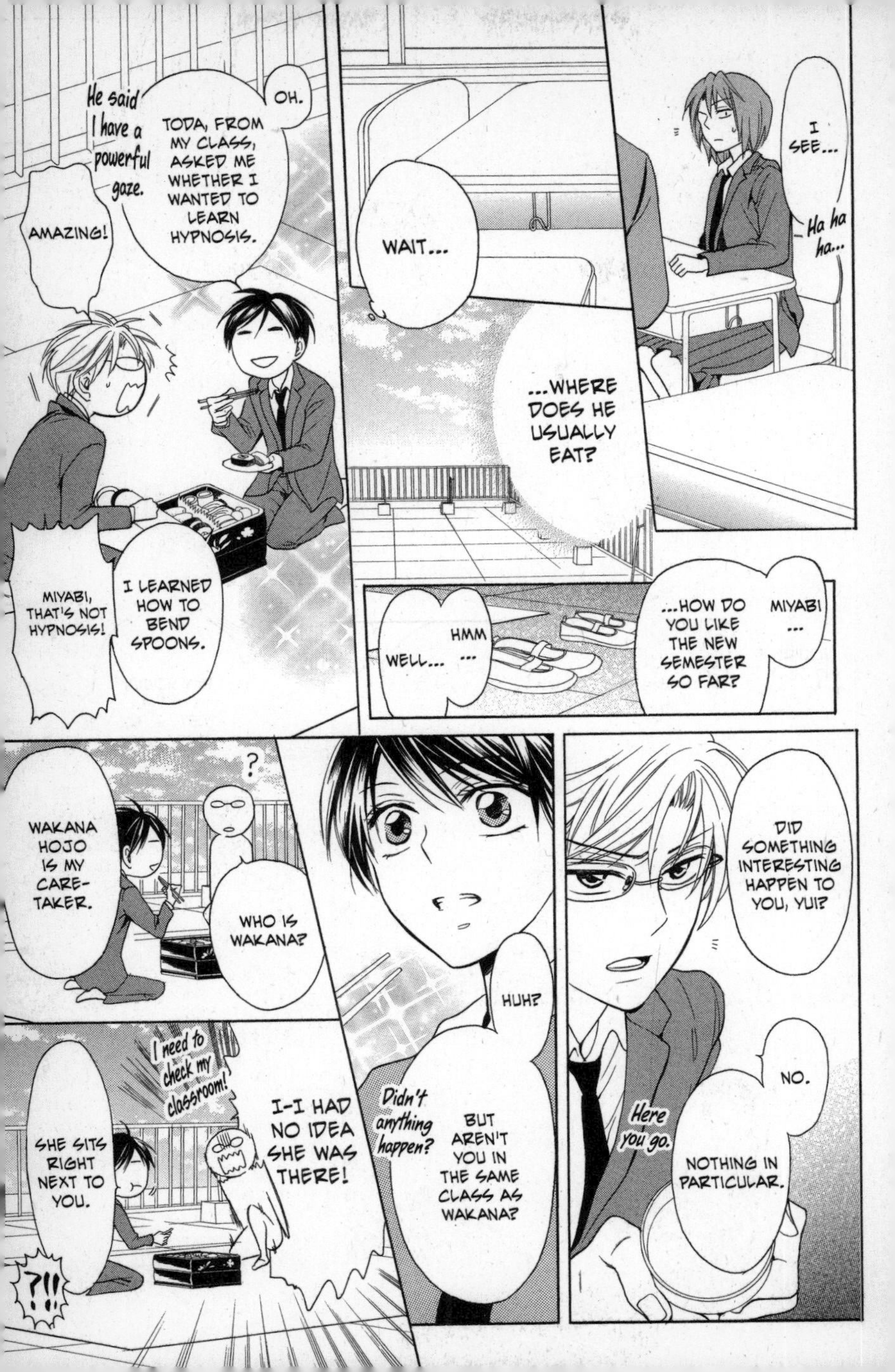

I SEE...
Ha ha ha...
WAIT...
...WHERE DOES HE USUALLY EAT?
MIYABI...
...HOW DO YOU LIKE THE NEW SEMESTER SO FAR?
HMM...
WELL...
OH.
TODA, FROM MY CLASS, ASKED ME WHETHER I WANTED TO LEARN HYPNOSIS.
He said I have a powerful gaze.
AMAZING!
I LEARNED HOW TO BEND SPOONS.
MIYABI, THAT'S NOT HYPNOSIS!
DID SOMETHING INTERESTING HAPPEN TO YOU, YUI?
NO.
NOTHING IN PARTICULAR.
Here you go.
HUH?
BUT AREN'T YOU IN THE SAME CLASS AS WAKANA?
Didn't anything happen?
?
WHO IS WAKANA?
WAKANA HOJO IS MY CARE-TAKER.
I-I HAD NO IDEA SHE WAS THERE!
I need to check my classroom!
SHE SITS RIGHT NEXT TO YOU.
?!!

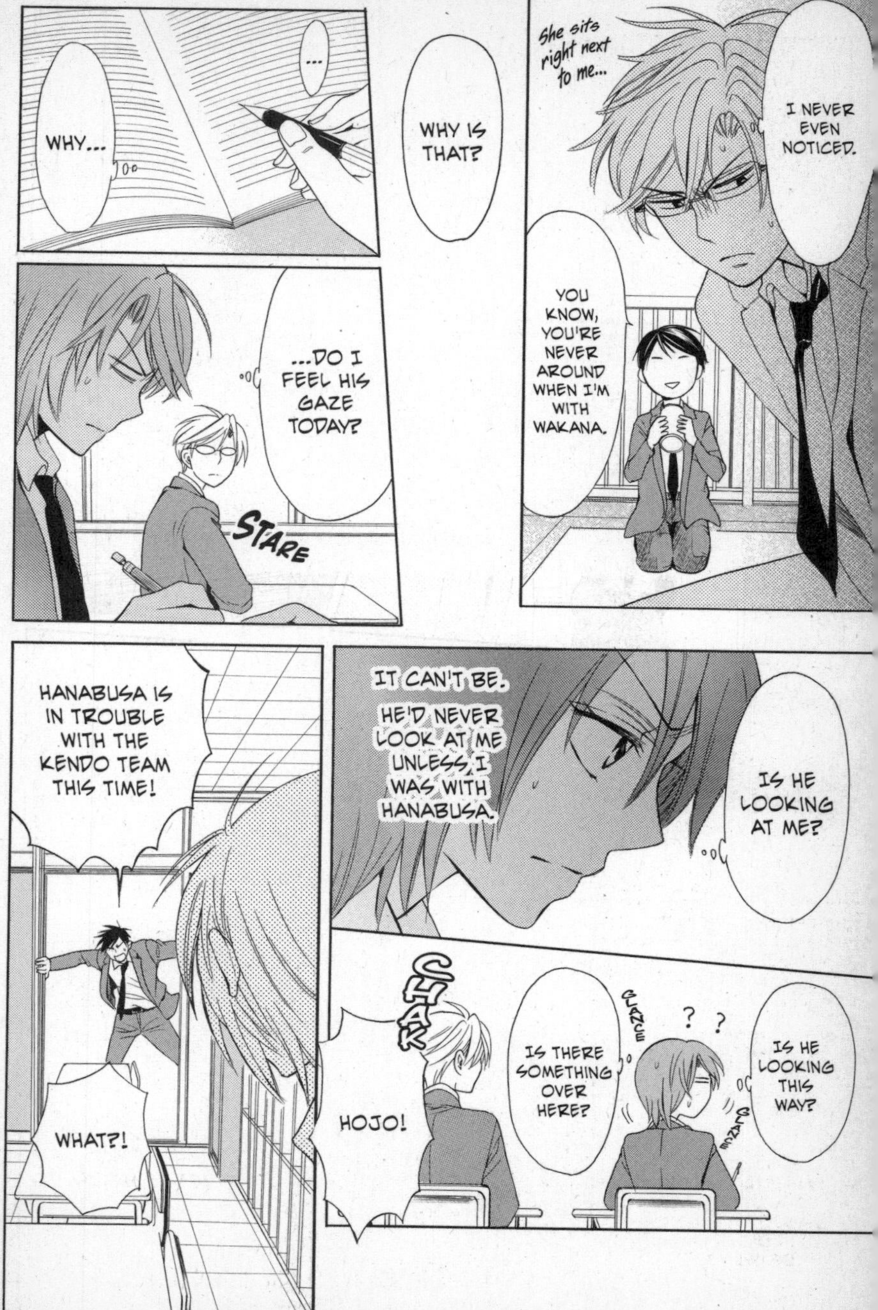
She sits right next to me...
I NEVER EVEN NOTICED.
YOU KNOW, YOU'RE NEVER AROUND WHEN I'M WITH WAKANA.
WHY IS THAT?
...
WHY...
...DO I FEEL HIS GAZE TODAY?
STARE
IS HE LOOKING AT ME?
IT CAN'T BE.
HE'D NEVER LOOK AT ME UNLESS I WAS WITH HANABUSA.
IS HE LOOKING THIS WAY?
GLANCE
? ?
GLANCE
IS THERE SOMETHING OVER HERE?
CHAK
HOJO!
HANABUSA IS IN TROUBLE WITH THE KENDO TEAM THIS TIME!
WHAT?!

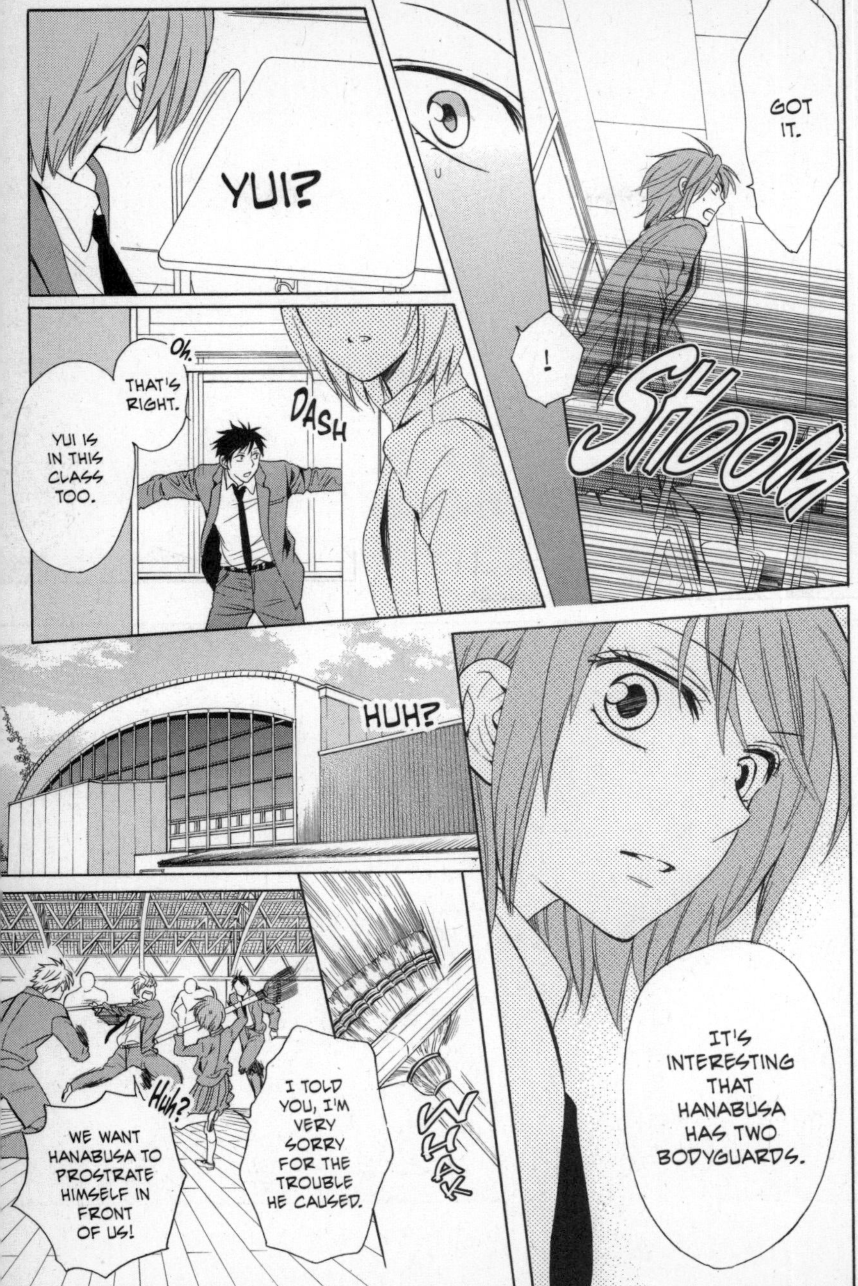
GOT IT.
!
SHOOM
YUI?
Oh.
THAT'S RIGHT.
YUI IS IN THIS CLASS TOO.
DASH
HUH?
IT'S INTERESTING THAT HANABUSA HAS TWO BODYGUARDS.
WHAK
I TOLD YOU, I'M VERY SORRY FOR THE TROUBLE HE CAUSED.
Huh?
WE WANT HANABUSA TO PROSTRATE HIMSELF IN FRONT OF US!

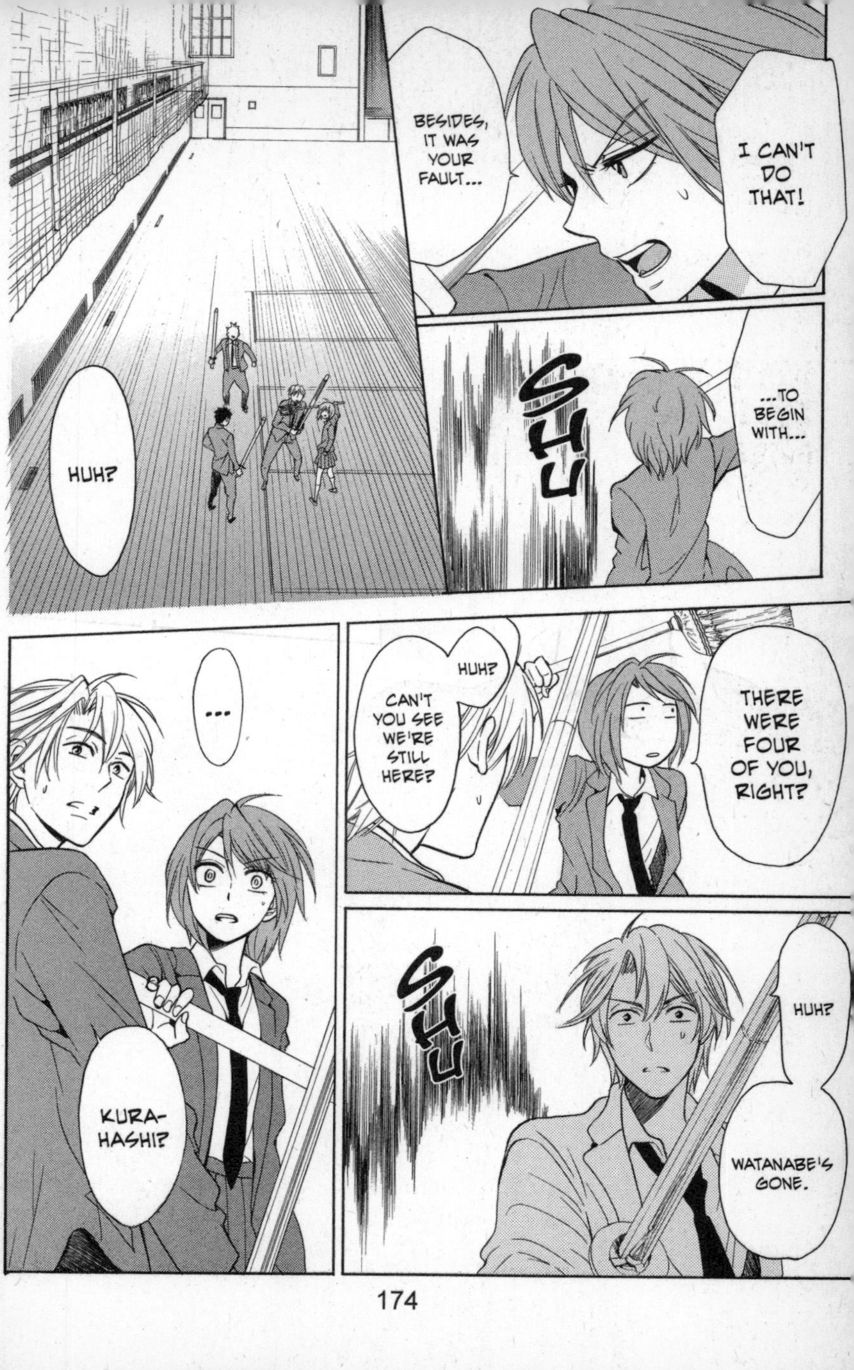
I CAN'T DO THAT!
BESIDES, IT WAS YOUR FAULT...
...TO BEGIN WITH...
SHU
HUH?
THERE WERE FOUR OF YOU, RIGHT?
HUH?
CAN'T YOU SEE WE'RE STILL HERE?
HUH?
WATANABE'S GONE.
SHU
...
KURA-HASHI?

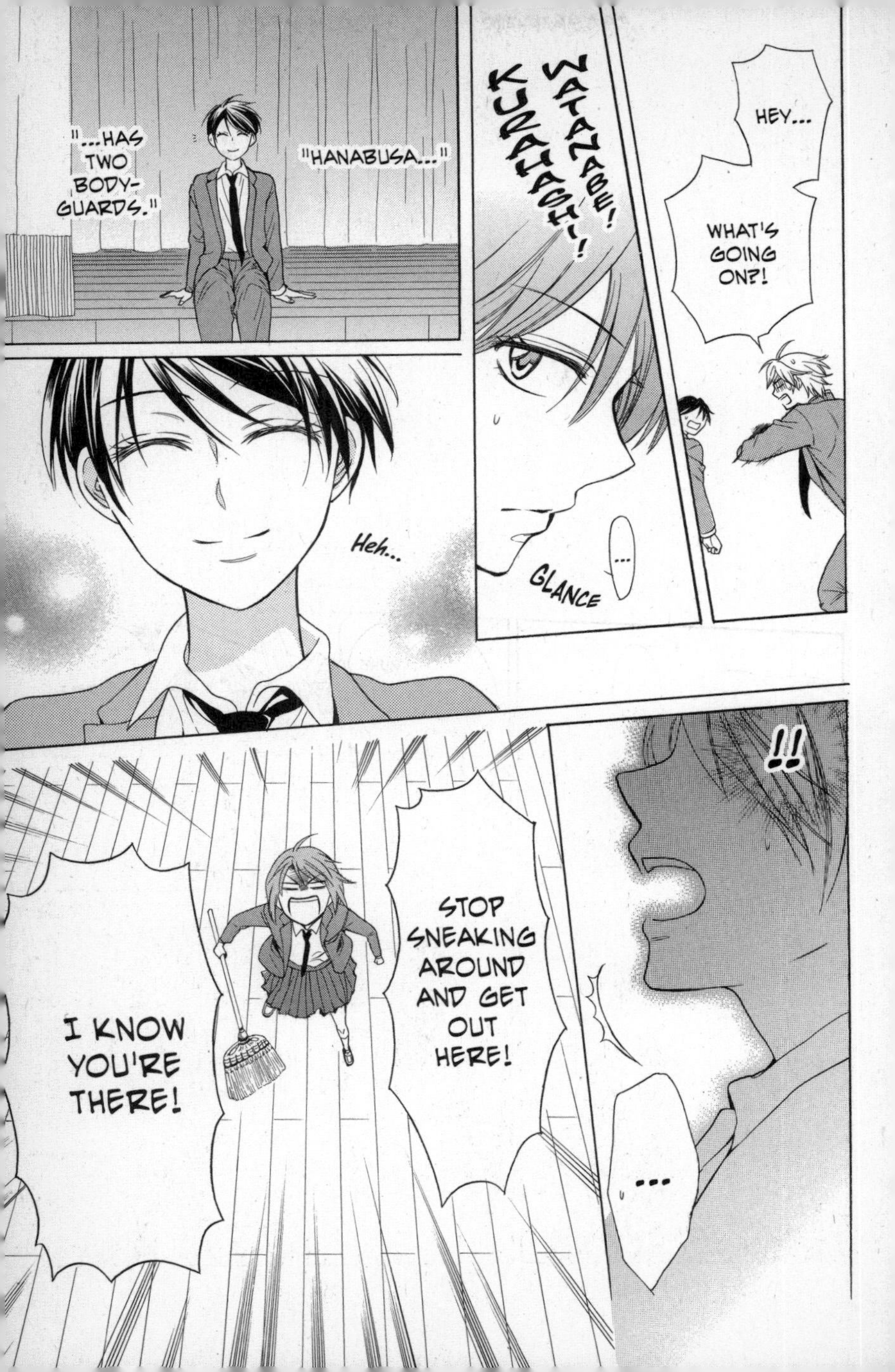
HEY...
WHAT'S GOING ON?!
WATANABE!
KURAHASHI!
...
GLANCE
"HANABUSA..."
"...HAS TWO BODY-GUARDS."
Heh...
!!
...
STOP SNEAKING AROUND AND GET OUT HERE!
I KNOW YOU'RE THERE!

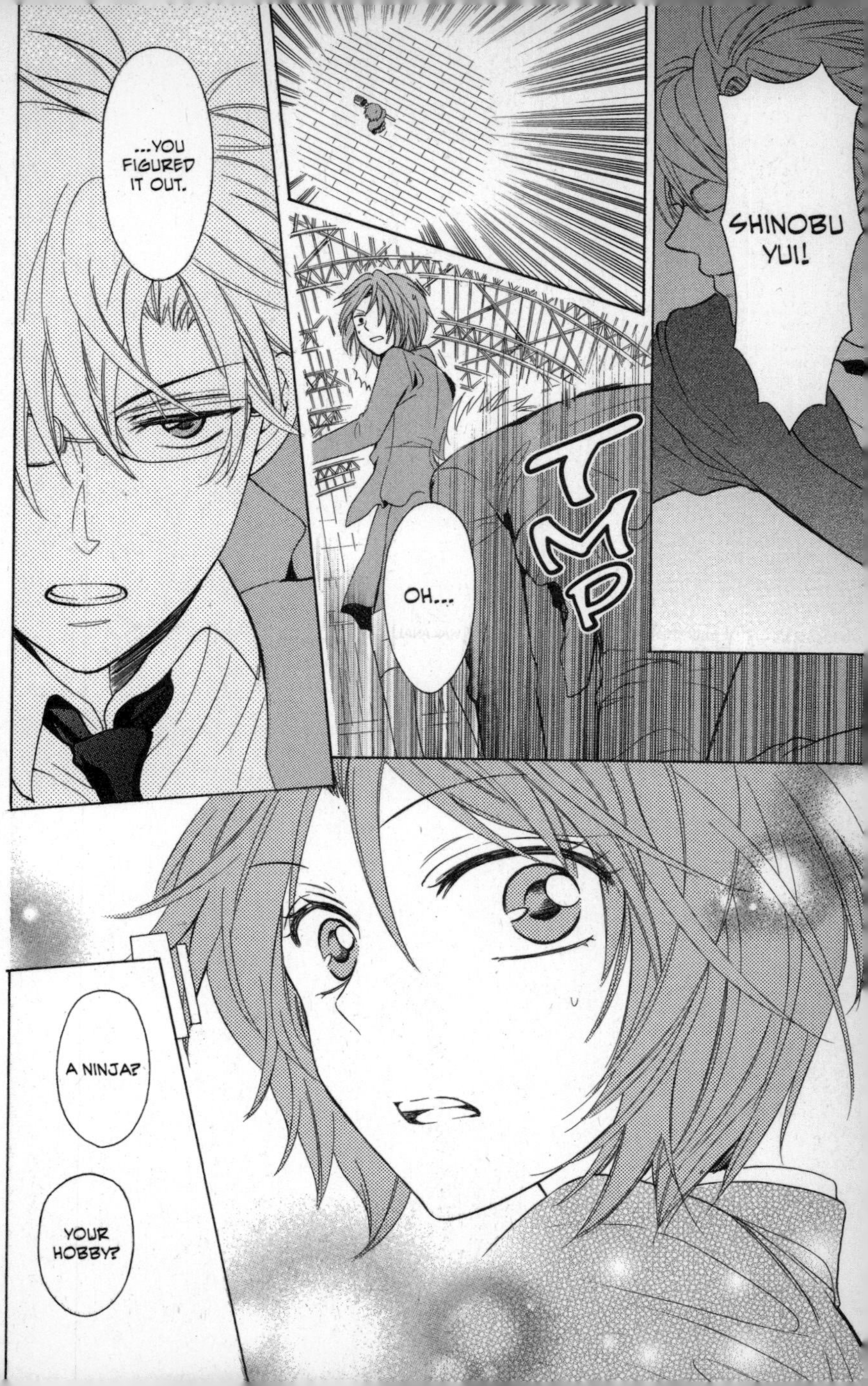

SHINOBU YUI!
TMP
OH...
...YOU FIGURED IT OUT.
A NINJA?
YOUR HOBBY?

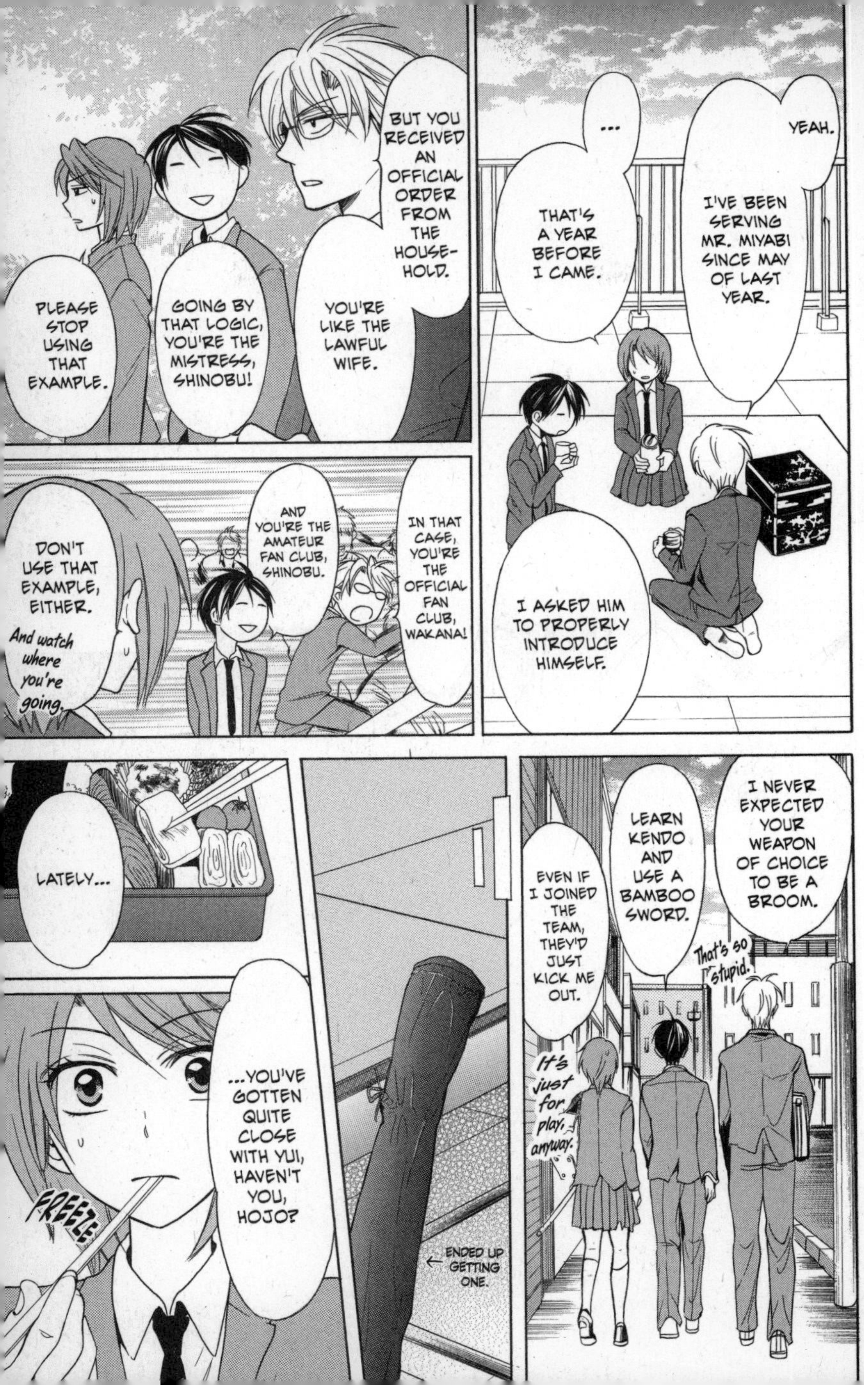
YEAH.
I'VE BEEN SERVING MR. MIYABI SINCE MAY OF LAST YEAR.
...
THAT'S A YEAR BEFORE I CAME.
I ASKED HIM TO PROPERLY INTRODUCE HIMSELF.
BUT YOU RECEIVED AN OFFICIAL ORDER FROM THE HOUSE-HOLD.
YOU'RE LIKE THE LAWFUL WIFE.
GOING BY THAT LOGIC, YOU'RE THE MISTRESS, SHINOBU!
PLEASE STOP USING THAT EXAMPLE.
IN THAT CASE, YOU'RE THE OFFICIAL FAN CLUB, WAKANA!
AND YOU'RE THE AMATEUR FAN CLUB, SHINOBU.
DON'T USE THAT EXAMPLE, EITHER.
And watch where you're going.
I NEVER EXPECTED YOUR WEAPON OF CHOICE TO BE A BROOM.
That's so stupid.
LEARN KENDO AND USE A BAMBOO SWORD.
EVEN IF I JOINED THE TEAM, THEY'D JUST KICK ME OUT.
It's just for play, anyway.
← ENDED UP GETTING ONE.
LATELY...
...YOU'VE GOTTEN QUITE CLOSE WITH YUI, HAVEN'T YOU, HOJO?
FREEZE

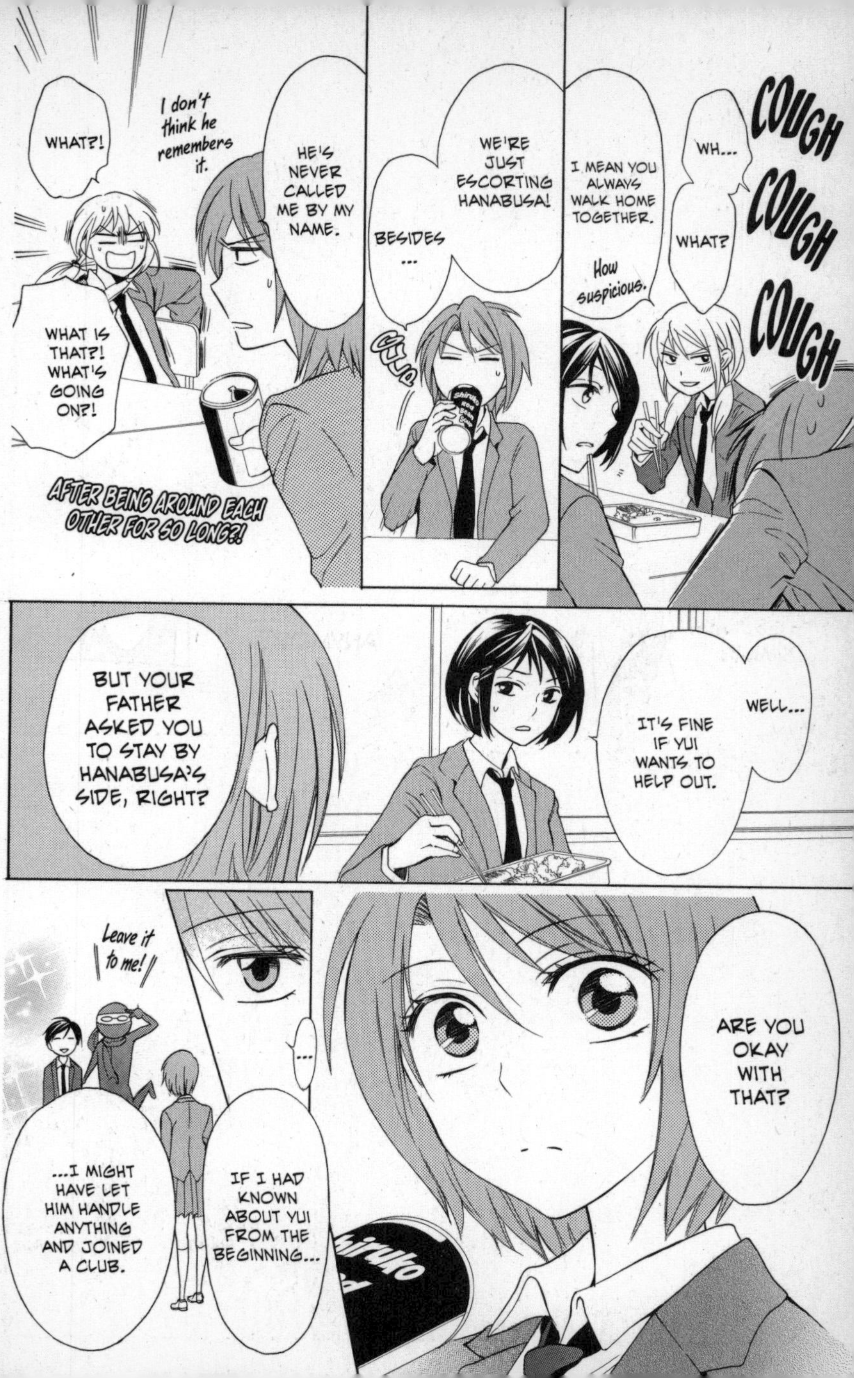
COUGH
COUGH
COUGH
WH...
WHAT?
I MEAN YOU ALWAYS WALK HOME TOGETHER.
How suspicious.
WE'RE JUST ESCORTING HANABUSA!
BESIDES...
HE'S NEVER CALLED ME BY MY NAME.
I don't think he remembers it.
WHAT?!
WHAT IS THAT?! WHAT'S GOING ON?!
AFTER BEING AROUND EACH OTHER FOR SO LONG?!
WELL...
IT'S FINE IF YUI WANTS TO HELP OUT.
BUT YOUR FATHER ASKED YOU TO STAY BY HANABUSA'S SIDE, RIGHT?
ARE YOU OKAY WITH THAT?
...
IF I HAD KNOWN ABOUT YUI FROM THE BEGINNING...
...I MIGHT HAVE LET HIM HANDLE ANYTHING AND JOINED A CLUB.
Leave it to me!

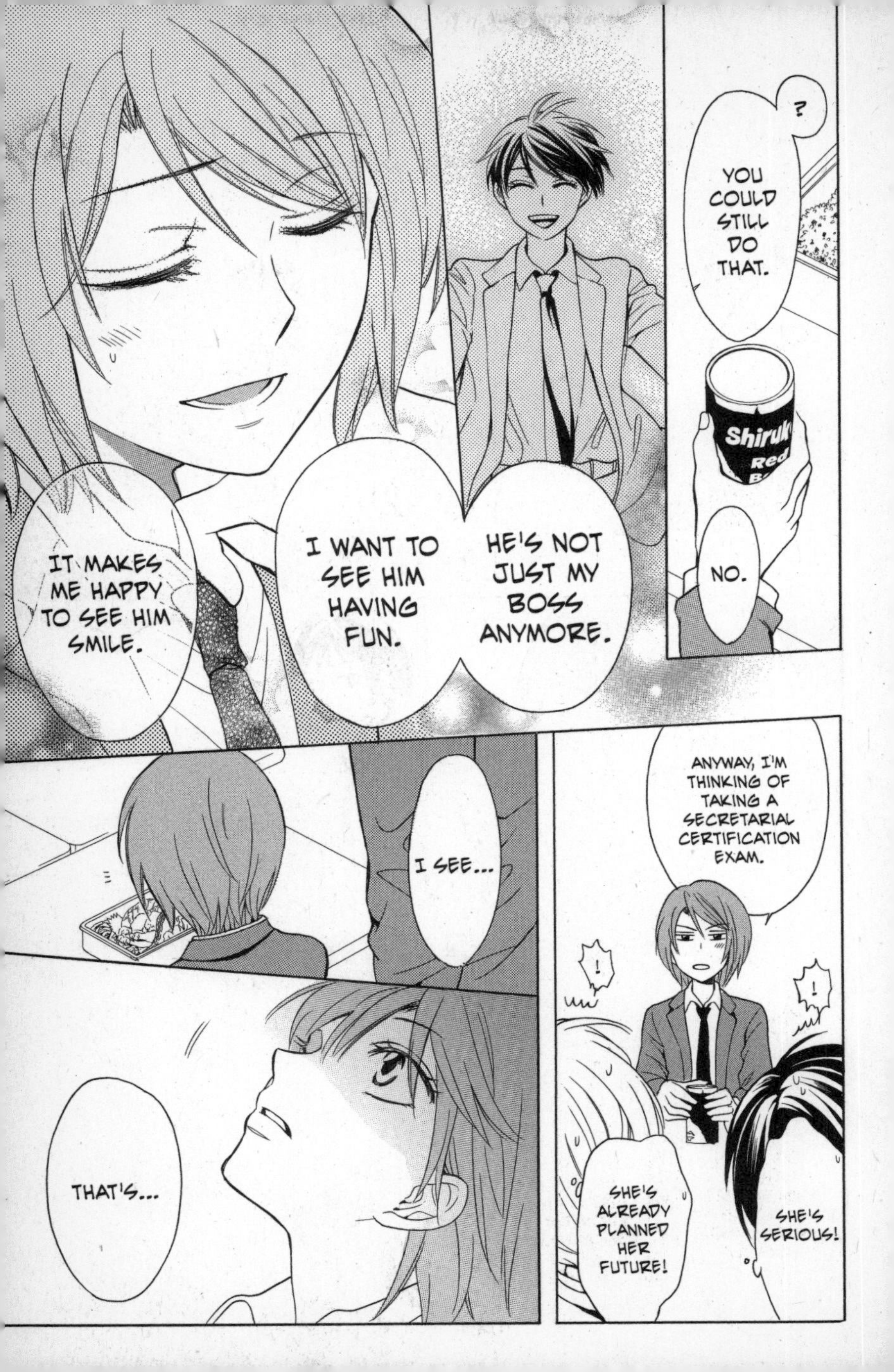
?
YOU COULD STILL DO THAT.
Shiruko Red B
NO.
HE'S NOT JUST MY BOSS ANYMORE.
I WANT TO SEE HIM HAVING FUN.
IT MAKES ME HAPPY TO SEE HIM SMILE.
ANYWAY, I'M THINKING OF TAKING A SECRETARIAL CERTIFICATION EXAM.
!
!
SHE'S SERIOUS!
SHE'S ALREADY PLANNED HER FUTURE!
I SEE...
THAT'S...

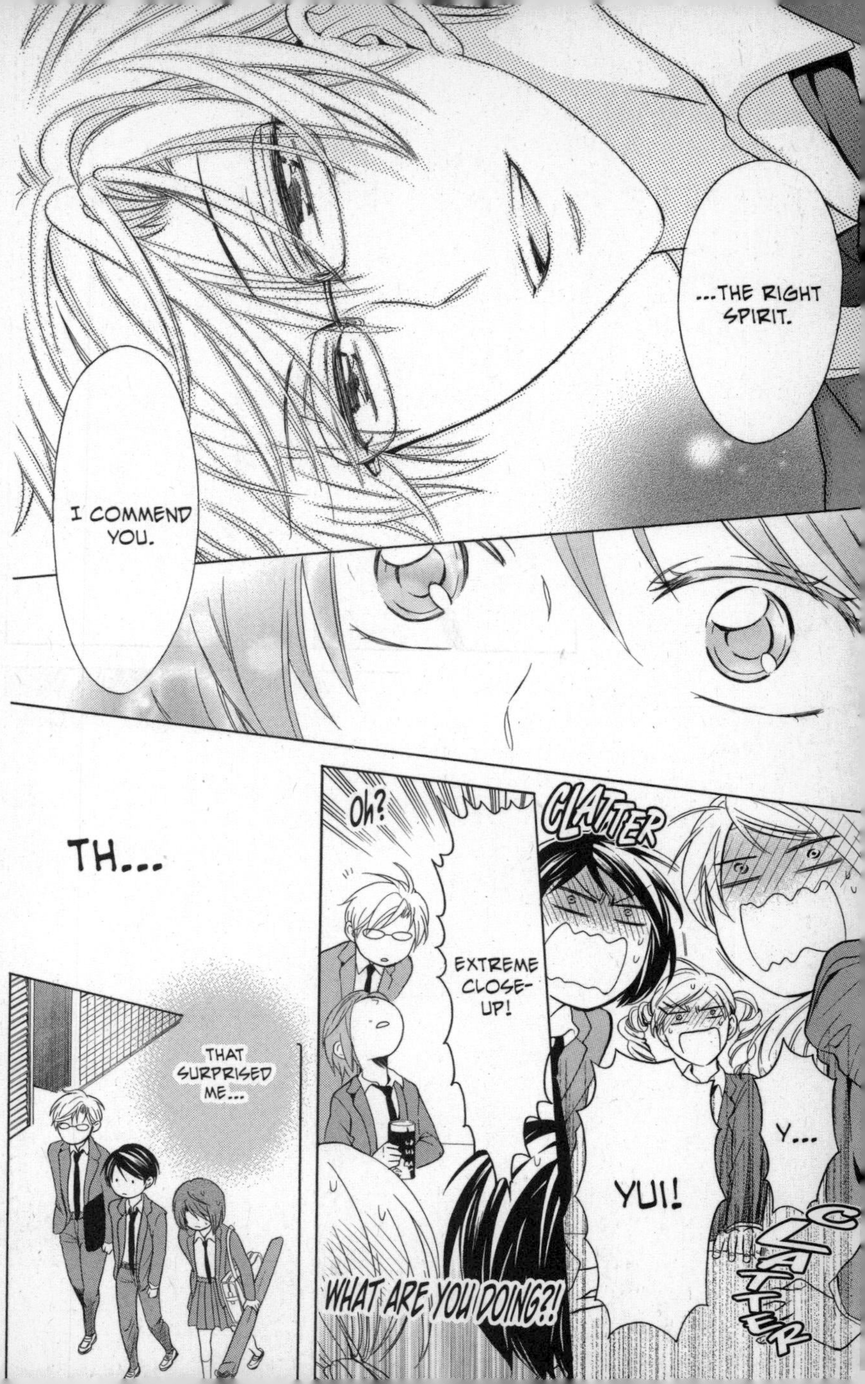
...THE RIGHT SPIRIT.
I COMMEND YOU.
CLATTER
Oh?
EXTREME CLOSE-UP!
Y...
YUI!
WHAT ARE YOU DOING?!
CLATTER
TH...
THAT SURPRISED ME...

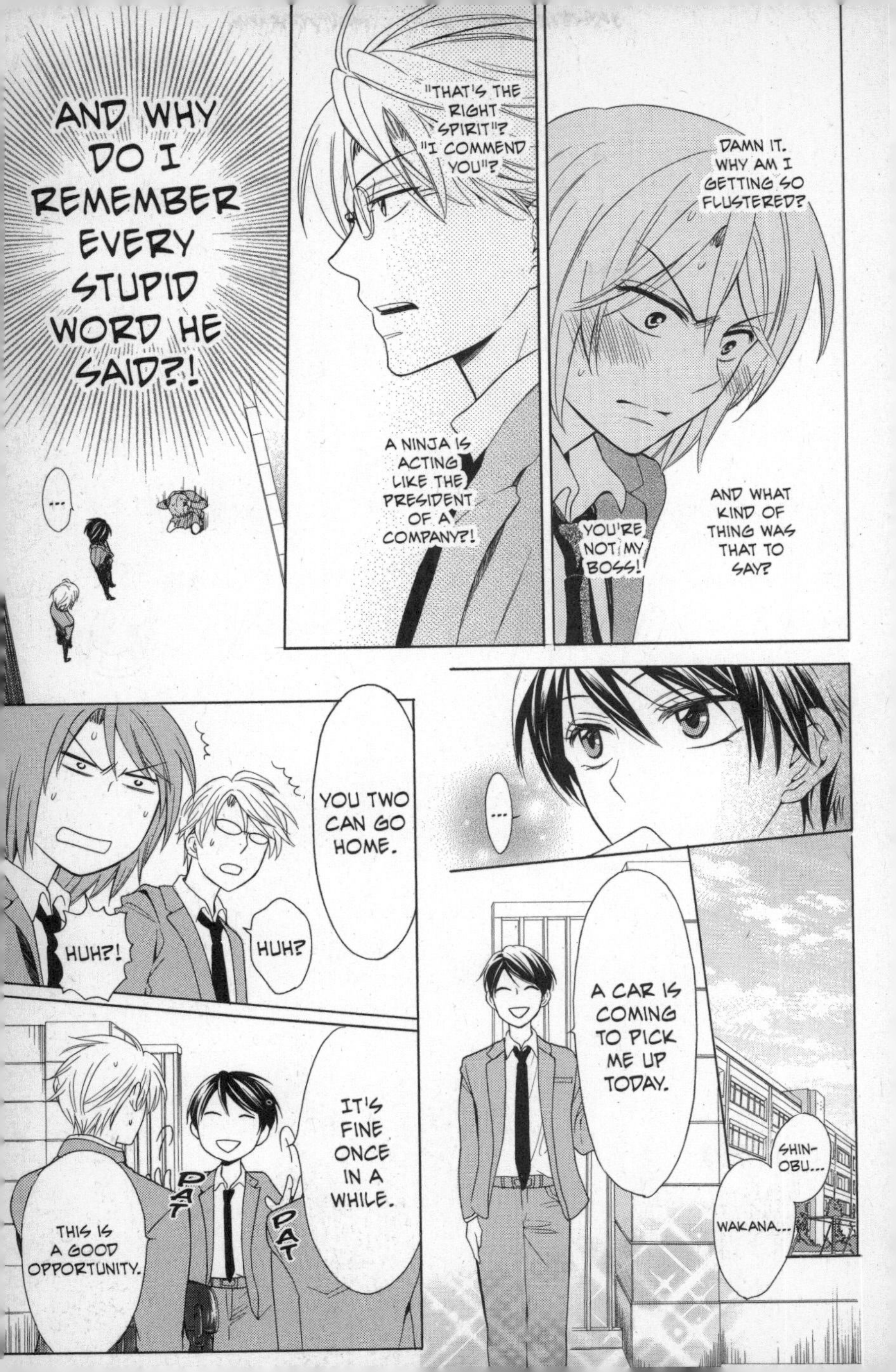
DAMN IT. WHY AM I GETTING SO FLUSTERED?
AND WHAT KIND OF THING WAS THAT TO SAY?
YOU'RE NOT MY BOSS!
"THAT'S THE RIGHT SPIRIT"? "I COMMEND YOU"?
A NINJA IS ACTING LIKE THE PRESIDENT OF A COMPANY?!
AND WHY DO I REMEMBER EVERY STUPID WORD HE SAID?!
...
...
YOU TWO CAN GO HOME.
HUH?
HUH?!
A CAR IS COMING TO PICK ME UP TODAY.
SHINOBU...
WAKANA...
IT'S FINE ONCE IN A WHILE.
PAT
PAT
THIS IS A GOOD OPPORTUNITY.

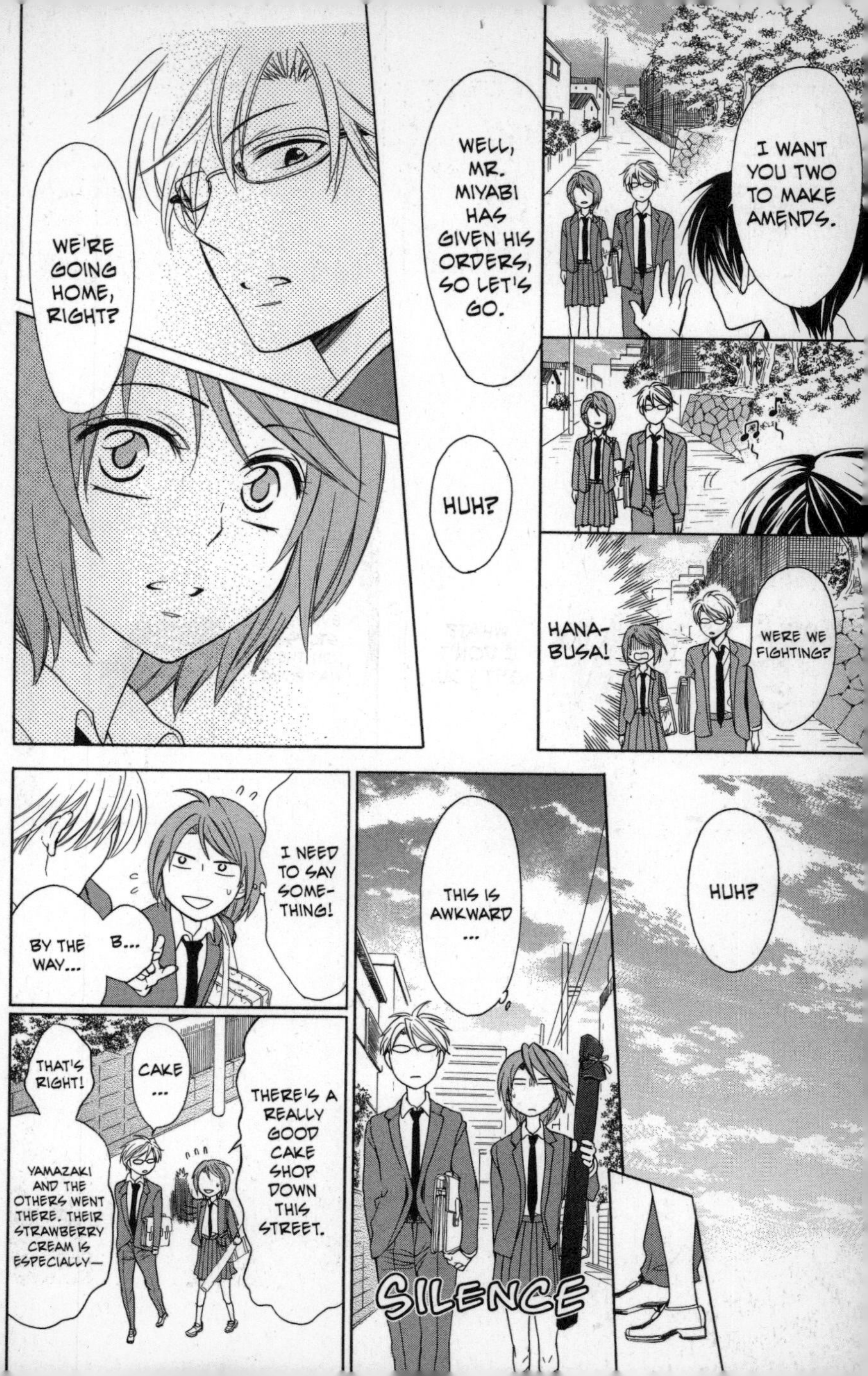
I WANT YOU TWO TO MAKE AMENDS.
HANA-BUSA!
WERE WE FIGHTING?
WELL, MR. MIYABI HAS GIVEN HIS ORDERS, SO LET'S GO.
WE'RE GOING HOME, RIGHT?
HUH?
HUH?
THIS IS AWKWARD...
SILENCE
I NEED TO SAY SOMETHING!
B...
BY THE WAY...
THAT'S RIGHT!
THERE'S A REALLY GOOD CAKE SHOP DOWN THIS STREET.
CAKE...
YAMAZAKI AND THE OTHERS WENT THERE. THEIR STRAWBERRY CREAM IS ESPECIALLY—

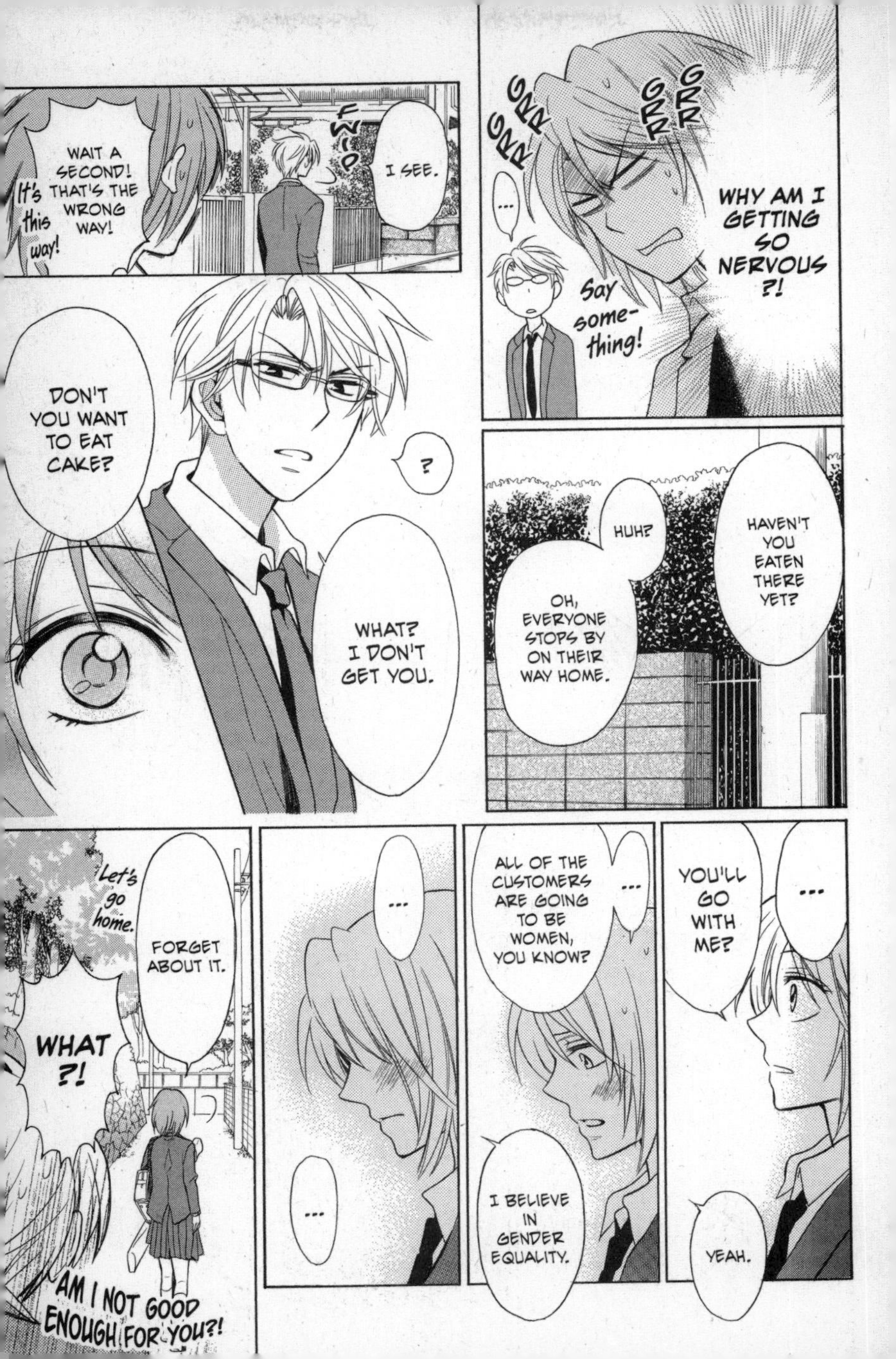
RRG GRR
RRG GRR
WHY AM I GETTING SO NERVOUS?!
...
Say something!
FWIP
I SEE.
WAIT A SECOND! THAT'S THE WRONG WAY!
It's this way!
HAVEN'T YOU EATEN THERE YET?
HUH?
OH, EVERYONE STOPS BY ON THEIR WAY HOME.
DON'T YOU WANT TO EAT CAKE?
?
WHAT? I DON'T GET YOU.
...
YOU'LL GO WITH ME?
YEAH.
...
ALL OF THE CUSTOMERS ARE GOING TO BE WOMEN, YOU KNOW?
I BELIEVE IN GENDER EQUALITY.
...
...
FORGET ABOUT IT.
Let's go home.
WHAT?!
AM I NOT GOOD ENOUGH FOR YOU?!

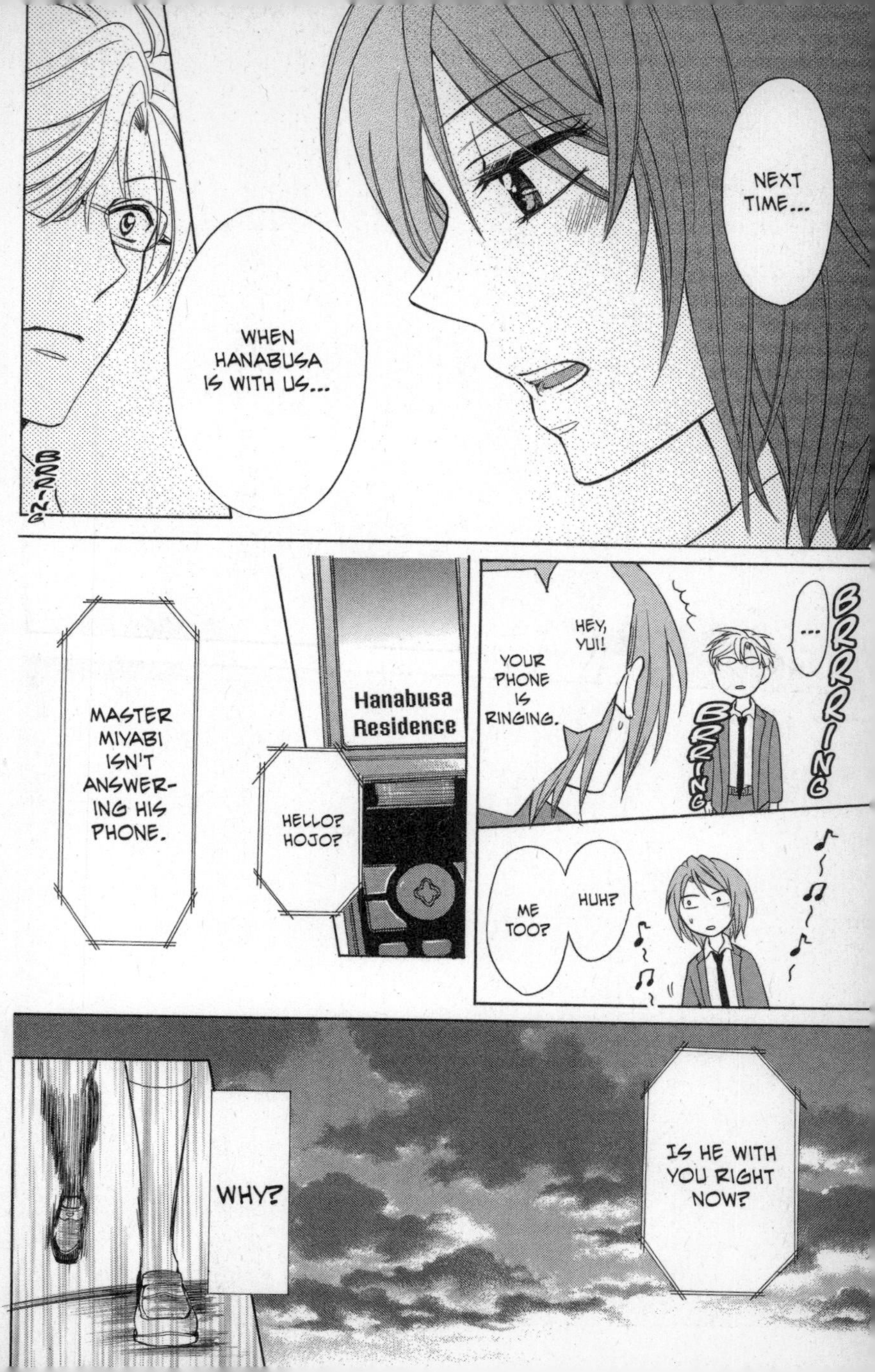
NEXT TIME...
WHEN HANABUSA IS WITH US...
BRRRING
BRRRRING
...
BRRRING
HEY, YUI!
YOUR PHONE IS RINGING.
HUH?
ME TOO?
Hanabusa Residence
HELLO? HOJO?
MASTER MIYABI ISN'T ANSWERING HIS PHONE.
IS HE WITH YOU RIGHT NOW?
WHY?

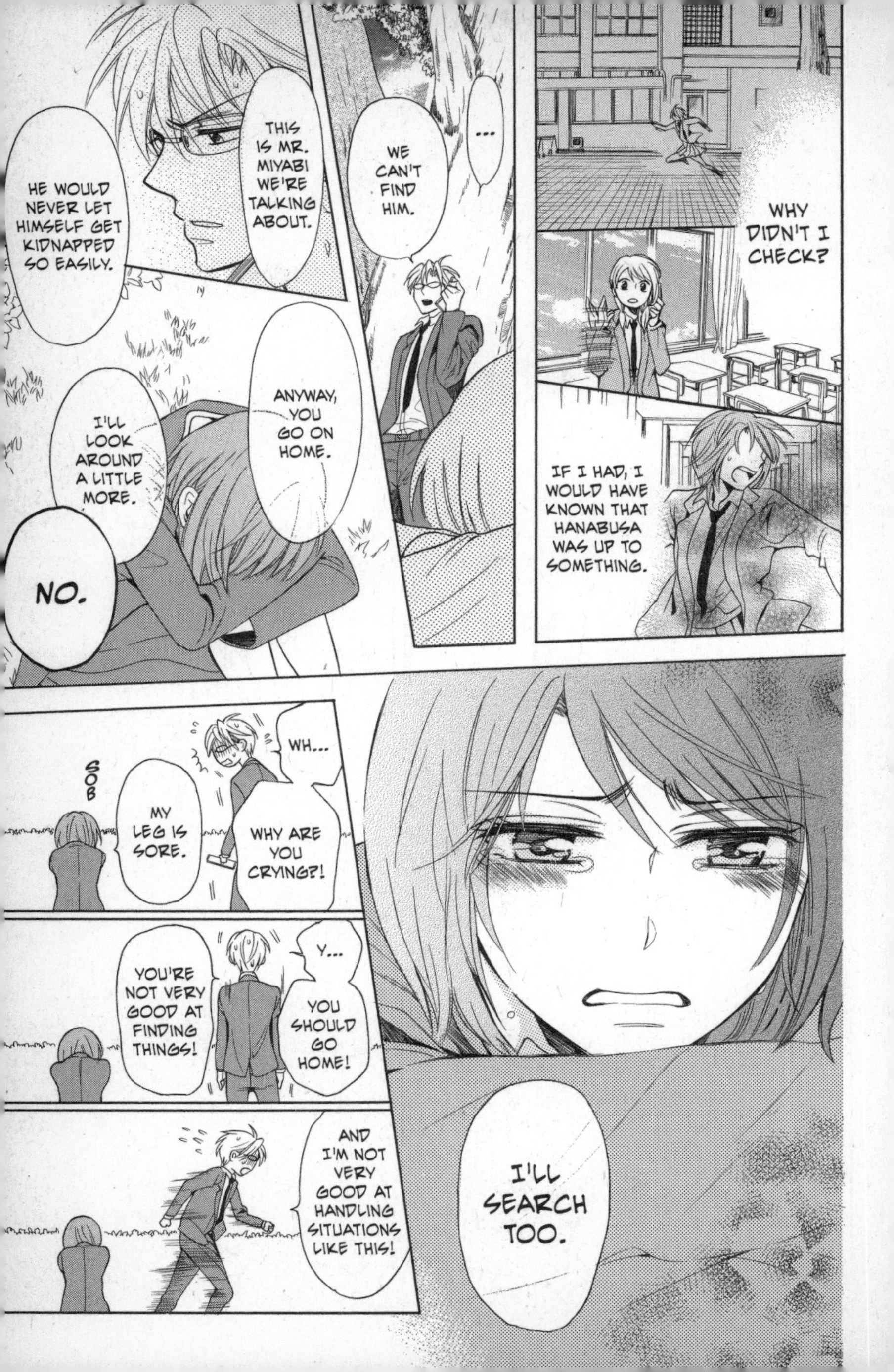
WHY DIDN'T I CHECK?
IF I HAD, I WOULD HAVE KNOWN THAT HANABUSA WAS UP TO SOMETHING.
...
WE CAN'T FIND HIM.
THIS IS MR. MIYABI WE'RE TALKING ABOUT.
HE WOULD NEVER LET HIMSELF GET KIDNAPPED SO EASILY.
ANYWAY, YOU GO ON HOME.
I'LL LOOK AROUND A LITTLE MORE.
NO.
I'LL SEARCH TOO.
WH...
WHY ARE YOU CRYING?!
MY LEG IS SORE.
SOB
Y...
YOU SHOULD GO HOME!
YOU'RE NOT VERY GOOD AT FINDING THINGS!
AND I'M NOT VERY GOOD AT HANDLING SITUATIONS LIKE THIS!

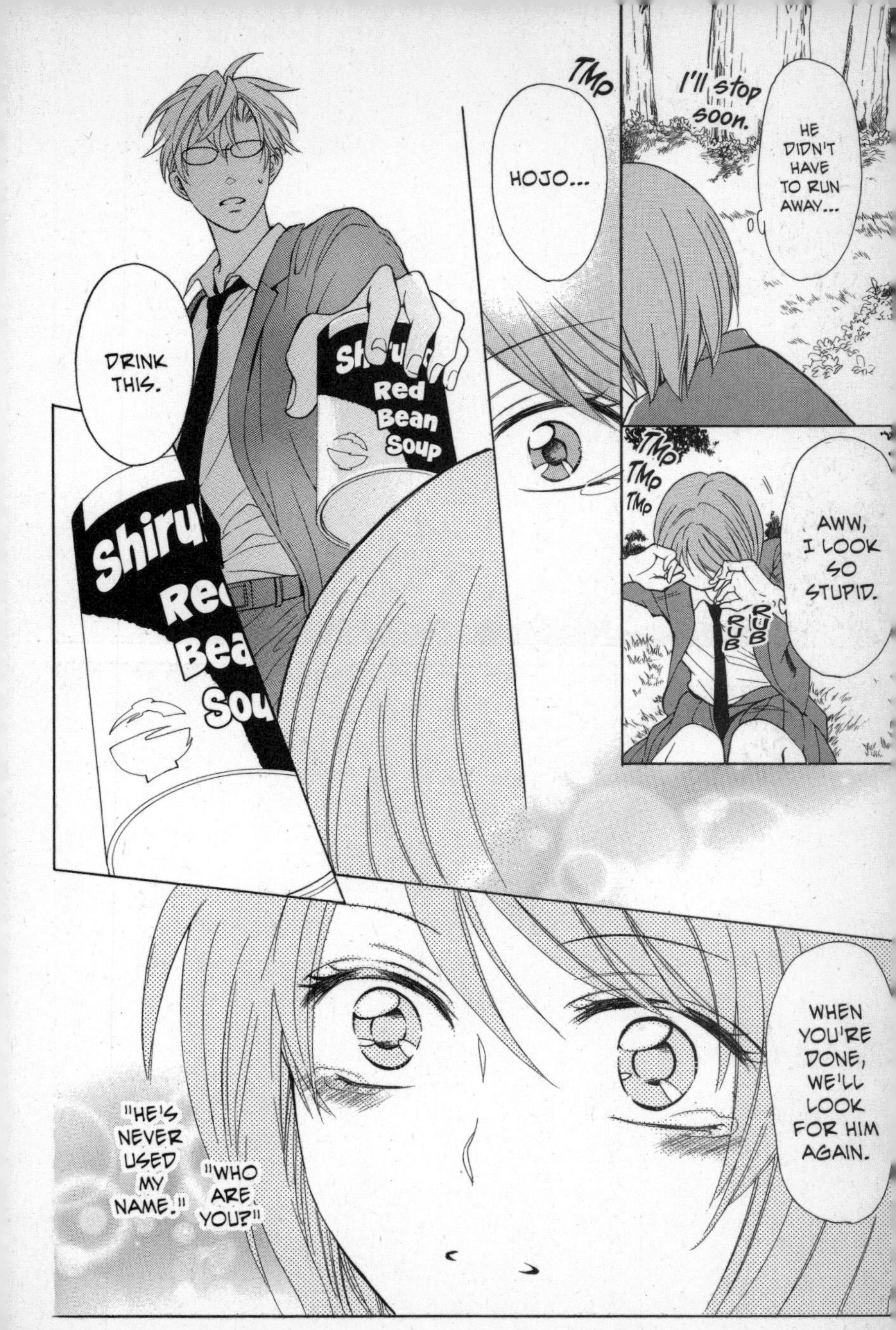
I'll stop soon.
HE DIDN'T HAVE TO RUN AWAY...
TMp TMp TMp
AWW, I LOOK SO STUPID.
RUB RUB
TMp
HOJO...
Red Bean Soup
DRINK THIS.
Shiru
Red Bean Soup
WHEN YOU'RE DONE, WE'LL LOOK FOR HIM AGAIN.
"WHO ARE YOU?"
"HE'S NEVER USED MY NAME."

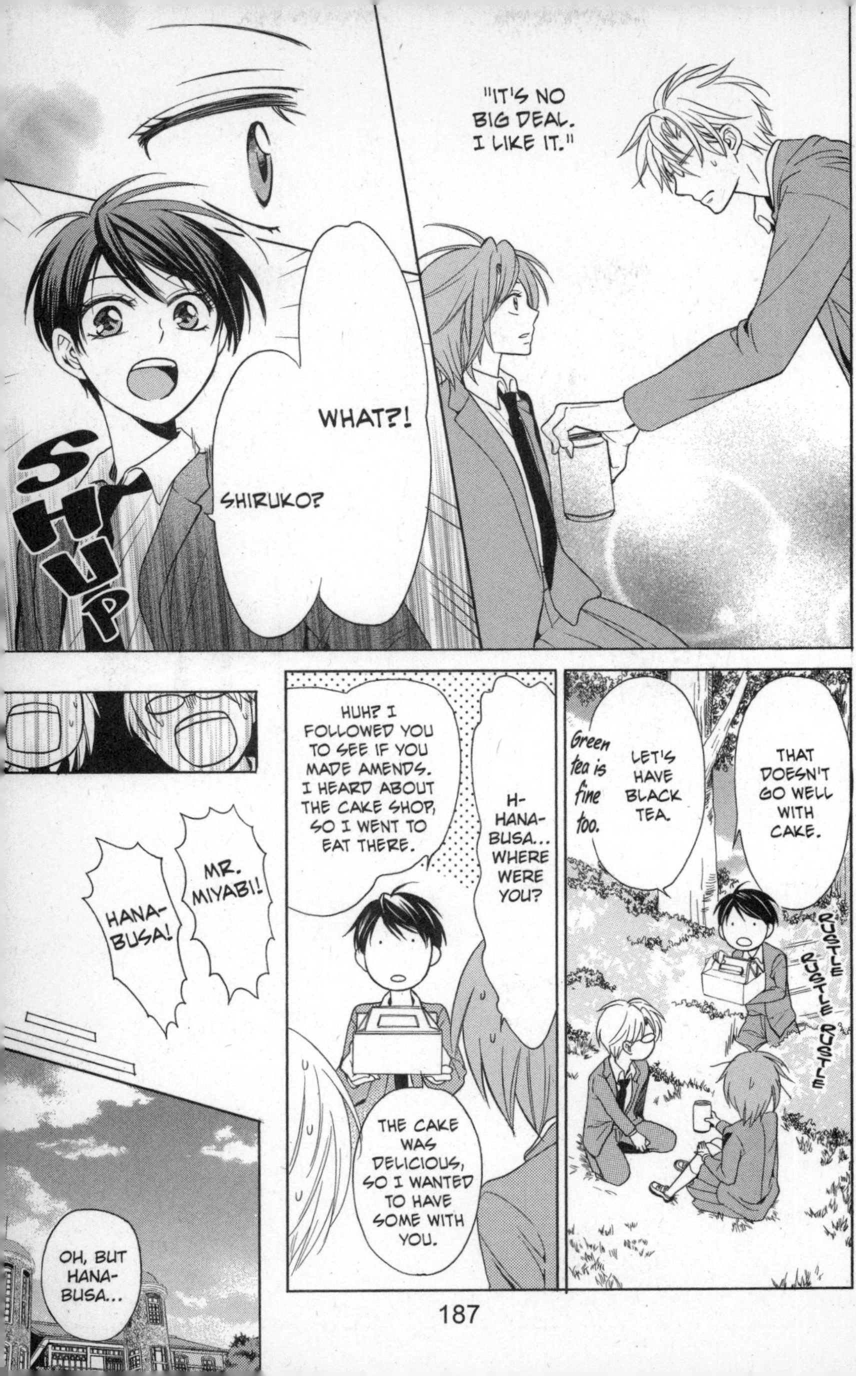
"IT'S NO BIG DEAL. I LIKE IT."
WHAT?!
SHIRUKO?
SHUP
THAT DOESN'T GO WELL WITH CAKE.
LET'S HAVE BLACK TEA.
Green tea is fine too.
RUSTLE RUSTLE RUSTLE
H-HANA-BUSA... WHERE WERE YOU?
HUH? I FOLLOWED YOU TO SEE IF YOU MADE AMENDS. I HEARD ABOUT THE CAKE SHOP, SO I WENT TO EAT THERE.
THE CAKE WAS DELICIOUS, SO I WANTED TO HAVE SOME WITH YOU.
MR. MIYABI!
HANA-BUSA!
OH, BUT HANA-BUSA...

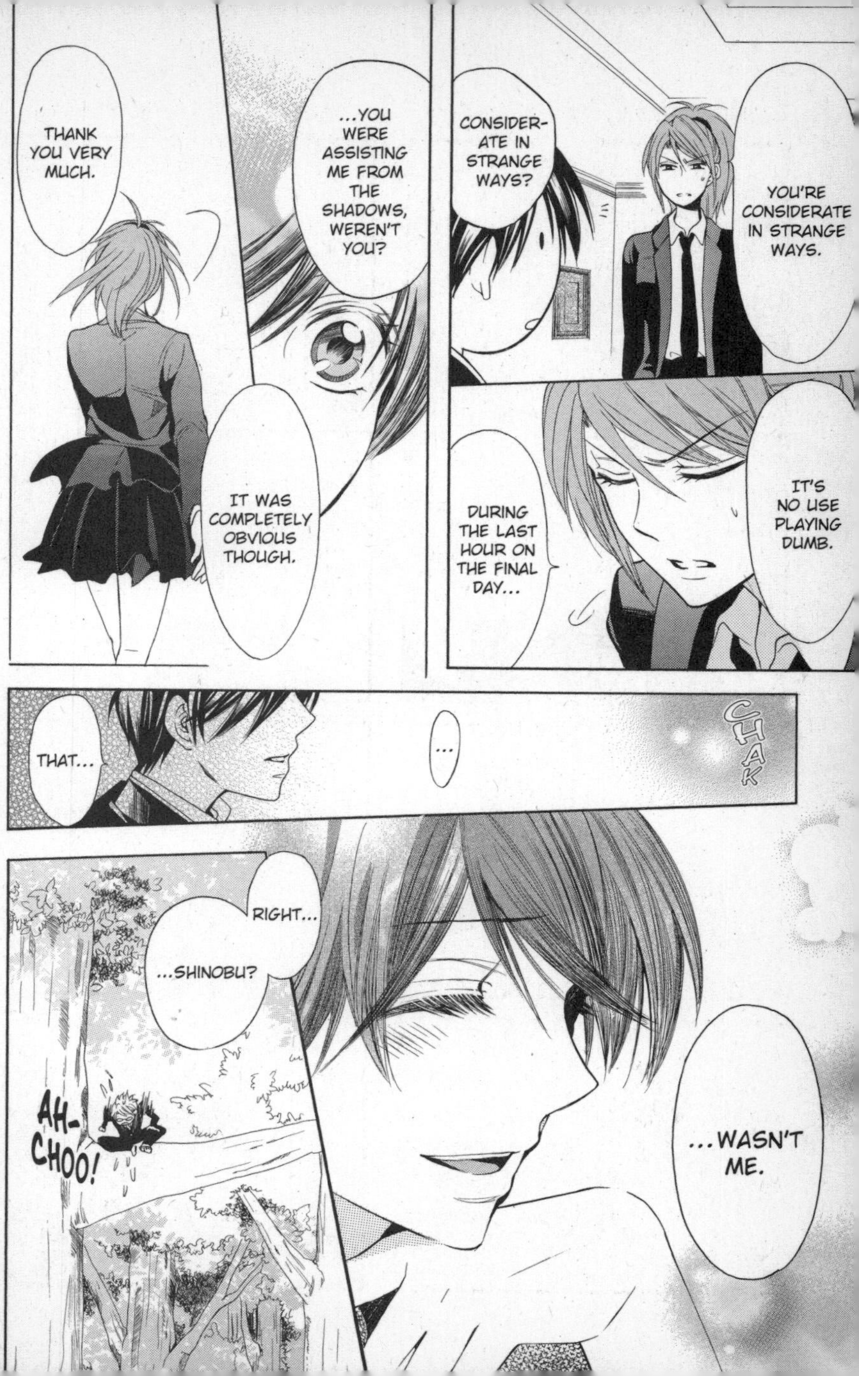
YOU'RE CONSIDERATE IN STRANGE WAYS.
CONSIDER-ATE IN STRANGE WAYS?
IT'S NO USE PLAYING DUMB.
DURING THE LAST HOUR ON THE FINAL DAY...
...YOU WERE ASSISTING ME FROM THE SHADOWS, WEREN'T YOU?
IT WAS COMPLETELY OBVIOUS THOUGH.
THANK YOU VERY MUCH.
CHAK
...
THAT...
RIGHT...
...SHINOBU?
...WASN'T ME.
AH-CHOO!

LIKE A SOAP OPERA

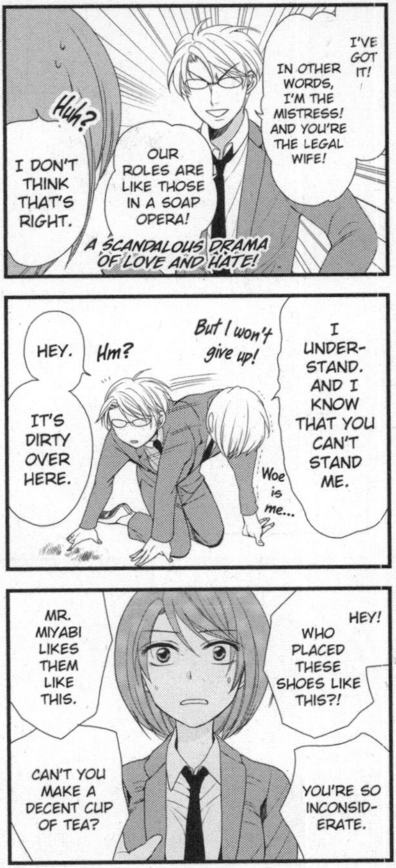
I'VE GOT IT!
IN OTHER WORDS, I'M THE MISTRESS! AND YOU'RE THE LEGAL WIFE!
OUR ROLES ARE LIKE THOSE IN A SOAP OPERA!
Huh?
I DON'T THINK THAT'S RIGHT.
A SCANDALOUS DRAMA OF LOVE AND HATE!
I UNDERSTAND. AND I KNOW THAT YOU CAN'T STAND ME.
But I won't give up!
Woe is me...
Hm?
HEY.
IT'S DIRTY OVER HERE.
HEY! WHO PLACED THESE SHOES LIKE THIS?!
YOU'RE SO INCONSIDERATE.
MR. MIYABI LIKES THEM LIKE THIS.
CAN'T YOU MAKE A DECENT CUP OF TEA?
I CAN'T TAKE IT ANYMORE.
WAAAH!
SHINOBU...
...THAT'S THE WRONG KIND OF SHOW.
This isn't a drama between a mother- and daughter-in-law.

THE MEANING OF SORRY

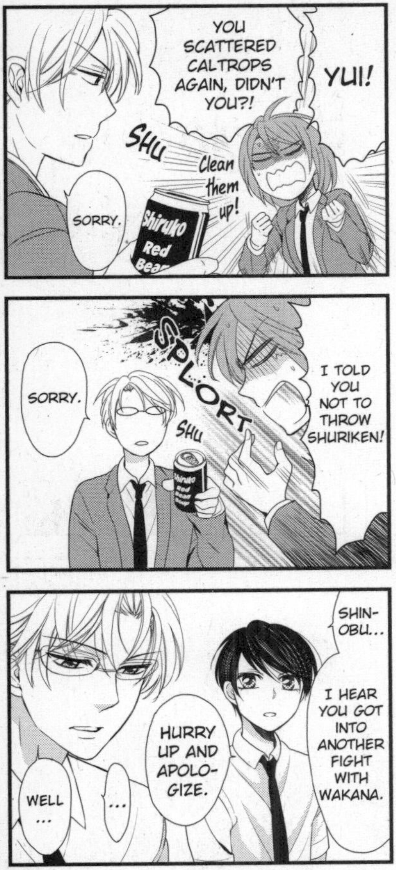
YUI!
YOU SCATTERED CALTROPS AGAIN, DIDN'T YOU?!
Clean them up!
SHU
Shiruko Red Bea
SORRY.
I TOLD YOU NOT TO THROW SHURIKEN!
SPLORT
SHU
SORRY.
SHINOBU...
I HEAR YOU GOT INTO ANOTHER FIGHT WITH WAKANA.
HURRY UP AND APOLOGIZE.
...
WELL...
SHIRUKO!
I CAN'T FIND ANY SHIRUKO!
Where did the hot drinks go?!
MIIN
MIIN
MIIN
IS THIS ABSOLUTELY NECESSARY?

THOSE LEFT BEHIND

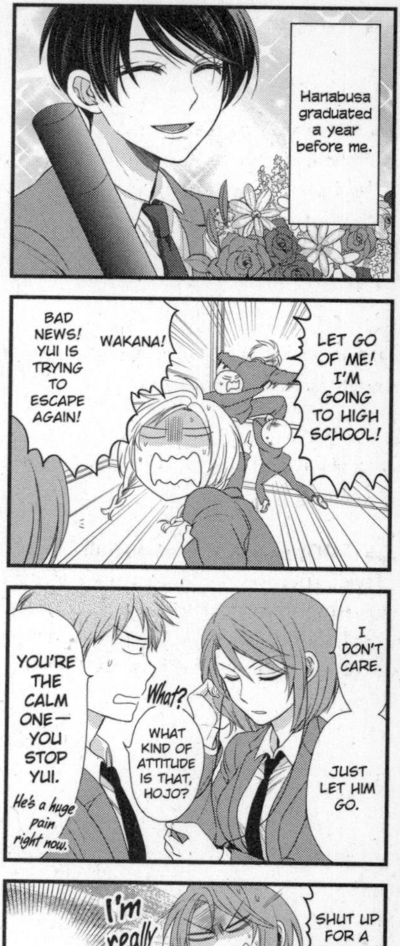

Hanabusa graduated a year before me.
LET GO OF ME! I'M GOING TO HIGH SCHOOL!
WAKANA!
BAD NEWS! YUI IS TRYING TO ESCAPE AGAIN!
I DON'T CARE.
JUST LET HIM GO.
What?
WHAT KIND OF ATTITUDE IS THAT, HOJO?
YOU'RE THE CALM ONE—YOU STOP YUI.
He's a huge pain right now.
SHUT UP FOR A SECOND!
HANABUSA IS GETTING HIS FIRST CAFETERIA MEAL NOW!
I'm really stressed out!
SLAM
WIRETAP
YOU TOO?!

THERE ARE SOME BATTLES YOU CAN'T LOSE

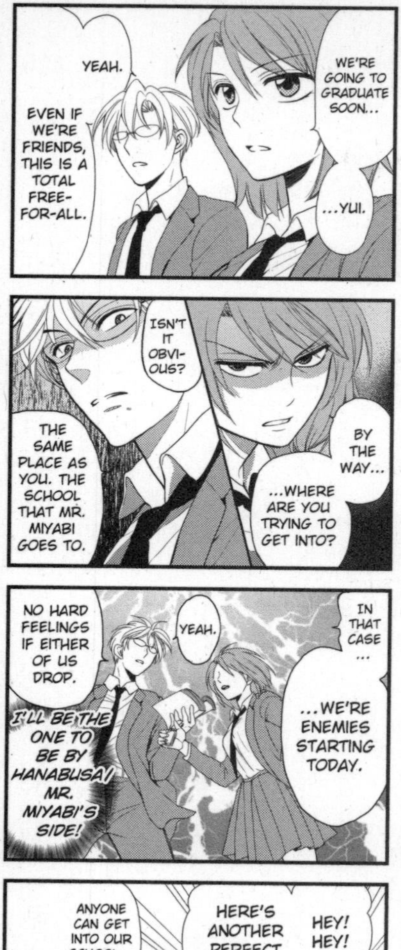

WE'RE GOING TO GRADUATE SOON...
...YUI.
YEAH.
EVEN IF WE'RE FRIENDS, THIS IS A TOTAL FREE-FOR-ALL.
BY THE WAY...
...WHERE ARE YOU TRYING TO GET INTO?
ISN'T IT OBVIOUS?
THE SAME PLACE AS YOU. THE SCHOOL THAT MR. MIYABI GOES TO.
IN THAT CASE...
...WE'RE ENEMIES STARTING TODAY.
YEAH.
NO HARD FEELINGS IF EITHER OF US DROP.
I'LL BE THE ONE TO BE BY HANABUSA/MR. MIYABI'S SIDE!
HEY! HEY!
HERE'S ANOTHER PERFECT SCORE!
ANYONE CAN GET INTO OUR SCHOOL...
...AS LONG AS THEY WRITE THEIR NAME.
Wow!
Amazing!
They didn't have to try so hard.

End Notes

Page 52, panel 5: Katsudon
A bowl of rice topped with deep-fried breaded pork cutlets, eggs and sauce.

Page 170, panel 3: Shiruko
Sweet Japanese soup made from red beans (azuki).

Page 188, panel 7: Ah-choo
In Japan, it's said that when you sneeze it means someone is talking about you.

Page 189, panel 8: Miin miin
This is the sound cicadas, a type of insect, make in the summer.

Page 190, panel 5: Free-for-all
In Japan, students don't matriculate into high school automatically like they do in the U.S. They must pass entrance exams or get letters of recommendation. Competition for the best schools is fierce.

Izumi Tsubaki began drawing manga in her first year of high school. She was soon selected to be in the top ten of *Hana to Yume*'s HMC (*Hana to Yume* Mangaka Course), and subsequently won *Hana to Yume*'s Big Challenge contest. Her debut title, *Chijimete Distance* (Shrink the Distance), ran in 2002 in *Hana to Yume* magazine, issue 17. Her other works include *The Magic Touch* (*Oyayubi kara Romance*) and *Oresama Teacher*, which she is currently working on.

ORESAMA TEACHER
Vol. 10
Shojo Beat Edition

STORY AND ART BY
Izumi Tsubaki

English Translation & Adaptation/JN Productions
Touch-up Art & Lettering/Eric Erbes
Design/Yukiko Whitley
Editor/Pancha Diaz

ORESAMA TEACHER by Izumi Tsubaki © Izumi Tsubaki 2011
All rights reserved. First published in Japan in 2011 by HAKUSENSHA, Inc., Tokyo.
English language translation rights arranged with HAKUSENSHA, Inc., Tokyo.

The rights of the author(s) of the work(s) in this publication to be so identified
have been asserted in accordance with the Copyright, Designs and Patents Act
1988. A CIP catalogue record for this book is available from the British Library.

The stories, characters and incidents mentioned in this publication are
entirely fictional.

No portion of this book may be reproduced or transmitted in any form or
by any means without written permission from the copyright holders.

Printed in Canada

Published by VIZ Media, LLC
P.O. Box 77010
San Francisco, CA 94107

10 9 8 7 6 5 4 3 2 1
First printing, September 2012

www.viz.com   www.shojobeat.com

PARENTAL ADVISORY
ORESAMA TEACHER is rated T for Teen and
is recommended for ages 13 and up. This
volume contains violence.
ratings.viz.com

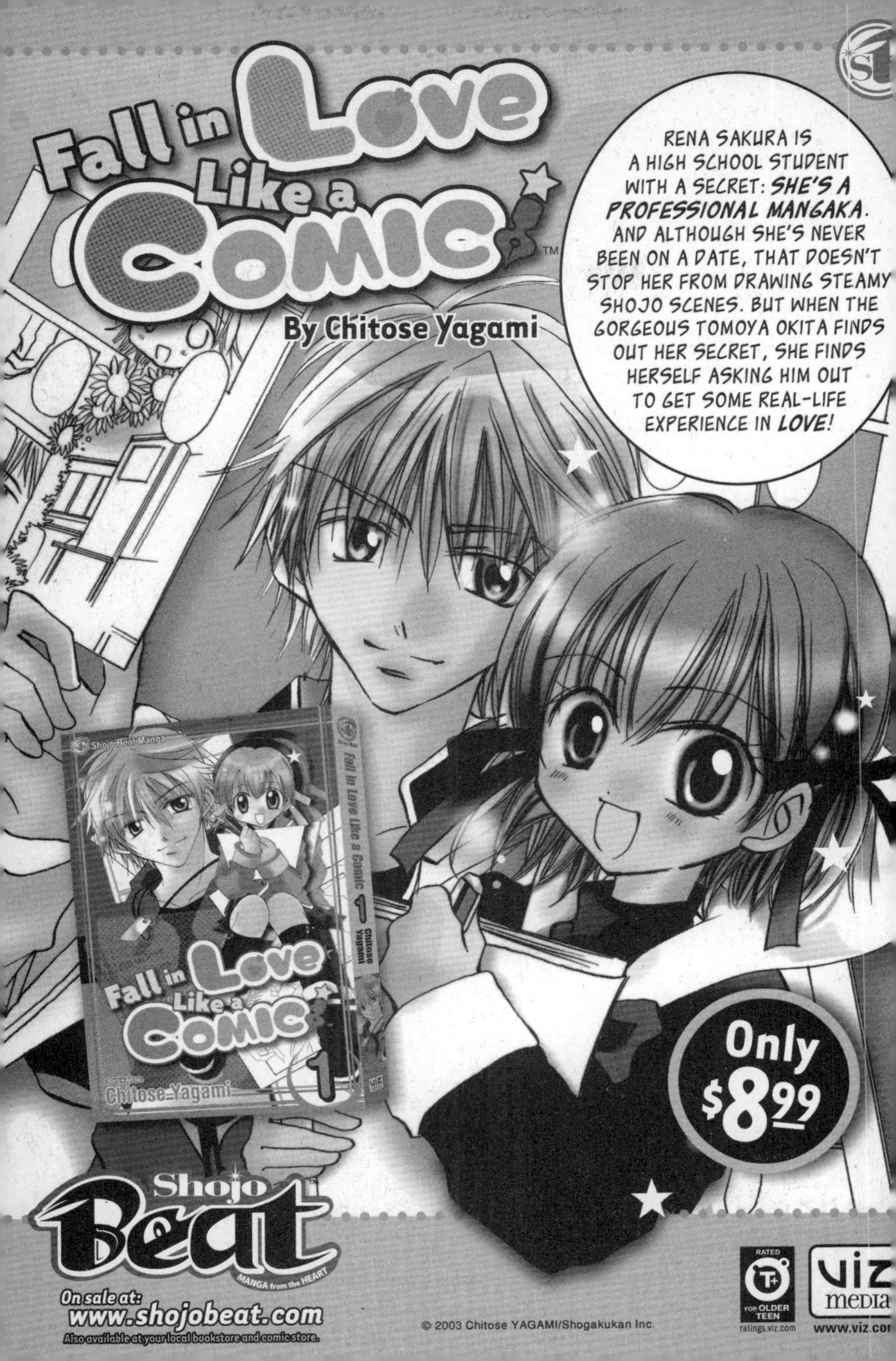

Fall in Love Like a Comic!™
By Chitose Yagami
RENA SAKURA IS A HIGH SCHOOL STUDENT WITH A SECRET: SHE'S A PROFESSIONAL MANGAKA. AND ALTHOUGH SHE'S NEVER BEEN ON A DATE, THAT DOESN'T STOP HER FROM DRAWING STEAMY SHOJO SCENES. BUT WHEN THE GORGEOUS TOMOYA OKITA FINDS OUT HER SECRET, SHE FINDS HERSELF ASKING HIM OUT TO GET SOME REAL-LIFE EXPERIENCE IN LOVE!
Shojo Beat Manga
Fall in Love Like a Comic 1 Chitose Yagami
Only $8.99
Shojo Beat MANGA from the HEART
On sale at:
www.shojobeat.com
Also available at your local bookstore and comic store.
© 2003 Chitose YAGAMI/Shogakukan Inc.
RATED T+ FOR OLDER TEEN
ratings.viz.com
VIZ media
www.viz.com

love ★ com

By Aya Nakahara

Class clowns Risa and Ôtani join forces to find love!

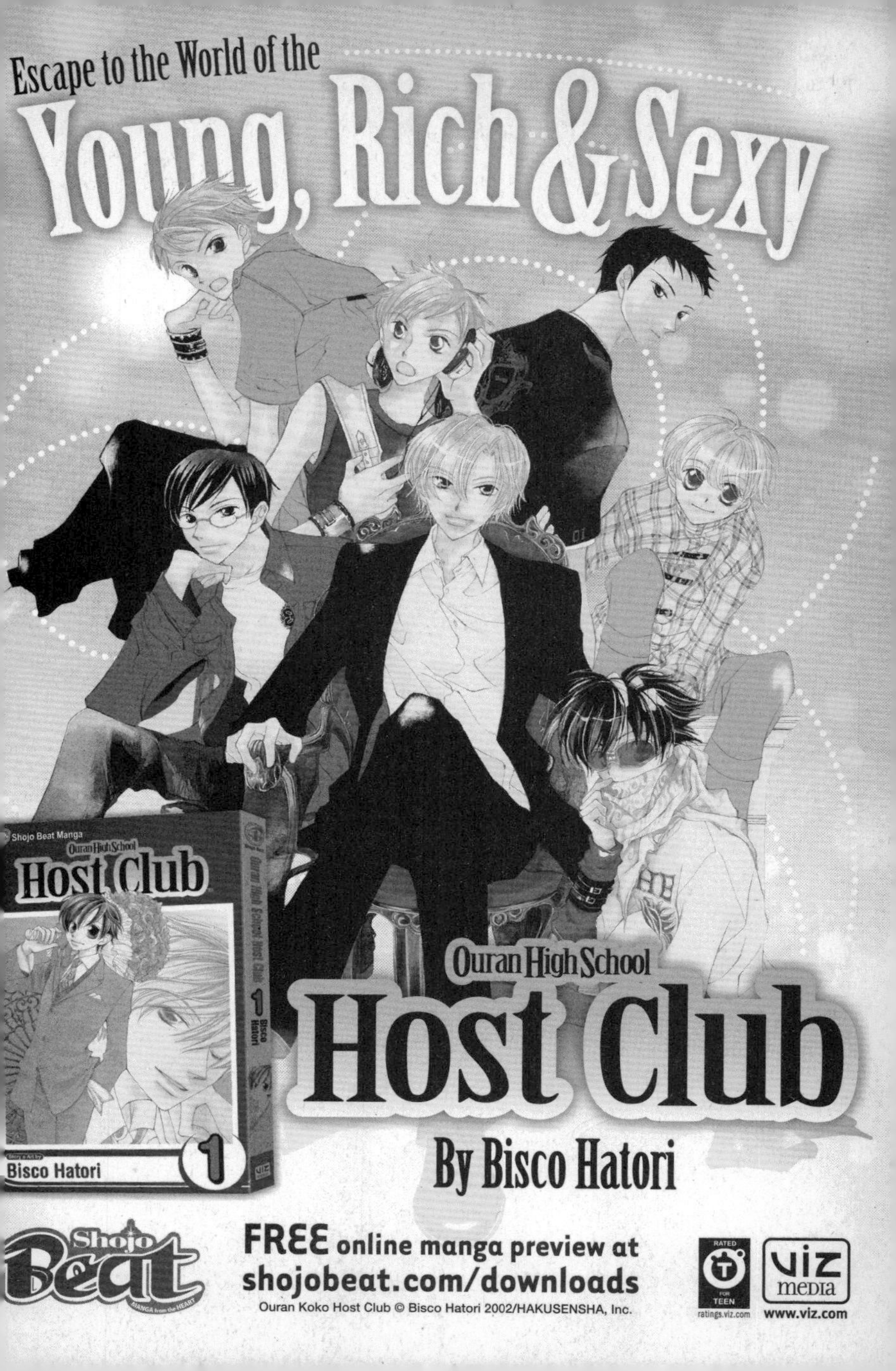
Escape to the World of the
Young, Rich & Sexy
Shojo Beat Manga
Ouran High School
Host Club
1
Bisco Hatori
Ouran High School
Host Club
By Bisco Hatori
Shojo Beat
FREE online manga preview at
shojobeat.com/downloads
Ouran Koko Host Club © Bisco Hatori 2002/HAKUSENSHA, Inc.
RATED T FOR TEEN
ratings.viz.com
VIZ media
www.viz.com

You may be reading the wrong way!

It's true: In keeping with the original Japanese comic format, this book reads from right to left—so action, sound effects, and word balloons are completely reversed. This preserves the orientation of the original artwork—plus, it's fun! Check out the diagram shown here to get the hang of things, and then turn to the other side of the book to get started!

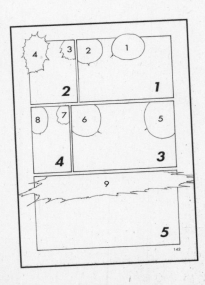